CONTEMPORARY CHRISTIAN RELIGIOUS RESPONSES TO THE SHOAH

CONTEMPORARY CHRISTIAN RELIGIOUS RESPONSES TO THE SHOAH

Edited by
Dr. Steven L. Jacobs, Rabbi

Studies in the Shoah

Volume VI

University Press of America
Lanham • New York • London

Copyright © 1993 by
University Press of America®, Inc.
4720 Boston Way
Lanham, Maryland 20706

3 Henrietta Street
London WC2E 8LU England

Library of Congress Cataloging-in-Publication Data

Contemporary Christian religious responses to the Shoah / edited by
Steven L. Jacobs.
p.   cm. — (Studies in the Shoah ; v. 6)
Includes bibliographical references.
1. Holocaust (Christian theology) I. Jacobs, Steven L. II. Series.
BT93.C66   1993   231.7'6—dc20   92–46070 CIP

ISBN 0–8191–8984–7 (cloth : alk. paper)

For

Leo and Ella Jacob,

Grandparents,

Married July 29, 1920,

Murdered by the Nazis,

Late 1941 or Early 1942.

With Love.

And for My
Father,
Ralph Albert Jacobs
[May 1, 1921– September 27, 1981],
The Saving Remnant

TABLE OF CONTENTS

INTRODUCTION

WHY THIS BOOK?

In 1988, there appeared a collection of philosophical essays dealing with the Shoah[1] entitled Echoes from the Holocaust: Philosophical Reflections of a Dark Time[2] . In examining its Table of Contents, only one of those essays, that of Hans Jonas--"The Concept of God After Auschwitz: A Jewish Voice" [pages 295-305]--reflected upon those years theologically. No "Christian voice" was heard. For, in truth, while many of those who had thought theologically and religiously as Christians about the implications of the Shoah, including many of those included here, had done so either in individual articles scattered about in a wide variety of publications, or in specific books, there did not exist a comparable collection of thoughtful essays from the perspective of Christian religious or theological thought. Contemporary Christian Religious Responses to the Shoah is an attempt to fill that void by bringing together many of the leading Christian religious thinkers about the Shoah, allowing them the freedom to respond to two questions uppermost in the mind of this Editor: [1] "What are the questions which you as Christian religious thinkers should be asking about the Shoah today?" and [2] "What are the answers which you yourself would give?" That all of those included were so readily willing to contribute their thinking to this project is an indication of the need for such a work.

Contemporary scholars in all disciplines have long recognized that the Shoah is a critical challenge to Christianity and Western Civilization, as well as a watershed event in Jewish history. The authors of the individual essays, as it were, speak of their own particular concerns to a wider audience than the Christian community. For this Editor, at least, these essays are nothing short of revelatory, challenging normative Christian thinking at a very basic and fundamental level. In so doing, these essays serve to broaden the base of the reader's own thinking about the theological implications of the Shoah for Christianity, and, thus, enter into dialogue with the reader. That the concerns expressed here are as varied as they are is a potent indication that now, five decades after the closure of the Second World War, there still exists no consensus as to the primary or central issues--theologically, philosophically or historically--when confronting the enormity of the Shoah in all of its many and varied aspects and dimensions.

When all is said and done, however, what comes through in these essays is the primacy of a renewed exploration of the ethical--in a very real and practical sense--over that of the intellectual task of "theologizing," in addition to the realization that, sadly, in truth, Christianity has yet to confront the Shoah "head on," as it were. Whether it will do so now is anyone's guess; whether these essays will aid in that confrontation is equally problematic. But such a confrontation must take place according to all those included here.

The Shoah presented humanity not with its successful evolution of both intellect and technology, but with its failure to use both for the improvement and betterment of all humankind. It equally presented Christianity with the most daring frontal assault to its own presentation of faith and salvation/redemption through the person of Jesus the Christ in modern times. What is now needed, given this reality of an historical experience testifying to the willingness of a given segment of the human community to go to any lengths whatsoever to eradicate another segment, is a renewed commitment to the teaching of ethics, at all levels of society, within a religious context, addressing the very concerns that should be the central focus of any faith, including Christianity: concern for the individual and group, regardless of their size and status; concern for the life's journey all humanity shares; and concern for that which is common among all peoples--recognition of the partnership of humanity and planet earth in a universe beyond itself. The all-too-frequent repetition of genocidal acts subsequent to the Second World War [e.g. Tibetans, Ibos, Kampucheans, Bosnians, etc.] is eloquent testimony and witness that the world--both Western and Eastern--has learned precious little from the Shoah. The inherent danger, however, in not learning from the Shoah is not merely repeating the "sins of the past," but, with ever-increasing and ever more sophisticated technology, encompassing wider and wider segments of humanity in the wake of its murderous design. Having committed itself continually to destroying specific portions of its own population, having increased the ability to do so exponentially, humanity appears to inch ever closer to turning in upon itself and destroying itself as well as its home. While no humanly crafted or created process is, ultimately, irreversible, one prays that Samuel Pisar, international lawyer and "graduate" of Auschwitz, author of the book Of Blood and Hope[3], is proven wrong by the work and resolve of collective humanity. Should he be proven correct, however, that "the Holocaust is the pilot program for the end of humanity," neither books such as this one, nor all the prayers of all the world's peoples, will prove capable of preventing the long, dark night of destruction which will engulf it.

*

Difficult as this project has proven to be, pain-filled as the subject itself has proven to be, profound thanks and grateful acknowledgement are herewith extended to all those without whom it would not have seen the light of day.

To those who contributed their thinking to this book and who met every deadline and expectation asked and from whom I have learned so much; to Professor Zev Garber of Los Angeles Valley College and General Editor "Studies in the <u>Shoah</u> Series" who saw merit both in this project and in its publication; to my wife Louanne, daughters Hannah and Naomi, and son Shea, for their understanding, encouragement, and love; to all those who continue to wrestle and to struggle with the <u>Shoah</u> and the world of faith; and to those who own reading of these essays <u>will</u> further all the dialogues which must now take place. May the thinking contained within this book serve to inspire others to address the issue of our collective human survival on spaceship earth before it is too late.[4]

Steven L. Jacobs

Huntsville, Alabama

14 December 1992

Harry James Cargas' essay responds to the contemporary phenomenon of those who would deny the very historicity of the Shoah, seeing in its "politi-cization" by "pro-Zionist Jews" [and others] an attempt to win support for a beleaguered Israel. He cites three "reasons" by these "historical im-provisationists"--preferred term--attempt to undermine the historical validity of the Shoah: "First, they wish to undermine the state of Israel; second, they wish to contribute to a resurgence of anti-Judaism; finally, they appear to want to rehabilitate the reputation of the Nazis." After presenting what he believes to be their arguments and demolishing them in the process, he next presents a brief history of Western Civilization's anti-Jewish journey, including that of the Church, thus forcing us to contemplate this so-called "historical revisionism" as an outgrowth of that which preceded it, namely centuries of antisemitic acts, thoughts, and writings. Sadly, in so doing, he forces us to diminish our naivete that such an absurdity could spring de novo on the world scene, and, therefore, obliquely, challenges the Christian [and Jewish] religious communities to rethink the long-range and extended implications of their theologies.[1]

REVISIONISM AND THEOLOGY:
TWO SIDES OF THE SAME COIN?

Harry James Cargas

I. Introduction: Who Are These Men?

It is not easy to think about the people who try to tell us that the Shoah never occurred. How should we speak of these men [there seems to be no women who are publicly advocating this position]. Do we call them liars? Shall we label them fools? Are they mad? Is it just that they are haters? Are they unbelievably stupid?

We may be tempted to treat them casually, even with mockery. After all, they are advocating that which is ridiculous. Intellectually, they are less than infants. They could be looked upon as partners in denial with members of the Flat Earth Society, and who have as much relevance. But while we tend to think the Flat Earth Society charming, knowing that many of its members cling to it for diversion and fun, no such description can be applied to the people who give themselves the respectable title of "Revis-ionist Historians." They are, rather, "Improvisationist Historians," men intent on distorting truth, on spitting on the graves of the dead--through the manipulation of evidence.

All historians select from the data available. But all decent historians make some attempt to approach the raw material of history with a certain detachment, a certain objectivity, a certain integrity. We do not find this to be the case with the Improvisers.

An outline of their charges gives us an idea of just who they are, just what these liars and/or fools and/or madmen and/or haters stand for. Or rather, what they stand against. Clearly, they oppose the continued existence of the state of Israel. They are so obsessed with the destruc-tion of that political entity that they will attempt the most illogical, inane kinds of argument in order to support their illogical, fraudulent history.

The Shoah--that massacre of nearly six million Jews and uncounted others at the hands of the Nazis and their collaborators in death camps deliberately designed for such a satanic purpose--never happened. Such is the Improvisationists' most sensational absurdity. They focus exclusively on the Jewish deaths, insisting that either they never occurred or that the numbers are greatly exaggerated. At most, some Improvisationists offer a figure of 200,000 Jewish deaths--"only 200,000" in their words--nearly none the result of deliberate murder but rather from typhus and other diseases.

But never do these fictioneers refer to the figures of the non-Jewish dead. What of them? Are their tragedies to be taken as accurate, only the numbers of the Jewish dead to be questioned?

But then, if the Shoah never was, why spread such a lie? The bogus historians tell us that the whole story is a giant conspiracy on the part of the pro-Zionists who wanted to make the world sorry for what was done to Jews. A post-war universal guilt would thus be a convenient basis from which Zionists would labor for the establishment of the state of Israel. So it seems a few Zionists came together and developed this fanciful tale about the Shoah and got every Jew in the world--every Jew in the world--to go along with the deceit. They are telling us that 18,000,000 Jews, 18,000,000 People of the Book, people whose very historical roots are in a profoundly moral tradition, that 18,000,000 Jews all agreed to a tremendous hoax. This would include, of course, many Jews who are not Zionists; this would have to include the Jews who are anti-Zionist. This would even have to number the Jewish survivors of Auschwitz and Buchenwald and Dora and Bergen-Belsen who are anti-Zionist. 18,000,000 Jews agree to the Big Lie. Indeed!

Add to this the fact that after the Second World War, Nazis and other Germans admitted to the atrocities done in the concentration camps. The Germans collaborated, the Improvisationists offer, because by doing so they guaranteed themselves Allied economic support in rebuilding their war-torn nation. "This means," the Allies said to the defeated Germans, "we French and Russian and British and American and other peoples are all of us pro-Zionists and we are all deliberately lying about the Shoah. We will help German economic recovery only if you Germans, too, join this otherwise incredible plot." And the Germans, according to feigned history, did so. The evidence for this: there is not one shred.

The reason, of course that the Allies were forced in cooperation with the Zionists was simple: continued Jewish control of the media. Can we imagine how Jews dominate the [former--Ed.] Soviet press, for example? Are the Improvisationists looking at the world media currently--that same media which they continue to claim is controlled by Jews. Former Defense Minister Ariel Sharon was unaware that the American press is managed by Jewish interests. Former Minister Menachem Begin did not think the French press is operated by Jews. A definite hostility can be detected towards the Jewish invasions of Lebanon by the media which, later, in much smaller print, corrected gross errors of fact in reporting events in Lebanon--errors which did not reflect glory on Jews. And what is the evidence that the disguised historians show us to prove Jewish control of the media? There is not one shred.

One must notice, also, the Improvisationists' determination to make us believe that the Soviets, too, went along with the Zionist plot about the Shoah. The Soviets, whose armaments surround Israel even today in such a threatening manner, were pro-Zionists and to this day have not let the cat out of the bag regarding fabrication. The evidence that the Soviets were in on the game: there is not one shred.

There is indeed a plot connected with the Shoah. But this conspiracy has naught to do with the Zionists, with the victims, with the Allies. A plot has been hatched by the Improvisationist Historians who would like to plant doubts in our minds regarding the truth, the pain, the suffering, the anguish, of the Shoah.

Nazi eyewitnesses of the most expert variety have testified to the horrors of the murders of millions of people in death camps. [One million of these were Jewish boys and girls not yet in their teens.] Rudolf Hoess, the commanding officer at Auschwitz, made a personal confession so enormous that he may be the one person in all history who might accurately say, "I directed more murders than anyone else who ever lived." Adolf Eichmann's testimony likewise was damning proof of the Shoah. Many, many other Nazis corroborated the truth of the massacres. The Improvisationists claim that these witnesses were coerced into convenient confessions. Their proof: there is not one shred.

II. Fantasy Extraordinaire

For a moment, let us imagine a contemporary world in which these fakers of history are correct. Let us pretend with them that the Shoah never occurred. What would it mean if they were right in saying that the deaths of millions of Jews never happened?

First, of course, it would mean that one awful lot of people are lying. And lying magnificently! You can compare the stories of Auschwitz survivors who have never met and they jibe, right down to the little, least significant details of existence in the death camp. Former inmates from Czechoslovakia, Poland, Norway, and other countries, people who have never heard of each other, corroborate each other's account, to a kind of perfection. That can only be described as "magnificent lying."

Think, too, of the Nazis who, at the Nuremberg War Trials, supported the lies of the Zionists--even before the Zionists invented them! Rudolf Hoess appeared to spill his guts in his confession which became the autobiographical book, Commandant at Auschwitz. This by the man who said, "I personally arranged the gassing of two million persons between June-July, 1941, and the end of 1943." The Improvisers would have us believe this man is a liar--not a killer!

Adolf Eichmann would also have to be transformed from a murderer to one who slaughtered words rather than people. Here is Eichmann's own somber recollection:

I was sent by my immediate superior, General Muller....He liked to send me around in his behalf. I was, in effect, a traveling salesman for the Gestapo, just as I once had been a traveling salesman for an oil company in Austria. Muller had heard that Jews were being shot near Minsk and wanted a report....they had already started, so I could see only the finish. Although I was wearing a leather coat which reached almost to my ankles, I was still very cold. I watched the last group of Jews undress, down to their shirts. They walked 100 or 200 yards--they were not driven--then they jumped into the pit. It was impressive to see them all jumping into the pit without offering any resistance whatsoever. Then the men of the squad banged away into the pit with their rifles and machine pistols. Why did that scene linger so long in my memory? Perhaps because I had children myself. And there were children in that pit. I saw a woman hold a child of a year or two into the air, pleading. At that moment all I wanted was to say, "Don't shoot, hand over the child." Then the child was hit. I was so close that later I found bits of brain splattered on my long leather coat. My driver helped me to remove them. Then we returned to Berlin.

These words could not be true according to history mocked--although they helped get Eichmann executed.

Historians galore participated in the great lie. We can name writers of such stature as Hugh Trevor-Roper, William L. Shirer, and Arnold Toynbee [none Jewish and the last named considered by some to be anti-Israel] who contrived a plot about the Shoah with the rest.

The Vatican, too, had to go along with the forgery of history. Catholic priests were everywhere. These clergypersons would have been able to see so very much. And, of course, Rome had been accused of failing to help Jews in their hours of desperate need. Pope Pius XII has been singled out particularly for harsh criticism concerning his so labeled "great silence," his alleged non-intervention on behalf of Jews during World War II. If ever the Catholic Church needed a defense for moral failure, some feel, here is the issue. Yet the Vatican never chose the easy way out. The moral center of world Catholicism could have saved itself serious embarrassment by merely telling the truth: Why should the Church have acted? There was no persecution of Jews; there was no Shoah. The fact that no Pope has offered this defense shows just how deeply that Rome is allied to the Zionist plot. [The fact that the Vatican does not officially recognize the State of Israel cannot be discussed here because it does not fit in with Improvisationist data.]

Many other liars could be mentioned, including all of those--all of those--Allied officials who participated in the various war crimes trials after the war, particularly those at Nuremberg. All judges, all prosecu-tors, and all lawyers would have to have been corrupted by the Zionists, and that, according to this view of synthetic history, is what happened.

And there are countless more prevaricators, but let us just consider one other group, the Shoah survivors who became parents. Victims who outlived the death camps tended to marry survivors. A shared, almost unutterable experience, tended to bring such coupled together. But in order to promote the Zionist myth, they all had to lie to their children about grandparents. They had to tell their infants that they had no grandmothers and grandfathers--all for the promulgation of Israel. What are Jewish holidays like in the homes of survivors of the Shoah? They are lonely. Their families are abbreviated. We have to wonder what the survivors did with their fathers and their mothers.

Arthur Butz, in his Improvisationist book The Hoax of the Twentieth Century[2], gives us a hint of how Jewish families reacted to the opportunity to advance the Shoah myth. This hero of the contemporary neo-Nazis writes that some Jews were sent to labor camps to help the German war effort. Then we read these words:

> In many cases deported Jewish families were broken up
> for what was undoubtedly intended by the Germans to be a period
> of limited duration. This was particularly the case when the
> husband seemed a good labor conscript; just as German men were
> conscripted for hazardous military service, Jews were con-
> scripted for unpleasant labor tasks. Under such conditions it is
> reasonable to expect that many of these lonely wives and husbands
> would have, during or at the end of the war, established other
> relations that seemed more valuable than previous relationships.
> In such cases, then, there would have been a strong motivation not
> to re-establish contact with the legal spouse.

Think of it! Many Jews who were married preferred not to return to their original families. Clearly Mr. Butz here destroys the myth of close-ness of Jewish families. [Butz has done much service for the Improvisers, by the way. Among his more brilliant analyses is his insight into the use of Zyklon gas at Auschwitz. Far from denying its availability, Butz informs us that Zyklon gas was "used as an insecticide at Ausch-witz." So Zyklon was employed to help Jews, not harm them, he tells us. He fails to document his claim, and he cannot defend the enormous quantities of "insecticides" ordered, but these are minor failings.]

III. The Shoah Could and Did Happen!

Let us continue to look at the world as if the Shoah never happened from another point of view: even if the Shoah had not occurred, it could have. The climate had been created, for centuries, which made a Shoah possible. There was a Shoah, so obviously it was possible. But we should look very keenly at what created an atmosphere which permitted, and more, encouraged a massacre of the proportions we know. Here is a paragraph from a book I published in 1976:

> Adolf Hitler, a baptized Catholic who was never excommunicated by Rome, implemented a policy of total destruction because, and only because, he was able to. Only because people willingly cooperated in individual and mass murders. Who, for example, were the architects who designed the ovens into which people were delivered for cremation? Who meticulously executed the plans for the efficient gas chambers into which naked men, women, and children were herded to die? Who originated the design for the camps, those models of economical, technological destruction? Which firms bid on the contracts to build the camps, the gas chambers, the ovens? Who bribed whom to win the coveted contracts, to gain the chance to make a profit and serve the Fuhrer by erecting houses of death and torture? Which doctors performed experiments on Jewish victims? Who shaved their heads, and all bodily hairs, to gain materials for clothes and rugs? We've heard of lampshades made from Jewish skins, of soap made from Jewish bodies, of enforcers throwing Jewish victims--most of them dead, but not all--into huge pits, of brutal guards crushing babies' skulls with rifle butts, and shooting aged and unhealthy Jews who couldn't keep up on forced marches, and making naked Jews stand for hours in freezing weather for either convenience or amusement. Who were these tormentors? What of the train engineers who guided the cattle cars packed with starving, dying, dead Jews to locales of internment? And what ordinary citizens of many European nations who, as the death trains passed through their communities, would throw bits of bread into the cattle cars to be entertained by watching famished Jews fight over the food in an agonizing display of attempts at survival?

What led up to these possibilities? Historically the picture is devastating. We can find seriously anti-Judaic passages in the words and acts of the Romans: Cicero, Seneca, Tiberius, Democritus, Trajan, Caligula, Quintilian, Juvenal, Tacitus--a list much too long.

Then came the Christians. Not all, numerically perhaps not even many. And yet far too many Christians of influence had terrible and erroneous things to say about that general group of people called "the Jews." Here follows only a sketch of a very tragic history of our inhumanity toward each other. And we recall as we reflect on this, not only must we be aware of the atrocities committed against Jews, we should also be conscious of what violence these words of Christians have done to the teachings of Jesus, the Jew. Here is Father Edward Flannery from his excellent book on Christian anti-Semitism, The Anguish of the Jews[3]:

> The first Christian Church, full of zeal and fervor, was a Jewish church in leadership, membership, and worship; and it remained within precincts of the Synagogue. But as the universalist implications of the Gospel message [not yet fully written] made themselves felt, a series of developments gradually brought this arrangement to an end. In the tones of a prophet, Stephen charged the people and their leaders with infidelity to Moses as well as to the Messiah [Acts 7:2-53]. By private revelation, Peter was instructed to accept the demi-proselyte, Cornelius, into the Church without committing him to the Law [Acts 10]. The council of the apostles at Jerusalem decreed that gentile converts were not to be held to the legal observances [Galatians 2; Acts 15:11]. Finally, at Antioch, Paul confronted Peter, insisting that while Jewish Christians might practice the Law, faith in Jesus Christ was necessary and sufficient for salvation [Galatians 2:11-21]. This was the final disposition of the matter. Judaeo-Christianity, thus rejected, was destined to become a snare to Christian and Jew alike and a source of conflict for both Church and Synagogue.

Early Christian-Jewish hostility grew and some Jewish persecution against Christians took place, although it was comparatively insignificant, mainly reactionary. Soon, a nearly two millennium assault on Judaism began. Ignatius of Antioch required that no Christians could keep the Jewish Sabbath. He claimed that the prophets of Israel were not truly of the Jewish religion but were Christians before their time. Nils Dahl has written that "The simplistic doctrine that Israel was rejected and the Church chosen to be a new people of God is not really found within the New Testament, although it is adumbrated in some of the later writings." However, Rosemary Radford Reuther in Faith and Fratricide[4] insists that the Church won historical existence for herself by negating Judaism and claiming to supersede the historical existence of Israel. Reuther claims that a new Christology offers a way out of anti-Judaism for Christians.

But back to the historical thread. Saint Justin was probably the first to claim that the Jews had to suffer because they killed Jesus. This is both bad history and bad theology and has been proven to be so repeatedly by theologians, but the errors have persisted through the centuries with all their tragic effects.

In the third century, Saint Cyprian insisted that "Now the peoplehood of the Jews has been cancelled." The next century gave us Saint John Chrysostom:

How can Christians dare "have the slightest converse with Jews, "Most miserable of all men" [Homily 4:1], men who are "....lustful, rapacious, greedy, perfidious bandits." Are they not "inveterate murderers, destroyers, men possessed by the devil," whom "debauchery and drunkenness have given them the manners of the pig and the lusty goat. They know only one thing, to satisfy their gullets, get drunk, to kill and maim one another...." [1:4]. Indeed, "they have surpassed the ferocity of wild beasts, for they murder their offspring and immolate them to the devil" [1:6]. "They are impure and impious...." [1:4].

They Synagogue? Not only is it a theatre and a house of prostitution, but a caravan of brigands, a "repair of wild beasts" [6:5], a place of "shame and ridicule" [1:3], "the domicile of the devil [1:6], as is also the souls of the Jews" [1:4, 6]. Indeed, Jews worship the devil; their rites are "criminal and impure," their religion is "A disease" [3:1]. Their synagogue, again, is "an assembly of criminals....den of thieves....a cavern of devils, and an abyss of perdition" [1:2; 6:6].

God hates the Jews and always hated the Jews [6:4; 1:7], and on Judgment Day He will say to Judaizers, "Depart from Me, for you have had intercourse with My murderers." It is the duty of Christians to hate the Jews; "He who can never love Christ enough will never have done fighting against those [Jews] who hate Him [7:11]. "Flee then, their assemblies, flee their houses, and keep far from venerating the synagogue because of the books it contains in it" [1:5]. "....I hate the Synagogue precisely because it has the law and prophets...." [6:6]. "....I hate the Jews also because they outrage against the law...."

Many other saints and church leaders could be quoted from this point on, but more than enough has been indicated already to illustrate what needs to be said here.

But there were more than words--actions based on those words. Forced baptism became a practice. Jewish children were taken from their parents, baptized and not returned to their homes. This was done in spite of condemnations of such acts by popes. Another ugly chapter is that of the Crusades, still pointed to with pride in the current Catholic Encyclopedia, it should be noted. Next came charges of Ritual Murder. They seem to have begun in the 12th Century. Ritual murder was first said to be the sacrifice of a Christian victim, by Jews, usually a child, during the Christian Holy Week, for religious purposes. All over Europe, for centuries, such absurdities were claimed and many Jews were massacred, raped, had their homes pillaged and destroyed. One such event took place behind the Iron Curtain just a few years ago. A Catholic priest and historian, a Father Vacandard, has established that not a single case of Ritual Murder has ever been proven--not one, not ever.

Pope Innocent III's Fourth Lateran Council ordered that Jews and Saracens had to wear distinctive clothing. This was seven and a half centuries before the Nazis forced the Jews to wear yellow stars. The Talmud was burned by Christians, and, in 1298, about 100,000 Jews were killed in Germany and Austria because of the unfounded allegation that a Jew--one Jew--had desecrated a communion host.

Then came one of the most tragic eras in Christian history, the Inquisition. Set up only to root out heresy among Christians, it was, as we know, turned against Jews as well. There is no need to give accounts of torture and executions at this point--the story is too familiar.

Then came the Reformation. Things did not get better for the Jews. Here are the words of Martin Luther. And remember: this is not a quote from some Nazi officer caught up in the spirit of trying to rid the world of Jews:

> First, their Synagogue or school is to be set on fire and what won't burn is to be heaped over with dirt and dumped on, so that on one can see a stone or chunk of it forever....Second, their houses are to be torn down and destroyed in the same way....- Third, they are to have all their prayerbooks and Talmudics taken from them....Fourth, their rabbis are to be forbidden publicly to praise God, to thank [God], to pray [to God], to teach [of God] among us and ours....And furthermore, they shall be forbidden to utter the name of God in our hearing; no value shall be accorded the Jewish mouth [Maul] by us Christians, so that he may utter the name of God in our hearing, but whoever hears it from a Jew shall report him to the authorities....Fifth, the Jews are to be deprived totally of walkways and streets....Sixth, they are to be forbidden the lending of interest and all cash and hold of silver and gold are to be taken from them and put to one side for safe keeping....Seventh, the young, strong Jews and Jewesses are to have flail, axe, and spade put into their hands.

The story gets no better. In 1700, Johann Eisenmenger published Judaism Unmasked which has been an inspired encyclopedia of anti-Juda-ism until now. Names of people pronouncing anti-Judaic sentiments include Schleiermacher, Fichte, Goethe, Marx [himself born a Jew], Voltaire, Diderot, Spinoza [another Jew], Hegel--what a long list! Then in 1884 came Arthur de Gobineau's Essay on the Inequality of the Human Races[5]. Jews, in the author's view, were distinctly inferior to German Aryans and Hitler's policy of destroying Jews was based in great part on de Gobi-neau's errors.

In Germany itself, the nation was saturated in anti-Jewish atmosphere, and few people spoke out on behalf of the vilified. From 1925-1927, over 700 racist anti-Jewish newspapers were published throughout the country. Even in children's books, passages such as this could be read: "Without solution of the Jewish question/No salvation of mankind."

The Jew was blamed for the loss of World War I, for Germany's economic woes, for being of impure blood and literally for being less than human. Adolf Hitler came onto the scene proclaiming that "by defending myself against the Jew, I am fighting for the work of the Lord." It was said of Der Fuhrer that "God had manifested himself not in Jesus Christ but in Adolf Hitler." The Minister for Church Affairs in Germany in 1937 urged that "A new authority has risen as to what Christ and Christianity really are--Adolf Hitler." The same man, Hans Kerrl, even went beyond this when he postulated that "As Christ in his twelve disciples raised a stock fortified into martyrdom, so in Germany today we are witnessing the same thing....Adolf Hitler is the true Holy Ghost!"

IV. Where Do We Go From Here?

Indeed, the climate was prepared. The fact is that the Shoah happened because it could have happened. It was not an effect of a one-time satanic interference in human events. The Shoah was centuries in the making. The responsibilities are enormous and widespread. Jews born in 1942 had been condemned in 342 and 1542 as well. And those who deny that the genocide took place are, indeed, participating in this ignominious continuity which helps to grant victories to the Nazis beyond their graves.

Why do the Improvisationist/Historians ply their sham trade? The answer may be seen as threefold: First, they wish to undermine the state of Israel; second, they wish to contribute to a resurgence of anti-Judaism; finally, they appear to want to rehabilitate the reputation of the Nazis. Willis Carto, a treasurer for Liberty Lobby, has written that Hitler's defeat was America's defeat. Austin App blames the United States for starting the Second World War and for fighting on the wrong side.

Actually, however, this turns out not to be too surprising. Here is part of a letter, written to U. S. Chief of Staff George Marshall by Dwight Eisenhower when he was the Supreme Commander of the Allied Forces in the European Theater. After visiting the newly-liberated camp at Ohrdruf, Eisenhower wrote:

> The things I saw beggar description....The visual evidence and the verbal testimony of starvation, cruelty, and bestiality were so overpowering as to leave me a bit sick. In one room there were piled up twenty or thirty naked men, killed by starvation; George Patton would not even enter. He said he would get sick if

he did so.. I made the visit deliberately, in order to be in a position to give first-hand evidence of these things if ever, in the future, there develops a tendency to charge these allegations merely to "propaganda."

Eisenhower somehow anticipated the appearance of nay-sayers in the future. But the most meaningful blow rendered against the bastardization of history by the Improvisationists occurred at an International Liberators Conference held at the State Department in October, 1981. I participated in the meeting and witnessed what I am about to relate.

Death camp survivors and those who freed them were among 500 men and women from fourteen nations who gathered in Washington for the emotion-laden assembly. Included were former soldiers, war correspondents and medical personnel from Russia, Poland, Czechoslovakia, France, Israel, Great Britain, Denmark, the Netherlands, Norway, Switzerland, Belgium, Canada, New Zealand, Yugoslavia, and the United States. All gave witness to what they saw upon liberating Auschwitz, Buchenwald, Bergen-Belsen, and Dachau. In so doing, they put an end to the lie of the pseudo-history of the Improvisationists.

Among those who testified to the truth was Soviet Lieutenant Vassily Petrenko, hardly with any Zionist purpose in mind. Yet Petrenko, who led the liberation of Auschwitz, did indeed acknowledge the truth of the death camps.

The evidence was so overwhelming that Polish Brigadier General Francizek Skibinki noted that "With every hour of this conference we are convinced that we came at the right time to the right place." The distinguished British jurist Colonel G. I. A. D. Draper urged that all nations adopt laws making it a crime to advocate the claim that the Shoah never occurred. He received an ovation for that remark.

Those who doubt the truth about the annihilation of more than a third of the world's Jews are either liars, fools, mad, haters, stupid, or a combination of these. The plethora of evidence presented at the Nuremberg War Crimes Trials is certainly enough to convince any reasonably rational person. So are the histories, the eyewitness accounts by Shoah survivors, the confessions by the Nazis. To question the reality of the Shoah ought to be unthinkable.

In his book Vatican Diplomacy and the Jews During the Holocaust, 1939-1943[6], a Catholic priest at Seton Hall University, John Morley, documents so much that condemns the Improvisationists. He quotes Catholic communiques from at least seven nations--letters, memos, directives, etc.--which affirm that high Vatican officials did indeed know what was happening to Jews through Europe. And what was happening was indeed horrendous, nearly unimaginable. The Vatican had hardly been a source of strong Zionist support. The documents which Father Morley quotes were not written to help establish the state of Israel. Anyone who says the opposite is a liar.

Even the Arabs today, many of whom feel that the Israelis are intruders on Arab territory, do not deny the Shoah.

In October, 1982, speaking at Webster University in Saint Louis, Dr. Hatem Husseni, the Palestine Liberation Organization's Deputy Observer to the United Nations, talked about the deprivations of his people since the recognition of Israel. He compared their suffering to those of the Jews during the Shoah. Dr. Husseni is hardly part of a Zionist conspiracy.

I myself am not a Zionist. [Nor am I anti-Zionist] I teach, write, and speak about the reality of the Shoah as a Christian failing--as the greatest Christian tragedy since the Crucifixion of Jesus. My basic purpose is to explore how so many persons in Christian nations could have acted in so un-Christian a manner, whether they were active persecutors or merely neutral observers who just "didn't want to get involved." I do not do work on behalf of the State of Israel. I do my work because I am obsessed by the fact that millions upon millions of mothers, grandparents, babies, fathers, doctors, laborers, teachers, rabbis, clerks, secretaries, and others were murdered by thousands of men who were baptized in Christ. I want to know how this can be true.

And, tangentially, I want to know about the pornographers as well. Who are they? How dare they write and speak their filth! Listen to the titles of the works they offer for sale:

Christ is Not a Jew

Our Nordic Race

The Negro and World Crises

A Gallery of Jewish Types

I. Q. and Racial Differences

Proof of Negro Inferiority

Who Brought Slaves to America
[Which pretends to prove that Jews
were responsible for the slave trade]

The South's Part in Mongrelizing the Nation

White Man Think Again!

Etc., etc., truly ad nauseam

Indeed, there is a conspiracy concerning the Shoah! But the plot was not hatched by Zionists to support the legitimization of Israel; nor do Soviets, Yugoslavs, anti-Zionist Jews, Vatican officials, and so many others I've quoted--including members of the PLO--join in any scheme to take territory away from Arabs.

The only conspiracy about the Shoah is entered into by the nay-sayers, those who take the blood of Hitler's victims willingly on their hands. They are the conspirators, they are those who make a forgery of history, who manipulate, contrive, counterfeit, fabricate, and mock not only the facts, but all people as well. We are poorer, as a human race, for their existence. Their only contribution has been, by prompting a reaction, to cause the Shoah to be the most validated, documented tragedy of all time. But the problem has absolutely nothing to do with whether or not the Shoah happened. The problem has to do with our response to the Shoah. What have we learned from that awesome event? What are we going to do about it?

The great Swiss theologian Karl Barth composed the famous section on evil in his <u>Church Dogmatics</u> in the immediate post-war years; consequently, he alone thought his thoughts after the terror. It is remarkable, therefore, and, in retrospect, extremely puzzling that this anti-Nazi theo-lo-gian never refers to the attempted annihilation of the Jews on the part of Nazi Germany in the course of this seminal discussion, although he does allude to the <u>Shoah</u> elsewhere.[2] Had Barth been either an antisemite or a German nationalist, the matter would not be in the least puzzling, but he was neither. In his eyes, antisemitism was a "sin against the Holy spirit"[3], and the National Socialist state with its totalitarian claims was "the Beast out of the Abyss"[4]. What, then, explains the omission? Are his chapters merely the continuation of pre-war reflections, written as if nothing significant had happened between 1939-1945, and thus uninformed by the experiences of his time? Are they merely an exercise in the history of ideas, a metaphysical discussion for its own sake--a defense of the faith against the atheistic philosophers Martin Heidegger and Jean-Paul Sartre? Or is the explanation of a different order? Perhaps the doctrine itself suggests an answer.

As Barth's translators have pointed out, the English language does not contain a satisfactory equivalent to the German das <u>Nichtige</u>: "nothingness" is too feeble, since the Barthian power of nothingness is not nothing: "the Nihil," which Otto Weber prefers, has the advantage of a semantic connection with the term "nihilism," with its evil and destructive connotations, but it is not an English word, and, in any case, the Barthian Nihil is deeper and more terrible than philosophical and moral nihilism.[5] For lack of a better alternative, the more familiar term will be employed here. What exactly is it intended to signify? It is intended to signify not merely evil, but [to adopt Immanuel Kant's expression] radical evil, or evil chosen and committed as an end in itself, rather than as a means to another end, because it is grounded in an evil will; radical evil is thus both mysterious and absolute in character.[6] Barth, however, unlike Kant, was a theologian, and not confined by the limits of philosophical language, which must avoid the assumptions and dogmas of religious faith. For the theo-logian, radical evil moves from philosophy into theology as soon as its mystery and absoluteness are taken seriously, since the characteristics raise essentially religious questions, and religious questions require religious answers. In Barth's theology, radical evil or nothingness is more than the sum total of the many antithetical aspects of the world: non-being, death, darkness, finitude, etc.--in short, the "shadow side" of creation [creation, of course, is a theological, not a philosophical category] that, of necessity, belongs to existence itself.[7] Can there be being without non-being, life without death, light without darkness, infinitude without finitude? Can even these concepts exist without their polar opposites? Indeed, these various "nots" or "frontiers" of creaturely, especially human, existence are not evil in themselves, although, when invaded by the power of nothingness, they become the instruments of evil, and hence easily confused with evil. Real evil, that which Barth designates nothingness, transcends natural evil, lying outside of the created order, being "neither God nor....creature, but possessing reality--a reality of its own--nevertheless"[8]. Nothingness owes nothing to God's will; rather it represents that which God does not will, or the choices that God does not make--all of the malignant possibilities spurned by a good Creator that lurk around the edges of the creation as its travesty and perversion, seeking to annul the divine decree.

> The character of nothingness derives from its ontic peculiarity. It is evil. What God positively wills and performs in the opus proprium of His election....is His grace....What God does not will and therefore negates and rejects, what can this be only the object of His opus alienum, of His jealousy, wrath, and judgment, is a being that refuses and resists and therefore lacks His grace. This being which is alien and adverse to grace and therefore without it, is that of nothingness. This negation of His grace is chaos, the world which He did not choose or will, which He could not and did not create, but which, as He created the actual world, He passed over and set aside, marking and excluding it as the eternal past, the eternal yesterday.[9]

Nothingness, therefore, which the Biblical era personified in the form of demons, and which the Christian Middle Ages personified as a single immensely powerful devil, is as real as the chaos that constantly overcomes life in a multitude of ways, turning order into disorder. Neurosis, psychosis, the disintegration of the spirit, the destruction of the body, the destruction of the body politic: all of these things are real--why, then, should nothingness, the power that strives to reduce everything to nothing, be regarded as unreal? Nothingness is sin, but, according to Barth, it is more than sin, since sin is a human matter whereas nothingness is more than simply human; in metaphorical and mythological language, it is God's enemy. As God's enemy, moreover, it is a power to be feared and taken seriously, not to be dismissed lightly as a figment of the imagination because demons and devils, interpreted literally, do not exist. In this respect, the modern mind is at a disadvantage, falling victim to rationalistic assumptions that invariably minimize the problem of evil by dismissing any notion that assigns evil any measure of transcendence. Barth does not argue in favor of these demons and devils, but he does not deny their existence either; they, too, are not nothing.[10] They symbolize transcendent evil, and radical evil--evil for evil's sake--is certainly transcendent. Whatever internal problems and contradictions the Barthian doctrine of nothingness may contain, its author cannot be accused of taking too mild a view of his subject in the context of the twentieth century. Even prior to the Shoah, Nazi Germany was the embodiment of nothingness, and doubtless the model in Barth's mind for much of his analysis. Nothingness has the capacity to charm, as did Hitler with his charisma and his mass audiences. Hence many Germans fell under his spell, including many churchpersons, almost including Barth himself, despite the latter's impassioned opposition to the regime: "We were in danger of bringing, first incense, and then the complete sacrifice to it as to a false god."[11]

The Shoah could have been and should have been the theologian's proof-text par excellence. Transcendent evil, mass murder as an end in itself, a delight in indescribable cruelty, the triumph of chaos over order, the victory of the irrational over the rational, the destruction of the spirit as well as the body, the reduction of everything to nothing--in short, all the works of das Nachtige in all of their perversity, all were present in superabundance. The power of nothingness scarcely requires further documentation. For this reason, perhaps, so many individuals, past and present, have averted their eyes from the event itself, and engaged in the art of denial; they cannot endure its metaphysical dimensions. Had Martin Heidegger, for example, ever allowed himself to gaze into the true depths of nothingness, according to Barth, he would never have deified "nothing" as the "pseudonym which conceals the Godhead."[12] Nothing, for Heidegger, consequently, is "not a dreadful, horrible dark abyss but something fruitful and salutary and radiant."[13] A philosopher whose thought was colored by the First World War, the greatest of the German existentialists, clearly evaded the lessons of the Second World War, and particularly the lessons of the Shoah. Is it merely coincidence that he found it possible to embrace National Socialism? Like Barth, Emil Fackenheim finds a connection between Heidegger's political sympathies and his ability, even in his old age, to recognize radical evil.[14] Today, the new school of [so-called--Ed.] "historical revisionism" or Shoah denial also refuses to recognize radical evil as a universal possibility. If men such as Arthur Butz in the United States and Ernest Zundel in Canada allowed themselves to encounter nothingness, the nothingness in themselves, their nationalist and racist gods would be shattered, and their personal identities as well.[15] What they fear is not history, but that which history reveals about the human condition. They fear the face of the Nihil.

Barth, of course, was a Christian, and his theology reflects this fact at every turn. In his eyes, even the knowledge of nothingness ultimately depends on a knowledge of God's self-revelation in Christ, or the divine decision against nothingness that, by virtue of its supreme light and glory, illumines the contours of the abyss as nothing else can. This does not mean that only Christians can recognize radical evil; it does seem to mean, however, that only Christians can discern its true spiritual depths. Naturally, Jews are likely to dispute this claim on both religious and historical grounds. Had Barth paid more real attention to the Shoah when he developed his doctrine, he might have hesitated before committing himself to such a dubious and even offensive conclusion. A great blind spot involving Judaism [and, incidentally, the other non-Christian religions] mars his entire system.[16] One mistake, moreover, leads to another, and it is not surprising that an interpretation of revelation that excludes the vast realm of religious experience outside the bounds of the Christian faith also excludes the possibility of anything ever challenging its central paradigm. Christ defeated das Nichtige on the cross; henceforth, "nothingness is routed and extirpated."[17] Henceforth, it is not to be feared, for its power to annihilate is no more; it possesses the semblance of power--admittedly, a dangerous semblance--but no longer the substance of power: its dominion has ended. God's "yes" to humanity is absolute and irrevocably, and to think otherwise is to deceive ourselves. Most people, of course, including most Christians do think otherwise, regarding the human situation with "anxious, legalistic, tragic, hesitant, doleful and basically pessimistic thoughts," but they are wrong.[18] "Jesus is Victor," and if Jesus is victor, "nothingness has no perpetuity."[19] To be sure, the final revelation of the destruction of nothingness has not taken place; for this reason, non-Christians, post-Christians, and Christians lacking in faith suffer from blindness, mistaking the true state of affairs. That, however, although a sad indictment of our times, does not really matter; truth matters. Nothingness, the "defeated, captured, and mastered enemy of God," is now God's servant, and exists only with God's permission, serving God as an instrument, however unwilling, of the divine will.[20] After the resurrection, even the demons are in chains.

On this note of cosmic optimism, Barth's discourse on evil ends. The optimism is the problem. How, after Auschwitz, can anyone seriously believe that nothingness has lost its dominion, possessing only the sem-blance of power? Does not history refute Barth? Was it not Barth who was blind to reality, a reality not far removed from his Swiss doorstep? The theologian was no fool; he was thoroughly acquainted with the horrors of his age, and, unlike Heidegger, he did not avert his gaze from the countenance of the Nihil. On the other hand, the character of his theological method, with its stress on transcendence and its suspicion of human experience, including even religious experience, invited a disregard of contemporary historical events as far as the great truths of revelation were concerned. Nazi Germany certainly colored his theology, as the Barmen Declaration that he composed against the German Christians prior to the war obviously demonstrated. This, after all, was the professor who refused in 1933 to being his lectures in a German university with the required Nazi salute, choosing instead a Christian prayer. His passionate opposition to natural theology in all its forms was inspired by his antipathy to the biological arguments employed by the pro-Nazi theologians and churchpersons who defended the Aryan paragraph. Justifiably he regarded Emmanuel Hirsch's attempt to sacralize the National Socialist revolution as a visitation of the Holy Spirit ["**die grossen heiligen Sturn gegenwartigen Volksdeschehens**"] as an outrage[21], and his repudiation of this kind of religious immanence had a great deal to do with his refusal to view history--except, of course, scriptural history--as religiously significant in either a positive or negative sense. As a consequence, as certain critics have noted, much of Barth's thought acquired a decided unhistorical cast, and this is its major weakness.[22] This weakness is apparent both in his failure to mention the Shoah--a manifesta-

tion of the power of nothingness sans pareil ["without exception"--Ed.]--
and in his failure to consider the implications for christology. If Jesus is
really victor, why is the devil so visibly out of control? To argue that we
suffer merely from blindness, mistaking the true state of affairs, seems
insufficient, to say the least. The "Holocaust Kingdom" [Alexander Donat]-
-the reign of radical evil--is difficult to reduce to a semblance of reality on
any ground.

Although Barth's tendency to dwell on the transcendent at the cost of the
historical is probably the main reason why he omitted the Shoah from his
study of evil, other reasons can be inferred. No one wrote much about the
Shoah before 1950; it was too soon, and the realization too difficult to grasp.
Moreover, the central principles of Barth's theology were formulated in an
earlier era, and, while he was willing to revise his ideas in light of criticism, he never altered their fundamental character. Had he been a younger
man, he might have made the "Tremendum" the subject of one of the in-
numerable brilliant essays that constitute the secondary text of his Church
Dogmatics, but this was not to be the case. The omission is unfortunate,
because it would have deepened his analysis immeasurably, as well as
enhanced his image as a Christian theologian whose heart and soul were
opposed to antisemitism. Nevertheless, much of what he did write on the
power of nothingness remains pertinent to any serious discussion of the
nature of evil today. It is also pertinent to the Shoah itself.

III. Paul Tillich: The Demonic

It was during a vacation in Paris in 1926 that Paul Tillich composed his
famous essay on the "demonic" ['Das Damonische'], thereby giving definitive expression to one of his most distinctive ideas.[23] Art, one of the great
passions of his life, is its matrix, since the artists of any society are usually
aware of the tremors beneath the surface, which they capture and portray in
their works. Art is also concerned with the elements of form and feeling,
or the rational and emotional aspects of existence, because it touches the
depths and thereby encounters the "holy" or the transcendent in all of its
possible configurations, including good and evil. Trivial art especially, as
Tillich points out, reveals something in its naivete and primitive power that
eludes the Western consciousness and its secular mentality, namely, a form-
distorting and form-destroying impulse, and which also has its roots in the
holy. "The organs of the will for power, such as hands, feet, teeth, eyes,
and the organs of procreation, such as breasts, thighs, sex organs, are given
a strength of expression which can mount to wild cruelty and orgiastic
ecstasy."[24] These organs are still recognizable--their basic forms are
maintained--but with a difference: they are exaggerated and out of propor-
tion, and thus acquire an evil aspect that is at once both religious and alien--
the demonic! What art reveals, moreover, is not confined to the artistic
realm alone. The demonic is present in the entire history of religion,
including the so-called higher religions, and of culture, including the so-

called civilizations. It is an illusion to believe that any religion or any civilization can ever escape the demonic and its sinister power; indeed, the more advanced they become, the more subtle and dangerous their distortions also become.

> Holy demonries in a highly purified form exist in the intoxicated laceration-myths and orgies, which re-echo in the sacral sacrifice of the divinity; they exist in the blood sacrifice to the god of earth who devours life in order to create life--the original model of the man-destroying demonry of economics. Holy demonries are present in the cult of war gods, who consume strength in order to give strength--the original model of demonry of war. An outstanding symbol of holy demony is Moloch, who for the sake of saving Polis devours their first-born--the original of all political demonry.[25]

In Tillich's theology, the demonic and the 'Satanic' are not the same. In one respect, the Satanic is worse than the demonic, since it stands for pure destruction devoid of any creative or positive aspect, i.e., total absolute non-being. In another respect, it is not worse than the demonic, since it contains no form and consequently has no actual existence [to exist requires some measure of form]. If the destructive impulse is completely isolated from the creative impulse, there is literally nothing to destroy, making Satan an empty symbol. Satan, however, in the Biblical and Christian tradition, is not an empty symbol; he is the father of lies and the author of evil--a demonic rather than a satanic function. There is always a "demonic residue" in his character; he is the tempter, but a temptation that lies outside creatureliness is not a temptation "because it contains no dialectics, no 'yes' and 'no'."[26] The prince of demons, according to Tillich, is really "the negative principle contained in the demonic;" otherwise, he is nothing.[27] Not a Satanic Satan, therefoi e, but a demonic Satan subverts and distorts the good, turning the forms of creation into forms of destruction in which life feeds on life and the kingdom of day becomes the kingdom of night. In religion, the demonic appears as a corruption of the holy: the "Grand Inquisitor" from Dostoevski's great novel The Brothers Karamazov who condemns the Christ in order to protect the Catholic Church--the "will to power of the sacred institutions."[28] In the economic order, the demonic appears as a corruption of the process of production, manifesting itself in what for Tillich was the archdemon of modern capitalism, which exploits and starves one segment of society for the benefit of another: a movement that is both creative and destructive at once.[29] In the political order, the demonic appears as a corruption of the drive toward community, producing what for Tillich was the archdemon of modern nationalism, in which nation preys upon nation and in which collective pride swells to inhuman size, with awful consequences for Moloch's victims.[30] Nationalism, like capitalism, with which it is closely linked, is also both creative and destructive at once.

Although social and institutional manifestations of the demonic are terrible enough, its zenith lies in the personal sphere, where the creative and destructive elements of life are elevated to the highest spiritual level. The possessed or twisted personality--the self that is divided against itself--is a source of obvious evil in history, especially when the possessed individual possesses charisma, as so often has been the case. Filled with demonic ecstasy, such persons wreak havoc, because a power from the abyss has gained control over their consciousness, giving rise to the old myth of demon-possession and its modern counterparts; the center of the soul has been invaded, and its rational unity has been shattered. The abyss, a term that Tillich adopted from the seventeenth-century German mystic Jacob Bohme[31], represents the inexhaustible character of the depths of existence, as well as its dark and menacing side. What causes the abyss to erupt is the idolatrous desire to make too much of oneself, confusing the finite with the infinite or the conditional with the unconditional, or the human with the divine. Sin, in other words, unleashes the demonic--"the creative ambition to be like God"--which, of course, in the Biblical narrative, leads to the Fall.[32] The demonic is not identical with sin, since many "sins" do not take a demonic form, but in Tillich's anal-ysis, it is closely linked to the Bibli-cal-Christian concept of sin as a fundamental rebellion against God who sets limits and boundaries in creation. Titanism, or the breaking of these boundaries, contains the seeds of self-destruction, for the self-inflated personality cannot endure; unless grace intervenes and overcomes the demonic, the fate of the fallen creature is sealed. In the end, even the divine acquires the face of the demonic: the "abyss of nothingness" into which everything sinks.[33] Did not Hitler, a demon-possessed man if ever there was one, seek Germany's destruction in the closing months of the Second World War? The nation was not to survive its Fuhrer, once the gods had turned into devils.

As sin is always present, so the demonic is always present, but it tends to express itself visibly more in some periods than in others. The end of an era, as Tillich wrote in one of his post-war books[34], is the dangerous time, since social disintegration--the crumbling of the old systems, old beliefs, and old values--invariably causes the underlying anxie-ties of life to rise to the surface in the form of a collective neurosis or psychosis. One system of this mood is the inclination to demonize one's enemies, real or imagined, as, for example, Europe demonized the Jews at the end of the Middle Ages and again at the end of the modern era [i.e. the collapse of European civiliza-tion into world war, revolution and economic and social chaos]. The National Socialist revolution in Germany was a massive explosion of the demonic in all of its form-creating and form-destroying power during a century of crisis when the world itself seemed threatened with every manner of ruin. Interestingly, to Tillich, a small sign of this ruin was Hitler's "vulgar and barbarous" use of the German language, as the disintegration of language means the disintegration of the human spirit, and a cultural capable of producing such a leader must be profoundly disturbed.[35] In The Socialist

Decision [Die sozialistische Entscheidung], a book published on the eve of the Third Reich, he de-scribed the demonic aspects of the nation's plunge into a new promethean-ism--the mystique of blood, Volk, and soil--in an attempt to recover its primordial energies or "powers of origin."[36] The concepts of "blood" and "race," arising from the animal sphere of existence, stir a naturalistic ecstasy that has its roots in a remote tribalism. Modernized in the form of a pseudo-scientific racial theory, these cries from the depths revitalize the soul in a distorted and dangerous fashion. Thus, "the superior power of being of one's own race is affirmed, foreign races and nations are disparaged, and the political and economic claims of supremacy for one's own nation are ideologically justified."[37] Since Judaism, by virtue of its prophetic genius, is the "eternal enemy" of political romanticism and its myths of origin, antisemitism is a necessary and inevitable component of the latter, especially in its Germanic anti-Christian expression.[38] Antisemitism, therefore, in Tillich's eyes, was the final and most deadly proof of the eruption of the demonic in the Germany of his lifetime. So infuriated did he become at the sight of a brownshirt at the University of Frankfort [where he was Dean of the philosophical faculty in 1932], that, we are told, he had to be forcibly restrained by his friends from embroiling himself in serious trouble.[39] National Socialism itself, Tillich believed, might have turned in a creative direction insofar as the movement contained an authentic socialist impulse, but its form-creating potential was devoured by its nationalistic and destructive instincts, so that "a self-annihilating struggle of the European peoples" was inevitable.[40]

If the National Socialist regime was demonic, and if its antisemitism was proof of its demonic character, then the Shoah, the most bitter fruit of the poisoned soil of modern German, culture must be regarded as the embodiment of the demonic in its deepest Tillichian sense. The demonic, not the Satanic! To regard the Shoah as Satanic is to eradicate every trace of human causality, transposing the evil to a purely abstract metaphysical plane where its reality disappears. To regard it as demonic, on the other hand, is to relate it to the human condition, where its essential roots surely lie. Anyone who wishes to understand the demonic, Tillich once declared in a post-war dialogue with American students, has only to gaze into the faces of Hitler's storm troopers! "I am not now thinking of the atrocities--they were consequences--but of the totally different human type those faces represent....The troopers belonged to another human category; you felt the absolute strangeness in their completely mechanized and perfectly willing obedience, the fanaticism in everything they did."[41] Evil, the kind of evil that instigates genocide, flows from perverted religion and perverted religious ideals. Did not Adolf Eichmann, Hitler's executioner, regard himself as an "idealist" who had lived his entire life in accordance with Kantian moral law, although, of course, interpreted in Nazi terms?[42] For this reason, at least in his own eyes, he was a misunderstood martyr at his trial--a sacrificial lamb on the altar of duty to the state. Idealism, therefore, at once form-creating and form-destroying, informed by a fanatical racist nationalism with its myth of origin, utterly heteronomous in its submission to authority, not unlike, according to Tillich, the total subjection of Loyola's Jesuits to the Counter-Reformation Church[43], robbed those Nazi faces of their humanity and turned them into ruthless killers. Hitler, intellectually a stupid man, was nevertheless intuitive enough to know that a spiritual vacuum existed in Germany during the Weimar Republic; he also knew how to fill it.[44] Empty spaces do not remain empty for long: demons soon rush in. The Shoah, to which Tillich seldom directly alluded, was the consequence of both an evil ideology and existential estrangement in its most terrible mode. Only if the post-war Germans accept complete responsibility for their demonic actions during the war, he insisted in a public lecture in Berlin in 1953, can the "German problem" be resolved.[45]

It cannot be said of Tillich, as it can be said of Barth, that his theology overwhelms history, causing the lessons of history to suffer neglect. On the contrary, Tillich's thought was profoundly influenced by the historical events of his age, as well as by their effect on the lives of his contemporaries and his own life. The concept of the demonic, with its psychological and religious connotations, owes as much to an experience of human decadence in a dying society as it does to mystical and metaphysical ideas borrowed from long-dead thinkers such as Jacob Bohme and Friedrich Schelling.[46] As Barth was a theologian of the transcendent, Tillich was a theologian of the imminent, and this gives his theology a different character. It saves him from Barth's christological dilemmas, in which everything, including the revelation of evil, is enclosed within the circle of faith, but it exposes him to the opposite criticism: in Tillich, according to Heinz Zahrnt, "God and the world are so interwoven that man can no longer tell the world from God, and can no longer tell God from the world."[47] To be sure, this is a general judgment, and must not be adopted unequivocally; nevertheless, it points to an authentic problem. Form-creation and form-destruction are the two sides of the demonic--the positive and the negative. In what sense, however, can the Shoah be regarded as form-creation? Was it not rather a manifestation of the purely destructive--in Tillichian language, the Satanic, rather than the demonic? Can any element of anything in the least good or positive be detected in its Satanic depths, any rationale, however perverted, any pragmatic purpose, however wrong? Some historians have argued in favor of a "functionalist" view of the Shoah, seeing it as a massive exercise in problem-solving that moved from one phase to another almost by accident, with Hitler more or less above it all, except as Germany's evil wizard.[48] If they are correct, if the mass murder of the European Jews was essentially the consequence of what sociologists since Max Weber have described as "functional rationality," then seemingly it did contain a rational or form-creating element after all. A bureaucratic machine wildly out of control and acting destructively certainly corresponds to the demonic. No doubt, there is some truth in this depiction, but any attempt to reduce the Shoah to little more than a large-scale case of Weber's social disease inevitably reduces its evil dimensions as well. The abyss disappears, and thus the mystery of radical evil: the Nihil in all its "dread, horror, and darkness"--in other words, in its transcendence. For Tillich, the divine and the demonic were always closely linked; for Barth, they were not. While Tillich was certainly correct in believing that evil must not be abstracted from human causality, the category of the demonic ultimately fails when confronted by a reality in which not even the perversion of the good can be described as present.

IV. Reinhold Niebuhr [Original Sin]

Because of its existential and Biblical foundations, Reinhold Nie-buhr's understanding of both sin and evil is similar in certain respects to Tillich's doctrine, although the American theologian dislikes the mystical and romantic ideas so important to the German theologian. Bohme and Schelling, Niebuhr believed, both erred in locating the "dark ground" of evil in the Godhead itself, making sin "a consequence of the divine nature."[49] Niebuhr, in fact, distrusted ontological thought in general; invariably, in his view, thinkers of this type [including Tillich] blur the distinction between faith and reason, losing the sharp cutting edge of the symbolic and dramatic language of the Bible.[50] Hence, his point of departure was the Biblical tale of Adam's fall and its parabolic meaning for human existence. Adam falls because the gift of freedom involved him in a profound contradiction: while bound to nature and necessity like the animals, he also knows--as the animals presumably do not know--that he is finite. Standing "at the juncture of nature and spirit," Adam is caught between their insatiable demands[51]; he can become neither pure nature nor pure spirit, but must live in the everlasting tension that they pose. Ambiguity, therefore, marks the human condition, together with tragedy, for it is impossible for a creature who recognizes his/her creatureliness not to attempt to secure himself/herself against the fate that awaits all finite things. Spirit is not content to perish; thus Adam grows anxious, and seeks a place where he cannot perish, which, of course, he cannot attain because he is Adam and not God. As a result, he falls. His anxiety, however, is not his sin, but merely its "internal precondition," or the "internal description of the state of temptation."[52] The sin is unbelief: a refusal to trust, and consequently the decision to set oneself up as God in lieu of the only true God. Anxiety produces sin, but, like Tillich's demonic, it also produces creative energy, and, indeed, all the works of culture and civilization are the fruits of Adam's determination to overcome the bondage to nature. Nor can the creative and destructive aspects of anxiety be easily separated: "The same action may reveal a creative effort to transcend natural limitations, and a sinful effort to give unconditioned value to contingent and limited factors in human existence."[53] Adam's fall is both upward and downward, and his progeny can never escape this tragic ambiguity: it is the shape of our situation.

The unbelief that lies at the root of all sin not only arises out of this situation, but points to a mystery of evil that precedes human existence itself. Sin rests on sin, and even the temptation that leads to the fall reflects some form of spiritual disorder in the universe prior to Adam. "Before man fell the devil fell."[64] In the Genesis myth, the devil is depicted as the serpent, or an evil principle in the paradisean garden, who plays the role of the tempter. The tempter, however, is also [in later theology] a fallen creature, in this case, a fallen angel: he is Lucifer, son of the morning, who rose in rebellion against the Most High, and, as a consequence, forfeited his exalted state in the heavens. Evil, therefore, is note merely the bad fruit of human sinfulness, although a sinful humanity engages repeatedly in evil actions; it is a dark shadow that falls over our lives from some trans-human zone that no theology or philosophy can really explain or fathom, and that can only be spoken of in a mythological frame. Even Kant, according to Niebuhr, caught a glimpse of this shadow in his doctrine of radical evil, in which he departed from the "moral complacency" of Enlightenment rationalism that otherwise dominates his thought, penetrating "spiritual intricacies and mysteries" in "complete contradiction to his general system."[55] Since a close analysis of sin always discovers these intricacies and mysteries, it still legitimate for Christians to conceive of "original sin," although not, of course, in literalistic terms, after the fashion of an older Christian orthodoxy. Original sin, in Niebuhrian thought, is an existential insight arising form a more profound understanding of the human condition than conventional modern wisdom with its rationalistic bias can achieve. It expresses a "dialectical truth:" we are destined to sin, as Adam was destined to fall, but, like Adam, we are held responsible nonetheless.[56] The power of the tempter is irresistible; however, the tempter appeals to our freedom, so that our freedom, not our bondage to nature, is the instrument of our fall. Our freedom, moreover, is never lost. Indeed, its highest expression, and the "final paradox" of human existence, lies in the discovery of the inevitability of sin, or the triumph of egotism, self-centeredness and the many forms of pride in human affairs.[57] One of these forms--the "pride of power"--leads readily to the kind of naked promethianism that Nazi Germany, with its "maniacal will-to-power," so perfectly exemplified.[58]

Pride is a sin of the spirit, and the sins of the spirit are always more heinous than the sins of the flesh. The pride of power, in particular, invariably indulges itself at the expense of other life. Nationalism, racism and antisemitism are ideological expressions of both individual and collective egotism, which, when combined with the tremendous might of the modern nation-state, provides a formula for catastrophe, as the Twentieth Century knows only too well. In this fashion, the Shoah and the related atrocities of the Second World War can be seen as the products of original sin in the arena of history, or the deadly harvest of the "pride of nations" run amuck. Niebuhr, of course, was not thinking of the German "Final Solution" of the Jewish problem when he delivered his Gifford Lectures in Edinburgh in 1939, although he certainly had the "daemonic" nationalism of the Third Reich in mind[59]--Edinburgh was actually bombed during one of his lectures[60]--and he was fully aware of current events in Germany. The

Final Solution, however, had not yet readily begun. Nevertheless, antisemitism was in the air, and, for Niebuhr, a life-long admirer of Judaism and friend of the Jewish people[61], it represented one of the cardinal evils of the age. "The Nazis," he wrote in 1942, "intend to decimate the Poles and to reduce other peoples to the status of helots; but they are bent upon the extermination of the Jews."[62]   To exterminate a people can hardly be regarded as anything but the most extreme of evil deeds by any moral criterion; at the same time, the murderous passions that swept the political and social order in Germany are misunderstood if they are assigned to National Socialism alone. "The Nazis....accentuated but they did not create racial pride."[63] Racial pride, and every other possible expression of radical homogeneity, arises when the ego of a group--any group--is too insecure to permit social pluralism. This insecurity drives its leaders and ideologies in a chauvinistic direction, and the masses soon follow. Consequently, as Niebuhr saw matters, one of the great tasks of civilization is to resist this instinct, employing every stratagem possible "to prompt humility and charity in the life of the majority."[64]   Otherwise, Nazi tribal primitivism, or some version of the same phenomenon, becomes a virtual certainty.[65]   Hence, it is a serious mistake for the anti-Nazi Western critics of Hitler's Germany to imagine that the crimes of the Third Reich are unique to the Germanic psyche; original sin is universal, and so are its effects.

The universality of original sin, and the mystery of radical evil to which it points, bestows an inconclusive and enigmatic character on the whole of history that contradicts every attempt to see the human epic in neat rational terms. "There are....tangents of moral meaning in history; but there are no clear or exact patterns."[66]   We have no choice except to live with this recognition. Faith, however, with its symbols of fulfillment beyond time and space, enables both Christians and Jews to discern the possibility of an ultimate resolution of the antinomies of life, although only in a glass darkly. In the case of Christianity, the central symbol of the cross, in a paradoxical fashion, reveals both the scandalous nature of history--the "abyss of meaninglessness" that crucifies goodness--and the divine mercy that saves us from falling into its depths. If the crucifixion of Jesus was a revelation of this abyss, and of the true character of the world in its depravity and evil, then the Shoah, not the least of the subsequent crimes that have victimized an innocent humanity, both confirms the Niebuhrian vision and supplies it with a new dimension. In the light of Auschwitz, to regard history as lacking in rational coherence and intelligibility, while filled with terror and death, is far from implausible, although Niebuhr did not rest his argument on this event. He could hardly have done so in his Gifford Lectures, and, in his post-World War II writings, his inclination was to see the fate of the Jews in the context of the many disasters and catastrophes of the age. It is not singled out for special treatment; however, it is not minimized either.[67] Evil is evil, and no Christian who understands the degree to which sin is interwoven with the fabric of human existence should be surprised at the diabolical ingenuity and fantastic scope of its inventions. Only the dogmatism of the Enlightenment, and the hubris of modern culture, serve as a barrier, but the unbridled optimism of yesterday has lost, or should have lost, all conviction today. We live in a genocidal world, and there were clues to this fact long before genocide and totalitarianism became the stuff of daily experience. At least one of these clues, according to Niebuhr, lies in the Christian revelation itself.

Whatever else he was, the great American theologian was a realist, and cannot be accused of writing theology as if history did not matter. It was history, and its tragic configurations, that prompted much of his thought, including his doctrine of original sin. Sin and evil were obvious realities; the critical question in Niebuhr's mind was whether an ancient and, from a modern perspective, obscurantist dogma was an appropriate theological setting for a meaningful examination of these realities in the mid-Twentieth Century. In his later years, he decided that his defense of original sin in The Nature and Destiny of Man was a "pedagogical error," not because his earlier discussion was invalid, but because modern ex-Christians were incapable of assimilating even the symbolic significance of ancient religious myths.[68] However, despite this failure, original sin, in his opinion, remained "the only empirically verifiable doctrine of the Christian faith."[69] Interestingly, at least one modern Jewish theo-logian, Will Herberg, has analyzed the human condition in much the same way as Niebuhr, with a similar stress on original sin.[70] Its profundity lies in its compound of freedom and necessity: we are free not to sin, and are therefore fully responsible for our sins; nevertheless, evil constrains us and renders our fall inevitable. The Nazis, in other words, were responsible for the Shoah, and nothing can diminish their responsibility; they acted out of their freedom. At the same time, the Shoah, in the radicality of its evil, ultimately defies rational explanation; there is something transcendent in the magnitude of the crime that points far beyond ordinary human wrongdoing--something that requires the language of mythology, because conceptual language is incapable of capturing its essence. The Nazis were grasped by this strange transcendence, and they became its agents. A tempter of some description whispered in their ears. Dr. Josef Mengele, for example [the so-called "Angel of Auschwitz"--Ed.], a man who certainly tasted of the fruit of the tree of the knowledge of good and evil, appears to have enjoyed the role of God in his death camp selections. In Mengele, a scientist with two earned doctorates, a child of modernity in every sense of the word, Auschwitz was personified, and the myth of the fall assumed a new meaning. Yet Adam is everyman, and everyman stands at the nexus of nature and spirit, subject to the anxiety that is the internal pre-condition of temptation. Mengele, therefore, the quintessential Nazi, cannot be seen as a case apart from the rest of the human race; his tragedy has universal overtones.

Since Niebuhr disagreed with both Barth's theology of the transcendent and Tillich's theology of the immanent, his understanding of evil does not suffer from the major defects of its Barthian and Tillichian counterparts.

On the other hand, it can be criticized for failing to explain why sin and evil are not always uniform, and why the tempter does not always succeed in turning the world into Mengele's "univers concentrationnaire." To be sure, there were various special factors to account for the disintegration of Western values in the mid-Twentieth Century, including the rise of nihilism. According to Niebuhr, National Socialism grew on the "soil of despair," a mood that America, unlike Europe, had managed to avoid.[71] Despair, of course, allows all the dark undercurrents of life to flow freely, and homicidal and suicidal impulses to rise to the surface. However, these special factors only beg the question. Our freedom not to sin is still paramount, and if we are fated to sin nonetheless, how is it that some sin more than others? Niebuhr does not answer this question, nor can it be answered within the framework of his theology. In all probability, it cannot be answered at all, but this is another matter. The strength of the doctrine of original sin is also its weakness. Adam is everyman, and everyman sins, and everyman's sin can take the form of murder, and everyman can find himself/herself on the wrong side of the barbed wire at Auschwitz, but, in fact, some Germans, including some Nazis, including even some members of the SS, did not. Why not? Was not Kurt Gerstein everyman, as well as Josef Mengele?[72] Did the tempter whisper less audibly in Gerstein's ear, or was he protected by grace? Here, we tres-pass on more mysterious ground, and no universalistic doctrine can assist us. Original sin illumines the human condition by explaining why evil--human, not cosmic evil--occurs, but it can never explain why it does not occur. Consequently, even Niebuhr's acute analysis does not do justice to all the paradoxes and illogicalities of life. Is not the Shoah a drama of extraordinary goodness as well as extraordinary evil?[73]

V. Conclusion

For Christians at least, Barth, Tillich, and Niebuhr are all helpful in understanding the "Tremendum." In different ways, the concept of nothingness, the concept of the demonic, and the concept of original sin ring true when tested against and evil that had not occurred when Tillich and Niebuhr composed their definitive statements, and that played no apparent part in the elaboration of Barth's post-World War II theology. This fact, in itself, demonstrates their profundity. None of the three expressions is without its problems: the concept of nothingness is attached to a cosmic optimism that is difficult to reconcile with the raw experiences of history; the concept of the demonic supplies evil--and the Shoah--with a divine ground; and the concept of original sin does not really explain Germany's fall. These deficiencies, however, must not be judged too harshly; it is doubtful if anyone, even today, could succeed where the three great Protestant theologians failed. The Shoah, in the final analysis, simply defeats both theology and philosophy. Its evil remains a mystery, and no attempt to unravel its threads by searching for the historical causes of antisemitism and mass murder in European culture will ever plumb its ultimate depths. Antisemitism is a murderous ideology, but the Nazis did not kill the Jews because they were antisemitic; they killed the Jews because they were evil. Antisemitism was a necessary, but not a sufficient, condition of the <u>Shoah</u>. The antisemitic edifice in Western thought must still be dismantled, but the devil is elusive and full of surprises. Our finitude defeats us, and we must live in fear and trembling.

For Alice Lyons Eckardt, who, together with her husband, A. Roy Eckardt, have assumed central roles in a re-thinking of Protestant theology in
light of the Shoah, attempts to find theological meaning in the suffering
which occurred during those nightmare years have been found wanting in both
the Jewish and Christian religious communities, though, to be sure, some
explanations from the past still find currency today [e.g. Ignaz Maybaum].
Her lengthy review of responses to historical suffering and attempts to find
positive meaning in suffering in terms of the redemptive process serve as
reminders that the "evil that men do" is hardly a new experience. And, while
she finds some small measure of comfort in Elie Wiesel's response of
protest to that of suffering--reminiscent of Dylan Thomas' well-known
poem "Do Not Go Gently into the Good Night"--her critique of Christian
theology is profoundly disturbing in its implications for further Jewish-
Christian dialogue: "Most of the books of Christian theology still are
written and read as if the ghastly murder of six million individuals had never
occurred. And those theologians who do mention the Shoah are apt to find a
nice little niche for it and then surround it with the same theology that could
have been written before 1933 or 1939."

SUFFERING, THEOLOGY AND THE SHOAH

Alice Lyons Eckardt

I. Introduction: Planet Auschwitz

The Kingdom of Night with its oppressive greyness, its frightening blackness, and its fire and pall of smoke was a man-made hell on earth. We no longer need Dante or Milton, the Book of Revelation, the lurid paintings of countless artists, Jonathan Edwards' hell and brimstone sermons, or the prophecies of present-day apocalypticists to conjure up the torments of hell to us. For it has all existed here on Planet Earth as "Planet Auschwitz"--a whole universe apart from our own and yet in our midst, directly linked to our world by railroad lines and roads and air-planes flying overhead taking aerial photographs, by the belongings of its victims that were sorted and shipped back to the Third Reich for reuse by its "worthy" citizens, by the products that were turned out of those factories of death: bone meal and ashes for fertilizer, hair for felt cloth and packing insulation, gold torn from the mouths and hands of victims to enrich the bank accounts of the Reich or private SS hoarders.

Moreover, its reality was far worse than the worst imaginings, for its anguish was much more than physical agony [though the extent of that was also beyond the worst nightmarish apprehensions]. From the early stages on, it included the day-to-day torment of parents who found themselves totally helpless to protect their children or their own elderly par-ents--those dearest to them who looked to them for safekeeping--from humiliation, beatings, exclusion, and the ever-increasing dangers that finally culminated in starvation, shooting, and deportation to the murder camps. In the ghetto stage [a beginning of the process of total annihilation though disguised from the victims], it encompassed the tortuous choice a father or mother sometimes had to make as to which child to give over to a rescuer, or which parent or spouse should receive the precious work permit or hiding place. Or, for a young person, the decision whether to join the partisans in the forests or to try to survive as a non-Jew outside the ghetto. In either case, such action required the youth abandoning his/her family.   The anguish involved day by day and hour by hour attempts to decide what was the best action to take, when, in fact, very few options were possible. In the exter-mination[1] camp stage it could place a person in a literal race of death in which losing meant immediate death but win-ning meant sentencing someone else to immediate death. It could force a father to make a decision as to whether it was morally permissible to ransom his son from the death barracks when that would mean another man's son being put there in his place.[2] In most cases, of course, an individual was given no opportunity to make any choice for herself/himself or other family members. Nevertheless, uncounted numbers of Jews thought they had such an opportunity on arrival at the death camps and used it to direct a younger sibling, or child, or parent to the line of mothers, children, and elderly, never dreaming that they were thus condemning this beloved individual to immediate death.

The camps of annihilation devised suffering that cannot be imagined by anyone who did not endure it, and that cannot be fully comprehended even by those who did. Ironically, the survivor's return "to the world of the living..-..makes it impossible for him to believe fully in his own past experience."[3] The reality the victims experienced every minute was that of atrocity, and the "worst" cruelty was always superseded by a still greater cruelty. Their "semi-life" was made possible only by a "hanging on, a resistance of the spirit, a clinging strength one never knew existed even in colossal circus freaks, let alone in the skeletal leftovers" of a tailor, a rabbi, a housewife."[4]

The overwhelming reality of the Shoah is embodied in the enormous suffering it imposed [perhaps even more than in its death statistics]. What are we to take of this suffering? Can our traditional theologies deal with it? Is it to be subsumed under the general category of suffering and evil? Or under God's special requirements of the children of Israel? Or does it defy or challenge earlier attempts to answer the questions raised by inordinate and inappropriate suffering? One answer is given by Andrew Schwartz-Bart in his The Last of the Just. "A suffering so great leaves nothing to be redeemed and precious little to forgive or be forgiven." In fact, the Shoah seems to signify for him humanity's faithfulness and God's unfaithfulness.[5]

Hell is conceived of as a "place" or condition where particularly wicked persons receive the punishment they deserve. Justice is seen to be satisfied at last and injustice rectified. For that reason the use of the term "hell" for the Shoah in my opening sentence is inappropriate. For surely we cannot conclude that the Jews of Europe deserved this hell on earth, even though some Jews drew this conclusion, as we will see. [Of course none of the other victims of the camps did either.[6]

Is there any purpose, human or divine, that can justify or compensate for such abysmal agony and despair? Is there any answer that could have given ease to the victims of that can reconcile the still-living survivors or their kin? If an answer cannot satisfy them, dare we let our-selves accept it? Dare we allow it to suffice? But even if some of those who perished and some of those who survived the Kingdom of Night are willing to accept the traditional answers, are we permitted to evade the difficult questions? Does not the history of the way in which Jews re-sponded to various catastrophic destructions require us to propound the questions anew and search for our own contemporary answers? Is this not how we grow in our understanding of God and of human responsibility? Perhaps only the survivors, those who have already experienced the worst that can be dealt out, have the right to cling to the older answers.

To be sure, it may be argued with considerable force that the Shoah raises no new religious questions. The questions had all been raised before--about evil, God's presence or absence, the covenant's continuing existence or its abrogation, repentance or impenitence, forgiveness, martyrdom and self-sacrifice.   And, above all, questions about suffering--especially suffering of the essentially innocent and righteous.

But if the Shoah does not produce new questions, it raises all of them with a new intensity, a demand for answers that can take the Shoah reality into account in all of its radicalness. Against the backdrop of such monstrous suffering, such inappropriate death, such widespread complicity and indifference, the traditional answers no longer satisfy many. They suddenly are seen to be as inadequate as the invisible clothing worn by the naked king in the story from our childhood.

Is there perhaps more to the present quandary than a new perception? Has a quantum change taken place? A transmutation of evil into a new and more deadly form of evil, as when deviant cells become cancerous and set out to destroy the body that is their host? Are we required then to deal with this new evil in new ways? At the very least, we are compelled to re-examine the traditional answers our faiths have supplied and on which they relied. Are we afraid that we may find that we have to reject them as deficient or, much worse, even as contributing to the evil that we deplore? Such fear does not permit us, I believe, to ignore the troubling questions or the search for appropriate answers.

II. The Claims of the Past

Both Judaism and Christianity claim there is an objective morality--i.e., an external reality that determines what is intrinsically right and good and what is wrong and evil. Therefore it must shape and define our fundamental values and what ought to be adhered to by the members of the [faith] community. There should be no quibbling over this. Reality and the society's "ought" [values and laws] say, for example, that people must not kill, steal, commit adultery, covet, etc. If they break these divine and social laws, either God or the society will punish the offenders. The Ten Commandments/Tablets of the Law and the moral value system they establish would seem to be a statement of external moral reality, insofar as they are said to originate from God, and therefore to represent the "ought."

But there are additional propositions that are also treated [generally] as fundamental within every social and especially religious community. Within Judaism and Christianity, for example, assertions are made that not only is there purposefulness in suffering but that it has positive and redemptive functions; and that virtue is attached to being among the powerless or oppressed, despite the suffering it may entail, and therefore it will ultimately be vindicated. Then there are Jesus' reported admonitions such as:

> Do not resist one who is evil....if any one strikes you o n the right cheek, turn to him the other also. [Matthew 5:39]

> ....if any man will....take your coat, let him have your cloak as well. [Matthew 5:40]

> Love your enemies, and pray for those who persecute you.... [Matthew 5:44]

> Take no thought for your life, what you shall eat; nor-....what you shall put on. [Matthew 6:25 & 3; Luke 12:22 & 29]

> Be perfect, even as your Father in heaven.... [Matthew 5:48]

> Judge not, that you be not judged. [Matthew 7:11]

> If your right eye causes you to sin, pluck it out and throw it away. [Matthew 5:29]

Are these to be considered of equal status with the Tablets of the Law? The question of whether these are apodictic [absolute] commands that are divinely undergirded or whether they are more in the nature of aggadah-- teachings about ethical standards toward which we are to strive--is one of the fundamental arguments within Christian circles.[7] However, generally Christianity has striven to speak of them as absolute commands, even though its representatives and adherents often have acted in quite contrary fashion. [Of course the Torah of the Tablets can also be subjected to hermeneutical treatment.]

If we can utilize Peter Haas' analysis of what constitutes an ethical system and what constitutes morality[8], we need to ask: Are these or similar admonitions and assertions part of foundational morality [an externally existing moral reality]? Insofar as they are claimed to repre-sent something less, an "ethic"--that is, the system of values by which a society actually shapes its behavior? If so, what is the rhetoric of this ethic, and the syntax and semantic of its discourse? What is the nature of the connection between the external moral reality and the ethic being followed? And how has the latter shaped behavior and history?

I am not convinced that the distinction can be a hard and fast one since communities usually insist that their values reflect external reality.

I want to consider one of the basic concepts that are in one way or another fundamental to Judaism and Christianity--suffering [and by extension pay a bit of attention to powerlessness].

Evil and suffering have always been, and doubtless will always be, subjects of great concern, not only to their victims but to any system of thought that postulates a good creator or a purposeful universe. Attempts to explain them are manifold. There is not space to do a thorough survey of these explanations. But I want to examine some of their consequences for both the public rhetoric and the public ethic, including the negative form of that ethic [which usually means as it is applied to "the other"], and for the way they get applied in faith and action.

III. Explanations

Explanations usually tend to put the burden on the sufferers: Either it is their fault [even if no one, except God, knows exactly what sin or wrongdoing has been committed by them or their predecessors!]. Or, it must be borne since God has decreed it in His infinite wisdom. Thus, explanations seek to make a virtue of or assign positive value to something that we instinctively believe to be wrong and evil. The "what is" is justified or assigned legitimacy. [If there is suffering or evil, there must be a reason for it.]

Then the "what is" [the reality] becomes a basis for establishing a system of ethical principles that is intended to determine behavior--what I am calling an "ethic of suffering," [along with an ethic of powerlessness, meekness, non-resistance, etc.].

Some questions that can be raised about the validity and viability of an ethic of suffering and powerlessness include: [a] To what extend have they genuinely been manifested by individuals or the community, especially by the dominant community or those with power and authority? Have these ethics been anything more than an idealized "ought" that have been lauded but ignored--except as something that others are advised to accept? [b] Have they helped the victims or abetted victimizers? In the spotlight of history-- especially of our century--have they helped to sustain life and hope, or to foster death and despair? [Have we sold ourselves--or been sold--a faulty bill of goods?] [c] Is there justification for continuing to assert an ethic of suffering [or ethics of suffering and powerlessness, if we need to distinguish between them]? [d] What do the victimized have to say?

If there is sufficient reason to challenge an ethic of suffering and powerlessness, we need to consider whether there are alternative ethics that are retrievable by Christians and Jews that are free of the faults or pitfalls of the prevailing and dominant ethic regardless of whether that ethic is actually practiced or only verbalized.

Without minimizing any of the suffering that in our century has been deliberately and cold-bloodedly inflicted on millions of humans in numerous other situations, we need to pay particular attention to what has been done within our own Western, primarily Christian, sphere since it is here that we can and must test our ideals, our ethics, and our profession of faith by their consequences. And Jews need to make this sphere their primary concern as well, since so much of their past experience has been at the hands of the Christian world, and so much of their present existence and future hope lie within the Western societies.

IV. Jewish Explanations

From the earliest recorded Jewish efforts to understand the rea-sons for the sufferings, defeats, and catastrophes that the covenant people experienced to even the most recent, we find a number of wide-ranging answers: [1]   suffering represents deserved punishment; [2]   or divine pedagogy: teaching, chastising, disciplining; [3] some suffering is incomprehensible but must be borne since God is trustworthy; [4] the next world will rectify the imbalances of this world; [4a] suffering will increase the reward of the righteous in Paradise; [5] the messianic future in this world will rectify present injustice; [6] suffering of the righteous is to purify and strengthen them, expiate their sins, and bring their faith into action; [6a] it represents "afflictions of love;" [7] natural evil is part of the ordering of, and is for the overall good of, the universe; [8] humans are responsible for causing suffering; [9] it is not the will of God, and God suffers with people; [10] it represents the birth pangs of Messiah and redemption; [11] or, does not represent the birth pangs of Messiah and redemption, and is meaningless [at least to humans]; [12] suffering of Israel is on behalf of others and/or God and therefore is vicarious suffering.

None of these explanations, arguments, or assertions stood alone, but were intermingled and called on by various persons and communities according to their perceived needs.   Above all, the conviction of God's absolute justice was firmly held, even during and despite the various assaults on the Ashkenazic Jewish community of Europe throughout the tenth to fourteenth centuries. The testimonies of the martyr-victims of the Crusades not only repeatedly attested that the Holy One's justice must not be questioned, that their own destruction was decreed by heavenly judgment, regardless of their inability to fathom that decree, but they also made use of other traditional explanations.   The chroniclers of the events speculated that these victims were the elite of all generations, chosen for their capacity to fulfill the highest duty, in order to "atone for the past deeds of Israel [and] to create a fund of good will for coming generations."[9]

Under the circumstances of unusual suffering the 18th century Poland, the Baal Shem Tov [Founder of Hasidic Judaism--Ed.] and his disciples did not attempt to offer reasons but sought to help their people transcend it, to find joy and even ecstasy in their relationship with God in spite of their plight. But the rebbes [Hasidic rabbis--Ed.] went a step further and struggled, on behalf of the people, to breach what appeared to be the closed door of Heaven and to "influence God and move Him to compassion and grace" towards His suffering children.[10]

V. Christian Explanations

The new Christian community had to answer the same difficult questions. Because of its rootedness in Judaism and in the shared scriptures, it came up with many of the same answers: [1]   divine punishment; [2] chastisement or warning; [3]   disciplining; or [4]   a purifying force; [5] suffering leads to hope and assurance via endurance and character[11]; [6]   it provides an opportunity to witness on behalf of Christ [thus this suffering allowed for redemptive possibilities that could find merit in the suffering]; [7]   it is evidence of divine love; [8]   suffering is the result of human disobedience.   Some other explanations differed more from Judaism: [9] redemption of suffering will be made only in the next life, hence there are no redemptive possibilities in present suffering[12]; [10]   suffering for the elect is part of the "natural order of events" as this world must be destroyed[13]; [11]   it offers a contrast by which humans can learn to know and choose good; [12]   it is punishment for sin, but only at the social level--that is, it need not be related to a person's sins; [13]   natural [physical] evil is attributed to the wisdom of God[14];   [14]   it is a corruption of the original creation and is purposeless, therefore only Christ can vanquish it; [15] suffering and evil do not disrupt creation as creation belongs to the Creator; and it is not "spiritually calamitous for persons of faith" who are assured of "eternal peace and justice."[15]

In general, we may say that the Christian emphasis and expectation lay with the hereafter, however near or far of that might be: "after this brief suffering" [I Peter 5:10].   As Carter Heyward has recently written, "the loudest Christian voices have spoken historically of God's justice as characteristic of another time [the eschaton] and/or another place [Heav-en-]....Christian theology's justification of God--theodicy--has been to direct our attention beyond the here and now...."[16]   Moreover, although in several branches of the church, Christian martyrs and saints have a function as vicarious sufferers and therefore intercessors, Christ bears the primary responsibility for redeeming innocent suffering.

By contrast, although Judaism also looks forward to the "messianic age" or the "world to come" when all will be put right, the predominant perspective is that the new age will take place in this world, not in some heavenly abode. Moreover, it is more insistent than Christianity that humanity and God have a mutual responsibility to bring about that perfected world.[17]

VI. Suffering as Redemptive and Its Function as an Ethic

One of the primary ways by which the problem of evil and suffering has been approached is to go beyond explanation and ask more directly whether suffering has any positive function in the process of redemption.   The answers to suffering that we have considered so far often touch on this question. But both Judaism and Christianity have additional and more explicit ways of affirming that there is some redemptive force in the suffering of the faithful.

VII. Judaism's Arguments for Redemptive Power in Suffering

[a] The Thirty-Six Just Ones: In Judaism a concept developed that there are in every generation Thirty-Six Just Ones[18] whose piety and righteousness sustain the world. This concept has received more attention in Jewish kabbalah [mystical literature--Ed.] and folklore than elsewhere. In Jewish folklore, these obscure lamed vov tzaddikim [Thirty-Six Just Ones] or "hidden saints" were believed to have special powers which they would utilize to save Israel in times of great peril.

[b] Binding of Isaac: More central to mainstream Judaism, however, is Isaac, who for at least two millennia has been assigned a central place as an intercessor or reconciler.   The primary lesson drawn from the Genesis account of the "binding" of Isaac was that God does not desire human sacrifice. Thus Isaac saved unnumbered humans from being made sacrificial victims.[19]   But other consequences were discerned as well.   In time, Isaac came to be seen as the archetypal martyr, and as the lamb of sacrifice who, though "fully and completely offered," was not killed. His sacrificial action, that is, his willingness to be a sacrifice, was held to serve a prior expiation for Israel's sins, God could be asked to remember the Akedah [Binding--Ed.] so that He would answer Israel's prayers, deflect His anger against the people, remember the divine mercy, and bring redemption to her. Indeed, Isaac's "sacrifice" would also be a blessing for all peoples.[20]

[c] Maccabean, Hadrianic, and Later Martyrs: In the Biblical telling the readiness of Abraham to obey this most outrageous of divine commands[21] is offset by the angelic intrusion that stayed Abraham's hand. But during the Maccabean period of resistance to Antiochus Epiphanes' efforts to force Jews to abandon their God in favor of the Hellenistic gods, more radical sacrifices were made. Many Jews accepted martyrdom for themselves and their kin as a way of remaining faithful to the One Holy God of Israel and of sanctifying the Name of God in the presence of idolaters. The stories of a woman [later called Hannah] and her seven sons, and Eleazar come from this time.[22]   These martyrs became the paradigm of loving acceptance of

suffering to the death for God's sake, even without God's saving intervention.

During the subsequent Hadrianic persecutions, the suffering and death of the Ten Martyrs [all Rabbis] became famous.[23]   And the earlier acts of martyrdom were reenacted many times as parents and offspring refused to give in to another attempt to force them to abandon the covenant with their Lord. As recounted in this new setting, the faithful mother comforted her sons by assuring them that they were created in order to "sanctify in the world the Name of the Holy One...." But the mother also recognized that Abraham and Isaac had had a relatively easy testing. And so as her sons prepared to die she admonished them, "Go and tell Father Abraham....You built one altar, but I have built seven altars and on them have offered up my seven sons. What is more: Your's was a trial; mine was an accomplished fact!"[24]

And in the mid-seventeenth century when the Chmielnicki massacres devastated the Jewish communities of the Ukraine and Poland, Nathan Hanover concluded in his chronicle: "if our fate be decreed from Heaven, let us accept the judgment with rejoicing."[25]

[d] Sacrifice of Isaac: Surprisingly, however, we find that early in the Common Era, the Talmudic sages began to hold that Isaac was not spared, contrary to the account in Genesis.[26]   Some sources said that before the knife was stayed a quarter of his blood was shed "as an atonement for Israel." In others, he was slain and his body reduced to ashes on the altar. In either case, the "blood of Isaac's Akedah" and "the ashes of Isaac" were held to serve "as atonement and advocate of Israel in every generation and advocate of Israel in every generation. And whenever Isaac's descendants are in straits [God], as it were, beholds the blood of his [Isaac's--Ed.] Akedah, and pity fills Him so that He turns away the wrath of His anger from His city and His people."[27]

The readiness of Jews to accept martyrdom as a way out of sanctifying God's Name [Kiddush Ha-Shem] became a problem for the Talmudic Rabbis as they sought to sustain Jewish life and faith after the devastation of the Roman wars. They tried to establish conditions under which martyrdom need not be enacted. Perhaps this new attention to the atoning value of Isaac's blood and ashes was, in part, a way of assuring the people that the necessary sacrifice had already been performed and that further ones were not required except under unusual circumstances.

In the generation of the First Crusade massacres, a synagogue poem pointed out that "Once, over one Akedah Ariel [synonym for Jerusalem--i.e. the Jewish people--Ed.] cries out before Thee ," and then asked the agonizing question, "But now how many are butchered and burned!/Why over the blood of children did they not raise a cry?" Despite this question, there were no real protests, no calling attention to "the radical difference between the unconsummated offering [of Isaac] and the offering mercilessly brought to completion [in their own case]." Can this be explained by their having been aware of the ancient tradition according to which the offering was consummated? Certainly the twelfth century poetic interpretation of the Akedah by Rabbi Ephraim and the commentary by Abraham ibn Ezra that "the father 'acted contrary to Scripture,' 'for he slaughtered and abandoned' Isaac on the altar" demonstrate that such an understanding was available to Jews in central and western Europe at the time.[28]

VIII. Christianity's Arguments for Redemptive Power in Suffering

[a] Jesus' sacrificial and atoning death: In the first and second centuries of the Common Era, Christianity gave new emphasis to the concept of the atoning function of a righteous one's death.[29] Thus Jesus' sacrificial and atoning death became the cornerstone of Christian faith.

Since Jesus' followers were convinced that his tragic end must have served a purposeful and divinely-ordained end, new consideration was given to the meaning that could be found in the suffering of the innocent: even, in the case of Jesus, the necessity of it.

For the apostate Paul, the death of "Christ Jesus" must have been necessary in order to overcome the sin and death that the first human, Adam, had introduced into the world [Romans 5:12-21]. No other means but Christ's "expiration by his blood" would suffice [Romans 5:8; 3:24-25].

Not surprisingly, Second Isaiah's figure of a vicariously suffering Servant of the Lord was appropriated by the Gospel writers and the early church and read as a foretelling of Jesus' role in the divine drama of salvation. The writers of the Synoptic Gospels were intent on "showing how Jesus summed up this whole long tradition of his people by his sacri-fice and death."[30]

And just as Second Isaiah had written five and one-half centuries earlier that "it was the will of the Lord to bruise him; he had put him to grief....," so also Paul and the Gospel accounts present Jesus' death and resurrection "as the supreme disclosure of God's love in offering his Son to die, the righteous for the unrighteous, to reconcile a sinful world to its God."[31] [At the same time, Jesus is also presented as one who voluntarily assumed and/or accepted his destiny, even death on the cross.[32]

The Epistle to the Hebrews makes much of the purpose of Jesus' suffering and his sacrificial role: He "learned obedience through what he suffered" [5:8]; he offered himself "once for all" as a sacrifice in place of the daily sacrifice at the Temple [7:27]; he "was crowned with glory and honor because of the suffering of death, so that by the grace of God he might taste death for every one" [2:9]; he was made "perfect through suffering [2:10]; he "entered once for all into the Holy Place, taking not the blood of goats and calves but his own blood, thus securing an eternal redemption" [9:11].

[b] Christian martyrs and emulators of Christ: Christ's death was a martyr's expiation and his sacrificial love overcame sin and death. But not only for himself: all are "heirs of God and fellow heirs with Christ, provided we suffer with him in order that we may also be glorified with him" [Romans 8:17]. [See also II Timothy 2:11-12 and Hebrews 10:8-10.]

By following his example, the faithful will find comfort even in this life if they endure their trials patiently [II Corinthians 1:6], and will be approved of by God if they endure pain "while suffering unjustly" [I Peter 2:19, 21]. A second century Hellenistic-Christian sermon affirmed that suffering at the hands of the authorities was "part of a pattern of events in which the people of God....opposed the worldly powers."[33] Sixteenth century Anabaptists went so far as to insist that the Christian pilgrim must suffer with Christs. It is not enough to believe that Christ died as an atonement for others.[34]

In any case, "the sufferings of this present time are not comparing with the glory that is to be revealed to us" [Romans 8:18]; "this slight momentary affliction is preparing for us an eternal weight of glory beyond all comparison" [II Corinthians 4:17].

In this way many of Jesus' followers in the first and second centuries were imbued with the conviction that they ought to emulate their Lord. As they suffered with Christ [and he suffered in them], so would they be glorified with him. Once they had "died 'for the glory of Christ,' the martyrs were assured of 'fellowship for ever with the living God'."[35]

But these Christian martyrs had other models in addition to their Christ: the Maccabean martyrs were specifically mentioned by the Christians of Lyon and Vienne who were prepared to die for their faith in 177. There is no question about the significant influence this Jewish martyr tradition come to have on the Christian theology of righteous suffering.[36]

However, as the church gained acceptance and recognition in the Eastern and Western empires, martyrdom became superfluous--except for those Christians who refused to conform to the official orthodoxy! The remembrance of the early martyrs continued as a part of the church's liturgy, iconography, and teaching, but most Christians no longer needed to be prepared to accept the martyr's role. The remembrance did nothing, however, to soften attitudes towards their neighbors who were forced to suffer and be martyred if they wished to remain true to their own faith convictions.

IX. The Isaac and Jesus Traditions

We cannot fail to notice a number of similarities between the [near--Ed.] sacrifice of Isaac and the sacrifice of Jesus as these two events were elaborated upon in the Jewish and Christian communities. In fact, the Church Fathers made a specific connection between the two, seeing the Akedah as a prefiguring of Golgotha: Isaac as the "prototype for the sufferings and trials of Jesus;" Isaac carrying the wood for the sacrificial pyre just as Jesus bore his cross; Isaac as the sheep for the burnt offering and Jesus as the lamb slain for others, even as the Paschal lamb.[37]

From the synagogue's perspective, there are differences between its claims regarding Isaac's [near--Ed] sacrifice and the church's claims regarding Jesus' sacrifice. For one thing, the Rabbis never "set up all salvation and hope of Israel on one man's grace in times gone by." Righteous persons of all times gain merit for the people before heaven. Moreover, the Rabbis acknowledged that there are times when the Akedah fails to be sufficient due to Israel's iniquities. "There are no merits in perpetuity on high without continuing good action below. Hence, he who cannot find favor through the acts of Torah cannot find favor through the Akedah either....The Akedah Merit proclaims and promises that....the sum of the righteousness of the Fathers is there to add to and complete the reward of sons who engage actively in Torah; and thereby redemption makes haste to come."[38]

By contrast, Augustine spelled out on behalf of the church the absolute uniqueness of the Christ event: it was [and remains] an absolute necessity and revolutionary "reversal of human history."[39] [Ireneaus's view that the Christ event was a further evidence of God's grace which had been present in the world from the beginning was rejected categorically by Augustine.]

X. A Negative Ethic

The church did not allow for any equivalency in Isaac's "sacrifice" and Jesus' crucifixion [despite the connection it made between the two events], for it used only the Genesis account, that is, the unconsummated sacrifice of Isaac. Therefore it could taunt the synagogue with the fact that Abraham was not forced to abandon his son and Isaac was not required to give up his life, whereas God did make the total sacrifice of His only Son and Jesus' sacrifice was actually carried out. Nor would the church consider any real comparison between the atoning value of Isaac's suffering and the atoning value of Jesus' death on the cross: Isaac's suffering served only Israel and only until the covenant was abrogated and replaced by the new covenant that Jesus established; Jesus' death was a once-for-all sacrifice sufficient for all peoples and all times; only Jesus' death conquered death [through his subsequent resurrection].

Furthermore, since the church, early in its history, came to the view that God had cast off the original covenant people because of their unfaithfulness and had chosen a new people--the people of Christ--the suffering of God's new people was celebrated as faithful testimony to God's truth [as embodied in Christ and in his church].[40] They suffered as faithful witnesses to God's love and Christ's power to save. But the suffering of the unfaithful--the people of the "old" covenant--was nothing less than deserved punishment for their "hardheartedness and unbelief."[41] Their suffering served as a negative witness, demonstrating what happens to those who reject God's gifts and verifying for Christians that God had indeed rejected His former people.

In this way the theme of the suffering of the righteous was turned into a weapon against the Jewish people who had originated both the concept of righteous suffering and the deed of martyrdom, and who continued to die as witnesses to God [in their own view]. Moreover, adding insult to injury, Christian persecutors often interpreted Jews' willing martyrdom as connivance with the devil.

With considerably more reason Jews also turned the concept of the suffering of the righteous against their Christian adversaries. During the persecutions of the tenth to fourteenth centuries, Jews saw their own martyrdom as suffering on behalf of the true faith whereas the religion whose representatives were forcing this choice on them was seen not only as false but also as contemptuous. The offers to spare them from death in exchange for conversion were rejected with bitter words. Or they pretended to accept baptism in order to have the opportunity to spit at the crucifix.[42]

XI. Responses to Shoah Suffering: Jewish

Since the vicarious suffering of the people Israel as part of God's "secret aim" of transforming the world had become the recurrent theme of Jewish writings from the Middle Ages on, particularly at times of intense Jewish suffering, it is not surprising to find that during and after the Shoah it continued to be expressed [along with many of the other themes, of course].

Rabbi Hirschler, who died in Mauthausen in 1943, is reported to have said, "To us [Jews] the world is like a crucible into which God plunges us in the course of time because we have forgotten Him and have not respected His laws, perhaps for our purification, perhaps for a sacrifice of atonement for the salvation of others. [Therefore,] it may be right and beautiful to suffer beyond one's own sins."[43] Notice, however, the lack of certitude with which he propounds the traditional views, an uncertainty that only partially hides his unspoken questions.

Rabbi Elchanan Wasserman restated the theme of atoning sacrifice with more assurance. As he and others awaited execution at the Ninth Fort outside Kovno [July 6, 1941], he said to his fellow Jews: "It would seem that in heaven we are considered Tzaddikim [Righteous Ones--Ed.]. For atonement is to be made with our bodies for Klal Yisroel [the world-wide Jewish people--Ed.]. As we do Teshuvah [Repentance--Ed.] we should [be concerned] with saving [the souls of] our American brothers and sisters so that they can continue as the Shearith Israel [the Saving Remnant]....We go carry out the greatest Mitzvah [Commandment--Ed.], Kiddush Ha-Shem [Sanctification of the Divine Name--Ed.]. The fire which will burn our bodies is the fire which will resurrect the Jewish people." For Rabbi Wasserman and his brother-in-law, Rabbi Chaim Ozer Grodensky of Vilna, the churban [destruction--Ed.] had a "positive meaning: the more evil/punishment, the closer the redemption. Each moment of cosmic catharsis, of suffering, is a moment of messianic entry into history." All of the actors in the drama were "instruments" of God's plan to transform history.[44]

Other rabbis used alternative explanations, such as that Israel's suffering was divine chastisement intended to turn the people back to God. The sin for which they were being punished was variously identified as assimilation, or the idolatry of Zionism[45], or the abandonment of Torah in favor of secularism or socialism. Writing in the Fall of 1939, after the pogrom [attack--Ed.] of Kristallnacht [Night of the Broken Glass, Berlin, November 10-11, 1939--Ed.] and the beginning of Polish Jewry's agony, Rabbi Wasserman put the blame on all of the foregoing "sins," and held that the punishment fitted the crime. Nevertheless, he added, the sufferings were all for the sake of reminding Jews of their Jewishness and recalling them to their intended role in redemption.[46]

Contrariwise, Rabbi Issachar Shlomo Teichtal of Budapest in late 1943 came to the conviction that opposition to political Zionism had indirectly contributed to and compounded the tragedy of European Jewry. The purpose of their suffering was to be a stimulant to the Jews in galut [exile--Ed.] to return to the Source--the land and his true Jewish self. In this way suffering could be the "prelude to redemption," the beginning of tikkun [repair--Ed.], by shattering defective reality.[47]

After the war Ignaz Maybaum also dared to speak of a constructive outflow from the horrors of the Shoah. By God's "severe decree" [gezirah], the history of humankind had been thrust into a new age. The old obstructions to progress and community were now removed: the medieval Christian dogma that outside the Church there is no salvation, and the medieval Jewish Codes that "worked on the principle: outside the din [law--Ed.], you cannot be a Jew." Now "Jew and Christian meet as equals...." The third churban [his designation for the Shoah] makes possible "messianic progress," just as the two earlier gezirot did [when the two Temples were destroyed].

Maybaum was driven to find some such meaning because he "refused to consider the possibility that Jewish history was devoid of meaning." For the Jew, "Auschwitz is the great trial. The Jew is tried, tested, like Abraham at Moriah," but the faithful remnant will pass the test. There was no question for Maybaum but that the six million "died an innocent death; they died because of the sins of other. Western man must, in repentance, say of the Jew what Isaiah says of the Servant of God: 'Surely, our diseases he did bear, and our pain he carried....he was wounded because of our transgressions, he was crushed because of our iniquities' [43:4, 5]. Jewish martyrdom explains the meaning [of this passage]....better than the medieval Christian dogma [of the cross] ever did."[48]

How do survivors of the Shoah respond to the various ways by which Jewish tradition and thinkers have sought to deal with suffering? There is, of course, no way to answer that question definitively. However, Reeve Robert Brenner's detailed survey of seven hundred survivors [camp inmates and those who survived outside the camps], and the effect or non-effect of the Shoah on these persons' religious beliefs and observances is most helpful.

With reference to the thesis that in the Shoah the Jewish people were the sacrifice for humanity's sins, only 11 percent gave affirmative responses. One who did said, "....the good and the best Jews died and the worst lived on. The only way you can make sense out of that is to assume that the one was sacrificed for the other...." But one who disagreed spoke out strongly against any concept of vicarious suffering: "God is not unjust and He is not a Christian God who can offer some third party, Jesus or the Jews of Europe, to die for the sins of others....there is no vicarious atonement in Judaism in a way which would have God sacrifice six million of the innocent for the guilty; nor were they sacrificial lambs, or goats dispatched to the wilderness to absolve the sins of others."

A significant 72 percent voiced the opinion that God was not involved at all and that the destruction was due entirely to human relationships.

Some of the traditional answers were not given by a single survivor in this study: for example, the explanation that evil--the radical evil of the Shoah--is illusory; or the idea that the sufferings of the righteous are "trials of Divine Love;" or that God permits or causes suffering in order to reveal the divine power; or that suffering is God's way of strengthening individuals or refining their nature or purifying their moral character. [The suffering of six million "for the benefit of those that lived? That's insane....What a great injustice to the dead that would be...."]

Not one of the survivors in this study "thought the world-to-come-- whether as afterlife, heaven, messianic future, resurrection, or whatever a survivor may conceive--was sufficient alone to make sense out of the Holocaust" [although some believed into a world-to-come]. As one said, "nothing, no possible reward however great which we may be entitled to and which we may receive in a world-to-come can ever compensate for the suffering which we endured in this world."

The single most overwhelming response showed that 98 percent of the survivors in this study rejected the theory that Jewish martyrdom in the Shoah was the result of divine judgment.[49]

Albert Friedlander echoes and reemphasizes this judgment. Any such conclusions are misuses of the Shoah, even if they were made by victims or survivors of the Shoah. They become "a defense for established position; a substitute for religion, and a substitute for thinking." Just as Jews had to reshape their theology after the previous churban, Jews of today must seek for new understanding. After Auschwitz, Jewish self-definition rejects "imposed concepts" of Jewish destiny "that view Israel as the vicarious-/atonement, as a lamb of God or a suffering messiah figure. The tremendum....may never be defined as Jewish destiny."[50]

Richard Rubenstein and John Roth agree with Friedlander and Emil Fackenheim and the majority of Brenner's survivors in insisting that while perhaps in some instances the belief that "human suffering may be considered instrumental or redemptive," the "Holocaust defies such hope. No imaginable good-to-come will ever make up completely for what was lost in the Nazi era."[51]

In a profound Jewish theological response to the Shoah and its questions, Andre Neher focuses on the silence of God wherever and whenever it has been felt. He affirms that the testing of Job and of Naomi [and by extension, of the Six Million] is "inauthentic" for, unlike Abraham, they were never asked for any decision or response. A destiny was simply imposed on them; their loved ones were taken from them and destroyed. "Job is alone, cut off from his children by the hurricane of death. And to the end of his experience and of his book, he will remain alone; and though he is given other children, none of his dead children will ever be given back to him....The testing of Job is marred by a failure, that supreme failure which is death."[52] [Compare, if you will, a comment from one of Brenner's survivors: "Ten more wives and a hundred more children will never replace the one beloved wife and the two precious children I lost to the Nazis."[53] And then, Neher protests, we are told, as if the burden of Job's innocent suffering were not enough, that Job was a substitute for Abraham; that God had transferred "all the trials of the combat" from Abraham to his nephew, Job; that Job suffered vicariously for Abraham [as Isaac suffered for Israel, and the Jewish people suffer for the world][54] Why? Because of Abraham's response to God's testing: Neher examines the text and concludes that Abraham decided that he had had enough [even though he had had a choice--whether to obey God's command, and even though Isaac was restored to him]. Having said "Yes" to the test of Mount Moriah, "Abraham could never again repeat his acquiescence, and, in fact, he was not to do so." He decided he was "willing to pay the price of the silence of God" rather than risk another test.[55] Therefore God needed Job.

Does such imposed vicarious suffering help us in our troubling quest for answers or does it only make the task more painful?

And Jews after the Shoah? Almost none of the six million were given any choice; and most [all?] experienced God's silence. Can or will Jews today say "Yes" to the continuation of the covenant relationship with its concomitant possibility of further testing or suffering on behalf of others" Or have they had enough of an ethic of suffering?[56] The answer is neither a simple "No" nor "Yes." In one very important sense, most Jews have said "Yes" by refusing to abandon their Jewish identity and by refusing to opt out of the community. Emil Fackenheim believes that Jews today are responding to the death camps as ancient rabbis would have done--by seeking "to meet the absolute evil of the death camps in the only way absolute evil can be met--by an absolute opposition on which one stakes one's life." As he so tellingly points out, "In the age after Auschwitz, for any Jew to survive as a Jew and bring up his children as any kind of Jew....is itself a monumental act of faithfulness." For every Jew today knows that Jews were murdered in Nazi Europe not because of their faith, or lack of faith, but because of the faith of their grandparents. And they cannot know whether their grandchildren will be sought out for destruction for that same reason. No one wishes to prepare a generation of sacrificial offerings; yet no one wishes to collaborate in finishing Hitler's job."[57]

Perhaps the resolution of the dilemma is the one already undertaken: a willingness to reaffirm the covenant, in spite of God's silence in the Shoah, as long as they have Jewish sovereignty.[58] The "Yes" is qualified by this condition. For most Jews are now convinced that martyrdom is no longer the way of sanctifying God's Name or of fulfilling Jewish existence. Therefore, Jewish powerlessness and vulnerability must at last come to an end along with martyrdom. Jews have learned that they will have to make their use of power in ways they dislike as part of the payment for their intention to survive, and to survive as a free people. Jews may have to die defending their right to life as a people but they will die fighting. For what function can martyrdom have when the entire people is being threatened with extinction? Can dead covenant partners witness to God's love or cooperate in perfecting the creation? Is not the covenant meant to be a means of sustaining life? [As the Warsaw Ghetto approached its final demise, a few of the surviving rabbis were troubled by such questions and came to somewhat similar conclusions: the surviving people were to do whatever they could to live as a way of sanctifying God's Name--Kiddush Ha-Shem--and preserving the covenant.[59]

As Gordon Tucker puts it, the State of Israel is intrinsic to the "restorative, history-respecting interpretation of redemption." It fits the Biblical meaning of geulah [redemption] in the very concrete meaning of that term: a state, a society, in time and history, that makes and is affected by history. It also fits with the Biblical understanding of "salvation" which encompassed the survival of the remnant and the return of those "saved" to their land. The modern State of Israel "is worthy of blessing and is precious because it is a restoration that breathes life into real human beings and into their collectivity. [Moreover, it demonstrates partial redemption is possible and has value.] Redemption need not be 'all or nothing'."[60]

Elie Wiesel is troubled by the traditional answers and tales particularly as they speak of suffering and determine response to it. Although Abraham dared to query God and remonstrate with Him on behalf of others, he was silent when God told him to make of his son an olah [a totally burnt offering]. Why did not Abraham protest on behalf of this innocent son?[61]

Must we not also wonder rather than celebrating Abraham's obedi-ence? By his not protesting in this instance, did Abraham consign his people to being perpetual victims? And even to their being participants in their own victimization? Was it not his silence before God that led the father in Auschwitz on the even or Rosh Ha-Shanah [Jewish New Year--Ed.], 1944, not only to conclude that he was prohibited from ransoming his son from the death barracks [because another father's son would be put there in his place], but also to conclude that it was a merit to offer his only son to God as Father Abraham had done?[62]

Wiesel also challenges Job--why did he not carry his protest, his accusations against God, to the end? Why did he suddenly give in? "His resignation as a man was an insult to man....He should have continued to protest...."[63]

The need to protest is one of Wiesel's major themes: protest against human injustice and protest against divine injustice. For Wiesel, failure to protest is a failure to be involved in the divine-human drama: it is a renunciation of responsibility, and thus it enables evil and suffering to prevail.[64] "In those years [of the Shoah], anyone who did not question God was not a true believer....I believe God himself became a question mark then."[65]

Though Wiesel remains within the tradition, he also goes beyond it by pushing the tradition into confronting the revolutionary difference with which it was faced in the years of the Third Reich and which it cannot ignore even now since the precedent has been set. His protests and reworking of the Bible stories are serious and existential attempts to make Biblical faith face that ultimate test.[66]

The precedent of the Shoah requires not only protest to and against God and against any social injustice, but it also requires that the Jewish people cannot ignore the consequences of powerlessness. Wiesel is convinced that "the Jewish people today could not survive physically or spiritually if it were not for Israel." "Israel is the cornerstone, the backbone of Jewish existence everywhere." [In 1970 he also said that he believed that if Israel were to "end in tragedy, it would be the end of the human race....that for the first time man's fate and the Jewish fate have converged....If the world will again try to kill the Jew, it will mean the end of the world."[67]

XII. Responses to Shoah Suffering: Christian

How do Christians speak of suffering after the Shoah?   Have their thoughts and words been changed at all by that cataclysm in history and human relations? Do they feel any need to change them? Or do they assume that their theology has said the final words on the subject based on their inherited understanding of Jesus death?

Most books of Christian theology still are written and read, and most sermons are preached, as if the ghastly slaughter of six million individuals had never occurred and certainly as if it has no relevance for Christian thought. Those "mainline" theologians who do not mention the Shoah are apt to find a nice little niche for it and then surround it with the same theology that could have been written before 1933 or 1939-1968. On the basis of the theologically-rooted conviction that Christ's experience on the cross encompasses [and even exceeds] all human agony whenever and wherever it occurs, theological constructs do not have to be altered in order to take something new into account for nothing new matters. For such Christians, Auschwitz can be identified as the Golgotha of the Jewish people in the twentieth century without considering whether there are any significant differences in that Golgotha and the original one, or wondering whether Auschwitz has something to say to us about how the church has been interpreting Golgotha all the intervening centuries.[68]

Yet that is exactly what facing the Shoah requires--a recognition that a rupture in history occurred.   The German Catholic theologian Johannes-Baptist Metz, who acknowledges the radical demands that the Shoah makes on Christianity, is insistent that Christianity cannot do theology with its back toward Auschwitz; and once facing Auschwitz, it must realize that Christian theology in its entirety must be revised. "We will have to forego the temptation to interpret the suffering of the Jewish people from our standpoint in terms of saving history. Under no circumstances is it our task to mystify this suffering!"[69] Robert McAfee Brown agrees: "No theology can encompass this event so that its wounds are closed, its scars healed. The event forever precludes easy faith in God or faith in humanity....Neither faith, I believe, can confront the Holocaust without in some ways being transformed."[70]

If one were to identify Auschwitz with Golgotha, what could the redemptive purpose of six million deaths be? [After all, in the Christian scheme, Christ has already made redemption available to all humanity, so what else can six million "crucifixions" accomplish?"]¹ Pope John Paul II and John Cardinal O'Conner have attempted to grapple with that question.

Addressing the Jews of Warsaw on June 14, 1987, the Pope confessed, "We believe in the purifying power of suffering. The more atrocious the suffering, the greater the purification. The more painful the experiences, the greater the hope....You continue your particular vocation [as a saving warning]....This is to be your mission in the contemporary world...." [It would appear that the Pope was saying that the Jewish people will and must continue to suffer according to the divide plan.] On June 25, 1988, after visiting Mauthausen, the People further observed that "the Jews 'enriched the world by their suffering' and their death was like the grain which must fall into the earth in order to bear fruit, in the words of Jesus who brings salvation."⁷²

Cardinal O'Conner confesses that he approaches the agonizing question of the Shoah within the context of his own theology of suffering. He is convinced that "the crucifixion and its enormous power continue mystically and spiritually in this world in our day, and will continue until the end of time. Christ....continues to suffer in His Body, the Church [and through the Church in all people]....quite, quite really. And this suffering has a purpose and an effect [on other persons elsewhere in the world], as does ours if we conjoin it with His, if we 'offer it up.'" Because of its effect [in the case of Christ's suffering, the "salvation of souls"], it is a gift to the world. Consequently, "if the suffering of the crucifixion was infinitely redemptive, the suffering of the Holocaust, potentially conjoined with it, is incalculably redemptive."⁷³

Two questions arise: How is the Jewish suffering in the Shoah to be conjoined to Christ's on the cross? [Can the suffering of those long since dead be offered up by someone else on their behalf?] And what if it was not then [or is not now] offered up? Although an unknown number of Jews went to their deaths affirming their trust in God, certainly a larger number of the victims would not have done so given the circumstances under which they perished, or would not even have been in a condition to do so, and certainly not with the name of Christ on their lips. Is their suffering then non-redemptive and hence meaningless? What is their fate? Is this theology consigning them to an even greater invisibility and non-being than the Nazi killers sought to achieve? Using Metz's dictum, we must ask whether the Cardinal's back is not turned to Auschwitz even though he thinks he is facing it?

Are Christians such as O'Conner asking Jews of today to offer up their own pain [as survivors, relatives of victims, or vicarious sufferers of

Hitler's obsessive hatred]? Does this mean their having to be accepting of that pain because of it having a possible positive effect somewhere in the world? Can such victims believe that? Is asking for such a response not further burdening those already victimized or intended for victimization? Would it not be more appropriate for such churchpersons to urge that their own community take on [in whatever ways are possible] the pain of the victims and survivors and vicariously bear that pain as fellow sufferers? Not in order to offer it up--which would be presumptuous--but simply by sharing the pain and fear perhaps slightly to alleviate it for the people of suffering.

But there are additional and perhaps even more troublesome questions raised by such a theology of suffering:

[1] Does it actually work? Does one person's suffering really alleviate someone else's condition, as Cardinals O'Connor and Cushing believe? If the amount of pain experienced in the Shoah really were to make a difference, should not the world be on a mountain peak of tranquility and joy? [In point of fact, the reality of the world condition is the exact opposite: The expertise of torture and mass killing has been exported and appropriated globally by individuals and political groups ready to murder for the sake of power or some ideology.] If someone were to respond to this objection by saying that the fault was that of the victims for not "offering up" their suffering, that person would be wrong insofar as we know that many numbers of the Shoah victims did exactly that in their own way of ultimate trust. But more importantly, such an observation would fault persons for not doing something that they had little or no basis for believing would be effective. Moreover, it would place an unendurable [and inexcusable] burden on the very people who suffered in extremis, not to mention the insuperable burden on anyone who might face such extremities in the future.

[2] Does the concept of vicarious suffering really help? Does one or more person's suffering really atone for the sins of others, as both Christianity and Judaism have affirmed? We have no way of proving that it does. Perhaps we need to ask whether the suffering of one should vicariously benefit another?[74] Is not the recognition of personal and group responsibility the most significant aspect of any kind of rehabilitation and betterment of society? And is not the acceptance of responsibility undercut by theologies of vicarious suffering?[75]

[3] Can we consider "Auschwitz" [the Nazis' whirlwind of mass destruction] in the same category as other suffering? Lawrence Langer points out that the Nazis removed any "exemplary" possibilities from the victims' sufferings and deaths when they cut them off from any appeal "for sympathy, status, or justice [or from] martyrdom." In the circumstances of "Auschwitz" the very word suffering is inappropriate; atrocity is more correct. "The Nazi evil not only subverted good as we know it; the forms it

took poisoned the possibility of a redemptive suffering to counteract the moral paralysis it generated."[76]

Terrence Des Pres insists that in such extremity death can never be a victory. "The luxury of sacrifice--[i.e.] the strategic choice of death to resolve irreconcilable moral conflicts--is meaningless in a world where any person's death only contributes to the success of evil."[77]

XIII. Against Finding Meaning in Unmerited Suffering

There is a danger in all efforts to find meaning in unmerited suffering--not just that of the Shoah. Just as the concept of martyrdom can be a veil to mask the reality of death, so we may be obscuring unacceptable agony by a veil of good results.

How much of the effort to give suffering a purifying or redemptive power is a result of our not knowing how else to cope with it? Trying desperately to make something good come out of evil? Trying to provide ourselves with reassurance that pain is not meaningless and that evil will not have the last word? And how much of the commendation of the meek and powerless is a result of our not wanting the status quo upset, or of fearing the uncertainty of change?

Instead of speaking about rediscovering the capacity to suffer, or about God's indebtedness to His people for allowing divine forbearance with human sin to persist[78], would we not be more advised to listen to the witness and warning of some contemporary spokespeople among the Blacks, women, Hispanics, poor, tortured [along with the victims and survivors of the Shoah]?[79]

Along with survivors of the death camps, these victims of oppression insist that suffering does not ennoble, does not provide moral stature or spiritual depth or refined sensibility. It does not make a person superior or more authentic than a non-sufferer. [In fact, many feel that they can never fulfill their potential to be human because of what they have been subjected to.] These people tell us that as long as we try to comfort ourselves or others with ideas about the positive effects of suffering--including a redemptive function--the less we will be inclined to reject it as the evil it is, and the less we may be inclined to fight against it.[80]

Similarly, these oppressed groups are insistent that powerlessness, and the admonition to find ultimate justification in their oppressed condition, is evil. In Des Pres' words, "In a landscape of disaster....where people die in thousands, where machines reduce courage to stupidity and dying to complicity with aggression, it makes no sense to speak of death's dignity or of its communal blessing."[81]

XIV. God's Pathos/Suffering

Does it help to say that God suffers because of the pain inflicted on Her/His human children, and suffers along with those persons? It appears to me that the only benefit in such a view can come from two realizations. The first would be the acknowledgement that suffering is not part of God's will or wish for the creation; that it is the reverse of what God intended. Therefore, all attempts to find God's beneficent action in any event involving suffering would be incoherent with the divine will.

The second would be a recognition that God's suffering represents the continual threat of destruction and dissolution that faces humankind. Of all the attempts to consider alternative ways of understanding the divine-human relationship and the theodicy question I find Hans Jonas essay "The Concept of God after Auschwitz" particularly appealing and perceptive [as well as succinct]. He has suggested that we recognize that God has been a suffering God who is altered from the moment of creation; is a becoming God who is altered by what happens in the world; is a caring God who is involved with what He cares about; is an endangered God who has risked Himself and thus made Himself vulnerable to human events. These events leave their mark on God. The cries of "the gassed and burnt children of Auschwitz, of the defaced, de-humanized phantoms of the camps, and of all the other number-less victims of the other man-made holocausts of our time" must now hang over our world "as a dark, mournful, and accusing cloud" and eternity must look down upon us "with a frown, wounded itself and perturbed in its depths." In turn, won't there always be "some resonance to that [heavenly] condition" in our own earthly condition?[82]

XV. Concluding Thoughts

Humans have a tendency to make comparisons and fit new happenings into existing thought patterns. But a contemporary Christian scholar argues that the "Holocaust and all other holocausts which followed in its train or preceded it....have rendered all our previous explanations of suffering either obsolete or insufficient." And death camp survivors attest to the "utter irreconcilability" of their experience with any "prior consoling system of values." Similarly, their anguish "teaches nothing about developing an enduring attitude toward suffering that might eventually lead toward some form of healing, forgiveness, or redemption. The atrocities they beheld or endured were beyond suffering, as they were beyond the framework of conventional theodicy."[83]

The ineradicable problem of the Shoah will not let us rest. We may be better advised to let it remain an unanswered question, forever troubling us, so that we do not hide the warning that it provides and do not obscure the mystery of evil to which it should make us ever more alert. At the same time, since it would be criminal to make the Shoah an event so totally apart from our world that it has nothing to say to us, the troubling questions it raises should make us rethink our traditional answers and propositions about suffering [and punishment]. We also need to be careful about the rhetoric we use about suffering [especially of others] in contrast to the reality by which most of us lead our own lives, so that the way we respond to the oppression and suffering of others will be coherent with what our own instinctive reactions would be were we in their shoes.

For Eugene Fisher, "remembering" [anamnesis in Greek; zikkaron in Hebrew] is a primary category of bridge-building between the Catholic and Jewish communities and leads him directly to a "theology of praxis," whereby he enumerates those categories of theology which now need be rethought in light of the Shoah: [a] forgiveness and reconciliation, [b] repentance, [c] the uniqueness of the Jewish experience in the Shoah and its meaning for Catholic [and other] Christians, [d] suffering, [e] the State of Israel, [f] hope, [g] love, and [h] Catholic teaching about the Shoah. Basing himself on contemporary post-Shoah events [e.g. Bitburg, Kurt Waldheim, the Auschwitz convent], which themselves are nevertheless pain-filled and difficult, he suggests possible directions and avenues of thought which may, possibly, transcend the barriers which seemingly presently exist, and offers new directions for increased dialogical understanding.

MYSTERIUM TREMENDUM:

Catholic Grapplings with the Shoah and Its

Theological Implications[1]

Eugene J. Fisher

I. Introduction: Anamnesis and Zikkaron

To speak of the Shoah, its witnesses remind us, is an impossible task. How can one encapsulate in words the absolute horror of the deaths of millions? Is not the very attempt to find meaning, even religious meaning, in such an event somehow blasphemous?

Yes. But not to speak may be worse. It would be, in the words of Emil Fackenheim, to commit the final blasphemy, to allow Hitler the posthumous victory of having silenced forever the voices of the prophets.

Judaism and Christianity are religions of remembering, of anamnesis and zikkaron, of wrestling out of the tragic vagaries of history the meaning to guide our divinely-covenanted peoples on the path toward hope. As Daniel Polish in a moving article arguing the possibility of "Witnessing God after Auschwitz" has said: "To be silent is a sin, doing violence to the Jewish imperative to remember. No, we must speak of the Shoah.... Had the generation of the Exodus been allowed the final say in understanding their experience, we would have found no redemption in it....[Only their] humiliation, despair, and terror."[2]

If there was a temptation to silence in the dialogue between Jews and Catholics in the face of the intractable realities of the Shoah, that silence has been shattered by the increasingly vocal controversies between our two communities in recent years. Even as Pope John Paul II on April 13, 1986, became the first Bishop of Rome since St. Peter to visit a syna-gogue, the seeds of those controversies were developing: the process of beatification of Edith Stein was moving toward its conclusion; a small group of Polish nuns were working to turn into a modest convent the interior of an abandoned theater adjacent to the infamous death camp at Auschwitz-Birkenau; and Kurt Waldheim, former General Secretary of the United Nations, was being proposed as President of Catholic Austria.

All three actions touched on the Shoah and thus on a memory sacred to the Jewish people today. Jewish nerves, rubbed raw by centuries of persecution, and the Jewish soul, scarred by the agony of the loss of one third of its entire people just fifty years ago, cried out with sincere anguish, an outcry of pain and accusation that threatened the rip apart the still delicate fabric of the new relationship Catholics and Jews have been weaving in patient dialogue for over twenty years in this country and throughout the world.

Despite the rhetoric, however, the fabric of our relations has not torn. Rather, in Rome and New York, Washington, D.C. and local parishes and synagogues throughout the country, Catholics and Jews continue to listen to one another's fears and hurts, breaking through, I believe, to a truer and deeper dialogue than ever before.

Catholic theologian David Tracy, following Arthur Cohen, fittingly describes the Shoah as "theologically the tremendum of our age."[3] Numerous Christian as well as Jewish thinkers have grappled in the wake of the Shoah with the implications of the Shoah for their respective theologies.[4] My point in this paper is not to rehearse that literature, but, rather, to focus on the more specific issues of misunderstanding and mistrust raised to the surface of our relationship by the recent controversies and their attendant rhetoric, and on how Catholic theology has and can react to it all. The present paper should be seen, then, not so much as an exercise in systematic theology, though organized thematically, as a "theology of praxis," seeking to draw out of recent events in Catholic-Jewish relations some of the underlying dynamics pertinent especially to a Catholic response to the Shoah.

Of necessity, then, rather more attention will be given to official Catholic documents and especially to the pronouncements of Pope John Paul II than might be typical of an academic approach to Shoah studies. But I believe that this Pope, perhaps more than any other, can show us the way to move beyond the blockages of the past toward reconciliation. Finally, though I have picked a major theme or two for each controversy, the reality is that most of the issues are present in each, with the concerns and misperceptions consequently intensified over the whole period.

II. Bitburg, Waldheim, and The Theology of Forgiveness

The first event, though not one primarily between Jews and Catho-lics, revealed an ongoing misunderstanding by Catholics of Jewish teaching and Jewish spirituality. So pervasive is this misunderstanding that it needs to be addressed before proceeding any further. This is the issue of forgiveness, a variation of which was heard also during the Waldheim affair.

Reacting to Jewish outcries over Bitburg, many Christians [not just Catholics] were heard to ask: "What's the matter with Jews? Hasn't there been enough on the Shoah? Why can't they forgive after all this time?" Underlying such plaints, at times quite explicitly, is one of the most ancient elements of the "teaching of contempt" against Jews and Judaism. That is the belief that Judaism [the "Old Law"] preaches justice and vengeance, while Christianity, following the teaching of Jesus, especially the Sermon on the Mount, proclaims mercy and forgiveness. The ironic fact that Christians over the centuries, because of our oppressive treatment of Jews, have needed far more forgiveness from Jews than they need from us, is seldom noted by Christian critics of "vindictive" Judaism.

But do Judaism and Christianity hold two entirely different, antithetical understandings of the theology of forgiveness as so many Christians presume? What, exactly, are Jews saying to us underneath the often hurtful rhetoric thrown at us via the media? The 1974 **Vatican Guidelines**[5] remind us that:

> The Old Testament and the Jewish tradition founded upon it must not be set against the New Testament in such a way that the former seems to constitute a religion of only justice, fear and leagalism, with no appeal to the love of God and neighbor.

As with the law of love [Matthew 22:34-40, which reiterates the commandments of Deuteronomy 6:5 and Leviticus 19:18], Jesus' saying on love of enemies in the Sermon on the Mount [5] [Matthew 5:43 ff] draws on Jewish sources. In point of fact, there is no command in the Hebrew Scriptures or in rabbinic tradition to "hate your enemy." Instead we find:

> Do not rejoice when your enemy falls, and let not your heart be glad when he stumbles! [Proverbs 24:17]

> If your enemy is hungry, give him bread to eat; if he is thirsty, give him water to drink. [Proverbs 25:21]

Rabbinic tradition in turn commented upon and reinforced these Biblical sayings:

> Rabbi Hama bar Hanina said: "Even though your enemy has risen up early to kill you, and he comes hungry and thirsty to your house, give him food and drink. God will make him at peace with you."

> Rabbi Simeon bar Abba said: "The verse [Proverbs 17:13] means that if a man returns evil for evil, evils shall not depart from his house...."

> Rabbi Nathan said: "Who is the most powerful? Whoever wins the love of his enemy."

Jewish tradition here is not total pacifism, as the minority position within Christianity would interpret and apply Jesus' words. Rather its theme, as in the High Holy Days of Rosh Ha-Shanah [Jewish New Year-- Ed.] and Yom Kippur [Day of Atonement--Ed.], is reconciliation, the great

Jewish theme stressing the reconciling power of divine love over hatreds: "God will make peace with you."

Like the commandment to "love your neighbor as yourself" [Leviti-cus 19:18], acts of loving kindness [hesed in Hebrew] toward one's ene-mies are considered in Judaism to be part of Biblical law: "If you see the ass of one who hates you lying under its burden, you shall help to lift it up" [Exodus 23:5]. Rabbinic tradition commented:

> A person goes along the road and sees that the ass of an enemy has fallen under its burden. The person goes over and gives the enemy a hand to unload and reload....Then they go over to an inn and the ass driver thinks: so and so loves me so much, and I thought he hated me. Immediately they talk with one another and make peace. [Midrashic commentary to Psalm 99:4; underlying its sentiments may be Amos 3:3: "Can two wander together without becoming one with one another?"][6]

If Judaism holds such a rich theology of forgiveness and recon-ciliation, the persistent Christian critic may still ask, why the outbursts over Bitburg and Waldheim? In the former case, Bitburg, the answer lies in the nature of the event itself: the Christian President of the United States and the Christian Chancellor of Germany got together over the graves of Nazi SS troops to forgive each other for acts of war. Jews were neither consulted nor invited to participate. The fact of the Shoah, therefore, was ignored. Trivialized. Not allowed to interfere with "more important matters of State" between the two countries. Jews were not to be present to forgive-- or even to tell their story--which is one reason why the United States Catholic Bishops' Conference, along with so many other non-Jews, urged the President to cancel the event.

III. Waldheim and The Theology of Repentance

The Jewish perception of a trivialization of the Shoah, of judging the systematic murder of six million innocents to be of such little present moment that it should not give pause to current affairs of state, also played a significant part in Jewish reactions to the granting of a papal audience to the President of Austria. Again, numerous Catholic voices could be heard calling on Jews to forgive Waldehim, whose crimes on the scale of Nazi butchery, after all, were not that great even he had based his career on lies about his relatively minor role in the Germany army.[7]

Again, let us look at little deeper into the rhetoric. What were Jews trying to tell us Catholics about the significance, to them and to us, of the audience? While I believe that the papal audience was justifiable for reasons of state that were given by the Holy See and because Mr. Wald-heim, who has not been convicted of any criminal charges is the duly-elected head of a democratic state and should be considered legally innocent until proven guilty, I also believe that we Catholics need to listen very closely to what has been said to us in this affair.

The Jewish accusation against Mr. Waldheim, if I understand it correctly, was not so much that he was a major war criminal of the Shoah, an Eichmann or a Klaus Barbie, but that he appears to remain entirely unrepentant about his arguably minor role in mass murder. This note of unrepentance was present in almost all of the Jewish statements of protest against the audience. It effectively challenges Catholics who would criticize Jews as "unforgiving" over the incident. Forgiveness, in Christian theology no less than in Jewish theology, requires repentance. While no human being can fully plumb the depths of Mr. Waldheim's heart to sit in judgment on his soul--only God can do that--still, his public posture and his grudging admissions of the truth as each new piece of evidence against his original story came out, has left the impression that he has not yet fully, at least in public, come to grips within his own conscience with the enormity of the evil perpetrated against the Jewish people and against humanity by the Nazi death machine of which he was certainly a part.

What Jews are saying in essence, then, is no more and no less than what the prophets and Jesus said to the world in earlier generations: "Repent and sin no more!" It is a timeless and timely message. For Christians to speak of reconciliation with Jews in this, as the Pope has rightly called it, "the century of the Shoah," we must take the first step, repentance, a heshbon ha-nefesh, an accounting of the soul. I believe we have begun to do this, in the Catholic community most clearly through the declaration of the Second Vatican Council, **Nostra Aetate,** and in the remarkable progress [not well known enough in the Jewish community, I fear] in implementing the Council's mandate in Catholic teaching and preaching in all levels of the Church's life, especially, perhaps in this country.[8]

Still, the words that Cardinal Eichinger of Strasbourg addressed to the Second Vatican Council retain their urgency for all Christians today:

> We cannot deny that not only during this century but also during past centuries crimes have been committed against the Jews by the Sons and Daughters of the Church....We cannot ignore that during the course of history, there have been persecutions and outrages against the Jews; there have been violations of conscience as well as forced conversions. Lastly, we cannot deny that up until recently, errors have insinuated themselves, too frequently, into preaching and into certain catechetical books in opposition to the spirit of the New Testament. In going back to the sources of the Gospels, why not draw sufficient greatness of soul to ask forgiveness in the name of numerous Christians for so many misdeeds and injustices?[9]

Pope John Paul II affirmed this attitude of repentance when he said to Catholic representatives of Episcopal Conferences meeting in Rome in 1982:

> Certainly, since a new bough appeared from the common root 2,000 years ago, we know that relations between our two communities have been marked by resentments and a lack of understanding. If there have been misunderstandings, errors and even insults since the day of separation, it is now a question of overcoming them with understanding, peace and mutual esteem. The terrible persecutions suffered by the Jews in various periods of history have finally opened many eyes and disturbed many hearts.[10]

IV. Pope John Paul II in Warsaw: The Uniqueness of

Jewish Witness to the Shoah

On June 14, 1987, the Pope met with representatives of the tiny remnant of the Jewish community of Warsaw. This address, I believe, provides a spiritual and theological basis for a Christian reflection on the Shoah. Decrying the "terrible reality" of the attempted extermination of the Jewish people, "an extermination carried out with premeditation," the Pope noted that "the threat against you was also a threat against us [Polish] Catholics," though "this latter was not realized to the same extent." The Pope clearly acknowledges here the uniqueness of the Jewish tragedy even while affirming the enormity of Polish Catholic suffering at the hands of the Nazi death machine:

> It was you who suffered this terrible sacrifice of extermination; one might say that you suffered it also on behalf of those who were likewise to have been exterminated.

The Pope also addressed the uniqueness of the Jewish witness to the Shoah, saying that "because of this terrible experience, you have become a loud warning voice for all humanity....More than anyone else, it is precisely you who have become a saving warning." A saving warning. Such words, to Catholics, are theologically pregnant, reminding us of the "saving warnings" of the prophets themselves. Drawing out this point, which takes the Shoah very seriously I believe as a mysterium tremendum, a "sign of the times" through which Christians may discern something of God's plan of salvation for all humanity, the Pope made a significant step in developing a Catholic theology of the Shoah and of Judaism's continuing unique role as the Chosen People of God:

I think that in this sense you continue your particular vocation, showing yourselves to be still the heirs of that election to which God is faithful.

This is your mission in the contemporary world before the peoples, the nations, all of humanity, the Church. And this Church, all peoples and nations feel united to you in this mission.

"Particular vocation" and "mission," of course, are part of the Catholic vocabulary of election and covenant. Here, very clearly, the Pope is framing an understanding of the continuing salvific validity of the Jewish people as God's people. It will be noted that the Pope reaches the universality of the Jewish witness to the world [and to the Church itself!] only through full acknowledgement of Jewish particularity. The mission of the Church in the world, its proclamation to the world, does not absorb Judaism's mission and witness. Rather, the Church united itself to that ongoing Jewish vocation which it acknowledges as divinely willed, and, indeed, an essential part of God's plan of salvation for all humanity.

It will also be noted that the Jewish witness to the Shoah is entirely a post-Christum vocation, not dependent on the teachings of the "Old Testament, but considered valid on its own, which is to say Jewish terms, even though coming to be considerably after the close of the New Testament period. So far as I know, this is the first time, the Church, whether Catholic or Protestant, has pointed to a specific aspect of Judaism's post-New Testament role in the history of salvation, giving concrete theological substance to the Second Vatican Council's general theme, as articulated in the 1974 "Guidelines," that "the history of Judaism did not end with the destruction of Jerusalem, but rather went on to develop a religious tradition rich in religious values." In the Pope's words in Warsaw, paying heed to the particular witness of the Jewish people today concerning the significance of the Shoah "helps me and all the Church become even more aware of what unites us in the disposition of the Divine Covenant." The story of the people Israel, today no less than in Biblical times, remains a story, with all its tragedies and hopes, that is a "light to the nations." Israel remains God's people. And Israel's story remains one that the Church, in developing its own theological visions, must address.

V. Cardinal John O'Connor and The Theology of Suffering

The Pope's Warsaw address raised also a theological issue given great prominence in the press during Cardinal John O'Connor's trip last January to Israel. That is the Christian theology of suffering. Coming out of Yad Vashem [Israel's Shoah Memorial--Ed.] in Jerusalem, Cardinal O'Connor gave an interview in which he mentioned that in a certain sense the Jewish suffering of the Shoah may be considered a "gift" to humanity.

Cardinal O'Connor's statement was jumped upon and denounced by Jewish leaders, I think unfairly, even before he returned to New York. This, then, is a case where the Jewish community has the responsibility to listen closely to what Catholics are saying, and to come to understand the Christian theological categories involved before reacting to it with denunciation in the press.

No devout Christian, I believe, can go to Yad Vashem, see there the moving evidence of the horrifying loss of innocent Jewish lives and the monstrous evil that the Shoah represents, and not be challenged to the core of his or her spiritual life. Inevitably, this will take the form of reflection upon the suffering of another Jew, Jesus of Nazareth, whose death, and we believe, resurrection is the bedrock for us of all our faith and hopes.

To us, the death of that Jew at the hands of Israel's Roman oppressors two millennia ago frames our very understanding of reality, all that we are and hope to be as Christians. To us, it is our essential mysterium tremendum. Out of despair can come hope, out of death renewed life. That Jesus' death is a divine gift bringing all humanity closer to God's love is the central paradox, the central mystery of Christian faith. Because of it we can proclaim with joy Adam's [which is to say humanity's] fall into evil, "O felix culpa!" "O happy fault!" We can, we believe, most deeply, discern some meaning, some hope in all human suffering.

If this sense of hope amidst despair is true because of the death of one Jew long ago, Christians will inevitably ask themselves, might it not also be true, and much more so, of the deaths of six million Jewish wo-men, men, and children consigned to the most diabolical hell humanity has ever created for itself?

This is not to equate the suffering and death of the one with the sufferings and deaths of the six million. Such an equation would be monstrous. Nor is it to seek to absorb the deaths of the six million into the theological categories developed by the Church to articulate its faith that the death of Jesus, and therefore death itself, has some purpose, that there is reason to hope even in the face of the most awesome evil, evil understood as a mysterium tremendum. It is more simply, and more profoundly, to struggle for the theological insights, the words, to help us cope with the awesomeness of the Jewish tragedy in ways that can link its significance to our deepest spirituality as Christians. Such attempts as Cardinal O'Connor's, then, should not, I believe, be viewed as either theologically flippant or as an attempt to subsume Jewish experience into Christian categories. Flawed as they are, and all attempts to derive significance from the Shoah, meaning from such massive, senseless tragedy, will be to some extent flawed by our incapacity as finite creatures to express in words what must be said, the attempts to use these words derived from the central mystery of the Church itself, must be seen as sincere and honest offerings of the Christian heart.

Pope John Paul II, in Warsaw, after proclaiming as a Pole and as a head of the Catholic Church, that Jews suffered in the Shoah "on behalf of those who were likewise to have been exterminated" had Hitler's plans been allowed to fulfill themselves on all non-Aryans, stated:

> We believe in the purifying power of suffering. The more atrocious the suffering, the greater the purification. The more painful the experiences, the greater the hope.

I suspect that many Jews today will find religious references such as "purification" and the "purifying power of suffering" applied to the Shoah to be somewhat mystifying, though they have solid precedent in the Hebrew Scriptures and close parallels with mystical Jewish literature through the ages.

Some Jewish thinkers, such as Elie Wiesel and Emil Fackenheim, feel that no theological framework can be adequate to absolute horror. For Wiesel, Jews can still utter the Ani Ma'amin ["I still believe...."--Ed.] of traditional faith in the coming of the Messiah, but never in the same sense as before. Now, there is always tension. Nothing, not even Israel reborn can justify those deaths. And still one prays--for to be a Jew is to pray: "Ani ma'amin, Isaac. Because of Belsen. Ani ma'amin, Jacob. Because of and in spite of Maidenek. Pray to God. Against God. For God."[11] For Fackenheim, the Shoah holds no salvific meaning. The deaths of so many must remain meaningless. There is only the commanding Voice, in one sense a new revelation, in another sense not, adding a 614th commandment to the Torah's 613: survive. But the Jew is commanded not just to survive, but to survive as a Jew, i.e. as a moral person in full historical consciousness and perpetual remembrance of the six million. Martyrdom, the traditional Kiddush Ha-Shem, "sanctification of the Name," is overtaken, exhausted of meaning, fulfilled, ended in the deaths of the innocent multitudes.[12] The Martyr has a choice: convert or die. The victims of the Shoah only died. None of the classical theological categories or images can any longer be considered authentic.

Fackenheim follows Buber in stressing that God cannot be replaced by theological "concepts of God," but must be encountered in the crucible of history. He accepts the reality of Biblical revelation, and challenges us to grapple with it in the tragedies of contemporary events. Fackenheim rejects Martin Buber's notion of a contemporary [and by implication temporary] "eclipse of God." "The God of Israel cannot be God of either past or future unless He is still God of the present."

The questions of theodicy and the meaning of suffering, of hope out of despair, life despite death, are raised by the Shoah for Christians as well as Jews. And for us Christians there is an addition challenge. Bishop James

Malone of Youngstown, Ohio, speaking to the National Workshop on Christian-Jewish Relations, put the distinctive Christian problem this way:

> Acknowledgement is due that all too many Catholics were,
> in fact, among the executioners of death-camp inmates. But
> equally to be acknowledged are the millions of Catholics and
> thousands of their clergy who were themselves victims of death-
> camp executioners. Part of the Christian tragedy is that untold
> numbers of Christians lost their lives attempting to shelter Jews.
> Part of the Christian tragedy, too, is that Christians were num-
> bered among the executioners and among the victims. At one and
> the same time, Christians were both oppressor and oppressed.[13]

Similarly, the Holy Father has stated that "reflection upon the Shoah....-
impels us to promote the necessary historical and religious studies on this
event which concerns the whole of humanity today....There is no doubt that
the sufferings endured by the Jews are also for the Catholic Church a motive
of sincere sorrow, especially when one thinks of the indifference and
sometimes resentment which, in particular historical circumstances, have
divided Jews and Christians" [John Paul II, August 8, 1987].

VI. The State of Israel and The Theology of Hope

Running like a blue thread through the white heat of Jewish responses to
Cardinal O'Connor's trip to Israel and to the Waldheim audience, and indeed
through all of the dialogues between our communities, is the Jewish insistence on full diplomatic recognition by the Holy See of the State of Israel.
An exchange of ambassadors, the Jewish community is telling us, would be
symbolic of the Church's acknowledgement of the Jewish peo-ple's right to
self-identity. Without going into details on the reasons of the Holy See's
posture on the diplomatic question, I would like to raise what for me is the
deeper issue: What can the Church say of the rebirth of a Jewish State in
Eretz Yisrael [Land of Israel--Ed.] theologically?

Interestingly and not coincidentally, this issue is linked in Catholic
reflection as in Jewish reflection with the theological question raised by the
Shoah.

For many Jews, Fackenheim among them[14], the religious dimension of
the Shoah has its sole, if only partial, resolution in the rebirth of the State
of Israel. The survivors of the death camps chose life over death, hope over
despair, and so founded a nation, tiny and insecure but their own, where
Jews could be Jews, religiously and morally, and where the Jewish spirit
could rediscover itself in the wake of the destruction of much of its traditional patterns of thought.

This is why for Jews, even those who live in other lands, the Land of Israel represents so crucial a part of religious survival. It is not solely a place of refuge, a place which, if it had existed in 1939, would have meant that much of European Jewry could have been saved. It is more deeply a sign [a 'sacrament' if we were to apply Catholic terminology] that moral life, the life to which Jews are called in covenant, remains possible after the absolute evil that was Auschwitz.

Irving Greenberg, building on Fackenheim, puts it this way:

> To raise a Jewish child today is to bind the child and t h e child's child on the altar, even as Father Abraham bound Isaac. Only, those who do so today know that there is no angel to stop the process and no ram to substitute for more than one and one-half million Jewish children in this lifetime. Such an act, then, can come only out of resources of faith, of ultimate meaningfulness-of Exodus trust....The reborn State of Israel is this fundamental act of life and meaning of the Jewish people after Auschwitz. To fail to grasp that inextricable connection and response is to utterly fail to comprehend the theological significance of Israel....
>
> The real point [of Israel] is that after Auschwitz, the existence of the Jew is a great affirmation and act of faith. The re-creation of the body of the people, Israel, is renewed testimony to Exodus as ultimate reality, to God's continuing presence in history proven by the fact that his people, despite the attempt to annihilate them, still exist.[15]

The Pope, speaking spontaneously to Jewish leaders in Castelgandolfo on September 1, 1987, himself used the paradigm of the Exodus in meditating upon the source for hope that through divine grace good can be discerned even after the awesome evil of the Shoah.[16] In Miami, the Pope acknowledged officially for the Church not only the existence of the State of Israel but the Biblical source for Jewish attachment to it and the "inextricable connection" between Israel and the Shoah as well:

> Catholics recognize among the elements of the Jewish experience that Jews have a religious attachment to the Land, which finds its roots in Biblical tradition. After the tragic extermination of the Shoah, the Jewish people began a new period in their history. They have a right to a homeland, as does any civil nation, according to international law. 'For the Jewish people who live in the State of Israel....we must ask the desired security and the due tranquility that is the right of every nation.'[17]

The meaning of Israel is a message of hope, not only for Jews, but for all peoples of faith throughout the world. Tragedy, however seemingly implacable, need not lead us to abandon the struggle for survival in a post-modern world. Nor does the nature of our survival need to be merely petty or self-serving. One can survive and still strive for the betterment of others. The cycle of victim and oppressor can be broken.

Israel thus exists as a burst of hope rising out of despair; as an affirmation of life spoken amid the vivid memories of death; as a cry of joy hurled in the face of doom; as a statement of love that survived an abysmal hatred.

The very existence of Israel can thus be a symbol of hope and faith for all struggling peoples. The Jewish people, descendants of those who lived through the first Exodus, have seen its meaning reaffirmed in our time. The Exodus serves as a powerful sign to all of the possibilities of true liberation from oppression. This is a fact which calls for profound reflection. To every person of faith it is a fact which elicits a response of faith, a renewal of our commitment to the best in our own traditions, and a deep sense of confidence in the ultimate meaningfulness of God's creation.[18]

VII. Edith Stein, the Auschwitz Convent, and The Theology of Love

In a famous rabbinical tale, a master asks his disciples if they love him. "Of course," they reply. "Then what hurts me?" "We do not know," they respond in some confusion. "If you loved me," the master concludes, "you would know what hurts me."

Catholic-Jewish relations after the Shoah, it can be said, is in somewhat this same situation. Catholics profess their love, but do not always understand the immense trauma of the Shoah for the Jewish people. Jews, struggling with their own grief, are not always aware of the pain their rhetoric can at times cause Catholics.

In late 1987, Rabbi Daniel Polish published an editorial entitled "A Painful Legacy: Jews and Catholics Struggle to Understand Edith Stein and Auschwitz."[19] In it, Polish attempts to articulate how Jews perceived and why they reacted the way they did to the news [not always accurately presented in the media] of Edith Stein's beatification and the establishment of a small Carmelite convent adjacent to the site of the major Nazi death camp in Poland.

Polish first captures the sense of perplexity among many Catholics to the Jewish outcry in the two cases: Are not, Catholics ask, the beatifi-cation of a Catholic and the establishment of a convent internal Church matters? Should not these symbolic gestures on the part of the Church to join its voice to that of the Jewish people in prayerful memory of the six million be acknowledged by Jews as sincerely motivated Catholic efforts to heal the wounds of the past and to heed the Jewish people's own call to the world to remember the Shoah?

"How difficult we must seem to Catholics to make sense of," Polish comments, "in both cases we [Jews] responded to what one could construe as expressions of fellow-feeling, even solidarity." Polish has it right. Catholics are confused, and hurt, by Jewish rebukes in these matters, and especially by the tendency on the part of some Jewish commentators to call into question the sincerity of the intentions of Catholic authorities, often without even first asking what the Catholic motivation might have been, but simply presuming an evil intent.

But before lapsing into righteous indignation on our part, we Catho-lics need to listen a bit more carefully to understand the very real fears that underlie the Jewish rhetoric that has caused so much pain over the last months. These fears are [and as a Catholic I can only say this with a profound sense of sadness and contrition] all too solidly founded in our history. Again, Rabbi Polish helps us to move beyond harmful rhetoric to the deeper sensitivities involved: "At the heart of the Jewish response to the beatification of Edith Stein is the perception that it has the effect of legiti-mizing efforts to promote conversion among the Jews."

From a Jewish point of view, Polish writes, it is very difficult to distinguish the Catholic Church's veneration of a Jewish convert and the blatantly proselytizing activities of extreme fundamentalist groups such as the "Jews for Jesus" and the "Messianic Jews." Catholics would quickly respond that such Jewish fears are groundless. As the Bishops' Committee for Ecumenical and Interreligious Affairs of the National Conference of Catholic Bishops [NCCB] stated on the occasion of the beatification itself:

> Catholic respect for the integrity of Judaism and for the ongoing validity of God's irrevocable covenant with the Jewish people is solidly founded on our faith in the unshakable faithful-ness of God's own word. Therefore, in no way can the beatifica-tion of Edith Stein be understood by Catholics as giving impetus to unwarranted proselytizing among the Jewish community. On the contrary, it urges us to ponder the continuing religious significance of Jewish traditions, with which we have so much in common, and to approach Jews not as potential 'objects' of conversion, but rather as bearers of a unique witness to the Name of the One God of Israel.[20]

The intent of the Church is seen in Pope John Paul II's repeated insis-tence on his homily during the beatification ceremony on May 1, 1987, that Edith Stein died as 'the daughter of a martyred people....a Jew....a daughter of Israel' and 'at the same time' a Catholic martyr who was sent to Ausch-witz by the Nazis in reprisal for the strong public protest issued by the Catholic bishops of the Netherlands against the deportation of Dutch Jews.

The Pope's careful phrasing acknowledges clearly the uniqueness of the Jewish tragedy as well as the obvious fact to the Nazis neither Jewish nor Catholic tradition held any authority. To the Nazis, Edith Stein was simply one more Jew to be murdered with bureaucratic efficiency. No more, no less than the rest of the six million. Catholics, then, according to the Bishops' statement cited above:

> ....see the beatification of Edith Stein as a unique occasion for joint Catholic-Jewish reflection and reconciliation. In honoring Edith Stein, the Church wishes to honor all the six million Jewish victims of the Shoah....Catholic veneration will necessarily contribute to a continuing and deepened examination of conscience regarding sins of commission and omission perpetrated by Christians against Jews during the dark years of World War II.[21]

This Catholic intent and predicted effect, one may say, is almost precisely the opposite of that feared by the Jewish community as articulated by Polish. It is at this point as well that our consideration in dialogue of Edith Stein merges with differing perceptions of the Auschwitz Carmel convent. Polish accurately reflects widespread Jewish opinion, I believe, when he states that Stein's beatification and the move by the Carmelites into the abandoned theater adjacent to Auschwitz are seen "as part of a pattern of Catholic actions....leaving the impression that the Catholic Church is trying to appropriate the Holocaust as its own."

Such an allegation will come as a surprise to Catholics, especially those not involved in dialogue with the Jewish community. Polish explains that for Jews the Shoah is a tremendum, "filled with import as any event in our millennia-long experience." Just as the Exodus, the Babylonian exile, and the destruction of the Jerusalem Temple were part of the sacred history of the Jewish people, "so do we perceive this tragedy wrought upon the body of our people as an intrusion of God, ineffably, into human history--a sanctum for us."

As the Catholic Church appropriated into itself the Sacred Scriptures and sacred story of Israel, Polish argues, and as it has continued to absorb "the very location of temples, shrines, and sacred graves of the various native traditions and cultures it has displaced," over the centuries, so, too, is it "appropriating the Holocaust--this sancta of the Jewish people--to itself." The essence of Catholic tradition, a tradition symbolized by the crucifix, Polish states, is to discern the transcendent meaning and "redemptive potential" of suffering. Having been born in an appropriation of the Jewish experience of suffering and redemption, Polish implies, it may be "inevitable" for the Church [and not necessarily with invidious intent] to wish to take as its own this latest chapter in the ongoing Jewish story. But in the process the particularity of that story as Jewish is once again lost, once again put to another, Christian purpose.

However, in neither case, would these very sincere Catholic expressions of reverence for Jewish victims have had the desired effect--the subsuming of the Shoah into Christian categories--that Polish and many in the Jewish community for whom he speaks seem to fear. Rather, they would and were intended to have the effect of supporting the Jewish particularity of the Shoah against those who would trivialize the Shoah, such as the Communist government of Poland, which seeks to universalize it, and the neo-Nazi revisionists who seek to deny it. They would stand as perpetual challenges to the Christian conscience and reminders of the evils of antisemitism and, indeed, of the ancient Christian "teaching of contempt" so strongly condemned by the Second Vatican Council and repeatedly by Pope John Paul II.

While the Edith Stein debate has died down as it has become apparent that her beatification has not led to any increased proselytism of Jews by Catholics, the Auschwitz convent has become increasingly controversial.

On February 22, 1987, four European Cardinals, including Franciscus Macharski of Krakow, committed the Church to moving the convent "within two years." When the anniversary came and went in 1989, with no ostensible movement on the part of the Carmelites, Jewish protests began.

These protests, in turn, have triggered Polish Catholic protests, since Auschwitz is also a major Polish symbol of the millions of Polish Catholics murdered during the Nazi occupation. While these arguments have real merit and need, I believe, to be brought into the dialogue between Catholics and Jews, so that the latter might begin to understand some of the deep pain experienced by the former, the issue for Catholics should not be who is "right" but what is the proper course of healing love.

Reverend Stanislau Musial, Secretary of the Polish Bishops' Commission for Dialogue with the Jews, answered the underlying question when asked whether he thought that "the Polish people are psychologically prepared to accept" moving the convent:

> The decision to move the Carmelite convent was the fruit of a dialogue. Some might ask whether this dialogue with the Jews was unilateral and....led to hasty concessions....However, the Catholic representatives did not enter into the [1987] talks in a calculating way. A sincere dialogue took place, conducted in a spirit of love and respect for all. Only this kind of dialogue can bear fruit.[22]

Cardinal Macharski, confirming the Church's intention to proceed with the move, but not committing himself to a specific timetable, put the matter even more succinctly and profoundly. The Church's renunciation of its rights to the present location, he said, is "a demand of charity, not of justice."[23]

In other words, while they may be arguments on both sides [a convent outside the camp, after all, hardly represents a "appropriation of Auschwitz-/Birkenau even if that <u>were</u> its intent], there are times for argument and times, in dialogue, for the simple response of love when confronted with another's very genuine pain. The <u>Shoah</u>, properly understood, reaches that bedrock level of what Christianity is all about: love. Christian acknowledgement of the reality of the other's deepest anguish is, as in the rabbinical tale, the beginning of love, of an understanding that is concrete in its actions and the opposite of sentimentality. One loves with healing deeds, not with hollow words.

VIII. Can Christians Teach About the Shoah?

The question posed here is deceptively simple. It is, in reality, a set of questions, each more difficult than the last. Some of them, at least the beginning ones, are:

--What is the <u>Shoah</u>?

--What is there about the <u>Shoah</u> that makes it distinctive?

--What challenges, religious, moral, historical, and social does it raise for the educator?

--Why can or should there be a distinctively <u>Catholic</u> educational response to the <u>Shoah</u>, as suggested by the 1985 <u>Vatican</u> **Notes** and even more strongly by Pope John Paul II in his address to the Jewish community of the United States in Miami, on September 11, 1987?

--What is the proper educational and catechetical goal f o r <u>Shoah</u> education in a Catholic setting?

In this section, I shall try to respond to these and related issues in a preliminary fashion, hoping to provide at least some ground for the larger discussion which must be initiated within the Catholic educational community and between that community and its counterparts in the Jewish community.

1. What is the Shoah and what makes it distinctive?

By the <u>Shoah</u>, I mean here specifically the <u>Shoah</u>, the events leading up to and including the Nazi decision to exterminate the entire Jewish population of Europe, even at the expense of the German war effort itself.

Why not other events? The Armenian genocide, for example? Or the equally devastating [in terms of numbers] Nazi slaughters of the Slavic population of Eastern Europe?   Or Stalin's or Cambodia's massacres of their own populations?   All of these deserve in their own way the title "genocide." Why could not any one of these or anyone of a hundred other ancient and modern examples serve just as well in the classroom to raise the question of human inhumanity and the reality of human evil?

In response, I would first agree that such questions are quite valid.   An honest educational approach ought to be inclusive rather than exclusive.   One must not fall into the trap of pitting the victims of Nazi and other brutality against one another.   Each and every human being is of infinite worth, formed in the image of God.   One does not, cannot, morally, try to tote up on some gruesome quantitative scale the pain and suffering of individuals or groups to see which was "worse" or "more deserving" of our compassion. Such judgments can be made by God alone. So, yes, it is quite appropriate, even necessary in Shoah education to speak of the suffering of non-Jews, of Poles and Slavs, Gypsies and resistance fighters, Seventh Day Adventists and homosexuals.   God, the Bible teaches us, hears the cries of all.   The Divine suffers with the suffering of all human beings.   On this level, no valid distinctions are permitted between the pain of one and the pain of another. Each human being is of infinite worth to the Creator of all.

Yet, there is something about the Shoah, the Jewish suffering of the Shoah, that enables, even impels us to see in it a paradigm for the suffer-ings of others, not more urgent or more serious or "more" anything, but in itself distinctive, arresting, compelling.

I suspect that both the Christian and Jewish communities today recognize the reality of this affirmation, even as both of our communities experience immense difficulty articulating why we feel this way. Part of the answer may lie in what has been called, whether helpfully or not, the "uniqueness" of the event. Both the scope [relatively speaking] and the method and manner of the process of the enslavement and mass murder pose historical and theological challenges that are nowhere else quite so clearly raised.   No-where else has racial genocide been so integrally woven into the ideological fabric of the state as in Nazi Germany. In no other case have the potentials for the evil of bureaucracy, modern technology, "objective" science, and higher education itself been more starkly revealed.

This is a negative revelation, certainly, but it is also a necessary one for our time. In the summer of 1987, as we have discussed above, Pope John Paul II returned to his native Poland, meeting in Warsaw with the tiny remnant of the once great Polish-Jewish community. He spoke there of the particular Jewish "witness" to the Shoah as a "saving warning" to the world and to the Church itself. The Pope linked this Jewish witness of Jewish suffering directly to the ancient prophetic witness, insisting on its distinctive, unique significance. To this Jewish witness, which, if heard, can be a saving witness for the Church and for the world, he stated, the Church can only "unite" with its own witness.

This is startlingly unprecedented language to hear from a Christian, no less from the Pope himself. The Church's saving proclamation "united" to that of another people, another proclamation, another saving witness? Yet the Pope has reaffirmed this Warsaw statement, referring to it time and again since then. He means it. We Catholics should, I believe, attend carefully to it.

2. Why the Jews?

This is a double-edged question which brings us closer to the heart of the mystery. The Jews, the Church has proclaimed with ever-greater clarity since the Second Vatican Council, not only were but are chosen by God to be a "light to the nations." They remain, now no less than before, "the Suffering Servant" of God. Given this clear and "irrevocable" divine calling, Christians cannot but strive to respond to the Jewish suffering with the eyes of faith. It addresses us, because of our very belief in God's Word, in a way that we cannot but seek to relate it to our own mystery as Church.

I will not here attempt to detail what a proper Catholic theological understanding of the Shoah might be like. I will only affirm as strongly as I can that one must be developed by us today. This is a clear mandate for us as Church, as ourselves "People of God." For we, too, in God's Spirit" are, in a very real way, in the line of the prophets.

I cannot, then, fully answer "why the Jews?" here. The answer, if there is one short of the eschaton [end of days--Ed.], is for the Jewish people themselves to utter. It is for us, as Church, to support that utterance, to attend to it, to listen and to respond to it in reliance on the Holy Spirit and Christ's salvific love for all humanity.

3. The Shoah raises distinct spiritual, moral, and social challenges.[24]

It took place in the heart of "Christian Europe." Christians were both among its victims and chief among its perpetrators [even if many of the latter are most accurately described as apostates].

On the one hand, this trenchant reality questions the basis of West-ern civilization as we know it. How could this monstrous event happen in "civilized" Europe in the twentieth century? Where were the limits, the moral restraints, the laws? How could civilization move from the repressive [but sadly familiar from Christian history] legislation of Nuremberg in the early 1930s to Auschwitz and Bergen-Belsen in less than a decade? The people that ran the death camps, that put in commercial bids to build the crematoria and provide the gas pellets for the death chambers, were not illiterate savages, not a "golden horde" of Mongols or Huns, but the graduates of the finest institutions of higher learning the world had known to that day. Stepped in Christian culture, they returned from a day of systematic, dispassionate murder of women and children to listen to Bach and Beethoven, and perhaps to read Goethe and Schiller. They were scholars and scientists, doctors and writers. Many had Ph.D.s and other advanced degrees.

If the best of our education, the heights of our culture, could not make them hesitate to participate in such ultimate depravities as whole-sale, calculated murder, of what benefit, really, is education? What reliance can we place upon it? Education itself, I believe, must raise and respond to these questions today.

4. The Shoah and the Church.

But if the Shoah raises chilling questions regarding our comfortable assumptions about twentieth century "civilization," it raises equally hard challenges regarding our understanding of religion and God. Many of the perpetrators saw themselves as "good" Christians, Protestants and Catho-l-ics. How could they? What was missing [or, more chillingly, present] in the Christian education they had received for centuries that allowed them to remain blind to what they were doing? Or indifferent to what others were doing in their name?

Many scholars point here to the ancient Christian "teaching of contempt" against Jews and Judaism as providing a negative framework, though not the direct cause, for the ease with which Hitler scapegoated the Jews. Without the medieval "demonization" of the Jews, they argue, modern racial antisemitism would not have been possible, much less so successful politically in Europe.

I believe there is truth in these assertions, uncomfortable as they are, though distinctions must be made. If the teachings of Christian preachers and Church leaders, bad as they sometimes were, were a sufficient cause for genocide, that would have happened, as many of these same scholars also point out, long before when the Churches had direct political power in ancient, medieval and Reformation Europe to implement their theology. But it did not happen then. Not for hundreds of years that their power held sway. It took the breakdown of that ecclesial authority, and with it the breakdown of its moral restraints by the Enlightenment and the "secularization" of Europe, to make possible the Shoah.

In medieval Christendom, Jews in extremis could always convert and survive. Often enough, they were able successfully to appeal to canon law and to the popes for legal protection or direct intervention to save them. But the Shoah, in our time, reveals how fragile civilization can be without such moral restraints. Secularity, no less than religion, it turns out, can have a dark side as well as a beneficial one. Interreligious and religious/secular dialogue, I would affirm, is not just a luxury in view of such awesome realities. It is a vital necessity for human survival as we approach the Third Millennium of the common era of Christian-Jewish interaction in history.

5. What, then, is the goal of Catholic teaching on the Shoah?

Again, I cannot here give a complete outline. This is up to Catholic educators themselves to develop. But I can give some indicators of directions to follow. An educational goal, as I see it, is not simply to expose evil, but to attract students to the good, to "act justly" as the prophet would say. It is not simply to list horrors, though confrontation with the horrors of humanity's inhumanity is necessary. Antisemitism is sinful--mortally so. This is a commandment for our generation and for all Christian generations that follow us.

But acknowledging evil is not in itself the point of Catholic catechesis [education--Ed.]. It is merely the counterpoint. Our educational goal, rather, is, first, to clarify for the students the deep challenges to our society and to our religion that the fact of the Shoah raises, and, second, to provide for students a structured and hope-filled environment within which they can begin to grapple with the issues of evil and goodness that the first of the crematoria cast in such painfully sharp relief.

The ultimate lesson of the Shoah for the believer is not evil but the mystery of the good, not despair but hope. Given the most implacable system ever devised for the destruction of the human spirit, how did so many [albeit relatively few] manage to maintain a sense of humanity in a world filled with corruption? What motivated those who risked their own lives to save Jews? How did so many [relatively and absolutely] of the victims maintain religious belief in the face of ultimate horror? Why did so many Jews go into the gas chambers singing the ancient Hebrew chant, Ani ma'amin [I believe....]? How were the survivors able to emerge from the camps and build new lives? Bear a new generation of the Jewish people? Build a new nation--the State of Israel--out of the ashes? In short, our teaching strategy must be one of hard challenges. It is one that accepts and cherishes the Jewish witness to us as Christians, that realizes in the Jewish witness a "saving warning" and, paradoxically, a saving hope as well.

IX. Conclusion

Finally, I would like to alert readers to three recent official documents of the Church that are pertinent to Shoah education. These are one statement of the Holy See and two issued by committees of the National Conference of Catholic Bishops.

All three of these documents need to be read within the context of the reassessment of official Catholic thought regarding Jews and Judaism begun by the Second Vatican Council.[25] Although the Second Vatican Council's declaration on the Jews, **Nostra Aetate, No. 4,** was very much precipitated by the Catholic reaction after the Shoah, it was not until 1974, in its implementing document for **Nostra Aetate**[26] that this crucial context for the Conciliar debate was first officially acknowledged at this level:

> ....the step taken by the [Second Vatican] Council finds its historical setting in circumstances deeply affected by the memory of the persecution and massacre of Jews which took place in Europe just before and during the Second World War.[27]

It was not, in turn, until 1985, that the **Notes** issued by the same Committee[28] for the first time universally mandated that Catholic religious education [properly, "catechesis"] "should help in understanding the meaning....of the extermination [of Jews] during the years 1939-1945, and its consequences," though Pope John Paul II had begun addressing the subject in some depth even earlier.[29]

It can be said, then, that many of the themes and issues first raised at scholars' conferences on the Shoah over the years are only now becoming embedded in the official teaching of the Roman Catholic Church. The other side of this same statement, of course, is that these crucial themes are becoming embedded in the very heart of the teaching of the Church, filling the catechetical "gap" left by the concurrent attempt to remove the vestiges of the old, pernicious "teaching of contempt" against Jews and Judaism condemned by the Second Vatican Council.

While perhaps relatively slow to act, the Church's institutional memory is long, and, once committed, correspondingly deep.

The first statement to which I draw your attention is primarily historical and moral, though it does rebut rather effectively one lingering element of the theology of contempt, the pernicious dichotomy between so-called Jewish particularity and Christian universalism. Both elements are to be found in both traditions, of course, as the document rightly points out.

The Pontifical Commission on Justice and Peace statement, "The Church and Racism," is, in many ways, a remarkable document for the Holy See to issue. It offers a survey of "racist behavior throughout history" that does not seek "to gloss over the weaknesses and even, at times, complicity of certain Church leaders....in this phenomenon," but rather analyzes the growth of intergroup antipathy to its apotheosis in modern antisemitism. Indeed, it calls antisemitism "the most tragic form that racist ideology has assumed in our century," citing specifically the Shoah in this context. [Section No. 15]

Nor does "The Church and Racism" shirk from including the Christian teaching of contempt in its pre-history of modern racial antisemitism, acknowledging that "within 'Christendom,' the Jews, considered the tenacious witnesses of a refusal to believe in Christ, were often the subject of serious humiliation, accusations and proscriptions" [Section No. 2]. It distinguishes, properly, this religious polemical stance from modern racial ideology as it appeared in the eighteenth and nineteenth centuries. It devotes a major section to the development of National Socialism in the twentieth century, citing it as "responsible for one of the greatest genocides in history." "This murderous folly," the statement continues, "struck first and foremost the Jewish people in unheard-of proportions," thus acknowledging the historical uniqueness of the Shoah, while also calling to memory Nazism's genocidal attacks "on the Gypsies and Tziganes and also categories of persons such as the handicapped and the mentally ill."

The Holy See's document recalls the stern opposition to these Nazi policies by Pope Pius XI [which has never been a subject for scholarly contention] and by Pope Pius XII [which has, though perhaps unfairly]. "The Church and Racism" is a timely statement that will be immediately of use to Catholic teachers not only in history, but in ethics and religion courses as well, providing them with the beginnings of a framework for the development of Shoah education on all levels, as Pope John Paul II called for during his visit to Miami on September 11, 1987.[30] I say "beginnings," because the Holy See's document on the Shoah, also promised by the Pope in Miami, is still forthcoming. This latter will be drafted, however, as is most appropriate, only after "serious studies" on the subject have been undertaken jointly by Christians and Jews through the mechanism of the International Catholic-Jewish Liaison Committee.[31]

The two American documents were issued by different Committees of the United States Bishops' Conference. It June of 1988, **Criteria for the Evaluation of Dramatization of the Passion**, by the Bishops' Committee for Ecumenical and Interreligious Affairs, was published in both Spanish and English. This document centers on depictions of Christ's death and spells out, in some detail, how it can be portrayed dramatically without having the implication, as in the past, of "collective guilt" of Jews for Jesus' death.[32]

In this, as with the second document to be discussed below, one can see how the Church is moving into a new stage in its implementation of **Nostra Aetate's** effort to eradicate antisemitism from Catholic teaching, reaching even the level of local passion plays and media presentations.

The second document, **God's Mercy Endures Forever: Guidelines on the Presentations of Jews and Judaism in Catholic Preaching**, published January, 1989, is a statement by the NCCB Committee on the Liturgy. Designed for homilists, it covers the entire spectrum of the Church's liturgical calendar. Bishop Joseph P. Delaney of Fort Worth, who chairs the Bishops' Committee on the Liturgy, begins his Preface to the document with the following words:

> Even in the twentieth century, the age of the Holocaust, the Shoah, the "scouring Wind," God's mercy endures forever.
> The Holocaust drew its fiery breath from the ancient, sometimes latent, but always persistent anti-Semitism which, over the centuries, found too large a place within the hearts of too many Christian men and women. Yet, since the Holocaust and since the Second Vatican Council, Christians have struggled to learn the reasons for such irrational and anti-Christian feelings against that special people for whom "God's mercy endures forever," to deal with those feelings, and to overcome them through knowledge, understanding, dialogue, and love.[33]

The purpose for these liturgical guidelines, Bishop Delaney continues, is thus "to see to it that our [Catholic] liturgical celebrations never again become occasions for that anti-Semitic or anti-Jewish sentiment that sometimes moved the liturgy in the past."[34]

Drawing on the 1974 Vatican **Guidelines**, the 1985 Vatican **Notes**, and a wealth of recent liturgical and Biblical scholarship, **God's Mercy** offers historical perspective and hermeneutical clarification to Christian preachers. It begins by noting the "Jewish roots of the Liturgy," not only Biblically but also in the synagogue and post-Biblical Jewish forms of worship. It rejects explicitly the false notions "that the New Covenant 'abrogated' or 'superseded' the Old, and that the Sinai Covenant was discarded by God and replaced with another" [Section 6], as well as the deicide [God killer--Ed.] charge [Second 7].

God's Mercy denounces "triumphalism" and instead frames a positive understanding of the Gospel message that affirms unequivocally the Church's teaching about Christ while affirming also the continuing validity of God's covenant with the Jewish people. It does this, it should be noted, on specifically Christian theological grounds:

> The Christian proclamation of the saving deeds of the One God through Jesus was formed in the context of Second Temple Judaism and cannot be understood thoroughly without that context. It is a proclamation that, at its heart, stands in solidarity with the continuing Jewish witness in affirming the One God as Lord of history. Further, false or demeaning portraits of a repudiated

Israel may undermine Christianity as well. How can one confidently affirm the truth of God's covenant with all humanity and
creation in Christ [See Romans 8:21] without at the same time
affirming God's faithfulness to the Covenant with Israel that also
lies at the heart of Biblical testimony? [Section 8]

God's Mercy tackles the often-abused "fulfillment" theme of the Advent
liturgy, noting that the Biblical prophecies are not to be understood as
"merely temporal predictions," but are also "profound expressions of
eschatological hope." They are "fulfilled" [i.e. irreversibly inaugurated] in
Christ's coming, but preachers must also note that "the fulfillment is not
completely worked out in each person's life or perfected in the world at
large." Hence, it concludes, "with the Jewish people, we await the complete realization of the messianic age." [Sections 11-12]

Similarly, **God's Mercy** affirms traditional Christian applications of
Biblical texts, such as typology, but notes that such interpretations, while
valid, do not exhaust the "unfathomable riches" and "inexhaustible context" of
the Hebrew Bible. The association of the Akedah [the Binding of Isaac] with
Christ's sacrifice, for example, is a natural one for Christians. But this
does not invalidate traditional Jewish applications of the same Biblical text,
from which Christians can continue to learn. [Section 14]

In these areas, I believe, **God's Mercy** is moving toward a positive, non-
triumphalist form of Christian anamnesis ["memory"] within the very
understanding of the Church's worship. Since, for Catholics, lex orandi is
indeed lex credendi, the significance of such liturgical hermeneutics is quite
apparent.[35]

God's Mercy, as does the Vatican **Notes**, stresses that the conflict
scenes in the Gospel between Jesus and "the Pharisees" often reflect later
Christian-Jewish disputes "long after the time of Jesus" [Sections 16-20],
and, like the BCEIA **Criteria**, takes particular care with the passion narratives of Holy Week [Sections 26-28]. The document concludes with a
summary listing of nine "general principles" applicable to all homilies
throughout the year. I would like to see this list posted on the bulletin boards
of every Catholic seminary, parish rectory, and school faculty lounge in the
country.

Finally, the Bishops, for the first time that I know of in any official
Church statement at this level, recommend joint Jewish/Christian Memorial
Services for the victims of the Shoah and offer specific examples of
prayers to be said at Mass on the Sunday closest to Yom Ha-Shoah:

> 29.   Also encouraged are joint memorial services com-
> memorating the victims of the Shoah [Holocaust]. These should be
> prepared for with catechetical and adult education programming to

ensure a proper spirit of shared reverence. Addressing the Jewish community of Warsaw, Pope John Paul II stressed the uniqueness and significance of Jewish memory of the <u>Shoah</u>: 'More than anyone else, it is precisely you who have become this saving warning. I think that in this sense you continue your particular vocation, showing yourselves to be still the heirs of that election to which God is faithful. This is your mission in the contemporary world before....all of humanity' [Warsaw, June 14, 1987]. On the Sunday closest to <u>Yom Ha-Shoah</u>, Catholics should pray for the victims of the Holocaust and their survivors. The following serve as examples of petititions for the general intercessions at Mass:

--For the victims of the Holocaust, their families, and all our Jewish brothers and sisters, that the violence and hatred they experienced may never again be repeated, we pray to the Lord.

--For the Church, that the Holocaust may be a reminder to us that we can never be indifferent to the sufferings of others, we pray to the Lord.

--For our Jewish brothers and sisters, that their confidence in the face of long-suffering may spur us on to greater faith and trust in God, we pray to the Lord.

For Presbyterian Douglas Huneke, Irving Greenberg's working principle to which he alludes in the title of his essay "In the Presence of Burning Children," has not produced "a radical, systemic institutional reformation of Christianity in Europe or America." After examining "The Ten Points of Seelisberg" [Switzerland, 1947] and their contemporary implications according to the following schema: [a] the Jewishness of Jesus [#1, #2, #3, #10]; [b] love of God and one's neighbor [#4]; and [c] theological antisemitism [#5, #6, #7, #8, #9], for him, the theological agenda of post-Shoah Christianity still must be framed by three tasks: [1] examination and repudiation of Christian antisemitism, [2] analysis of the theological and social implications of the Nazis' murder of the Jews; and [3] a "re-ordering" of education for both laity and clergy. Significantly, at the heart of his essay Jesus the Christ still remains as the model to be emulated, based on his exhaustive study and interviews with those Christians who were themselves "rescuers."

IN THE PRESENCE OF BURNING CHILDREN:

The Reformation Of Christianity After The <u>Shoah</u>

Douglas K. Huneke

[With Admiration for Sergey Lyzov, Christian, <u>Shoah</u> Scholar, and Op-

ponent of Antisemitism, Moscow]

I. In Their Presence

Throughout history, warriors have reserved special terrors for mothers and children. Early in the history of Israel, Elisha prophesied that when Hazael became King of Syria, he would "....dash in pieces their [Israelite] little children and rip up their women who were with child" [II Kings 8:12]. The brutality of Hazael's soldiers pales next to the record of Hitler's SS. It became a routine Nazi practice, particularly among the <u>Einsatzgruppen</u> [mobile killing units], to snatch an infant from its mother and, before her eyes, smash her child's head against a wall, or impale an infant on a bayonet, or execute a mother and child together. When I wrote the biography of Herman F. Graebe, a German railroad engineer who rescued hundreds of Jews in the Ukraine, Graebe described carefully and with tremendous emotion how the strength of his decision to rescue Jews and, later, to testify at the Nuremberg trials, was solidified when he witnessed his co-nationals smashing infants against pillars and impaling them on bayonets. His vivid accounts recalled a painting that hangs in the administration center of the Israeli <u>Shoah</u> memorial, Yad Vashem. It depicts a battered infant lying askew in the corner of a stone wall, a trail of blood begins mid-wall and traces the child's passage to the ground.

A. At Watch on Buchenwald's Perimeter

In spite of its setting, on a hill looking out over a lush and beautiful valley and beyond to the historic city of Weimar, Buchenwald is a desolate memorial to the Jews who were murdered there. On the north perimeter of the camp, outside the rusting barbed wire, is a thick stand of poplar trees. Just inside the wire fence are memorials to the Soviet prisoners of war, Communist anti-Fascists, and Jews who were exterminated by the Nazis. In 1976, as I stood reading the monuments, my eyes caught a movement near the fence. A woman with a wizened face, wearing a long black coat and bandanna, paced in the small clearing between the poplars and the once-electrified fence. Keeping a discrete distance, I watched this woman walk up and down the fence line. Her body bent and contorted as she moved; her arms flew up in the air and then drove down toward the ground. She twisted her hands as if in deep, agonizing grief and her lips moved as if praying or conversing. This ritual continued for several hours each of the days that I was visiting the camp.

Why was she there? What past torments compelled her presence on this mountain? Had someone she loved been tortured on the infamous whipping block? Was she mourning the death of a parent or husband who was led into the gassing rooms only to exist through the chimney? Was she mourning the death of her child? Who could wipe away the horrible vision, the haunting eyes of the small ones in Buchenwald's special children's camp? Has she walked hundreds of streets and scanned bundles of Red Cross photographs searching for the face of her child? Alone now, does the Mourner's Kaddish [Jewish memorial prayer--Ed.] cross her lips? Does she find solace in her prayers?

The Shoah covers its students with a shroud of pained silence, surrounds them with unanswerable questions, and casts them into haunting, wordless encounters. It is painful to see the faces, to look into the wide, vacant eyes of the nine hundred little children who survived Buchenwald's gas chambers. It is worse for those who survey the endless enlargements for a single recognizable family trait. The source of this woman's anguish remained a mystery; her sorrow and prayers were private by her choice. An invisible wall blocked the visitor from the survivor. So I kept a discrete distance, reciting the Kaddish under my breath, and prayed for wizened old women in long black coats and bandannas.

B. A Defiant Prayer at Majdanek

The suffering of mothers and children confronted me in a powerful way again at the former extermination camp, Majdanek, in Lublin, Poland. There was a large, grassy field at the entrance to the camp. As I left the Visitors' Office and walked along the promenade to the main camp monument, I passed three women peacefully pushing their babies in strollers. Near them, on a curved park bench, in the shade of a tree, sat another woman who gazed into the camp serenely, a baby nursing at her breast. Beyond them, the sky was split by the largest and most imposing Polish monuments to the victims of Nazi terror. In the distance, antiquated, but perfectly preserved guard towers cast long shadows across tall barbed wire fences and swaying pine tree hid the camp from its nearby neighbors.

While the yes of her nursing infant stared gently and contentedly at her, she looked out at a universe that betrayed the tranquility of the moment: the barracks [cramped and stagnant], disinfection showers [public undressing],

barbed wire [calculated ravaging of the spirit as parents and children were
separated violently], gas chambers [the dash, shaved and naked, under
flailing truncheons to the release of death], crematorium chimney [gross,
posthumous examinations for jewels and money]. How could this woman
nurse her child under such a dark cloud of history? Why did these women
come to this place? Certainly there were other places infinitely more
pastoral and certainly easier to reach from Lublin's town square. Then it
struck me: They brought the consummation of sexual love, the new gift of
their wombs, and paraded defiantly at the edges of the citadels of death.
The nursing mother brought the most vulnerable symbol of life and peacefully sat before death's kingdom, proclaiming:

> See! Look at my baby--You shall
> > never smash another one against one wall!
> Look! My breast, full of milk--you will
> > never cause another woman's breast to wither and dry!
> > I am
> here to declare to you that you shall
> never again separate children from parents!
> You imposed death, but I gave life--
> > I live beyond you! Against you!
> They were innocent women and children--not a danger to you;
> > now,
> > I am
> a threat to your memory because
> I exist and
> I create beyond your life and death.
> For the souls of women and children who knew your whips,
> > your humiliations, your terrors,
> > I am!
> For my child and for 1,500,000 children
> I offer the warmth and nourishment of my breast,
> the rich milk of human love and hope.
> Do you see me?
> > I am here!
> > I am nursing!
> In spite of you, because of you,
> > I am!

II. A Fatal Alliance: Nationalism and Triumphalism

The sense of hope that I drew from the women's presence and their
defiance of death is tempered by Adolf Hitler's declaration in Mein Kampf:
"Today I believe that I am acting in accord with the will of the Almighty
Creator: by defending myself against the Jews, I am fighting for the work
of the Lord."[1] Hitler's sense of a "holy war" joined with the growing and
militant nationalism that took root in the fertile soil of racism, permeated

nearly every level of ecclesiastical leadership, and profoundly influenced the life of the German churches. Prominent theologians gave special credibility to this nationalistic way of uniting God's Word with the theory of the Volk, sounding more like the emerging political preacher of hatred and division that ministers of the Gospel. An example is a lecture in 1937 by Lutheran theologian, Paul Althaus, who has been described as a distinguished and influential figure in German theology at that time:

> As a creation of God, the Volk is a law of our life....We are unconditionally bound to faithfulness, to responsibility, so that the life of the Volk as it has come down to us not be contaminated or weakened through our fault. We are bound to stand up for the life of our Volk, even to the point of risking our own life....Our life in our Volk is not our eternal life; but we have no eternal life if we do not live for our Volk. This is not a question of the absolute value of the Volk, but of our absolute obligation to the Volk.[2]

In an apparent attempt to discredit the then newly-released Theological Declaration at Barmen [1934], Althaus signed the Ansbacher Ratchlag, which included the following lines underscoring a theological and ecclesiastical support for Hitler's holy war:

> In this knowledge we as believing Christians thank God our Father that He has given to our Volk in its time of need the Fuhrer as a pious and faithful sovereign, and that he wants to prepare for us in the National Socialist system of government 'good rule,' a government with discipline and honor.
>   Accordingly, we know that we are responsible before God to assist the work of the Fuhrer in our calling and in our station in life.[3]

Only a small remnant of theologians, pastors, and church leaders publicly challenged the blatant linking of the law of God with the laws of the German state and the nationalistic fervor of the Volk. Those who dared to disapprove publicly were quickly silenced by the Reich and most paid with their lives. The majority of German Christians remained secure in their silence. The others turned their words to the service of the Reich and continued on a course that legitimated the bonding of German national-ism and Christian triumphalism. The effect of this silence and the unifi-cation of nationalism and triumphalism opened a fatal new chapter in the history of Christian antisemitism and gave tacit legitimacy to those who were preparing the design for Hitler's "Final Solution."

A. Fatal Loyalties

Could these theologians and preachers have known that Hitler and his colleagues took the fearful silence of the many and the support of the complicit as a license for genocide? Could they have known that their words might afford special encouragement to men like Pastor Ernest Biberstein? Biberstein, a student of theology and for eleven years a parish minister, commanded the brutal and efficient Einsatzcommando 6 in Einsatzgruppe C.[4] Could they have imagined that their words and activities would be taken as a sign permitting well-educated, religious men and women to put Jews to death in mass graves, in sealed chambers, in silent forests; to smash children against walls or force them to be held in front of their mothers so that two persons might be dispatched by one bullet--a strange economy of death in a universe devoted to death?

Could they have foreseen that a young survivor of Auschwitz would one day bear witness to the systematic institutionalization of Nazi horrors against women and children, to the end result of unchecked racism, nationalism, Christian triumphalism, and antisemitism?

> Not far from us, flames were leaping up from a ditch, gigantic flames. They were burning something. A lorry drew up at the pit and delivered its load--little children. Babies! I saw it--saw it with my own eyes....those children in the flames. [Is it surprising that I could not sleep after that? Sleep had fled from my eyes]....
> Never shall I forget that night, the first night in camp, which has turned my life into one long night, seven times cursed and seven times times sealed. Never shall I forget that smoke. Never shall I forget the little faces of the children, whose bodies I saw turned into wreaths of smoke beneath a silent blue sky.[5]

In 1943, a year after Auschwitz opened, Althaus learned for the first time that German soldiers were routinely killing civilians in occupied lands. That revelation reported repulsed him, but not so much that he was provoked by the offense nor compelled morally to speak out against the killings or the Reich. Instead, he and the others continued knowingly to place their words and ministries in the service of genocide.

III. The Geography of Genocide: In Their Presence

Drawing a lesson from the silence of the majority of the German churches and from the active complicity of theologians, preachers, and ecclesiastical bureaucrats, Rabbi Irving Greenberg drafted a "working principle" to guide Jews and Christians who probe the implications of the Shoah: who seek a humane, informed, and faithful response to the victims and survivors. Greenberg's "working principle," given wide public voice for the first time in 1974, is the foundation for a long ignored, but essential radical reformation of Christianity after the Shoah. In light of the impotence of most of

Christianity before the Nazis, his words must be understood to be the definitive mandate for post-Shoah Christianity:

> Let us offer, then, as working principle the following: No statement, theological or otherwise, should be made that would not be credible in the presence of burning children.[6]

A post-Shoah Christian theology, if it is to have integrity and credibility, must begin at the edge of a mass grave, at the entrance to a gas chamber, besides a bloodstained wall, in the presence of burning children.

A. Agenda for Post-Shoah Christianity

The agenda for post-Shoah Christianity has remained virtually unchanged since the Nuremberg Tribunal weighed the evidence and pro-nounced its verdict on genocidal crimes against humanity. The tragedy is that the presence of burning children did not bring about a radical, systemic institutional reformation of Christianity in Europe or America. The post-Shoah agenda is framed by three central tasks: first, a careful study of the origins of and a full repudiation of Christian antisemitism which found its complete and most violent expression between 1933 and 1945; second, a thorough analysis of the theological and social implications of the Nazi destruction of European Jewry; and finally, a re-ordering of theological education for laity and clergy to the end that the church never again acts freely and destructively on triumphalist beliefs, is not a perpetrator of antisemitic or other divisive teachings, nor a willing partner conforming to the political, social, or theological directives of ill-intentioned authorities.

B. The Seelisberg Paradigm

In August, 1947, the Third Commission of the International Emergency Conference of Christians and Jews met in Seelisberg, Switzerland. French historian Jules Isaac provided the commission with a study document entitled, "The Rectification Necessary In Christian Teaching: Eighteen Points."[7] Isaac's paper served as the basis for the final statement of the conference, "The Ten Points of Seelisberg."[8] The Commission distinguished itself by its very early date relative to the end of the war, by the participation of Protestants and Catholics, and by the decision of the Commission to have Jews review and comment on the various points. The very factors that distinguished the work of the Commission appear to have worked against its noble purposes. The meeting may have brought forth its product too near the end of the war and the beginning of a generalized public awareness of the horrors of the Shoah. In 1947, survivors were still slowly piercing their daily lives back together and few had begun to process what they had lived through or plumb the Shoah's implications. Those who spoke of the unspeakable offered their testimony to a world that had no means to comprehend the brutality and immensity of the "Final Solution." More importantly, survivors quickly discovered that words were inadequate for their experience.

Also in 1947, Protestants and Catholics did not have a familiar basis for dialogue and common pronouncement. It was most likely too early for institutional Christianity to make the necessary connection between centuries of antisemitism and the work of the camps. Another indication that the Seelisberg document was premature is the absence of any reference to the Shoah. This is most surprising considering that many participants knew that Isaac's wife and daughter had died in a concentration camp. None of these observations are intended to diminish the importance of the Seelisberg Points, but rather to indicate why the points did not lead to the changes imagined by the participants.

The drafters of the "Ten Points of Seelisberg" were visionaries who sensed the urgent need for what Paul van Buren would describe twenty-eight years later:

> ....at least a few Christians have begun to realize that a reconsideration of what Christians have been saying about Judaism and of Christian-Jewish relations must lead to a reconsideration of Christianity itself....Theology can shut its eyes and pretend that the Holocaust never happened and that Israel doesn't exist. Theology has shown itself capable of such blindness before! But if there are prospects for serious theology, for a theology not hopelessly blind to matters that pertain to the heart of its task, then the time has come for a reconsideration of the whole theological and Christian enterprise of the most radical sort.[9]

Mindful of the presence and witness of burning children, I shall now examine several of the Seelisberg points as the basis for the study and repudiation of Christian antisemitism. The implications of the "Ten Points of Seelisberg" may yet serve to launch a radical reformation of the whole theological and Christian enterprise.

C. The Challenge of the Shoah to Christianity

The first three and the tenth points of the Seelisberg document address the Jewishness of Jesus and his movement by affirming that "it is the same living God who speaks to us all" through the Hebrew and Christian Scriptures[10]; that "Jesus was born of a Jewish mother" in the lineage of David and lovingly embraced "his own people and the whole world;" identifies the first followers of Jesus as Jews; and the tenth point calls Christians to keep from speaking of the "first members of the Church as if they were not Jews." Tragically, centuries before and during the time of the Shoah, the vast majority of theologians and preachers rejected out of hand or ignored the truth of these points. The few preachers and theologians who did attend to these details met strong resistance. In their important study of the Shoah, Richard Rubenstein and John Roth recount the time when, in December, 1933, Reformed theologian, Karl Barth, preached a sermon entitled, "Jesus Christ was a Jew."   This courageous message predictably caused a rift in the membership of the church. Shortly thereafter, Barth wrote a member of the church, "anyone who believes in Christ, who was himself a Jew, and died for Gentiles and Jews, simply cannot be involved in the contempt for Jews and ill-treatment of them which is now the order of the day."[11]

The implication of the first three Seelisberg Points is that Christian antisemitism and any harmful or destructive acts which follow from it are, by definition, fratricidal attacks upon the history of God's covenantal relationships [the Hebrew and Christian Scriptural record of the cove-nants], upon those who live under God's unaltered promises [Jews], and, ultimately, upon the Creator of the universe. The prophetic texts in Hebrew Scripture and the Christian Gospels portray clearly the God who shares fully the wholeness and humiliation, suffering and joy, freedom and bondage of the covenant peoples. If Jews suffered and died at the hands of Christians during the Shoah, God, who identifies fully with God's people, suffered and died, as victim of these same Christians. God was murdered with each and every Jew who died during the Shoah. This is to say that those baptized believers whose antisemitism led them to be silent, complicit, or active participants in the Shoah were guilty not only of antisemitic fratricide, but also of Deicide. Any form or expression of antisemitism, no matter if it is fatal or subtle, must be regarded as an expression of Christian self-hatred that has the capacity to destroy those who practice it and those who are its targets of abuse, including God who is never divided from God's people.

The presence of the God whose fate is inextricably bound to the fate of the covenant peoples finds a powerful statement in Elie Wiesel's memoir. At Buna, three inmates, two adults and a child, were to be hung as suspected saboteurs. Jews in the camp were forced to watch as ropes were placed around the necks of the adults who shouted, "Long live liberty!" The child was silent, but behind Wiesel a voice asked, "Where is God? Where is He?" The child was slow to die and Wiesel concludes the account:

> For more than half an hour he stayed there, struggling between life and death, dying the slow agony under our eyes. And we had to look him full in the face. He was still alive when I passed in front of him. His tongue was still red, his eyes were not yet glazed. Behind me, I heard the same man asking: "Where is God now?" And I heard a voice within me answer him: "Where is He? Here He is--He is hanging here on this gallows...."[12]

A Protestant theologian in the mid-1970's, perhaps moved by Wie-sel's experience at Buna, expressed a Christian understanding of the link between

God's fate and the fate of God's people. He wrote that the most compelling contemporary image of the Passion is of a Jew hanging cruci-fied on an electrified barbed wire fence at Auschwitz. A theology that dares to separate God from God's people; that denies or diminishes the promises of God to humanity; that ignores or contributes to the suffering of others; or that fails to perceive in the suffering of another human being, the pain and suffering of God, has failed to comprehend the pathos communicated by the prophets and the commitment of God in the various covenants.

D. Two Faithful Remnants Honor A Commandment

The fourth of the Seelisberg Points calls Christians to remember that the "fundamental commandment....to love God and one's neighbors" is contained in the Hebrew Scripture and confirmed by Jesus, and is "binding upon both Christians and Jews in all human relationships, without any exception." In Elie Wiesel's novel, The Oath, the narrator describes the thoughts of Moshe the madman:

> He knew that nothing justifies the pain man causes another. Any messiah in whose name men are tortured can only be a false messiah. It is by diminishing evil, present and real evil, experienced evil, that one builds the city of the sun. It is by helping the person who looks at you with tears in his eyes, needing help, needing you or at least your presence, that you may attain perfection.[13]

Not all German Christians followed a false messiah or the political preacher of hatred and division. A faithful remnant resisted actively and publicly the rise of National Socialism and Adolf Hitler. Some created and signed the Theological Declaration of Barmen, while others preached against the idolatry, falsehood, and folly of nationalism. Many of their stories are memorialized movingly in the book, Dying We Live, edited by Helmut Gollwitzer. In his Forward to the book, theologian Reinhold Niebuhr described these religiously-motivated dissidents, lovers of spiritual and civic freedom, as "Revelations of the heroic heights to which the human spirit may rise when it is informed by 'grace,' a power that tran-scends the sense of duty and that is infused into those lives which have a sure hold of the meaning of human existence, which transcends their own lives and survival...."[14]

A second remnant of Christians, a distinct minority numbering fewer than ten thousand persons among the millions of people living in all of Central and Eastern Europe, responded directly to the tears, the need for help or at least offered the presence described by Moshe. These women, men, and children intervened personally and directly on behalf of desperately endangered Jews, dissidents, peasants, and others. The rescuers of Jews embodied the practice of a Christian faith called for in the fourth Seelisberg Point and grounded in the Biblical teachings to "love your neighbor" and "care for the sojourner in your midst." These Christians defied laws, endangered themselves and their families, and resisted successfully the combined forces of culture, nationalism, state authority, and misguided theologies. Their actions answered in the affirmation Cain's question, "Am I my brother's keeper?" and removed any limitations or barriers to the lawyer's question in the Gospel of Luke, "Who is my neighbor?"

Most of the rescuers were unlikely characters who did not stand out in their religious, social, vocational, or political settings. For the most part, they were common people who performed their daily routines until some act of brutality or the arrival of a frightened stranger, a survivor, galvanized their compassionate spirits and propelled them into activities that most others were unwilling or unable to consider. In spite of almost insurmountable odds and dangers, they managed to act honorably in an evil era. They were not perfect nor was that their goal, and they did not see themselves as heroic. On the contrary, they were people who simply remained faithful and human. A person does not fulfill the Biblical mandates to love one's neighbor and care for the sojourner without certain predispositions and skills which are structured on a radical understanding of faith. A warning is in order. As the case of Pastor Ernst Biberstein, commander of a mobile killing unit, illustrates dramatically, it is not sufficient to have a formal theological education and an articulated faith based on Biblical values and teachings. Those values and teachings are useless unless they can be translated into behaviors that protect, sustain, and sanctify human life.

In 1980, I began a study of the moral and spiritual development of Nazi era rescuers. In the succeeding years I interviewed rescuers and those whom they saved, and conducted case studies in the archives of the Department of the Righteous at Yad Vashem. The findings influence significantly the practical application of the fourth Seelisberg Point.[15] Nazi-era rescuers had a discernible spirit of adventurousness. These people were risk-takers in multiple, overlapping areas of their lives. They were not, however, reckless or impulsive. Numerous rescuers reported that they engaged in elaborate planning procedures and calculated their actions carefully in order to maximize security and reduce the risk to the people they were helping. A Dutch rescuer who was an award-winning skier is an example. He regularly waited for nightfall and then skied the route he would take the next morning with refugees. Skiing entails certain risks which are magnified when the conditions become extreme, as when this rescuer skied in the dark. He did this to be certain that military snow patrols had not moved into the area he and the Jews would be traveling, thereby minimizing the risks to everyone.

Nazi-era rescuers had an intense identification with a parental model of moral conduct. Virtually all of the rescuers in my study reported a close, significant relationship with one or both parents who acted morally, who made use of a decidedly moral vocabulary, and who actively practiced their values in the presence of their children. Numerous rescuers recall their parents based their moral teachings on religious concepts and frequently quoted one or more passages from Hebrew and Christian Scriptures that illustrated and supported their beliefs and actions. There was also a useful and practical folk wisdom or common sense of quality about the moralizing. One rescuer reported that the Bible lessons his father frequently read to him dealt with kindly behavior and how to get along with people and life. Another rescuer told how his father connected the feeing of strangers and the care of widows and orphans with the Biblical mandates for such behavior.

A significant factor disposing Christians to act altruistically was a religiously-inspired non-conformity that was linked to Biblical directives to compassionately care for those who are vulnerable, disenfranchised, and who suffer oppression and injustice. A Dutch rescuer summed up the matter of religiously-inspired non-conformity when she explained the foundation of her altruistic actions by quoting Saint Paul's admonition in Romans 12:2, "Be not conformed to this world, but be transformed to a completely new way of thinking so as to know what is the good and acceptable and perfect will of God." She went on to say that, "For me to kill or betray Jews would have been to conform to evil. I had no choice but to follow God's will and save Jews from the Nazis."

Religiously-inspired non-conformity coupled with the social ethics of the Christian Scripture became intellectual mandates to intervene on behalf of desperately endangered people. A German rescuer noted that his interventions, which he justified using Biblical passages, afforded him an important and comforting sense that there was consistency between his religious beliefs and how he lived his life. We have already seen the discontinuity that existed for those who made a connection between nation-alism [das Volk] and Christianity. The effect of the discontinuity led to conformity, complicity, silence, and indifference. Their allegiance was to a transitory and inhuman political order rather than to the ethical and spiritual teaching of their faith.

Many Nazi-era rescuers had sophisticated empathic imaginations. The essence of the empathic imagination is the ability to place oneself in the actual situation or role of another person and actively visualize the long-term consequences of the situation of that person. The so-called "Golden Rule" of Matthew 7:12 is the Biblical model for the empathic imagination, "Do unto others what you would have them do unto you." The German rescuer Herman Graebe had one of the most effective empathic imaginations of the rescuers I interviewed. It was nurtured by his mother who always asked him in situations of moral choice, "Fritz, what would you do?" Her questions were neither idle nor rhetorical.

Graebe's empathic imagination served him at the edge of a mass grave in Dubno, Ukraine, where he watched his contemporary, an anonymous, naked Jewish man point to the sky and speak to his son moments before the two descended a ledge in the mass grave and were murdered. In Graebe's empathic imagination, he and his own young son became the two Jews standing before the pit. Forty years later, Graebe vividly remembered thinking at the time what he would say to his son if they had been the ones waiting to be murdered. As he walked from the scene, heartsick, his mother's question crossed his consciousness: "And Fritz, what would you do?" Graebe went on from this encounter to establish a successful rescue network in the Ukraine.

Rescuers were quite adept at hospitality. They removed endangered people from intensely hostile environments, offering them a respite from the forces that sought their destruction. They shared food, drink, warmth, rest, protection, and presence. Hospitality is the specific training ground of religiously-motivated altruism. Henri Nouwen, a Roman Catholic theologian, has written the following description of this quality:

> In a world full of strangers, estranged from their own past, culture, and country, from their neighbors, friends, and family, from their deepest self and their God, we witness a painful search for a hospitable place where life can be lived without fear....That is our vocation, to covert the hostis into a hospis, the enemy into a guest and to create the free and fearless space where brotherhood and sisterhood can be formed and fully expressed.[16]

Finally, rescuers of Jews had all learned to confront and manage their prejudice. Entrenched and culturally validated stereotypes of Jews determined the political, social, and legal actions that resulted in centuries of dehumanizing attitudes, injury, or death. When such stereotypes are set aside in deference to a greater consideration of human dignity or a more egalitarian worldview, the effects of prejudice and brutality can be avoided. Moral parents, humane Biblical teachings, and a worldview that enabled the rescuers to interpret the persecution of Jews as morally repugnant all contributed to the containment of prejudice.

It must be noted that there were very few communal rescue efforts during the Nazi era. Communal rescues were orchestrated by religiously-based groups with credible and inspiring leaders. It is clear from the few examples of communal rescue [i.e. Le Chambon and Assisi] that compassionate interventions leading to the protection of victims will be most successful when there is a community of like-minded persons with an organized ethic that supports such interventions. Institutional Christianity reaps a justifiable condemnation when it fails to prepare people to act in a pro-human manner or fails to build both an ethic and a structure that protects human life and ensures the dignity of persons.

Nazi-era rescuers are models for the mandate set forth in the fourth Seelisberg Point: they had the skills and predispositions that empowered them to love God and their neighbors. Any form of religious or secular education that fails to take Nazi-era rescuers into consideration has abandoned the past, neglected the present, and risks defaulting on a faithful and humane future.

E. Additional Challenges to Christianity Today

The remaining five points of the Seelisberg document address important specific forms of theological antisemitism. Point five calls Christians to avoid "disparaging Biblical or post-Biblical Judaism" in order to extol Christianity. This common form of triumphalism holds that Christianity is the fulfillment and completion of Judaism and incorrectly concluded that all covenants between God and the Jews were breached and, therefore, revoked. Christianity is seen by those who accept this flawed line of reasoning as superior to Judaism. This reasoning has served historically as the basis for countless evangelistic "missions to the Jews." No Christian who stands in the presence of burning children would dare to seek the conversion of Jews. Such a Christian must struggle with the contradictions implicit in speaking of a God of love whose followers were the architects of mass murder and genocide; of a covenantal God who did not save the covenantal people, who did not extinguish the flames or dispel the gas or vanquish the adversaries. These irresolvable contradictions will quench the evangelistic fervor and humble the triumphalist spirit of any believer who stands before the Shoah.

The implication of the fifth Seelisberg point is harsh, but it must be said. Christians who pursue the conversion of the Jews fail to hear the screaming, tortured anguish of the victims, they fail to comprehend to fragile rebirth of post-Shoah Judaism, and they fail to confront the powerful questions about God and faith and promise that arise from the ovens and mass graves. Whether acting out of a mistaken benevolence or self-righteous triumphalism, these Christians seek to do to the Jews spiritually what Hitler sought to accomplish physically.

The sixth, seventh, and ninth Seelisberg Points are closely related. The sixth point confronts the issue of using the word "Jews" in the context of "the enemies of Jesus," and the words "the enemies of Jesus" to identify the whole of the Jewish people. It should be noted that the Gospel according to John frequently employed the "collective term 'the Jews' in a restricted and pejorative sense to mean Jesus' enemies."[17] The drafters of the Ten Seelisberg Points preferred to keep the warning unlimited, but the Gospel of John does pose the greatest difficulty for exegetes and preachers who wish to eliminate this problem. The seventh point urges Christians to "Avoid presenting the Passion in such a way as to bring the odium of the killing of Jesus upon all the Jews or upon the Jews alone." The drafters correctly note that the Jews were not the only ones demanding Jesus's death, that they alone were not responsible. The point ends with a lengthy and impassioned plea for responsible religious education that avoids inflaming believers and leading them into "an undiscriminating hatred of the Jews at all times, including those of our own day." The ninth point challenges the perpetuation of the "superstitious notion that the Jewish people is reprobate, accursed, reserved for a destiny of suffering."

Much of the legacy of the hatred of the Jews can be traced to the teaching of the church that Jews were and continue to be responsible for the crime of Deicide in the crucifixion of Jesus. For centuries, clergy and theologians have solidified their power by distorting the historicity of the crucifixion. They have deflected responsibility from a few Jewish leaders who worked in concert with the political leaders of the Roman occupation government to a transhistoric collective Jewish responsibility. This dishonesty was the fertile soil in which the seeds of the Shoah were planted early in the development of the church. Even Hitler tried to capitalize on this fatal harvest when, in Mein Kampf, he asserted that Jesus' attitude toward Jews was displayed at the end of a whip in the Temple. Hitler concluded that the Jews sealed Jesus' fate on the cross to protect their business interests and he compared Jews of his day with those who arranged Jesus' death.[18]

In his study paper for the Commission, Jules Isaac asserted that "those who had him [Jesus] arrested and sentenced, the chief priests, were representatives of a narrow oligarchic caste, subjugated to Rome and detested by the people...."[19] The Seelisberg drafters elected to avoid placing blame anywhere. In retrospect, this is a serious shortcoming. It is not possible to avoid the question of responsibility for the crucifixion, just as it is irresponsible to tolerate the willful and fatal distortion of history. Ellis Rivkin has written a persuasive volume in which he offers a political, social, and religious challenge to the charges of Deicide leveled against the Jews. Addressing the confluence of events leading to the death of Jesus, Rivkin writes:

> The times were no ordinary times; the tempests, no ordinary tempests; the bedlam, no ordinary bedlam; the derangements, no ordinary derangements. The chaos that gave birth to a charismatic like Jesus was the very chaos that rendered clarity of judgment impossible....Everyone was entangled within a web of circumstance from which there was no way out....The emperor sought to govern an empire; the procurator sought to hold anarchy in check; the high priest sought to hold his office; the members of the high priest's sanhedrin [governing council--Ed.] sought to spare the people the dangerous consequences of a charismatic's innocent visions of the kingdom of God, which they themselves believed was really at hand....

It is in this maelstrom of time, place, and circumstance, in tandem with impulse-ridden, tempest-tossed, and blinded sons of men, that the tragedy of Jesus' crucifixion is to be found. It was not the Jewish people who crucified Jesus, and it was not the Roman people--it was the imperial system, a system which victimized the Jews, victimized the Romans, and victimized the Spirit of God.[20]

Jews were not the enemies of the Jesus nor of the emerging church. To blame all Jews in all eras for the crucifixion and to use the death of Jesus to justify the centuries of inhumanity that culminated in the Shoah is to completely fail to understand the meaning of Jesus' death on a Roman cross. The message of the cross proclaims the end of imposed, officially sanctioned death. For Christians, the crucifixion and resurrection compose an inseparable unit of belief that bears witness to the love of God overcoming corrupt power and defeating death in all its myriad forms. The crucifixion and resurrection are a direct challenge to the systems that perpetuate oppression, anarchy, and faithlessness.

On the basis of distorted historical accounts and a misunderstanding of the meaning of the crucifixion, Christians have fallen into the erroneous belief that Jews and Judaism are, in the words of Seelisberg Point Nine, "reprobate, accursed, reserved for a destiny of suffering." Christians who subscribe to this belief have taken God's place and substituted their own moral and eternal judgment on Jews for God's more compassionate quest to be reunited with the covenant people. In the words of Seelisberg Point Eight, these Christians refer to limited, suspect "scriptural curses" and elect to hear only "the cry of a raging mob, 'His blood be on us and on our children!'" Seelisberg and Ellis Rivkin find agreement in Jesus' response to his fate. After indicting the imperial system of Rome which victimized Jews, Romans, and the Spirit of God, Rivkin concludes:

And Jesus understood. Twisted in agony on the cross-- that symbol of imperial Roman cruelty and ruthless disregard of the human spirit--Jesus lifted his head upward toward God and pleaded, "Father, forgive them; for they know not what they do."[21]

The Ninth Seelisberg Point does not directly address the humiliation and suffering experienced by Jesus during the process of the crucifixion, but does caution that misrepresentation of the Passion can lead to timeless, indiscriminate hatred of Jews. Jules Isaac warned in his study paper that the cruelty was a result of the normative procedures in Roman executions and certain excesses by Roman soldiers. The emphasis on the suffering of Jesus, a central motif in many observances of the Passion, has contributed to the anger many Christians have felt toward Jews. This has been most notable in the Holy Week Programs that terrorized Jews over the cen-

turies. Careless rendering of history and inaccurate ascription of responsibility for the crucifixion resulted in vigilante-like revenge.

Christians who claim that Jesus' humiliation and suffering was without
compare, risk perpetuating through this hyperbole, a contempt for Jews who
had no part in the crucifixion and who would not have participated in it had
they lived in Jerusalem at the time. It is inappropriate and terribly insensitive to compare suffering. The suffering of one person does not negate or
justify the suffering of another person. The only faithful response to
suffering is to oppose and transform it. It is faithless and cynical to exalt
the humiliation and suffering of Jesus to legitimate violence against Jews
and attacks upon Judaism. Christians who do so must stand in the presence
of burning children and say to them that their humiliation and suffering does
not compare to Jesus' suffering on the cross; that their suffering is not real
suffering.

The implications of Seelisberg Points five through nine judge institutional Christianity whenever it uses Jesus to isolate, torture, and kill
Jews. Those Christians who believe that Jews are the enemies of Jesus and
the church for all time, who blame Jews for the crucifixion, who hear the
cry "his blood...." and ignore the prayer "Father, forgive them....," and who
replace God's mercy with their judgment, must stand in the presence of
burning children and say to them, "You deserve this fate because you and
your ancestors crucified Jesus and because you have crucified him anew by
refusing to accept him as your messiah."

IV. The Unfinished Agenda: A View from the Parish

For its time, the Ten Points of Seelisberg were bold and visionary.
Forty-two years later, with the specter of burning children still before us,
their cries still echoing in our ears, Seelisberg commands implications that
should ignite a revolution in theological education, preaching, and teaching,
and in the daily lives of believers. Burning children, tortured mothers, and
gassed fathers should be the source of heretofore unimagined questions about
the nature of God and covenant. They should be the reason behind a transformation of education that begins by examining the moral and humane uses
of knowledge. They should disrupt and challenge not only Judaism, but
values-neutral humanism, and the religion that turned murderously on its own
roots. Gas chambers and crematoria should be relentless witnesses against
unquestioned obedience to authority, uncritical conformity to nationalistic and
triumphalist ideologies, and unconditional loyalty to a state or ruler.

My students at the University of Oregon helped me to understand why
such changes come so slowly and they showed me that there was both a
tremendous will to confront the implications of the Shoah and a profound and
costly transformation awaiting those who examined their lives and futures in
the presence of burning children. The struggle of one student illustrates the

will and the cost, not only for academics, but any who allow their lives to be challenged by the Shoah. She was a pre-med major when she enrolled in my class on the literature of the Shoah. Her view of medical practice was only informed by an idealistic understanding of the Hippocratic Oath. All of the students read a history of the Shoah and a variety of books by survivors. At the end of the course, the students were required to submit a paper in which they addressed the implications of the Shoah relative to their vocational aspirations. She read sections from several volumes on the medical experiments at Auschwitz. Her innocent view of medicine and humanity was overturned by the Nazi medical doctors who conducted the experiments. Having confronted the dark side of her calling, she wrote of the awareness and fragile hope arising from her painful studies:

> As a pre-medical student and scientist, any future avenue I might take will require that I look closely at how I will apply my knowledge. I must be aware and cautious of possible inhumane uses of my knowledge and research. I hope I will be strong enough to use my knowledge for the benefit of the human community.

If my personal experience and that of the majority of my students can be generalized, Christians and their religious institutions that undertake such a confrontation must expect that it will send crushing seismic waves through the structures of their lives and most likely shatter the paradigms with which they have built their values and worldviews. That cost will be seen as a small price to pay for standing in the presence of, truly listening to, and changing because of the experience of victims and survivors. Historically, Christianity has made important advances based on reform movements that sought religious and human freedoms, protection of human life and dignity, and civic responsibility. Once past the initial wrenching and pain, I expect that a genuine encounter with the Shoah would give Christianity a just and humane footing from which to enter the next century and the courage and strength to join with post-Shoah Judaism to confront the powerful forces of death at work in history.

A. The Difference the Shoah Makes: Obedience

What shall be different because we begin our theology and live our faith in the presence or burning children? One antecedent contributing to the role of Christianity in the Shoah was the misplaced loyalty of many leading theologians, clergy, and laity. Instead of a complete commitment to Jesus and his compassionate and humane teachings, the loyalty of these Christians was to a religiosity that almost uniformly submitted to the emerging political order, to nationalism, and to the Volk. A Christian is called to follow Jesus exclusively and seek to know and hold fast to Jesus' teachings and the commandments [the Decalogue and Jesus' commandment to "love the Lord your God....and your neighbor as yourself"]. This loyalty is the essential security for believers who live in periods of great insecurity, turmoil, and evil. When one is faced by malevolent authorities, this loyalty is the liberating source of critical thinking and constructive suspicion [as contrasted to cynicism which robs people of power and causes them to disengage from difficult situations in which there are great social pressures to conform, competing interpretations, and ambiguous outcomes]. This loyalty will lead Christians to resist actively those laws--both civil and church laws--strategies, programs, and officials that foster mistrust and division, that contribute to injustice and oppression, leading ultimately to the destruction of human life. In order to measure the effects of Christian loyalties, one need only contrast the misplaced loyalty, the failure of critical thought and constructive suspicion, and the fatal equivocations of theologians like Paul Althaus and Ernst Biberstein with the unambiguous commitment and courage of theologians like Dietrich Bonhoeffer and clergy like Martin Niemoeller [and those whose lives are memorialized by Gollwitzer].

B. A Problem of Loyalty

A concomitant to misplaced loyalty was obedience to ill-willed authorities. When their religious commitment was diluted and their spiritual and ethical grounding was eclipsed, many Christians found themselves bereft of the resources with which to question or resist the directives and policies of the Nazis. Challenged by the murderous acquiescence of Nazi soldiers to their leaders, Stanley Milgram reached a chilling conclusion in his study on obedience to authority:

> ....ordinary people, simply doing their jobs, and without any particular hostility on their part, can become agents of a terrible destructive process. Moreover, even when the destructive effects of their work become patently clear, and they are asked to carry out actions incompatible with fundamental standards of morality, relatively few people have the resources needed to resist authority.[22]

Institutional Christianity did not help its adherents understand that loyalty to Jesus and obedience to the Biblical mandate to sanctify and preserve life have irreversible significance. A tragic lesson of the Shoah was the widespread failure of the seminaries and churches to ready the preponderance of the faithful to recognize and resist the evils of the National Socialist movement. Worse than that, it failed baptized believers who experienced no incongruity between their faith and the acts of burning children, shooting women in mass grave, and gassing whole families. A politically astute remnant of Christians whose commitment led them to resist National Socialism did not establish their own laws, but rather followed a greater mandate, God's law of grace and love. These Christians knew that for their obedience to God, they must be prepared to spend years in prison, as Niemoeller and others did, or even to die, as Bonhoeffer and others did.

Nazi era rescuers, like the Christians who resisted the political rise of National Socialism, stand in stark contrast to those who were silent, complicit, or active participants in the Shoah. The rescuers had minimal ambiguity about their allegiance to Jesus and his teachings, no uncertainty about the Biblical origins of their resistance, no naivete about the possible consequences of their actions, and no confusion about their responsibility for others. Milgram concluded from his study on obedience to authority that: The disappearance of a sense of responsibility is the most far-reaching consequence of submission to authority.'[23] Those who could not resist ill-willed authority, passed responsibility to the representative of authority, saying, in effect, "I only did what I was told to do," or "I was only following orders." They were also unable to assume responsibility for the fate of their victims because their loyalty had shifted its locus from a Biblically-based ethical and humanitarian commitment to concern for satisfying fully the demands of the authority figure.

By contrast, Nazi era rescuers operated in a universe of Christian and humanitarian obligation that was without boundaries or limitations.   The most moving example of this was a Polish woman who with her family hid thirteen Jewish refugees on their farm. A neighbor betrayed them for a reward. Warned that the Nazis and militia were enroute, they were able to send the Jews into the forest. When the soldiers could find no hidden Jews, they shot the woman's husband and eldest son as a warning to those who might consider giving aid or comfort to Jews. The next morning, before she had buried her loved ones, this woman had a new group of refugees hiding on the farm. By the end of the war she had saved forty-two more Jews. The course of the war turned against Germany and in the retreat soldiers were separated from their units. Many of the stragglers were killed by partisans or civilians. This woman hid several young German soldiers, and, in order to protect them, sent them on their way wearing the clothing of her murdered husband and son. She explained that the foot soldiers were innocent of the killings at her home or of Jews and that they should not suffer because of their leaders. Her behavior gives profound new meaning to Jesus' admonition "to love your enemies."

It must be noted that rescuers did not subscribe to a sentimental standardless altruism. After the war, rescuers actively sought justice for the victims of Nazi crimes against humanity. Herman Graebe's testimony, read before the Nuremberg Tribunal, set the tone for the trials and he spent the years until his death in 1986 pursuing War Criminals who evaded justice and challenging historical revisionists who denied the reality of the Shoah.

C. Christians With and Without the Church Support

It is interesting to note that nearly half of the Nazi-era rescuers in my sample described themselves as post-institutional Christians. They emphasized that they considered themselves to be "good Christians" who read the Bible and were spiritual and prayerful, but could not bring themselves to attend church or did so only faintheartedly and occasionally because, during the war years, they did not receive the support or encouragement of the church. Two examples will illustrate their concerns. A Polish woman who lost her life saving Jewish children did not return to the church after her priest refused to provide her with baptismal certificates for the children. A devout German rescuer disdained the Lutheran tradition after his pastor refused his request for help in hiding Jews. A number of rescuers indicated that they did not turn to the churches for help because, one rescuer put it, "I did not even think of the church as a place to look for support of my efforts." The implication of this finding is that many of the most faithful, moral, and compassionate people are driven out of the very institution that should sustain their values and work! What is to become of the individual churches that discourage altruists, but not the indifferent and not the killers?

A significant counterpoint to those who became post-institutional Christians are those who found strength and support within their parishes. A Dutch woman who saved some forty Jews is an example of the many. I spent several days interviewing her at Yad Vashem. During the second day of interviews she began looking at her watch. Several times I inquired about her fatigue or other commitments she might have. Finally, this eighty year old woman said, "I have truly enjoyed my time here, the reun-ions with those I love, but I am anxious to return home. You see, I am the coordinator of refugee settlements for my church and tomorrow we are welcoming two families who have lived on the South China Sea for months. I think I need to be there even though I am scheduled to remain here for another week." With strong loyalty to Jesus, clear values, an active religious life, and the ongoing support of her church, this woman, like so many others, continued to be a caring and helpful person.

The Nazi-era rescuers revive a healing view of humanity, they lift up the cause of kindness and human dignity, and they redeem our weakened hope for the future. Those who study the Shoah and live in the nuclear age must understand what enabled the rescuers to act as they did and realize that their actions did not come about ex nihilo, but rather were learned, grounded, rehearsed, and affirmed in ways that ensured their continued refining and practice. Our schools, colleges, universities, seminaries, churches, and synagogues cannot give less than that to their peoples. It is imperative that these primary institutions of society understand the work of the rescuers as an antidote to the tremendous death instinct at work in our times.

D. The End is the Beginning

I am compelled to end where I began, asserting that the location from which Christian theology and ministry must start and conduct their work is in the presence or burning children. If this is not the beginning point, I fear

that theology and ministry will fail to prepare believers to resist the com-
partmentalization of labor, knowledge, and society which encourages reliance on external authority; the debilitating threats of thermonuclear war; the
ravages of Apartheid; the new breeds of totalitarianism; the resurgence of
racism, nationalism, and religious triumphalism; and the attraction of a self-
interested indifference to the momentous problems and opportunities leading
the world into the new century. If theology and ministry begin with the
Shoah, the new paradigm which is birthed will restore hope and vision,
loyalty and obedience.   Then Christians will be better able to confront
powers and principalities with constructive suspicion; to respond to the cries
for help from torture cells around the globe and to the supplications of
refugees from Central Ameri-ca, Southeast Asia, and the Eastern Bloc; and
to resist those forces which deprive people of dignity, freedom, and life.

E. What the Shoah Reveals

The presence of burning children was a unique revelation to Christianity. It revealed that much of the Christian understanding of God was
embarrassingly meager, untested in the face of murderous suffering, and
often sublimely individualistic and self-serving. It revealed that before,
during, and after the Shoah, much of what was heard from pulpits was "civil
religion" which lacked relevance and the prophetic passion for justice and
dignity. Civil religion neither challenged the political will of those in power
nor commanded a humane response to the atrocities. Accompanying this
revelation that religion and government had crafted a separate peace which
virtually eliminated the ability of the church to have an influential or moder-
ating voice in politics and government.   The Protestant origins of this
unofficial concordat can be traced to 1525 when Martin Luther sided with the
landlords and governors in the Swabian Peasant Revolt. Luther wrote and
circulated a polemic entitled, "Against the Robbing and Murdering Hordes of
Peasants," in which he attacked the peasants for abandoning their loyalty to
their rulers under the banner of Jesus. In 1933, Luther's treatise was placed
in certain jail cells occupied by Germans who questioned or opposed the
policies of the Reich. The message to dissenters was clear: loyalty to the
state was paramount. It is little wonder that Christian leaders did not
actively disassociate themselves from dependence on the state and state
privileges.

The Shoah revealed the prevalence of the "cheap grace" Dietrich Bonhoeffer warned of in 1937 when he wrote:

> Cheap grace is the deadly enemy of our church....The
> sacraments, the forgiveness of sin, and the consolation of religion
> are thrown away at cut prices.   Grace is represented as the
> Church's inexhaustible treasury, from which she showers bless-
> ings with generous hands, without asking questions or fixing
> limits. Grace without price; grace without cost![24]

He went on to describe the opposite, "costly grace:"

> Such grace is costly because it calls us to follow, and it is grace because it calls us to follow Jesus Christ. It is costly because it costs a life, and it is grace because it gives man the only true life. It is costly because it condemns sin, and grace because it justifies the sinner.[25]

Evangelical theologian Helmut Thielicke wrote a critique of post-war church services, that was certainly accurate for the war years as well, "Despite the times, from many pulpits we heard only very conventional, pallid sermons which did not reach men's hearts and left them cold. We seemed to be denied a prophetic awakening."[26]

Not everything that the Shoah revealed was negative. In revealed that in the absence of a powerful prophetic voice there was, once again, a remnant who refused to abdicate their faith and their humanity. In the histories of Judaism and Christianity, very often it is the faithful remnant that perseveres and saves the hour, redeems the community, restores hope, and lights a way into the future. Post-Shoah Christianity can begin its rebuilding on the foundation of the loyalty, freedom, spiritual values, egalitarian worldview, compassion, and courage of Christian dissenters, victims and martyrs, rescuers, and drafters of such declarations as Barmen and Seelisberg.

F. Final Thoughts

Two concluding observations seem necessary as I review what I have written. First, I have assumed throughout that the Shoah is a uniquely Jewish experience in history and that is implications and lessons are universal. Politicians, peace activists, environmentalists, revisionists, and others have co-opted the name associated with Hitler's genocide, "the Holocaust," without sensitivity to the offense and pain this corruption of language causes. To speak of the "Holocaust" in relationship to anything other than the Jewish experience under National Socialism is a clear indication that the one so employing the term has not stood in the presence of burning children. The term "the Holocaust" does not belong to the world, but if there is to be a future free of such suffering, its implications and lessons must belong to the world.

Finally, Helmut Thielicke observed that in post-war Germany, "Instead of preaching of repentance and salvation, we had the proclamation of a collective guilt and a hysteria of self-accusation which was in need of psychological understanding rather than having any theological justification, and this led to a hardening of men's hearts."[27] While I do not agree that collective guilt and the hysteria of self-accusation have no theological justification or lesson, I am painfully aware of the way in which people's hearts can be hardened when they read about the Shoah ["read about" as contrasted to "learning from" its victims and survivors]. This chapter contains what may appear to some to be harsh conclusions bluntly stated. It is not my intention, estimable reader, to create a defensive barrier to the very reformation I seek, nor to be discordant or judgmental. I long for a greater reformation of Christianity than has occurred since 8 May 1945. It is my great love for Christianity and the church and my restrained hope for the future, not only of the church, but also the human family, that moves me to impatience and candor. It is also the case that for twenty years I have not found an acceptable or polite way to say what I feel must be said in the presence of burning children.

I recently came upon the poetry of Wendell Berry. There is one particular poem that has become my prayer as I continue to probe the Shoah. I wish I had had it earlier and share for those contemplating beginning or who are mid-course in the reformation.

> ....These times we know much evil, little good
> To steady us in faith
> And comfort when our losses press
> Hard on us, and we choose,
> In panic or despair or both,
> To keep what we will lose.
> For we are fallen like the trees, our peace
> Broken, and so we must
> Love where we cannot trust,
> Trust where we cannot know,
> And must await the wayward-coming grace
> That joins living and dead,
> Taking us where we would not go--
> Into the boundless dark.
> When what was made has been unmade
> The Maker comes to His work.[28]

In re-examining the theological implications of the Shoah for Christian faith, Thomas Idinopulos raises two questions of radically different perspective and proceeds to further clarify them in his essay: [1] What if Christ's atoning death did not defeat sin, but, rather, led to more crucifixions, more sin, as evidenced by the playing out of history itself? Does not its very power, therefore, lay in its defeat rather than in its victory, and, thus, continues to serve as a warning to and for all humanity? And [2] What is the proper interrelationship between literature and history, art and the Shoah? Can those who write and create this "literature of atrocity" truly illumine, and thereby improve, the human condition, and avoid repetition--the very goal of sanctified Christian and Christ-like [and Jewish] existence?

HOW THE SHOAH AFFECTS CHRISTIAN BELIEF

Thomas A. Idinopulos

I. Introduction: Christian Antisemitism and Anti-Judaism

If there is one thing we learn from history, it is that the forces which shape human destiny are slow in building; that when they finally burst forth with all their capacity for making and unmaking the life of humanity, one is saddened to realize how little they were understood, how poorly perceived in their beginnings. Antisemitism is one such force. The oppression of the Jewish people in the past 2,000 years is connected to the disdain for Jews that one finds in the catechism, preaching and teaching of Christian churches from earliest times. If a history of Christian theological anti-Judaism did not exactly "cause" modern racial antisemitism, unquestionably it helped to prepare the way.

It has been the habit of Christian theologians in recent years, especially since the Shoah, to treat antisemitism less as a matter for which Christians as Christians ought to regard themselves as guilty, much more as an expression of racial idolaters posing as Christians. However, the record of Christian thought makes unmistakable the hostility to the Jew in the canonical Gospels, in the sermons of such church fathers as John Chrysostom, Saint Jerome, and Augustine of Hippo, in the edicts of Christian emperors and the policies of influential popes and bishops, in the later writings of Martin Luther, in the ambivalent postures of theologians as recent as Karl Adam and Karl Barth. What one learns from this record is that subtle, powerful, essentially murderous inner-connections exist between Christian self-witness and political oppression of Jews. As Jules Isaac [the French Jewish historian who pioneered in research demonstrating the connection between Christianity and antisemitism] put it, "without centuries of Christian catechism, propaganda, vituperation, the Hitlerian teachings, propaganda and vituperation would not have been possible."

It is important to keep two things in mind when we address the Shoah. The first is conveyed by the striking assertion of Elie Wiesel, "....the Holocaust teaches nothing." I interpret Wiesel to mean that after we have patiently read through the history books and considered the explanations, we must not be surprised if we are brought back in disbelief to where we began, with an awful sense of the dark, impenetrable mystery of the event. For when the killers were average, law-abiding citizens who carried out their deeds impersonally, with little or no hatred for their victims, when the crime proved so massive that the names of the victims were erased by the abstractness of the number 6,000,000, when one cannot consult the grisly details of the crime without experiencing a revulsion mixed with rage, fright and shame--when one is thus confronted by the truth of the Shoah, one cannot help but realize that there are but two impenetrable mysteries for human contemplation: the depth of evil and the will of God.

The second thing to keep in mind in turning to the Shoah is the matter of respect, what I should like to call--existential respect. There are pure and impure ways to read about the Shoah. We must resist the temptation to rend our study of the Shoah a convenient and unceasing vehicle of blame and praise. For it is quite simply true that no amount of moral judgment on the part of the living can in any way rouse the dead or return a shred of the humanity ripped from them. It seems to me that moral perception of the past proves sound only when it is tied to the present; in other words, what the living should learn from the dead is something of truth worth living for. This is what I mean by existential respect. The dead retain their secrets. A suffering so great leaves little to understand, nothing to be redeemed. It is we the living who write the books, the words are ours, and we shape them in the hope that the past, with all its tragic mystery, can illumine the experiences of our lives here and now.

The great truth we have to learn from the Shoah is how to keep the human spirit alive; it is also the central truth to the matter of education in America. The evil of the Shoah was not a dark, Satanic evil of the medieval imagination; it was a modern evil, technological and antiseptic, "a vast crater of emptiness opened up by a betrayal of spirit." The alternative to spirit is chaos. Chaos prevails when human beings conform to their own techniques and inventions, turning themselves into objects, divesting themselves of individual self-identity. Here the spirit of humanity withers and dies, the spirit which ennobles intelligence with sensitivity and often inspires a human being to act courageously. When chaos replaces spirit, intelligence is put to insensitive uses, moral restraint crumbles, institutional safeguards of life and liberty are abolished, creating a situation which makes anything and everything possible, including wholesale death.

II. Studying the Problem

There are two major areas of scholarly inquiry which seek to establish the relationship between the history of Christianity on the one hand, and the developments of anti-Judaism and antisemitism on the other, a relationship which culminates in the twentieth century destruction of European Jews under Hitler. There are many scholars who have concentrated their attention on the role of Christian institutions, among them James Parkes, Alice and Roy Eckardt, Franklin Littell, and Guenter Lewy. A second line of inquiry, focusing more specifically on Christian scriptures and doctrines, was pioneered by the French historian, Jules Isaac, and developed more recently by John Oesterreicher, Alan Davies, Gregory Baum, Edward Flannery, Fred Bratton, and Rosemary Radford Reuther. The unifying aim of all this research is to document, clarify, and explain the extent of Christian guilt vis-a-vis Judaism and the Jewish people. I should like to make it clear that my paper is not intended to be a contribution to this research. It has a different aim: the Shoah in its specifically theological implications for Christian faith. I will not take up here the historical question of Christian ideas and actions in their connection to crimes against Jews; the focus of my attention is the constructive, theological question of the Shoah as it affects or should affect Christian belief.

If one examines the works of the most influential Christian theologians who wrote before, during, and after the Second World War, one will find references to the Shoah, but no extended discussion of the matter, nothing that takes the form of an essay. Karl Barth, Rudolf Bultmann, Emil Brunner, Paul Tillich, Karl Rahner, Teilhard de Chardin, Reinhold Niebuhr: none of them felt compelled by the events of the Nazi tyranny to re-examine the fundamental principles of their theologies. In the generation that followed these giants, some American religious thinkers startled the public in the 1960's by announcing the death of God. Here one would have expected that the connection would have been made with the Shoah. But the opposite happened. The "death-of-God" was interpreted by Thomas Altizer, William Hamilton, Harvey Cox, and Paul van Buren, not as a symbol of historical disaster, but as an injunction for Christians to break their ties with tired, discredited institutions and doctrines, and confidently to create new history as free, secular, mature men [and women] of the modern world. Not unexpectedly, it took a Jew, Richard Rubenstein, to remind his Christian colleagues [It always seems to take a Jew!] that the "death-of-God" means, what in essence Nietzsche said it meant, the breakdown of human culture witnessed in the catastrophes of history.

It does not surprise me that it took a Jew to make the connection between the death of God and the Shoah, thence to remind Christians that the death of God should be an occasion not for joy but for lamentation. I am afraid that the Shoah strikes Christian theologians as it strikes all other Christians, as a particularly Jewish subject, not just in the obvious sense that overwhelming numbers of Jews were involved in the event, but in the deeper sense which should trouble everyone, that whatever questions are raised by the Shoah, whatever institutions, values, beliefs are to be re-examined in the aftermath--these are matters about which properly Jews alone should concern themselves. There is in this, of course, the ordinary, inescapable element of human indifference; we really do not weep over the suffering death that touches not us but others. But I also recognize in the indifference the profound difficulty, perhaps impossibility, for Christian theology to risk confrontation with the worst disaster of Jewish history, indeed, to risk confrontation with great disasters afflicting many human communities throughout history. I will attempt to account for this.

III. Suffering and Indifference

Saint Paul, in his letter to the Romans, writes that "God....shows his love for us in that while we yet sinners Christ died for us." And he concludes, "Since, therefore, we are not justified by his blood, much more should we be saved by him from the wrath of God." [Romans 5:8-9, Revised Standard Version] It is uncertain if Paul was the first Christian to proclaim the conquest of sin in and through Jesus Christ, but he was unquestionably the most influential for all subsequent Christian thinking, starting with the Gospels, whose Passion narratives are constructed on Paul's view of the Cross's victory over sin and death. However, "realistically" the Christian recognizes the facts of human sinning since the death and resurrection of Christ, he seeks to bring his moral assessment of history into harmony with the Cross's victory and its message of accomplished redemption. This holds true even of the most liberally-oriented American Protestant thinkers. One distinguished American thinker who struggled to reconcile his own keen sense of the brutality of human history with the message of accomplished redemption drew an analogy from Second World War history. He argued that Christ's defeat of sin was like the Russians' defeat of the Germans at Stalingrad: there would be more fighting, but the decisive battle had been won, the tide of the history turned.[1] Would that it were true! It would be good to believe that history were like a great war where Christ could win the decisive battle. But if history shows anything, it shows that Christ did not win but rather lost the decisive battle, not once, but over and over again.

It is reasonable to ask, "What would remain distinctive of Christian belief if somehow incontestable proof were provided in history that Christ's cross did not defeat sin, but rather led to more crosses, more sin?" From a Jewish point of view, this is precisely what happened in Jewish-Christian relations. Nevertheless, one must acknowledge that Christian redemption is a matter of faith which, as a religious faith, strengthens, not weakens, in adversity. The Christian is bidden to draw closer to Christ precisely in response to the worsening corruption of the world. One recalls that the Rabbis, upon the destruction of the Second Temple, urged Jews to grow stronger, not weaker, in faith, for God himself had brought about this disaster as punishment for sin. Thus for the Christian, no less than for the Jew, the central truths of faith are revealed by God himself; they are a priori truths, established independently of history, faithfully adhered to in spite of history. I will not presume to speak of Judaism, but in the case of Christianity, this "a priorism" of faith leads to a homogenization of sin, a certain flattening out of human guilt.

The Christian doctrine of redemption makes it clear that Christ died for all human beings, whatever their sins, however great or small. No distinctions are made or should be made in human culpability, in the magnitude of guilt. The medieval symbol of purgatory was an insightful, if vengeful, acknowledgement of the differences in wickedness. But Martin Luther and the Reformers, led by Paul's words, "All have sinned and fallen short of the Law," did away with these differences. The liberalization and secularization of modern Western culture completed the process begun in the sixteenth century, by not only doing away with the differences between sin, but by doing away with sin itself.

In this homogenization of sin, in my judgment, stemming as it does from the gospel of the victorious cross, that often leads Christian theologians to utter the words Auschwitz and Hiroshima in one breath. I believe there is an authentic way to associate the two events, to compare the way in which each is an expression of the modern tendency to commit what Camus called "administrative murder," wherein human beings are regarded as objects to be cleanly and neatly disposed of by way of "a few freight trains, a few engineers, a few chemists." [Andre Schwarz-Bart] But there is also an unauthentic linking of Auschwitz and Hiroshima, to suggest that one crime is no worse than the other. When this assumption is made consciously or unconsciously, the Christian is "off the hook." If he is persuaded to believe that Auschwitz is no worse than Hiroshima, then he can treat the destruction of six million Jews and one million Gypsies as another instance of universal evil: which really means that he does not have to treat it in its particularity, to look at it right there where all the terror, all the truth lies.

IV. Jacques Maritain

Jacques Maritain, the French Roman Catholic philosopher, might well be regarded as an exception to the prevailing pattern of Christian indifference vis-a-vis the Shoah. Shortly before the Second World War, in 1938, he authored an essay detailing the rise of antisemitic actions from one European country to another; it is a remarkable statement, containing a presentiment of the extermination of Europe's Jews. Discussing the savagery loosed on German Jewry by the Nazis in reprisal for the assassination of one of their diplomats by a Jew, Maritain concludes with this observation:

> ....when we learned these things, we thought that truly armed men can do precisely what they will with unarmed men, we thought that we must thank the National Socialists for not having decreed that all Jews today--and tomorrow, all Christians who prefer to obey God rather than men--be simply reduced to ashes by the most scientific means; for in the world today who can stop them.[2]

The full truth of the expressed "reduced to ashes by scientific means" unfolded like a shroud in the next seven years, a truth not wasted on Maritain. If the facts of the Shoah did little to shake his belief in the victorious cross, they did seem to expose him to ambiguities about the relationship between suffering and salvation. In order to appreciate the change, one must note Maritain's attitude toward Judaism before the war, comparing it with what he later said.

In an essay of 1937, "The Mystery of Israel," Maritain refers to "the basic weakness of the mystical communion of Israel," which is "its failure to understand the cross, its refusal of the cross." He also speaks of the passion or historical suffering of the Jewish people:

> It is the passion of a scapegoat, enmeshed in the earthy destiny of the world and in ways of the world mixed with sin, a scapegoat against which the impure sufferings of the world strike back, when the world seeks vengeance for the misfortunes of its history upon what activates that history. Israel thus suffers the repercussion of the activation it produces, or which the world feels it is destined to produce....[3]

When one looks beneath the involution of the writing, one recognizes that the author repeats the argument of the ancient church fathers: The Jewish people, in rejecting Christ, antagonizes the Christian world, thereby bringing down on itself calamity and woe. The clear implication is that if the Jewish people accepts the message of the victorious cross, if Israel ceases to be Israel, antisemitism will stop, Jewish suffering will cease.

It is impossible to know if the events of the Second World War and the Shoah made Maritain recognize that Christian triumphalism is a greater case of antisemitism than Jewish rejection of Christ. What is clear is that, after the war, Maritain seems somehow more realistic in his attitude toward suffering, particularly Jewish suffering. There is the first hint that some suffering is unexplainable, useless, serving no higher, no greater purpose. In an essay of 1946, which takes its title from Jesus' eighth beatitude, "Blessed are they that suffer persecution for justice's sake: for theirs is the kingdom of heaven," Maritain speaks of the classical Christian equation between suffering and salvation. Those who choose to suffer in imitation of Christ's cross, share his victory, inheriting the kingdom of heaven. But what of those who do not so choose: Indeed, what of those who were never permitted a choice? After reciting instances of Nazi atrocities, including references to the destruction of the Jews, Maritain asks:

> Where lay the consolation of these persecuted innocents? And how many others died completely forsaken. They did not give their lives; their lives were taken from them, and under the shadow of horror. They suffered without having wanted to suffer. They did not know why they died. Those who know why they die are greatly priviledged.[4]

What is significant about this statement is its spirit: it represents that rare instance in which a Christian thinker felt compelled to search within his own theological system for a specific answer to the specific question raised by the knowledge of manifestly useless suffering. What is re-markable is not the answer given, but the honest facing of the question.

Reflecting on the meaningless suffering of innocent people, Maritain speaks differently of the relationship between Jews and Christians. Now they constitute a kind of fellowship of suffering. "Like strange companions," he writes, they "have together journeyed along the road to Calvary." He continues, "The great mysterious fact is that the sufferings of Israel have more and more distinctly taken the shape of the cross." Here the point is no longer Jewish suffering caused by the rejection of Christ; there is a new emphasis on the Jew's sharing of Christ's cross as the result of this innocent, unjustified suffering. Perhaps it is only that--a change of emphasis, not an essentially altering of the mind. One cannot be sure.

Maritain concludes his essay by suggesting that those who suffer and die without consolation are one with Christ precisely at the point of Christ's own dereliction, his own despairing agony on the cross. He goes on to argue that if they are one with Christ in dereliction, they are one with him in the grace that rises victorious from the cross. And he concludes with these words, "It's in the invisible world, beyond everything earthly, that the kingdom of God is given to these persecuted ones, and that every-thing becomes theirs." It is just where Maritain addresses himself to the question of useless suffering that I see the implications of Elie Wiesel's works for Christian theology: pointing to dereliction, not to victory, as the authentic, universal, and perennial meaning of Christ's cross.

V. Elie Wiesel

The writings of Elie Wiesel have great implication for Christian faith, but not because one can find in them answers to theological questions. What one finds is a deepening of the question. But is this not the power and genius of the artist--to deepen the question?

When one seeks to understand the role of the Shoah in Wiesel's early works, one must constantly bear in mind that the Shoah never appears as an event simply as such, but rather is transmuted by the imagination into a sensibility through which the author speaks. Thomas Lask, the New York Times literary critic, put his finger on this when he says, "There is surprisingly little physical horror in [Wiesel's] books. It is the mind that is outraged, the spirit that is degraded. When an emaciated father gives his bowl of soup to his starving son, when a naked mother covers her child's body with her own against the expected spray of bullets, pain and death pale before the suffering and humiliation in these events."[5]

Through the exercise of imaginative writing, Wiesel transmutes the historical and physical events of the Shoah into a moral and spiritual event. The finest example of this is one of the first in Wiesel's books, the description of the burning children in Night. In the way he builds his recollection of the event on the refrain "Never shall I forget....," feeling is intensified, physical horror is transmuted by a moral and spiritual perception. His words take the form of both a curse and a prayer, a form shaping the style of his later writing. Wiesel understands that the ultimate crime of the Shoah was the crime against the spirit. "Guilt was not invented at Auschwitz," he writes, "it was disfigured there." In Wiesel's own effort to restore a sense of guilt about this event, he gives a clue to the relation between literature and history, art and the Shoah. Art restores us to the realm of the particular and human, what is in essence an inhuman or "abstract" event. Let me clarify this.

Anyone who wishes to write clearly, perceptively and persuasively on the stories whose theme is the Nazi destruction of European Jewry should begin with one honest, if painful, admission. We human beings are drawn to stories of concentration camp events out of the same mixture of fascination and repulsion which we experience in reading of the torment and anguish of other human beings, whoever they are, whatever the circumstances of their misfortunes. No one should deny these feelings in himself. In facing the pain, suffering and death of others, we face ourselves. Dostoevsky, who was as good a psychologist as he was a story-teller, understood these feelings. He once accused his fellow Russian writer Turgenev of cowardice for refusing to witness a public execution of a murderer. In his biography of Dostoevsky, David Magarshak writes that Dostoevsky

> would have watched, open-eyed and pale-face, the chopping off of a criminal's head as he did the tearing off of heads of sparrows as a boy--so as to experience [as he put it] 'during the very process of torture a sort of inexplicable pit and the consciousness of one's inhumanity,' the sort of 'cruel sensuality' to which as he declared....'almost everyone on earth' was prone and which was 'the only source of almost all the sins of mankind.'[6]

"Inexplicable pity....the consciousness of one's own inhumanity:" these perceptions directed Dostoevsky's portrayal of the tortuous lives of crime, guilt and suffering led by his most famous characters. In my judgment, it is the same combination of inexplicable pity before abject suffering and a sense of one's own inhuman capacity for cruelty that influences the artistic imagination of Elie Wiesel.

VI. Shoah Literature as Art

One should not underestimate the difficulty in achieving critical appreciation of Shoah literature. When the traditional conventions or forms of literature are applied to events of great historical catastrophe, there is the tendency for morality to overwhelm art, or worse, for art to be judged by morality. With respect to the Shoah, one can rightly ask if art can illumine pain, suffering and death of this magnitude? Should art even dare to portray such misery? This is not an easy question to answer. It is the question in back of Theodor Adorno's famous dictum "to write poetry after Auschwitz is barbaric" [a dictum, incidentally, which Adorno himself as a writer did not follow]. Should one not feel ashamed to seize the suffering of so many, to transform it through the artistic imagination into creation of beauty and pleasure? Adorno writes that "the so-called artistic representations of naked bodily pain, of victim felled by rifle butts, contains, however remote, the potentiality of wringing pleasure from it."[7] This might indeed be so, unless that in tearing the veil from the unspeakable, art, as perhaps nothing else, makes us sense that of which Dostoevksy spoke--"inexplicable pity....-the consciousness of our own inhumanity." If there is a truth to art, as I believe there is, then it consists of the way in which art's distinct forms can be wielded to reveal what is hidden, to illumine our experience to make us see what we cannot otherwise see or are afraid to see, to touch us at the points at which we share a common life, a common humanity. There are, after all, major differences in technique and vision between, on the one hand, the depiction of "cruel sensuality" which exposes us accurately to ourselves, and, on he other, the depiction of "cruel sensuality" which whets our appetite for more cruelty, teaching us nothing; it is the difference between the spiritual and the salacious, the difference between art and pornography.

George Steiner, the American literary critic who is in part influenced by Adorno, asks whether language itself breaks down when employed to depict events of such enormity, of such appalling ugliness. "The world of Auschwitz," he writes, "lies outside speech as it lies outside reason."[8] There is considerable truth in this statement. Those who have had the patience to study the matter recognize that the destruction of six million human beings, methodically, without passion, was not an act of blood lust or vengefulness, or even of simple hatred. Lacking these elements, it is virtually impossible to discover a motive for such murder, and without motive, there is little basis for rational comprehension. But the facts are there and what one learns from them leaves him speechless. It is precisely to these facts that Steiner contends that silence not language is the only legitimate response to the Shoah.

But any careful examination of the best of Shoah literature suggests that Steiner's maxim, "Auschwitz lies outside speech as it lies outside reason," has not been wasted. For artists like Wiesel in Night, and Andre Schwarz-Bart in The Last of the Just, do not so much portray the Shoah itself, as an objective historical event; they seek rather to convey the personal experiences of individual human beings, caught up in fantastic events beyond their control, beyond even their comprehension, and most especially to record their own deepest feelings about these events. There is an inescapable biographical aspect to Shoah literature. An effect is made to depict the Shoah from the side of the victim, more precisely, from the side of the survivor. Little attention is paid to the assassins, to their motives, or the politics behind them. Moreover, in the delicacy with which they treat their subject, in the effort at intimate detail, at restrained narrative, in the absence of melodrama, in the consistent refusal to introduce judgment, whether in praise or condemnation, in the effort to describe actions accurately, in the wish above all to search for moral and spiritual depths amidst vast emptiness--in all this I sense in Wiesel [and also in Schwarz-Bart] precisely that quality of silence which Steiner says is the only respectful response to the Shoah. The writings of these two authors do not really conform to the "literature of atrocity"--a category introduced by critic Lawrence Langer.

Let me return for a moment to Steiner's statement that "the world of Auschwitz lies outside speech as it lies outside reason." He concludes with this thought: "To speak of the unspeakable is to risk the survivance of language as creator and bearer of humane, rational truth. Words that are saturated with lies or atrocity do not easily resume life." In Stein-er's judgment, Auschwitz is an event which brings to an abrupt halt the movement of the creative spirit that has shaped Western civilization. Until the Shoah, writers were able to discern in suffering something of significance, some-thing they could mold in relation to the dreams and illusions and tragedies of human life. But after the Shoah, one is confronted by a suffering so abys-mal, that nothing, literally nothing can come from it, nothing that is instruc-tive and creative, nothing redemptive and healing. The manufacturer of death produces only statistics and you cannot make poetry of statistics. Eric Kahler understands this when he writes that "The most frightening aspect of our present world is not the horrors in themselves, the atrocities, the technological exterminations, but the one fact at the very root of it all: the fading away of any human criterion...."[9] And, of course, if the human criterion fades, so does the artistic imagination. In this respect, I fully share the view of Adorno and Steiner that one must create artistic beauty out of the Shoah, not because the Shoah was evil, but because it was abstractly evil, so inhumanly evil. In this same vein, Wiesel says, that the Shoah teaches nothing. This is a significant statement. For I view the major achievement of his early works, the creation of a style in which what is by nature mute is given a kind of voice--not its own voice, but a kind of voice. As Wiesel said of his own writing, he writes not with words, but against words.

The literature that has arisen from the ashes of the Shoah has as its unifying purpose the translation of the abstract into the particular. It takes the number six million and divides it into the story of the living, suffering and dying of individual souls. It seeks to discern within abject despair an ultimate significance which can revive the spirit, so that a human being can face the truth and not turn away from it in disgust. The best of this litera-ture avoids judgment, whether by praise or condemnation. Like much other literature, it salvages something of worth from the wreckage of human history. As art, it does not aim to propagate the truth. The aim of art, Joseph Conrad once said, is to speak "to our capacity for delight and wonder, to the sense of mystery surrounding our lives; to our sense of pity and beauty and pain." And this the literature of the Shoah does. Investing with significant form the raw materials of human experience, it gives us on the outside a relation to what is deeply hidden and mysterious. By steady reflection not so much on the truth as on the shape and feel of the truth, this art succeeds in discerning a profound human tragedy within the crushing mediocrity of the evil it depicts.

If, as most agree, the Shoah cannot be wholly or easily or ever understood, I do not believe that art provides some sort of special understandings where other efforts fail. But then it is not the purpose of art, as such to understand. The significant form--that is, the meaning--which art bestows on the raw materials of experience is compounded of imagination, intelligence, feeling and sheer craftspersonship. This does not mean that art makes us understand what may not be understandable. Nevertheless, what is not understood is shaped by human hands and minds; impenetrable evil is penetrated with meaning. And we who attend to what Wiesel has artistically accomplished, are by virtue of our own imagination, feeling, intelligence and appreciation of craft, put into intimate relationship, as he has been, to what we do not understand. Thus, the mystery of the Shoah is not dissolved; it is deepened, made to be part of our lives.

VII. Wiesel and Christianity

The one scene in Wiesel's works to have the greatest implication for Christian faith is the hanging of the three Jewish saboteurs in Night. Here Wiesel, precisely as an artist, deepens immeasurably the theological question--"Did Jesus succeed in saving the world by the shedding of his blood?"

> The SS seemed more preoccupied, more disturbed than usual. To hang a young boy in front of thousands of spectators was no light matter. The head of the camp read the verdict. All eyes were on the child. He was lividly pale, almost calm, biting his lips.
> The gallows threw its shadow over him.
> ....
> The three victims mounted together on the chairs.
> The three necks were placed at the same moment within the nooses.
> "Long live liberty!" cried the two adults.
> But the child was silent.
> "Where is God? Where is He?" someone behind me asked.
> At a sign from the head of the camp, the three chairs tipped over.
> Total silence throughout the camp. On the horizon, the sun was setting.
> "Bare your heads!" yelled the head of the camp. His voice was raucous. We were weeping.
> "Cover your heads!"

Then the march past began. The two adults were no longer alive.

Their tongues hung swollen, blue-tinged. But the third rope was still moving; being so light, the child was still alive....For more than half an hour, he stayed there, struggling between life and death, dying in slow agony under our eyes. And we had to look him full in the face. He was still alive when I passed in front of him. His tongue was still red, his eyes not yet glazed. Behind me, I heard the same man asking:

"Where is God now?"

And I heard a voice within me answer him:

"Where is He? Here He is--He is hanging here on this gallows."

I do not know if Wiesel consciously employed images from the story of Christ's crucifixion to tell his own story. Perhaps it does not matter. The same formal elements are there: three Jews, each accused of crimes, one a youth and the symbol of innocence, all forsaken by God. I have been told that some Christian theologians interpret this story as a Jewish vindication of the Christian belief of salvation through Christ's cross. I interpret this story differently. It seems to me a parody of the Christian teaching of the Cross. Christians never teach the cross without also teaching the empty tomb. The Christian story of the cross does not end in defeat, but in victory, in resurrection. But there is no empty tomb in Wiesel's story, no resurrection; the story of the cross ends not in new life, but with more death. What this story suggests is that if the world waits to be healed, if God and humanity wait to be reconciled by the blood of a young innocent Jew in the twentieth century, as in the first century, perhaps salvation is not worth the price. Dostoevsky sensed something of the same when he had Ivan Karamazov say to Alyosha, "....I renounce the higher harmony altogether. It's not worth the tears of....one tortured child...."

If Wiesel's story is a parody of the Christian theology of the victorious cross, it is also a penetrating insight into the perennial truth of the cross. For each day of the earth's history, countless, unnamed human beings suffer their crosses unwillingly and die without hope. The Gospel writers wrote of the empty tomb because they sincerely believed that Jesus was the Messiah and rose to heaven upon his death. But in telling their story, they did not overlook one of the deepest, most human episodes in Christ's Passion. They wrote of Jesus' disciples fleeing the scene of his arrest in mortal fear of their own lives. It is a marvelous symbol of the simple truth that no human being chooses his cross gladly; rather, he suffers it in humiliation and defeat. Wiesel communicates this truth in the history of the hanged boy, thus symbolically joining the Shoah victims to all the victims of history.

The same truth is obscured for Christian theologians by their insistence that despite the evidence of history, that the cross ended not in defeat but in victory. But the sixteenth century Christian painter Matthias Gruenewald seems to have understood it differently. In Gruenewald's Isenheim altarpiece, we are given to see the distinctly human reality of Jesus' Cross. Jesus is nailed to pieces of wood, suffering torments that will bring about his death, a wretched figure alone and forgotten. In this depiction of the Crucifixion, there is no effort at softening, at blurring, at using the soft blues and warm pinks that idealize what is hard and real. There is no stretching and smoothing of the body to make it appear fully and lovely, to give it that strangely erotic appearance that one finds in the abominable crucifixion art hanging everywhere in Christian institutions. In Gruenewald's picture, there is twisted sinew, the bones are bruised, the body pallid, the head hangs limply from the shoulders, the open mouth exudes the odor of impending death. There is all about the air of humiliation and defeat. What Gruenewald depicts in his portrait of the Crucifix-ion is the crushing truth of common suffering.

Gruenewald depicts in his painting what Wiesel expresses in his story: that it lies within the power of art to take the muteness of suffering and give it voice, to proclaim a kind of gospel which speaks of human suffering, a suffering in which one recognizes both God's helplessness in the world and man's imaginative efforts to respond to that helplessness.

Reflecting upon the title of this volume, Michael McGarry enjoins us to consider two paralleling responsibilities: [1] the internalization of the memories of the Shoah by those who experienced it first-hand, a "sacred trust" for Christians, especially Catholics, and for Jews; and [2] a re-thinking of the role of prayer in our post-Auschwitz world as it related to the fate of God, the very meaning of community, and the very purpose of worship within the Church itself. Summarizing his own thoughts, he writes, "Christians' contemporary religious response to the Shoah is to pray for the Jews, not supposing that an interventionist God will reach out to support them--that possibility was shown to be futile in Auschwitz; rather they do so in order to align themselves with the intentionalist God who has chosen the Jews as God's very own and stands with them in their suffering, in their triumph, and in their calling."[1]

A CONTEMPORARY RELIGIOUS RESPONSE TO THE SHOAH:

The Crisis of Prayer

Michael McGarry

I. Introduction

In an address in Sydney, Australia, Pope John Paul II reminded his hearers that "this is still the century of the Shoah."[2] Many other events besides the Shoah might be marshalled forward to characterize the past hundred years: the introduction of mass communications, the era of possible nuclear annihilation, the beginning of space exploration, or the shrinking of the planet into the "global village." In a most profound sense, however, the cloud of the Shoah hangs over the Western Hemisphere and eclipses even those other epoch-making events. The Shoah is the reference point, the historical caesura, the mysterium tremendum of the century.[3]

For the religious person, the Shoah stands as a particularly difficult moment. It is a radically "re-orienting event" for both Christian and Jew; it has become the overarching reference point for personal and theological self-understanding. The purpose of my remarks in this essay, therefore, are to reflect as one religious person, a Roman Catholic, on some dimensions of this epochal event as we approach the third millennium. I do not suggest or give this unique event religious meaning as such; I do not even suggest to find religious meaning within it. Rather, I propose to take the title of this volume--Contemporary Christian Religious Responses to the Shoah--quite literally and to meditate with the reader on some of its aspects. I do not propose to give a survey of what others have seen as the religious responses; those have been done quite competently and completely.[4] My aim is to reflect thoughtfully on, first, what it means to be a contemporary person thinking about this subject, and, second, what religious [not philosophical or even "professionally theological"] responses might be, specifically the crisis of prayer after the Shoah.

II. Some Dimensions of Contemporary Reflections on the Shoah

While attending the very significant "Remembering for the Future" Conference at Oxford, England, in the Summer of 1988, I pondered the demographics of the other attenders. Most of them, it appeared to me, had been alive, even adults, during the Shoah years. For them, "remembering" was the primary category for grasping it. They sought desperately to cling to those years lest they be lost to future generations by irresponsible forgetting. This sense of "remembering" was heightened by the presence of many survivors who chillingly prefaced their remarks with "I remember when...." As a community forced over a few days, committed to a corporate remembering process, they offered compelling testimony which seemed to be almost a sacred trust to then be handed on to the next generation.

At the same time, I noticed a not insignificant number of young scholars like myself who sought to absorb the memory of the survivors. For this younger generation, the goal was not so much to keep a memory alive as it was to make someone else's memory their own. Or, to put it another way, they were seeking to solidify individual memories into a corporate memory, whether that be of the Jewish people, the Christian community, or people of Western Civilization. They--we--felt strongly that "remembering" this episode in our century was an urgent mission, not only to escape trivializing the six million Jews who were executed, not only to avoid marginalizing the five million others who were obliterated in the Nazi attack, but to insure that such a memory will act as a bulwark to prevent such genocide from happening again.

To reflect a contemporary response to the Shoah, it seems to me that we must recognize the critical moment before us: We are at the threshold of the post-survivor period after which there will be no living voice to say what the Shoah was like, no voice to correct the record, no witness to corroborate the evidence about horror of The Night. Now is that fragile moment when a generation passes on a personally-owned, and often individually experienced, memory into the minds and hearts of the generation which must first learn the memory and then make it its own.

Some other unique dimensions of this moment are to be recognized in the controversies surrounding the building of the National Holocaust Memorial Museum in Washington, D.C. These disputes revolve, in part, around the following question: who owns the Shoah--the survivors, who are fewer and fewer in number? The survivors' children--who have pledged to their parents never to mislay their legacy? The educators of the future--who may wish to use the Shoah for their own agenda and exposition of "its lessons?"

However we answer the question as to who owns the Shoah, our moment witnesses the erecting of Shoah Memorials now to be found in almost every major city in the United States, dozens of sites in Europe, and a few sites in Israel.[5] What is one to make of this contemporary development? What does it, then, mean to be surrounded by these memorials while, at the same time, the reality and meaning of the Shoah, once missing from our historical and religious courses of study, are increasingly finding a place, even a place of honor, in our curricula?[6]

At the same time, while the Shoah seeks it rightful place in American civic and educational life, a confluence of other powerful Jewish concerns emerges: the lower birth rate of American Jews, the worrisome dilution of

Jewish commitment through intermarriage, the ongoing anxiety for Israel's security, and the emerging wonderment at the wisdom and the tactic of using the <u>Shoah</u> as the reference point for Jewish life into the 1990s. There are other concerns which characterize our contemporary situation. So at the very time when a generation is asked to pass on the memory and the lessons of the <u>Shoah</u>, these other concerns are calling it into question or diverting its energy.

As a comparison for dilemma, one may well recall the generation who grew up in the United States after the Great Depression: their fiscal habits were marked by frugality, measured vision, and dogged work. The next generation, despite multiple warnings from those who had struggled out of poverty so heroically, look for quick, professional ways of making money, often quite unconcerned about the long term effects of their way of life. Analogously, Jews who emerged from Auschitz's ashes forged new lives and helped to create national policies which secured their freedoms. Now they often find a new generation who does not appreciate the battles that have been won for them. This new generation sometimes sees the focus on the past as morbid and the wrong center of gravity for the Jewish people. For many of them, "never again" does not carry the emotional anxiety of what less vigilance caused their grandparents' generation. In other words, the hard won victories of a certain generation are taken for granted by the next. At the same time, the contemporary generation--those who learn of the <u>Shoah</u> rather than remember it, who must be vigilant on the basis of the warnings of others and not because of a gut wrenching experience of their own--must find ways to make this event of the century their own.

In this situation, the Jewish community has its work cut out for itself, but the Christian community may find its tasks even more difficult. For many Christians, the <u>Shoah</u> does not even register in their universe of moral concern. Many think it should be shrugged off as an event from another generation, on another continent, and perpetrated by barbarians now extinct. For them to "remember," to learn about the time when the Christian community failed its Jewish brothers and sisters and, indeed, itself seems like an almost impossible and unfair burden.[7] The challenge for Christians [and I must be even more particular--for Catholics] is to situate the <u>Shoah</u> squarely within <u>their own</u> history, even as they study it within larger world history. This is a delicate task because post-World War II American Catholics, educated in a post-Vatican II Church, do not respond well to appeals to guilt or even global responsibility. They eschew, for better or worse, anything which hints of "guilt-tripping," and they have been forged, like other Americans, in a very individualistic climate which makes historical and relational ideas difficult to grasp, must less appreciate.[8]

The Roman Catholic Church has begun to educate its members about the <u>Shoah</u>, at least in terms of official directives. In 1985, a very important Church document counselled that religious "Catechesis should....help in understanding the meaning for the Jews of the extermination during the years 1939-1945, and its consequences."[9] The challenge, then, for the Catholic Church is to heed its own guidance on the inescapable necessity of studying the Shoah, not just for better Christian-Jewish relations, but, more importantly, for better and more authentic self understanding.[10]

Emil Fackenheim has written that we are all "situated in the post-Holocaust world. We must accept our situatedness. We must live with it."[11] Together, Jews and Christians of this contemporary generation--from different perspectives and for different reasons--must come to grips with our post-Shoah situation. They must study a history free of ideological distortions, one which invites not only remembering and grieving but also commitment and courage. The danger abides, however, that the ecclesiastical directives might become a burial place rather than a spur to such a process. Thus the task of making the Shoah part of collective Catholic memory, while intended and promised, has only just begun.

III. A Contemporary Religious Response

My organizing principle in considering the dimensions of a contemporary religious response to the Shoah may be something of a surprise in a "scholarly" article. That is, I suggest that prayer--the believer's and the Church's articulated relation with the Creator--is a prime casualty since and because of the Shoah and thus needs to be addressed.[12] And this not simply for academic interest: prayer imposes itself as an existentially insistent question related to the fate of God, the meaning of community, and the purpose of worship within the Church.

In reading other articles of this genre, one often gets the impression that the fate of God in and after the Shoah does not matter much to the writers. Rather, they describe, quite antiseptically, what theologically and rationally has happened to God because of the Shoah. One seldom gets the impression that the writers care much personally because they themselves are not all that affected. Without giving up a systematic approach, I hope to avoid such a distancing from my subject. What I mean by "distancing" may be compared to the difference between the journalist's account of a woman losing her husband in an automobile accident and the description by the widow of the ache she feels at her husband's absence. And so, I hope that my addressing the religious response to the Shoah through the prism of prayer may be seen as a more personal exploration of mourning God lost through the "accident" of the Shoah. And that God, not coincidentally, is a spouse--the spouse of the Jewish people [Hosea 2], the spouse of the Church [Ephesians 5:25-30]. My reflections, therefore, are not the dispassionate notes of the learned "observer of the religious scene." Rather, I hope to speak as one whose passionate "spouse God" has been perhaps mortally wounded or revealed to be less than faithful within that tragic darkness in Christian and Jewish history known as the Shoah.

My starting premise is that prayer, the believer's fundamental activity, has been shattered by recognizing the Shoah as part of Christian history.[13] From my perspective, these questions need to be addressed, and they constitute the outline for the rest of this essay.

A. What did prayer mean in the Shoah world?

B. How does prayer's Addressee--God during and after the Shoah-- resemble the God revealed in the Hebrew and Christian Scriptures?

C. What might our prayer be in the post-Shoah world?

A. What did Prayer Mean in the Shoah World?

The contemporary crisis of prayer looks for clues to its solution by first asking what prayer might have meant within and during the Shoah. And, as one would expect, this question arises in different wordings and urgency for the Jewish and Christian communities.

During the Shoah, most Jews found their prayers fruitless. They screamed out to the God of their ancestors for the Nazi onslaught to be reversed; they cried out to be saved. They wailed at God that He would deliver them from the plague of forced evictions, family ruptures, burned synagogues, and dreaded boxcars to death. Prayer, for most of them, seemed not to find responsive ears. Many felt their access to the Divine had been somehow severed. Many others felt even that the God of their ancestors had been unmasked as nonexistent. Roth and Rubenstein describe it as follows:

> For if Auschwitz made it no longer possible to trust God's goodness simply, it made questions about God and wrestling with God all the more important. Wiesel has been heard to say: 'If I told you I believed in God, I would be lying; if I told you I did not believe in God, I would be lying.'[14]

Other Jews, too small in number, felt that their petitions had indeed been answered through escapes, rescue, family reunions, or release for their children. These Jews regarded the [and sadly few] righteous Gentiles almost as messengers from a merciful God who hid them in blackened cellars or offered them asylum from the catastrophe's fury. And prayers of gratitude were offered.

From still others, unanswered prayers, regardless of results, rose with energy and enthusiasm. Fackenheim recalls the Hasidim at Buchenwald who purchased [with four rations of bread] confiscated tefillin [phylacteries-- Ed.] with which they "prayed with an ecstasy which it would be impossible ever to experience again in....[their] lives." This act of faith Fackenheim calls a kind of resistance, responding to God's command to live, to live as Jews. The Hasidim, by their prayer, refused the Nazi redefinition of their identities and their dignity.[15]

In the end, however, one has to say that the vast majority of Jewish prayers in the Shoah appear fruitless. Indecent, it would be obscene to enter into some sort of accounting exercise, weighing, on the one hand, those whose desperate prayers for escape were followed by exhausted prayers of gratitude with, on the other hand, the millions whose prayers dissipated as surely and as quickly as the smoke from the crematoria. This, indeed, would be grisly bookkeeping. But what does one do with either of these prayers? Where does one go? Are the survivors' prayers of gratitude meaningless babble because so many other co-religionists were annihilated? At very least, one must honor the faith and dignity of those Jews who prayed during and after the Shoah by not dismissing them as naive fools. Indeed, in our own dilemma, the prayer within the Shoah might be the very foundation for the possibility and meaning of prayer now. To paraphrase Fackenheim's kabbalistic [i.e. mystical--Ed.] principle, perhaps "prayer here and now is meaningful only because prayer then and there in the Shoah was actual."[16]

For Christians, similar questions arise. First, the Christian experience of the Shoah was that of seeing God's Chosen abandoned, even as many of them prayed for survival and deliverance. From a distance, Christian's beheld God's first Chosen threatened with annihilation, and God did not come to their rescue. They saw God's elect stunned by the wall of God's silence. The sensitive Christian must ask, "I claim that the Jews' God is my God and where was my God?"

A second Christian question arises: "What about their prayer in the Shoah world?" Again we turn to Fackenheim who recalls the time when a simple invocation for the Jews took on prophetic character and caused the death of one Christian leader. This prayer was that of Domprobst [Prior] Bernhard Lichtenberg who offered liturgical intercessions for the Jews in Berlin's Hedwigkirche. His prayers were marked by two critical characteristics: they were public and they disclosed a possible counterforce to the Nazi death machine. As Fackenheim notes, had Christian Europe joined in sincerity and in chorus with Lichtenberg to pray for the Jews by name, "they would have caused the collapse of the kingdom of the Antichrist."[17]

Third, if only a few German Christians uttered public intercession for the Jew, what were American Christians praying about during World War II? Surely it was not concentrated on the plight of the Jews in the Nazi onslaught. Numerous scholars have chronicled American preoccupations during the Second World War.[18] Understandably, Americans focused on defeating the Axis powers, which defeat would entail the end of the concentration camps. Thus, Americans prayed for victory even as they knew of so much suffering on the part of the Jews and other persecuted peoples.

Fourth, to complete the inquiry about prayers during the Shoah, one has to ask the terrifying question, "What kind of God were the Germans and their collaborators imagining when they prayed for victory?" A God who helped the good overcome the bad? A God who took sides in international conflicts? What flowed through the religious imagination of some SS guards as they bounced their infant on their knee on Saturday, went to Church on Sunday, and returned to work on Monday? Of what possibly could they have been thinking when they prayed? I have found no answers to this dreadful question in my research; I am even afraid to come across any.

These reflections about the prayer life of those who invoked God during the Shoah are very disturbing to those of us who pray for deliverance from war and other harmful threats. But whatever else one might say about the God to whom all these people prayed, in the end this God did not seem strong enough

[1] to transform the majority of German and Austrian Christians into people who would refuse to take part, directly or indirectly, in the extermination of Jewish people;

[2] to move Roman Catholic leadership to do more to influence Axis nations to cease persecuting the Jews;

[3] to save six million of His First Chosen.

Which brings us to the next major question....

B. How Does Prayer's Addressee--God During and After the Shoah--Resemble the God Revealed in the Hebrew and Christian Scriptures?

Whatever else they said, Biblical writers depicted God as radically and directly involved in history.[19] In the Hebrew Scriptures, God is repeatedly credited with changing history's course for the sake, and/or at the beckoning, of His beloved, the Jewish people. Oftentimes historical events were depicted as the consequence of the people's action. When they had been faithful to the covenant, God rewarded the people's goodness. When they turned to other gods or ignored the widow, orphan, or poor, God punished them. Perhaps more accurately, one might say that in the wake of a calamity--as, for example, a flood, drought, or attack of locusts--the people sought the cause of God's anger disclosed in those events. This theme of Divine retribution constitutes one important theme in the Hebrew Scriptures. One readily thinks of examples: Isaiah 8:5-8; Baruch 2:22 ff; Hosea 13:7-15; Ezekiel 11:1-13; Amos 3:2; Noah, and many others. [This theme, obviously, is not missing from the New Testament; cf. Luke 13:34, 19:41-44; Matthew 11:20-24; etc.]. Indeed, some contemporary Jews have sought to explain the Shoah precisely as God's chastisement because European Jews had not been faithful to God, and therefore God allowed more than one-third of them to perish.[20] Most Jews [and Christians] vehemently reject this interpretation, particularly before the inexcusable fact of the one and a half million children tossed into the crematoria's flames. A God who would cause--even allow--such to happen ceases to be a God in whom to believe.[21]

One cannot leave this notion of Divine retribution, however, without adverting to certain Christian tendencies to interpret in general Jewish misfortune to God's punishment for various infidelities. The Christian Scriptures themselves predict great Jewish calamity for not following Jesus. Most obvious is the way Gospel writers interpreted the destruction of the Second Temple as a sign of God's wrath for the Jews' "unbelief" at the time of their messianic visitation. Most Scripture scholars today would read Gospel threats of destruction and scattering as predictions ex eventu, prophecies made after the fact in the polemical situation of the early Christian community asserting its superiority after the Jewish calamity. This line of reasoning, however, one must leave behind in the wake of the Shoah. Rosemary Radford Reuther is correct where she states, "By applying prophetic judgment to 'the Jews' and messianic hope to 'the Church,' Christianity deprived the Jews of their future."[22] This penchant for applying all Hebrew Scripture prophecies of destruction to the Jews and all those of blessedness to the Church needs to be seen as part of the very teaching of contempt which provided part of the atmosphere which made the Shoah possible.

Despite the uselessness of Divine retribution as a viable description of God's hand in the Shoah, Christians can retrieve from their religious heritage a different, more productive Divine portrait. This is the image of a God who is said to "abandon"--not punish--his beloved.

Christians can perceive abandonment by God most dramatically in the very life of the Jew Jesus. Christians believe that Jesus was God's "beloved son" [Mark 1:11]. The Gospel writers recount numerous events and words which attest to Jesus' intimacy with the Father, most notably his almost unique "abba" experience.[23] But this same believed Chosen One experienced abandonment from his God during his agony in Gethsemane [even as he desperately implored God to deliver him][24] and his subsequent crucifixion on Golgotha.

Ironically, the Shoah may be the event which suggests that Gethsemane and Golgotha require an interpretation different from that of the tradition. We concluded at the end of Section A that God-within-the-Shoah was limited insofar as God did little more for the Jews strangling in the Nazi vise than God did for "his only begotten son" seized by Roman despots. The tentative, correct disclosure of Gethsemane and Golgotha, then, is not that God could have saved Jesus and did not, but that God was <u>unable</u> to save him....just as God was unable to save his first chosen, the Jewish people, during their agony. I am not saying that God put a kind of strait jacket on His/Her own loving, rescuing arms at the time of the Agony or the <u>Shoah</u>. Rather, each event reveals that long before either, God created humans in such a relation to Him/Herself that God would respect their freedom, even to the point of appearing impotent in rescuing His beloved. By creation's prior arrangement, the Creator could not intervene since the history's interim course had been handed over to human responsibility.

Other parts of the Scripture speak to God's way in creation. The author of Genesis describes how God, in mysterious wisdom, chose to create humans in freedom. Indeed, the second creation story in Genesis hints at the self-determined limitation of God who did nothing to prevent Adam and Eve from swiftly using their freedom for evil, with all its tragic consequences.

Or one can see in the Book of Job this same insight about the God refraining from intervention in human adversity. Whether this wisdom parable is about God's patience, faith, or Divine absence[25], God's answer to Job's desperate plight is framed in a litany of creation language:

> Where were you when I laid the
> foundation of the earth?
> Tell me, if you have understanding,
> Who determined its measurements--
> --surely you know!
> ***
> Or who shut in the sea with doors,
> when it burst forth from the womb;
> when I made clouds its garment,
> and thick darkness its swaddling band?
> --Job 38:4-5, 8-9 [RSV]

The answer to Job's current strife is to be found not in some explanation about good deeds rewarded, infidelity punished, but in reflection on God's role in the very moment of creation. God says to Job, in essence, "This is the way I created the world and you have to remember: I am God and you are not. My non-interventions in your sorrow have their explanation in creation. <u>This is the way things are.</u>"

Similar to God's absence from Job are God's role during the Flood, during the Exile, during the Crucifixion, and during the <u>Shoah</u>. Human implorings could not move God to renege on a "policy of non-intervention" in order to turn around these and other catastrophes. From the very beginning the consistent Biblical message reveals that God would not, could not, intervene, even when such could have saved the people from harm or from themselves. The creating God, strange to say, made Him/Herself semi-impotent by the very act of creating the free human being. Rather than becoming an instant rescuer, God chose the more puzzling course of imparting His/Her intentions about creation through the Torah and, Christians must add, Jesus. And this would have to suffice. Regarded more positively, however, one may say that God fashioned a partner through creation. This perspective is similar to Paul van Buren's:

> [We Christians] lacked the audacity to see God precisely in the suffering and failure of the cross. God steps back to leave us free to work His will, if we will, and suffers with us in all our failures. Therein lies the power and majesty of His infinite freedom, that He is free in the fullest power of personal love to hold back, to sit still and to suffer in agony as His children move so slowly to exercise in a personal and loving way the freedom which He has willed for them to have and exercise.[26]

In a profound and frightening way, God chooses to depend on humans for God's purposes in creation. It is our responsibility to live before Him according to His will.

Or, as Etty Hillesum's words, written shortly before she was taken to Auschwitz, more poetically affirm: "And yet I don't think life is meaningless. And God is not accountable to us for the senseless harm we cause one another. We are accountable to Him!....[It has been a] hard day, a very hard day....But I keep finding myself in prayer. And that is something I shall always be able to do, even in the smallest space: pray....And if God does not help me to go on, then I shall have to help God."[27]

As I have already indicated, for the Christian, Jesus' praying for deliverance at Gethsemane relies on the same Biblical God who was unable, by prior creation arrangement, to rescue His beloved. Jesus, seeing the almost inevitable consequence of his threat to the Romans[28], prayed to be spared execution. As the faithful Jews, he begs for rescue....indeed his last cry from the cross acknowledged his feeling of God's abandoning him [Mark 15:34]. The God who was absent in so many ways in the crises of Israel was absent again in the cry of His Chosen.

I am quite aware that many will find this comparison exceedingly improper, even monstrous: that is, the comparison between the death at Roman hands of one seemingly failed prophet and the systematic and inexorable crush of the Nazi slaughter of six million, including one and a half million children. However, the single, but crucial point I wish to make is for Christians to see that the God of Jesus is the same God of Abraham and Sarah, of Moses and Miriam....who is the same God revealed, by absence and silence, in the Shoah. It is not as if God had physically and regularly intervened in history for centuries before 1933 and stopped; rather the God of the Hebrew Scriptures and of the New Testament has always been experienced and believed in through God's absence.

It must be admitted that the theme of God's absence and silence is not completely new. Rubenstein and Roth write at careful length what many have written on "the silence of God."[29] What I suggest that goes beyond their report is that, not only is God's absence not new in the Shoah, it is a fundamental mode of the Biblical God's way of being since, and because of, the creation.

But God was not completely absent from Auschwitz. Most eloquently, Elie Wiesel describes the search for the Absent One in the camps. As the SS hanged two adults and one young boy, all inmates were forced to watch:

> The three victims mounted together on the chairs.
> The three necks were placed at the same moment within the nooses.
> 'Long live liberty!' cried the two adults.
> But the child was silent.
> 'Where is God? Where is he?' someone behind me asked.
> At a sign from the head of the camp, the three chairs tipped over. [The observers were forced to gaze closer.] Then the march past began. The two adults were no longer alive. Their tongues hung swollen, blue-tipped. But the third rope was still moving; being so light the child was still alive....
> For more than half an hour he stayed there, struggling between life and death, dying in slow agony under our eyes. And we had to look him full in the face. He was still alive when I passed in front of him. His tongue was still red, his eyes were not yet glazed.
> Behind me, I heard the same man asking:
> 'Where is God now?'
> And I heard a voice within me answer him:
> 'Where is He? Here He is--He is hanging here on this gallows....'[30]

This is no distant echo from the God of Job, the Psalms of lament, and the God of Jesus' crucifixion. Commenting on this oft-quoted passage, German Luthera Jurgen Moltmann said, "Any other answer would be blasphemy....To speak here of a God who could not suffer would make God a demon. To speak here of an absolute God would make God an annihilating nothingness. To speak here of an indifferent God would condemn men to indifference."[31] Besides Moltmann, many other commentators have put the experience of God-within-the-Shoah under the rubric of Divine suffering.[32] But God as suffering with the Chosen or as absent/silent at the catastrophe of the beloved are not contradictory; indeed, they are two expressions of the same lived experience. That is, "Where is he? Where is God when God's beloved are suffering?" God is with them, silent and suffering.

On a more theoretical plane, Chicago Catholic theologian John Shea offers a very helpful construct for systematizing this discovery of God's Biblical and Shoah resemblance. Shea distinguishes between the "interventionist God" and the "intentionalist God." The former is the God who is naively and unreflectively believed to change the course of nature and history by directly but intermittently interrupting the workings of the world. This God is said to cure cancer, bring rain, and save people from accidents. After the Shoah, a Deity who could have rescued the six million and did not is hardly the God who would turn around a single person's lung cancer. Such a God seems to be totally without credibility. And, as we have intimated above, such a description of God may well be a misreading of much of the Hebrew and Christian Scriptures.

The "intentionalist God" is the Creator God who fashions the cosmos in a particular way. Through a relation with this God, the Jewish people first and the Christians later came to understand that God's purpose in creation is to serve life and justice. Scripture's function has less to do with what God has done to change history as to show God's concerns.

> The [Biblical] story of hope and justice is a tale of God's heart not his hands. Paradoxically, for our age, the [Biblical] stories of the intervening God do not reveal his modus operandi but the concerns which obsess Him....The story of hope and justice chronicles the values of the Biblical God.[33]

The Biblical God's values are known through both the commandments and narratives of the Hebrew Scriptures and, for the Christian, the commandments and stories of Jesus. For the latter, the prime locus for Jesus' intention is his answer to the lawyer's question, "What is the greatest commandment?" Jesus replies that it is to know that God is one and God we must love with all our hearts and mind; a second is likened to it, to love our neighbor as ourselves. [Luke 10:25-28] In narrative form, the center of gravity is the Last Judgment scene in Matthew 25 where Jesus asserts that when one feeds the hungry, clothes the naked, or visits the imprisoned, one is indeed doing so to Christ himself. These are the values of the intentionalist God revealed in the Hebrew Scriptures and the New Testament.[34]

Finally, in thinking about the resemblance between the Biblical God and God during the Shoah, it would be incomplete to reflect only on God's silence or absence. One must return also to those extraordinary moments of liberation remembered in our respective traditions. In the Jewish tradition, most significant is the Exodus wherein Moses' experience of God was so overwhelming and immediate that he was empowered to lead a reluctant people out of more than four hundred years of slavery through forty years' journey to the land "flowing with milk and honey." Without being glib or simplistic, without implying that the Shoah was the price to be paid, the rebirth of Israel may be seen as another such liberation. On the Christian side, one must return, of course, to Jesus' resurrection. However one might explain its historicity, the resurrection of Jesus is the Christian way of saying that, in the end, the self-imposed limitations of God's acting in history are themselves limited. The final creative act of God is to embrace creation, never finally leaving it to ruin. For the Christian, the Resurrection is the cause and foundation of hope that life is not meaningless, short, or without final vindication. Here I do not wish to compare, much less equate, Jewish and Christian views of the afterlife or the teleological meaning of the cosmos. The point simply is that both traditions cling to these corporate memories which reveal God both as limited and as finally victorious.

C. What Might Our Prayer be in Post-Shoah World?

According to St. Augustine, "The best disposition for praying is that of being desolate, forsaken, stripped of everything." Surely the Shoah world provoked such disposition. And in the circumstance of the Buchenwald Hasidim and Domprobst Lichtenberg, we overheard prayers that spoke out defiantly against the rumble of the death machine. The post-Shoah world, too, is replete with broken lives and pained voices, echoes of the Shoah. Today, to become aware of the Shoah--in a time when it has to be learned before it can be remembered--is to attend to the cries of those in the camps, of those mothers torn from their children, and those babies' bloodcurdling screams quickly extinguished by lapping flames. It is to allow those voices to sensitize us to contemporary suffering. Contemporary prayer is not a matter of substituting concern for the Shoah with concern for contemporary events. Simply speaking, it is to reckon with our "situatedness" of living in a post-Shoah world in order to get in touch with the purpose of the "intentionalist God" who has made us partners in creation.

Often in such articles about "God after the Shoah," one reads a survey of what theologians have to say about the fate of God in and after the Shoah. These articles are eminently important, and I owe much to their insights. But I suggest the wisdom of the aphorism, "Those who take religion seriously should beware of those who take it professionally," applies quite poignantly here. Has one been "desolate, forsaken, stripped of everything" enough to be terrified at the possibility of losing one's God? Has the Christian Church allowed the experience of the Shoah to seep into its soul deep enough to pray to the God revealed therein, which we have discovered to be the same God revealed in Hebrew and Christian Scriptures? Can one turn oneself over, even a little, to feel empathically the desolation of a survivor? Although his faith seemed to have been destroyed by the flames of the Night, Elie Wiesel argues that he had to continue his dialogue-feeling-like-monologue with God:

Master of the Universe, I know what You want--I under-
stand What You are doing. You want despair to overwhelm me.
You want me to cease believing in You, to cease praying to you,
to cease invoking Your name to glorify and sanctify it. Well, I tell
You: No, no--a thousand times no! You shall not succeed! In spite
of me and in spite of Yu, I recite the Kaddish [Memorial Prayer--
Ed.], which is a song of faith, for You and against You. This song
You shall not still, God of Israel.[35]

From a very different place on the Christian side, French Reform
theologian Jacques Ellul has relentlessly pursued the question of the crisis of
prayer for the modern person.[36] In a world racked by enormous tragedy,
including the Shoah, Ellul candidly admits, "It is futile to pretend that prayer
is indispensable to man. Today he gets along very well without it. When he
does not pray he lacks nothing, and when he prays it looks to him like a
superfluous action reminiscent of former superstitions. He can live perfectly well without prayer."[37] After dismissing various reassuring views of
prayer [self-discipline, to obtain favors, to obtain consolation, to express
resignation, and so forth], Ellul concludes that the only reason for praying in
the modern age--or any age, for that matter--cannot be found in rational
justifications in the world or in seeking God's enlistment to develop one's
projects. What does one do when one is "desolate, forsaken, stripped of
everything?"

No, at those times I have in fact to cling to 'a reason'
outside myself, objective, which I find compelling, which pushes
me along, in other words, like a hand in my back forcing me
ahead, constraining me to pray. It is the commandment which God
in his mercy has granted to make up for the void in my heart and
in my life. 'Watch and pray;' that is the sole reason for praying
which remains for modern man.[38]

Like the survivor, for Ellul, there is no guarantee that prayers will be
answered....or even that they will be listened to. One does not question the
commander. One obeys, not out of simple duty or compulsive reaction, but
simply because of the personally addressed command from the Creator God
heard through the Jewish and Christian traditions.

Whether, like Wiesel, a Jew must pray after the Shoah so as not let God
"off the hook," or whether, like Ellul, one must pray after the Shoah
because the personal command to do so has not been retracted, one might be
left with a simple, but profound, conclusion. After the Shoah, one can pray
to the Creator God who has unleashed humankind into freedom, one can utter
entreaties to the Deity because the Buchenwald Hasidim, draped in tefillin
[phylacteries--Ed.], danced during the Shoah. Today, Christians must pray
Domprobst Lichtenberg's prayer because cruelly too few Christians even
whispered it during the Shoah. With the Domprobst, we Catholics must pray

publicly "on behalf of the Jews and the poor concentration camp prisoners." Lichtenberg stated at his trial, "I told myself that only one thing could still help, namely, prayer....for the Jews."[39] By praying with him, albeit sadly belatedly, Christians align themselves with the intention of our Creator God that the Jews survive, that they survive as Jews.

Here, then, the first and second parts of our essay come together. Christians' contemporary religious response to the Shoah is to pray for the Jews, not supposing that an interventionist God will reach out to support them--that possibility was shown to be futile in Auschwitz; rather they do so in order to align themselves with the intentionalist God who has chosen the Jews as God's very own and stands with them in their suffering, in their triumph, and in their calling. Prayer is the way, then, for believers to keep reminding themselves of God's creative will so they will live according to it. Frighteningly and lovingly, since the Shoah, it is clear that there is no other way for the world to be influenced by God than through the lives of God's creatures. As van Buren reflects:

> That the Creator should so love His creatures as to make His own heart's desire depend upon their longing to fulfill His plan bespeaks a love that surpasses understanding. That the Creator can choose to make us creatures His co-workers means that He, in His freedom, has chosen to make Himself our co-worker....He suffers in His own right over our failure to recognize that when we are most fully taking responsibility, we are only cooperating with Him who is most fully present and active when we are fully present and active.[40]

And now, if enough Christians recite the Domprobst Lichtenberg's prayer, God's will may be done. It has been revealed in creation and in the covenant, and tenderly left in our hands. God's will is that the Jews survive as Jews.[41] Already the Good Friday liturgy directs Catholics to pray that the Jewish people "may continue to grow in the love of....[God's] name and in faithfulness to his covenant."[42] It is a prayer we desper-ately wish the Christian community had uttered loudly and with conviction in 1935. Today it is a prayer which must be seared into the regular, public prayer of the Church.

For John Pawlikowski, for whom the <u>Shoah</u> represents "the ultimate expression of human freedom and human evil," the question now remains whether or not there exists <u>any</u> significant role for God in its aftermath in the construction of a moral schema with which to prevent the reoccurrence of radical evil. Surveying the major Jewish and Christian thinkers, including many less well-known, he finds both communities have not devoted sufficient discussion to any role for God, and would substitute the notion of the "compelling God" for that of the "commanding God." He likewise finds meaning both in the centrality of humility in the post-<u>Shoah</u> world and in the "theology of divine vulnerability," and would, following McGarry, Ruether, and others, present the need for a reformulation of Christology, cautioning us ever that the appropriate uses of power--political, religious, military, economic--must be addressed in any meaningful contemporary Christian or Jewish theology.

THE SHOAH: CONTINUING THEOLOGICAL CHALLENGE FOR
CHRISTIANITY

John T. Pawlikowski

I. Setting the Context

What follows is an attempt by one Christian scholar to confront some of
the overarching theological challenges posed by the Shoah which we are
gradually coming to understand as an epochal event in the history of Western
society, including the Western church, with decided implications for the
future of all of humanity. It is truly an "orienting experience" for contemporary human existence, to speak in the words of Irving Greenberg. We
shall probe the Shoah's impact on our sense of God, the Christ Event, the
church, morality, and theological methodology. But as we undertake this
necessary task of theological and social analysis, we must never let our
minds and hearts stray very far from the memory of the six million Jews,
including one million children, who were annihilated simply because they
were Jews, nor of the up to five million Poles, Rom people, Gays, mentally
and physically incapacitated and others who joined them in victimhood as part
of the Nazi effort to purify humanity. Likewise, Christians must never lose
sight of the fact that the Shoah continues to strain Christian credibility.
While contemporary scholarship has adequately documented that the Shoah
was primarily parented by currents within certain modern secular philoso-
phies and by social theories which at their core were often profoundly anti-
Christian, little doubt remains that classical Christian teaching and preaching
constituted an indispensable seedbed for the success of the Nazi effort.
Even a scholar such as the late Uriel Tal, who strongly argued for the
predominance of secular [and anti-Christian] antisemitism in the genesis of
Nazism, continued to underscore the pivotal contribution of the Christian
tradition. He insisted that Nazi racial antisemitism was not totally original
when subjected to careful analysis. Rather, traditional Christian stereotypes
of Jews and Judaism were clothed in new pseudoscientific jargon and applied
to specific historical realities of the period. In summation, Tal says that
"racial anti-Semitism and the subsequent Nazi movement were not the result
of mass hysteria or the work of single propagandists. The racial antisemites, despite their antagonism toward traditional Christianity, learned
much from it, and succeeded in producing a well-prepared, systematic
ideology with a logic of its own that reached its culmination in the Third
Reich."[1]

Christianity cannot equivocate regarding its responsibility for the spread
of Nazism if it is to enter authentically the continuing debate about the
broader theological implications of the Shoah. Achieving such authenticity
clearly will involve a commitment to the full and final purge of all remaining

antisemitism from its theological statements, catechetical teachings, and liturgical expressions. The church must likewise be willing to submit its World War II record to a thorough scrutiny by respected scholars. Ultimately, it cannot avoid confronting the question of a fellow inmate posed to Alexander Donat, author of The Holocaust Kingdom: "How can Christianity survive the discovery that after a thousand years of its being Europe's official religion, Europe remains pagan at heart?"[2]

Not raising the specific issues involved with the Christian response to the Shoah in no way is meant to convey the impression that they are of secondary importance. On the contrary, they remain absolutely central and critical for any meaningful encounter with this whirlwind of evil that so engulfed European civilization in our century. It would be presumptuous for any Christian to treat the overarching theological issues of the Shoah without first having addressed forthrightly the question of Christian culpability during the Nazi era. Having attempted to discharge this moral responsibility in other writings[3], the following reflections will concentrate on more generalized theological concerns.

II. A New Human Condition

In the final analysis the Shoah represented the beginning of a new era in human self-awareness and human possibility over which hung the specter of either unprecedented destruction or unparalleled hope. With the rise of Nazism the mass extermination of human life in a guiltless fashion became thinkable and technologically feasible. The door was now ajar for an era when dispassionate torture and the murder of millions could become not merely the act of a crazed despot, not just a desire for national security, not merely an irrational outbreak of xenophobic fear, but a calculated effort to reshape history supported by intellectual argumentation from the best and brightest minds in a society. It was an attempt, Emil Fackenheim has said, to wipe out the "divine image" in history. "The murder camp," Fackenheim insists, "was not an accidental by-product of the Nazi empire. It was its essence."[4]

The fundamental challenge of the Shoah lies in our altered perception of the relationship between God and humanity and its implications for the basis of moral behavior. What emerges as a central reality from the study of the Shoah is the Nazi effort to create the "superperson," to develop a truly liberated humanity, to be shared only by a select group, namely, the Aryan race. This new humanity would be released from the moral restraints previously imposed by religious beliefs and would be capable of exerting virtually unlimited power in the shaping of the world and its inhabitants. In a somewhat indirect, though still powerful, way the Nazis had proclaimed the death of God as a guiding force in the governance of the universe.

In pursuit of their objective, the Nazis became convinced that all the "dregs of humanity" had to be eliminated or at least their influence on culture and human development significantly curtailed. The Jews fell into this "dregs" category first and foremost. They were classified as "vermin." The Nazis could not imagine even a minimally useful role for Jews in the new society to which they hoped to give birth. The Polish and Romani peoples as well as gay persons and those suffering mental or physical disabilities were also looked upon as polluters of the new level of humanity envisioned by the Nazis. While proper distinction between these victims and the Jewish people needs to be maintained because, with the possible exception of the Rom community [or "Gypsies"], none were slated for the same kind of wholesale extermination that was to be the ultimate fate of the Jews, they, too, were considered obstacles to the advancement of human consciousness to new levels of insight, power and self-control. Their extermination under the rubric of humankind's purification assumes a theological significance intimately related to the Jewish question. Regrettably the non-Jewish victims are generally ignored in the emerging theological reflections on the Shoah whether by Christian or Jewish scholars.[5]

Uriel Tal captured as well as anyone the basic theological challenge presented by the Shoah. In his understanding, the so-called "Final Solution" had as its ultimate objective the total transformation of human values. Its stated intent was liberating humanity from all previous moral ideals and codes. When the liberating process was complete, humanity would be once and for all rescued from the imprisonment of a God concept and its related notions of moral responsibility, redemption, sin and revelation. Nazi ideology sought to transform theological ideas into exclusively anthropological and political concepts. In Tal's interpretation of the Shoah the Nazis adopted a kind of "incarnational" ideology, but not in the New Testament sense of the term. Rather, for the Nazis, "God becomes man in a political sense as a member of the Aryan race whose highest representative on earth is the Fuhrer."[6]

Tal's research led him to conclude that this new Nazi consciousness emerged only gradually in the decades following World War I. Its roots, however, were somewhat earlier. It was undeniably related to the general process of social secularization that had been transforming Germany since the latter part of the nineteenth century. Its philosophic parents included the Deists, the French encyclopedists, Feuerbach, the Young Hegelians, and the evolutionary thinkers in concert with the developing corps of scientists who, through their many new discoveries, were creating the impression that a triumphant material civilization was on the verge of dawning in Western Europe. In the end, Tal argued, "these intellectual and social movements struck a responsive chord in a rebellious generation, altered the traditional views of God, man, and society, and ultimately led to the pseudo-religious, pseudomessianic movement of Nazism."[7]

III. The Post-Shoah Theological Dilemma

The principal theological problem raised by the Shoah is how does humankind properly appropriate the genuine sense of human liberation that lay at the heart of Nazi ideology without surrendering its soul to massive evil. However horrendous their legacy, the Nazis were correct in at least one respect. They rightly perceived that some basic changes were under- way in human consciousness. The impact of the new science and technol- ogy, with its underlying assumption of freedom, was beginning to provide the human community on a mass scale with a Promethean-type experience of escape from prior moral chains. People were starting to perceive, however dimly, an enhanced sense of dignity and autonomy far more than most of Western Christian theology had previously conceded. Traditional theological concepts that had shaped much of the Christian moral perspective, notions such as divine punishment, hell, and divine wrath and provi-dence were losing some of the hold they had exercised over moral decis-ion-making since Biblical times. Christian theology had tended to accentuate the om- nipotence of God which in turn intensified the impotence of the human person and the rather inconsequential role played by the human community in main- taining the sustainability of the earth. The Nazis totally rejected this previous relationship. In fact, they were literally trying to turn it upside down.

Michael Ryan has emphasized this direction of Nazism in his theo-lo- gical analysis of Hitler's Mein Kampf. For Ryan, the most striking aspect of the "salvation history" found in this volume is Hitler's willingness to confine humanity in an absolute way to the limits of time. In the Hitlerian perspective humankind must resign itself to the conditions of finitude. But this resignation is accompanied by the assertion of all-pervasive power for itself within those conditions. The end result of all this was the self- deification of Hitler who proclaimed himself the new "Savior" of the German nation. It is this Hitlerian mindset that allows us, in Ryan's judg- ment, to term Mein Kampf a "theological" treatise. In the final analysis, in Ryan's words, Hitler's worldview "amounted to the deliberate decision on the part of mass man to live within the limits of finitude without either the moral restraints or the hopes of traditional religion--in this case, Chris- tianity."[8]

The challenge facing theology after the Shoah is to discover a way whereby the new sense of human freedom that is continuing to dawn might be affirmed but channeled into constructive rather than humanly-destructive purposes. The understanding of the God-human person relationship must be significantly altered in light of the Shoah. The intensified sense of power and human enhancement that the Nazis championed as a novum of our age needs to be acknowledged as a crucial and inescapable element in the ongoing process of humanity's salvation. There is simply no way of reversing the consciousness of a profound readjustment in the nature of the divine-human relationship. That is why the mere repetition of Biblical images and precepts is insufficient as a response to the Shoah. Contemporary humanity perceives itself in a far more liberated condition relative to divine power and authority than the authors of the Biblical texts could ever imagine. There exists today an awareness of dimensions of the Genesis notion of co-creatorship which the Biblical world was unable to grasp in any way. As the moral philosopher Hans Jonas has reminded us, we constitute the first generation with the responsibility for insuring the future of all forms of life in the universe. No previous generation had in its grasp the possibilities for massive destruction that are open to us. In the past, nature had sufficient recuperative powers to heal whatever wounds humanity's capitulation to evil might inflict. This is no longer so to the same extent. That is why, while it is important to consider the Shoah separately so as to properly illustrate its profound distinctiveness as a historical and theological event, it is equally necessary to establish a link with the other shattering experience of World War II--Hiroshima. In one sense, the two events are of a significantly different order; but, in anoth-er, as expressions of the newly-found power of humanity to destroy, they remain profoundly intertwined.

The question at hand is whether post-Shoah theology can develop an expression of God and religion which will help prevent the newly-recognized creative power of humanity from being transformed into the destructive force unveiled in all its ugliness during the Nazi era. Put another way, can post-Shoah humanity discover a relationship with God which will provide warrants for the use of its vast new power to shape itself and the creation it has inherited? This fundamental issue has been basically ignored by most Christian theologians up till now.

Reflections on the divine-human encounter in light of the Shoah have emerged in the last decade or so as one of the central theological discussions in Judaism. Unfortunately, as David Tracy has regretted, no parallel development has occurred within Christian theological circles. Few church theologians, says Tracy, are focusing on the ultimate religious question for all believers, including Christians--the problem of God--which, as Schleiermacher perceptively insisted, can never be treated as one among many doctrines but must pervade all other statements of belief. In this regard, Tracy is convinced that "Jewish theology, in its reflections on the reality of God since the Tremendum of the Holocaust, has led the way for all serious theological reflection."[9]

IV. Post-Shoah Approaches to God

Theological discussion about God in light of the Shoah has generated a variety of viewpoints among Jewish scholars. It is impossible to treat them in a comprehensive fashion in this discussion. Hence we will focus on a select number of figures whose writings has proven influential in the past several years.

The basic division among Jewish scholars has come over the question of how central a role the Shoah should assume in the contemporary reconstruction of Jewish belief. Most Orthodox Jewish scholars have tended to downplay the Shoah as a major turning point in the understanding of the divine-human relationship. While they remain acutely sensitive that the annihilation of six million innocent men, women and children has traumatized the Jewish People, they hold fast to the belief that the experience ultimately can still be incorporated into classical religious categories of evil. A few Reform Jewish scholars such as Eugene Boro-witz have likewise deemphasized the Shoah has a theological issue in favor of the more traditional concern in Reform Judaism with the problem of how belief in God is to be reconciled with what enhanced awareness of human autonomy in modern times.

David Hartman remains an articulate, creative spokesperson for the above point of view. In a number of writings, including the book A Living Covenant: The Innovative Spirit in Traditional Judaism[10], he opts for the contemporary renewal of traditional covenantal religion, rather than the Shoah, as central to the generation of the faith commitment required to guarantee Jewish survival. Adopting a position similar to that advocated by the Christian ethicist James Gustafson about humankind's inability really to know God ultimately intends for creation, Hartman stresses the development of a new faithfulness to Torah observance as the only way of assuring communal survival and a measure of meaning in a frequently chaotic world. The Shoah was certainly a part of this chaos. And its continued remembrance is vital. But in no way should it provide the basis for contemporary belief. For Hartman, "Auschwitz, like all Jewish suffering of the past, must be absorbed and understood within the normative framework of Sinai." Jews will mourn forever the memory of the victims, but they "will build a healthy new society because of the memory of Sinai."[11]

There is reason to show some sympathy for the stance of Hartman and his colleagues. No post-Shoah faith expression can totally divorce itself from the covenantal experience and promises. And to the extent that Hartman means to direct his remarks against those in the Jewish community who would use the Shoah as a basis for the development of a chauvinistic nationalism in the midst of the current Israeli-Palestinian crisis, he deserves applause. Yet, in the final analysis, Hartman's position falls short because of his inability to grasp that the reality of the Shoah no longer allows us to speak of covenantal faith in the same way as did the Biblical or Rabbinic traditions. The Shoah was not merely the most extreme example of the classical theological problem of evil. It had burst asunder the traditional position. To confine our response to the Shoah to the renewal of covenantal faith as Hartman prescribes would be to endanger human survival. For we would remain unprepared to deal with the magnitude of the power and consequent responsibility that has come into the hands of humanity. And failure on the part of humankind to recognize these new post-Shoah realities may allow this power to pass once again into the hands of a new class of Nazis. The frontispiece to Alexander Donat's The Holocaust Kingdom, based on Revelation 6:8, poignantly reminds us of that continuing potential: "And I looked, and behold a pale horse and his name that sat on him was Death, and Hell followed with him. And power was given unto them over the fourth part of the earth, to kill with sword, and with hunger, and with death and with the beasts of the earth."

Among those Jewish scholars who have argued for major theological re-interpretation of the divine-human relationship in response to the Shoah the names of Richard Rubenstein, Emil Fackenheim, Arthur Cohen and Irving Greenberg stand out. Brief attention will be given to the first three followed by a somewhat more detailed discussion of Greenberg's approach.

Rubenstein's volume After Auschwitz[12] caused a great stir in Jewish circles when it first appeared. Its boldly stated claim that the Shoah had buried any possibility of continued belief in a covenantal God of history and that, in place of traditional faith, Jews must now turn to a creed of "paganism" which defines human existence as wholly and totally an earthly existence shook the foundations of Judaism. When the dust had somewhat settled, the prevailing opinion was that Rubenstein had gone much too far, a point that he himself seemingly acknowledges [at least implicitly] in some of his more recent writings. Today, Rubenstein's position seems somewhat closer to a mystical approach to God. The cosmos is no longer as cold, silent, and unfeeling a reality as he projected in After Auschwitz. As John Roth presumably writes in the volume co-authored by Rubenstein and himself, "Today, Rubenstein would balance the elements of creativeness and love in the cosmos somewhat more evenly with those of destruction and hate than he was prepared to do in 1966. What has not changed is his affirmation of a view of God quite different from the mainstream view of biblical and rabbinic Judaism and his rejection of the notion that the Jews are in any sense a people either chosen or rejected by God."[13]

Whatever else may be said in judgment about Rubenstein's initial or more refined perspective, he is credited by a number of fellow scholars with at least one major contribution. Steven Katz, who rejects Ruben-stein's original summons to "paganism," is a case in point. He considers Rubenstein "absolutely correct" in his judgment that classical categories of evil no longer are convincing relative to the God-human relationship when confronted by the immensity of the Shoah.[14]

Fackenheim, Cohen and Greenberg, in their approaches to the post-Shoah divine reality, stop far short of Rubenstein's total rejection of a covenantal God. But, despite some significant differences among them, they speak with unified voice regarding the need for a major restatement of this relationship in light of the Shoah.

In his numerous writings, but especially in the volume The Jewish Return into History[15], Emil Fackenheim states his conviction that the image of God was destroyed during the Shoah. Our task today, a mandate incumbent in a special way upon the survivors of the Shoah, is to restore the divine image, but in a way that conveys a sense of a new curtailment of God's power in comparison with past images.

Arthur Cohen picked upon on this same theme, but used more philosophically-oriented language to make his point. In The Tremendum: A Theological Interpretation of the Holocaust[16], Cohen pointedly rejected the continued viability of any image of God as the strategist of human history. A post-Shoah God can legitimately be perceived [and must be perceived if radical evil is to remain in check] as "the mystery of our futurity, always our posse, never our acts. If we can begin to see God less as an interferer whose insertion is welcome [when it accords with our needs] and more as the immensity whose reality is our prefiguration, whose speech and silence are metaphors for our language and distortion, whose plenitude and unfolding are the hope of our futurity, we shall have won a sense of God whom we may love and honor, but whom we no longer fear and from whom we no longer demand."[17]

Turning now to Irving Greenberg, we find that his language about the effects of the Shoah on the divine image are not as blunt as those of Fackenheim's, but he shares the conviction that a major readjustment is required of our statement of the force of the covenantal obligations upon humanity in light of the Shoah. "The Nazis," he says, "unleashed all-out violence against the covenant...." Their program for the 'Final Solution' involved a total assault on Jewish life and values. For Greenberg, "the degree of success of this attack constitutes a fundamental contradiction to the covenant of life and redemption."[18]

The reality of the Nazi fury forces a thorough reconsideration of the nature of moral obligation upon the contemporary Jewish community and seemingly by implication upon all those other believers [Christian and Muslim] who in some way regard the Sinai covenant as foundation for their faith expression. For this covenant has called Jews as witnesses to the world for God and for a final perfection. "In light of the Holocaust," insists Greenberg, "it is obvious that this role opened the Jews to a murderous fury from which there was no escape. Yet the Divine could not or would not save them from this fate. Therefore, morally speaking, God must repent of the covenant, i.e., do teshuvah [repentance--Ed.] for having given his chosen people a task that was unbearably cruel and dangerous without having provided for their protection. Morally speaking, then, God can have no claims on the Jews by dint of the covenant."[19]

The end result of any serious reflection on the Sinai covenant in light of the Shoah experience, as Greenberg sees it, is simply the disappearance of any "commanded" dimension on the part of God. "Covenantally speaking, one cannot order another to step forward to die."[20] Any understanding of cove- nantal obligation must now be voluntary: "One cannot order another to go on a suicide mission. Out of shared values, one can only ask for volunteers....- No divine punishment can enforce the covenant, for there is no risked punishment so terrible that it can match the punishment risked by continuing faithfulness to the covenant."[21]

The voluntary nature of the post-Shoah covenantal relationship unques- tionably heightens human responsibility in the eyes of Greenberg: "If after the Temple's destruction, Israel moved from junior partner to true partner in the covenant, then after the Holocaust, the Jewish people is called upon to become the senior partner in action. In effect, God was saying to humans: you stop the Holocaust. You bring the redemption. You act to ensure that it will never again occur. I will be with you totally in whatever happens, but you must do it."[22]

My basic response to the post-Shoah reflections of Fackenheim, Cohen and especially Greenberg is that, despite some reservations, they provide the basic parameters within which we need to understand the God-human relationship today and its connection with the foundations for contemporary morality. For one, consciousness of the role of the human community in preserving human history from further eruptions of radical evil akin to Nazism has been greatly enhanced, as all three have rightly insisted. Hu- manity find itself after the Shoah facing the realization that "future" is no longer something God will guarantee. Survival, whether for the People Israel or humanity at large, is now more than ever a human proposition. In their differing ways, Fackenheim, Cohen and Greenberg have made this fact abundantly clear. And we need to be profoundly grateful for that. They have clearly confronted us with the post-Shoah reality that any simplistic belief in an interventionist God of history was buried in the ashes of Nazi Germany. Preventing massive human destruction is now far more evidently than before a burden primarily incumbent upon the human community. We must learn to save ourselves from future instances of holocaust, nuclear or otherwise. We are summoned to answer "right now" to D.H. Lawrence's plea, "God of Justice, when wilt Thou teach them to save themselves?"[23] We no longer have the luxury, fact it would be the height of human irresponsibility after the Shoah, to imagine that God will do it in response to simple petitions of prayer. Perhaps because of the freedom God has granted humanity he cannot do it. It might be added here that a fruitful source in our search for a post- Shoah vision of God that would strengthen the human role in the process of salvation might be the Jewish mystical literature with its notion of divine self-constriction in the act of creation.

But despite my gratitude to Fackenheim, Cohen and Greenberg their prescriptions for God-belief after the Shoah are not wholly satisfactory in the end. They would appear to have left humanity too much to its own whims after the Shoah. They have not adequately explored whether God continues to play a significant role after the Shoah in the development of a moral ethos within humanity that can restrain radical evil. The role they have in fact assigned to God is not potent enough.

V. Moving Towards the "Compelling" God

The post-Shoah theological vision must be one that recognizes both the new creative possibilities inherent in the human condition as well as the utter necessity for this creative potential to be brought under the sway of an encounter with the living and judging God. Only such an encounter will direct the use of this creative potential away from the destruction represented by Nazism. We need to find a way of articulating a notion of a transcendent God which can counterbalance the potential for evil that remains very much a live possibility in the contemporary human situation. In other words, we shall have to recover a fresh sense of transcendence to accompany our heightened sense of human responsibility after the Shoah. This is something basically absent from the reflections of Fackenheim, Cohen and Greenberg. Men and women will once more need to experience contact with a personal power beyond themselves, a power that heals the destructive tendencies still lurking within humanity. The newly-liberated person, to be able to work consistently for the creation of a just and sustainable society, must begin to sense a judgment upon human endeavors that goes beyond mere human judgment. Such a sense of judgment is missing in Fackenheim's emphasis on human restoration of the divine image, in Cohen's language about God as our "posse," and in Greenberg's notion of the voluntary covenant, as valid as each notion is in itself.

The Shoah has shattered all simplistic notions of a "commanding God." On this point, Fackenheim, Cohen and Greenberg are perfectly correct. Such a "commanding" God can no longer be the touchstone of ethical behavior. But the Shoah has also exposed humanity's desperate need to restore a relationship with a "compelling" God, compelling because we have experienced, through symbolic encounter with this God, a healing, a strengthening, an affirming that buries any need to assert our humanity through the destructive, even deadly, use of human power. This sense of a compelling Parent God who has gifted humanity, whose vulnerability for the Christian has been shown in the Cross, is the meaningful foundation for any adequate moral ethos after the Shoah.

Some have suggested that "compelling" may be too strong a replacement adjective for "commanding" in speaking about the post-Shoah God. Perhaps they are right. Perhaps "compelling" does tip the scales too much back towards a pre-Shoah vision of divine reality. These critics have offered the alternative of speaking of a "God to whom we are drawn" which admittedly is more cumbersome than "compelling." This inherent and enduring "drawing" power of God would substitute for pre-Shoah models which emphasized God's "imposition" upon humanity.

At this point, the "compelling" vocabulary seems preferable. But whatever image eventually wins the day, the basic point must be made that post-Shoah humanity needs to rediscover a permanent relationship with God who remains a direct source of strength and influence in the conduct of human affairs.

In speaking of the need to rediscover a "compelling" God, I believe I am close to the stage Elie Wiesel has reached as he has probed the depth of the Shoah these many years. Despite the remaining ambiguities, despite the apparent divine failures in covenantal responsibility, atheism is not the answer for contemporary humanity according to Wiesel. After we have exhausted ourselves in protesting against God's non-intervention during this period of night, we still are unable to let God go away permanently. Any attempt, Wiesel insists, to make the Shoah "fit" into a divine plan, any belief that somehow we can imagine a universe congruent with it, renders God a moral monster and the universe a nightmare beyond endurance. But, theologian Robert McAfee Brown, has put it, "....for Wiesel and for many others the issue will not go away. He must contest with God, concerning the moral outrage that somehow seems to be within the divine plan. How can one affirm a God whose 'divine plan' could include such barbarity? For Wiesel, the true 'contemporary' is not the modern skeptic, but the ancient Job, the one who dares to ask questions of God, even though Wiesel feels that Job gave in a little too quickly at the end."[24]

Wiesel hints that after all is said and done the Shoah may reveal that divine and human liberation are very much intertwined and that, despite continuing tension, both God and humanity yearn for each other as a result. In consequence of this linkage, Wiesel is prepared to say that human acts of justice and compassion help to liberate God, to restore the divine image as Fackenheim has phrased it. Job, says Wiesel, "did not suffer in vain; thanks to him, we know that it is given to man to transform divine injustice into human justice and compassion."[25] But they also show the need for God's continuing presence, for the human person who claims total freedom from God will not likely pursue such a ministry of justice and compassion for very long. So the human person is also liberated from the corrupting desire to cut all ties to the Creator.

At this point the inevitable question must be posed: How can this "compelling" God serve as the ground of contemporary morality? Strange as it may seem, the Shoah provides us with some assistance in responding to this question. For if the Shoah reveals one permanent quality of human life, it is the enduring presence of, the continuing human need for, symbolic affirmation and communication. What Reinhold Niebuhr called the "vitalistic side of humanity" has not been permanently obliterated. But increasingly in the West, it has been relegated almost exclusively to the realm of play and recreation. The Enlightenment and its aftermath caused a bifurcation in Western humanity which has catapulted reason to a place of overwhelming dominance in the self-definition of the person. All other human dimensions tend to be relegated to an inferior position. In this setting, ethics has become too exclusively rational a discipline and far too dominated by the scientific mentality. The liberals in Germany were powerless in fighting Nazism, not because they did not care, but because they naively assumed that the masses would respond to mere rational moral argumentation. The Nazis were far more perceptive in recognizing the centrality of the vitalistic in human life.

Recovery of abiding contact with the personal Creator God first revealed in the Hebrew Scriptures is as indispensable a starting point for social ethics in the post-Shoah era as recognition of our enhanced co-creational responsibility for the world. The two go hand-in-hand. Any attempt to construct a social ethic for our age by merely assuming the continued reality of this divine presence, however, will not succeed. Neither will efforts built around natural law, Kantian rational consistency models or psychoanalysis provide the requisite moral grounding. The kind of post-Shoah relationship between God and humanity pivotal for the development of social morality in our time will come only through divine-human encounter in worship and prayer. The failure of nearly all contemporary forms of social ethics to deal constructively with the role of symbols, especially liturgical symbols, in fostering social morality, to recognize how crucial they are for overcoming the prevailing one-dimensionality infecting Western society has left us with an increasingly barren public morality.

We may not need to return to the tradition of medieval morality plays. But we desperately need to understand that without liturgy and prayer there is no real way of overcoming self-centeredness and the destructive use of power evidenced in the Shoah save for the kind of spiritless centralization of authority proposed by Robert Heilbroner in his An Inquiry into the Human Prospect.[26] Psychoanalysis can uncover humanity's neuroses. But by itself it cannot fully heal. Sacramental celebration and prayer are crucial to this end. God is a Person experienced through symbolic encounter. This revolutionary revelation of the Hebrew Scriptures and the New Testament remains a touchstone for a sound social ethic for our society.

Much more could be said about the God-problem in light of the Shoah. But in the interest of addressing several other issues, we shall end the discussion at this point and turn to the question of Christianity.

VI. Christology and the Shoah

In the almost quarter century since the Second Vatican Council passed its historic declaration on the church and the Jewish People in its document **Nostra Aetate**, considerable progress has been made on the constructive restatement within the church of the theological relationship between Christianity and the People Israel. Individual theologians both in Europe and America have led the way, but some important developments have occurred in official ecclesiastical pronouncements as well. Paul van Buren, Franz Mussner, Clemens Thoma, A. Roy [and Alice L.] Eckardt and Peter von der Osten-Sacken, to name but a few, have made extremely important contributions in this regard. My own volumes Christ in Light of the Christian-Jewish Dialogue[27] and Jesus and the Theology of Israel[28] are modest attempts to survey recent theological developments and propose the outlines of a new theological model. This model is grounded in several key convictions. They are: [1] that the Christ Event did not invalidate the Jewish faith perspective; [2] that Christianity is not superior to Judaism, nor is it the fulfillment of Judaism as previously maintained; [3] that the Sinai covenant is in principle as crucial to Christian faith expression as the covenant in Christ; [4] that Christianity needs to reincorporate dimensions from its original Jewish context as an integral part of its creed; and [5] that the "uniqueness" of the Christ Event, a limited "uniqueness" at that, consists primarily in the enhanced understanding of the linkage between humanity and divinity and its impact on salvation expressed through what Christians have termed "Incarnation." Whether this new Christian-Jewish relationship is best expressed through the notion of a single covenant notion, as most ecclesiastical documents and some theologians such as van Buren propose, or a double covenant model as Mussner and I would have it, remains an open question. What is not debatable is that in light of the Shoah the church's moral integrity will not allow it to retain the classical supercessionist models of the relationship which generated antisemitism for centuries and which, while not the primary cause of the Shoah as was argued earlier, nonetheless played a decisive role in stimulating public acquiescence to the 'Final Solution'.

Johannes Baptist Metz in particular has stressed the church's responsibility to adjust its basic Christological formulations insofar as they impinge on the fate of the Jewish People in response to the Shoah. He proposes three theses as indispensable for theological reflection in the church in this post-Shoah era: [1] "Christian theology after Auschwitz must--at long last--be guided by the insight that Christians can form and sufficiently understand their identity only in the face of the Jews;" [2] "Because of Auschwitz the statement 'Christians can only form and appropriately understand their identity in the face of the Jews' has been sharpened as follows: 'Christians can protect their identity only in front of and together with the history of the beliefs of the Jews';" and [3] "Christian theology after Auschwitz must stress anew the Jewish dimension in Christian beliefs and must overcome the forced blocking-out of the Jewish heritage within Christianity."[29] Certainly Metz is moving in the right direction in his strong advocacy of these three theses. However, he still needs to apply them much more specifically and in much greater detail to an exposition of the meaning of God and Christ for contemporary Christianity than he has done to date.

Metz is not alone in his failure on the above point. It is generally true of most of the theologians who have undertaken a re-examination of the traditional statements of the Jewish-Christian relationship. While they may be consciously responding to the Shoah through their efforts in this regard, they do little to relate their new Christological statements directly to the Shoah experience and its impact on the God question. And yet, as David Tracy has rightly reminded us, the God question, not the Christ question, is the ultimate theological issue for Christians. A case in point is Paul van Buren who has undertaken the most comprehensive restatement of the covenantal links between the church and the Jewish People yet available. Even in his most recently volume, his constructive Christological statement, fails to treat of the Shoah in any significant way.[30] Rubenstein and Roth are on target in their criticism of van Buren's otherwise monumental contribution on this score.[31]

A few Christian theologians have tried to take up the specific challenge posed by the Shoah for Christological understanding. Lutheran ethicist Franklin Sherman has uncovered in the Cross of Christ "the symbol of the agonizing God." The only legitimate Christology for Sherman in light of the Shoah is one that sees in the Christ Event the revelation of divine participation in the sufferings of people who are in turn summoned to take part in the sufferings of God. "We speak of God after Auschwitz," Sherman insists, "only as the one who calls us to a new unity as between brothers--not only between Jews and Christians, but especially between Jews and Christians."[32] For Sherman, Christ crucified becomes the symbol of the agonizing God. Sherman laments the fact that this symbol of the Cross has become such a source of division, rather than reconciliation, between Jews and Christians throughout history. For, in fact, the Cross points to a very Jewish reality-- suffering and martyrdom.

An Israeli Catholic scholar, Marcel Dubois, O.P., moves in a vein somewhat parallel to that of Sherman.[33] While acutely conscious of the difficulty Christians have in setting the reality of the Shoah within the context of a theology of the Cross, and recognizing that such a linkage may appear as an obscenity to Jews whose sufferings in the Shoah the church helped to perpetrate, Dubois nonetheless feels that this is the direction in which Christian theology ought to move: "....in the person of the suffering servant there appears to take place an effable change. Our vision of Jewish destiny and our understanding of the Holocaust in particular depend on our compassion; the Calvary of the Jewish people, whose summit is the Holocaust, can help us to understand a little better the mystery of the Cross."[34]

Douglas Hall is yet a third Christian theologian focusing post-Shoah Christological interpretations around the Cross. His reflections on the Nazi period of night have left him convinced that only a theology of the Cross can express the thorough meaning of the Incarnation today. This Christological emphasis alone establishes the authentic divine-human link implied in the Word becoming flesh by highlighting the solidarity of God with suffering humanity. Such a Christological direction establishes a soteriology if solidarity which sets up the Cross of Jesus as a point of fraternal union with the Jewish people, as well as with all who seek human liberation and peace. Thus, for Hall as for Sherman, Jesus becomes a potential source of union rather than exclusion between Jews and Christians in this post-Shoah era. "The faith of Israel is incomprehensible," says Hall, "unless one sees at its heart a suffering God whose solidarity with humanity is so abysmal that the 'cross in the heart of God' [H. Wheeler Robinson] must always be incarnating itself in history. Reading the words of Elie Wiesel, one knows, as a Christian, that he bears this indelible resemblance to the people of Israel."[35]

The most comprehensive treatment of the Christology-Shoah link thus far appears in the writings of Jurgen Moltmann, especially The Crucified God. He interprets the Shoah as the most dramatic revelation to date of the fundamental meaning of the Christ-Event--God can save people, including Israel, because through the Cross he participated in their very suffering. To theologize after the Shoah would prove a futile enterprise in Moltmann's view "....were not the Sh'ma Israel and the Lord's Prayer prayed in Ausch- witz itself, were not God himself in Auschwitz, suffering with the martyred and murdered. Every other answer would be blasphemy. An absolute God would make us indifferent. The God of action and success would let us forget the dead, which we still cannot forget. God as nothingness would make the entire world into a concentration camp."[36]

Moltmann adds that the "theology of divine vulnerability" that emerges from a reflection on the Shoah has deep roots in both rabbinic theology and in Abraham Joshua Heschel's notion of divine pathos.

This "theology of divine vulnerability" clearly provides an important starting point for a post-Shoah Christology. For one, it establishes the close link between Christology and the more fundamental God-problem. It like- wise opens up the whole question of dual responsibility--divine and human-- during the Shoah. Too often, as Elie Wiesel has noted, the onus has been placed exclusively on God's shoulders. The Shoah, let it be said clearly, remains a challenge to any overly positive interpretation of human capacity. The Cross emphasis in Shoah theology exposes us to the notion that God had to pay a price during the Shoah for the freedom accorded humanity in the original act of creation.

But there are aspects to a Shoah theology centered on the Cross that leave the sensitive Christian uneasy. Certainly the propriety of the linkage comes into some question when we consider the significant Christian complicity in the Nazi effort. A. Roy Eckardt is especially strong on this point, arguing that it approaches blasphemy to make such a claim. He also believes that "in comparison with certain other sufferings, Jesus' death becomes relatively non-significant."   Another danger Eckardt sees in the Cross Christology model is that it may generate an exaggeratedly "powerless" plan for human living within a religious context that could result in the annihilation of both Jews and Christians.[37] Additionally, Christian theology has always described the Cross as a voluntary act on the part of God and of Jesus. And the Cross can be properly interpreted in a redemptive fashion only when viewed as the culmination and consequence of Jesus' active ministry. The Shoah was neither voluntary nor part of a redemptive mission in any sense. Finally, some doubts have also been raised whether the theology of divine suffering found in Jewish religious thought is as similar to the Shoah Cross theology as Moltmann and Sherman claim. This remains an open question in need of further exploration.

In the final analysis we have to say that Sherman, Hall, and especially Moltmann are collectively responsible for an important breakthrough in understanding the direct connection between the Shoah and Christology. But their perspectives need to be incorporated into a somewhat broader vision, something I have tried to do in my own writings. Understanding the ministry of Jesus as emerging from the heightened sense of divine-human intimacy that surfaced during the Pharisaic revolution in Second Temple Judaism, the Christological claims advanced by the Church in light of that ministry become an expression of a new sense of how profoundly humanity is intertwined in the divine self-definition. The ultimate significance of this Christology lies in its revelation of the grandeur of humanity, a necessary corrective to the demeaning paternalism that often characterized descriptions of the divine-human relationship in the past.

In my view the fear and paternalism previously associated with the statement of the divine-human relationship were at least partially responsible for the attempt by Nazism to produce a total reversal of human meaning, to hearken back to Uriel Tal's analysis, and finally "overpower" the Creator God. Incarnational Christology can help people recognize that they share in the very life and existence of God. The human person remains creature; the gulf between humanity in people and humanity in the Godhead has not been bridged. But it is also clear that a direct link exists; the two humanities can touch. The human struggle for self-identity vis-a-vis the Creator God has come to an end in principle, though its full realization still lies ahead. In this sense one can truly say that Christ continues to bring humankind salvation in its root meaning--wholeness.

With a proper understanding of the meaning of the Christ Event men and women can be healed; they can finally overcome the primal sin of pride, the desire to supplant the Creator in power and status that was at the heart of Nazism. Critical to this awareness is the sense of God's self-imposed limitation as manifested in the Cross. This is where Moltmann's theology becomes absolutely critical, if still incomplete. People now see, through Christ, that their destiny is eternal in their uniqueness and individuality. God will not finally try to absorb them back totally into the divine being. In fact, it has become apparent that God must allow men and women this degree of eternal distinctiveness and freedom of action in order to reach full maturity, to become finally and fully God. This is a viewpoint that bears at least some similarities to the notion of divine self-constriction in the Jewish mystical tradition spoken of earlier.

What I am claiming is that the Shoah represents at one and the same time the ultimate expression of human freedom and of human evil--the two are intimately linked. The initial divine action of creation constituted the liberation of humanity from its total encasement in the Godhead. The Creator God acknowledged that there is need to let go part of divine human- ity in the development of divine creative potential. But that part of God's humanity that now assumed an independent existence was faced with the task of establishing its own identity. At times, particularly during the Nazi era, there arose a strong desire to supplant the Creator. Here lies the roots of human evil. But until the modern age, fear of divine punishment kept such desire in check. But the Enlightenment, Nietzsche and contemporary move- ments for human liberation have changed all that. People began to shed the fear of divine retribution that had controlled human behavior in the past. The Nazis clearly believed they had become the final arbiters of right and wrong. This new sense of freedom, this growing Prometheus Unbound experience, in Western society, coupled with unresolved identity problems, resulted in a catastrophic plan of human destruction in Nazi Germany.

The ultimate assertion of human freedom from God in our time that the Shoah represents may in fact prove the beginning of the final resolution of the conflict. When humanity finally acknowledges the destruction it is capable of producing when it totally rejects the Creator, as the Nazis did during the Shoah, when it recognizes such rejection as a perversion not an affirmation of human freedom, a new stage in human consciousness may be dawning. We may finally be coming to grips with evil at its roots, the centuries-long struggle of the human community to work out its identity by overcoming God. The power of evil will wane only when humankind develops along with a sense of its own inherent dignity because of its links with God through Christ, a corresponding sense of humility occasioned by a searching encounter with the devastation that absence of such humility can occasion. A sense of profound humility evoked by the experience of the healing power present in the ultimate Creator of human power--this is crucial for human survival. On this point of humility as a central response to the Shoah experience I join hands with the ethicist Stanley Hauerwas in his reflections on the event even though we part company on several other of its implications.[38]

Only the integration of this awareness of humility into human conscious-ness will finally overcome evil and neutralize eruptions such as the Shoah in which humanity tries to "elevate" itself above the Creator. This necessary human self-realization will come more easily in light of the understanding of divine vulnerability manifested through the Shoah in such dramatic fashion. It is no longer "ungodly" to express dependence upon others--the Creator has done it. The full maturity vital for the humane exercise of human co-creatorship requires the assertion of this interdependence to which the Nazis were blind.

Let me add that the ultimate personal healing resulting from a proper understanding of Incarnational Christology must also be tied, for full whole-ness and salvation, to the sense of communal interdependence revealed by the Sinai covenant. Here is where the two aspects of the required post-Shoah reformulation of Christology intersect. Any post-Shoah significance for Christology must be stated in the context of Christianity's renewed apprecia-tion of its continuing bonds with the Jewish tradition and the Jewish people. It must also be said that at this point in human history the believing Jew and the believing Christian will likely develop their post-Shoah reflections in somewhat different ways. The Incarnational Christology approach discussed above is meant as the response of a Christian theologian for members of the church. There is no claim that a theological response to the experience is impossible save through Christology. This appears to be a trap into which Moltmann has wandered in The Crucified God.

VII. Ethics After the Shoah

In our previous discussion of the God question in light of the Shoah two major components of any discussion about ethics came to the forefront. The first had to do with how can God truly serve as the ultimate ground for ethics in this post-Shoah age. The second issue, intimately related to the first, revolved around the need for a greater recognition of the vitalistic dimension of human life and its role in ethical behavior. This also involved the recognition that if God were to provide moral grounding for the vitalistic dimension of humanity, this would have to be done through symbolic en-counters with God, principally in community worship. While more can certainly be said about each of these topics, we shall move on to some other issues at this point. Related to our discussion of ethics in this section will also be a consideration of the Shoah's implications for theological metho-dology. As will be seen very quickly, the methodological issues and the ethical questions inevitably impact upon one another.

One important result of the increased theological reflections on the Shoah has been an enhanced appreciation for the significance of history. Its events, including the Shoah, must be taken with great seriousness in any considerations of fundamental theological and ethical beliefs. David Tracy has spoken of how such encounter with the Shoah has personally convinced him of this need which will inevitably demand some alteration in previous theological positions in both Christianity and Judaism. He identifies with the call for a post-Shoah return to history found in the writings of Irving Greenberg and Emil Fackenheim. His exact words are these: "We Christian theologians have honestly come to terms with historical consciousness and historicity; we have developed a theological hermeneutics where the subject matter--the event itself--is once again allowed to rule in theological hermeneutic; we have recognized the Sach-Kritik that the religious event itself demands. But we have not returned to history--the real, concrete thing where events like the Holocaust have happened, where events like the state of Israel do exist."[39]

Johannes Baptist Metz, following up on his three fundamental theses discussed previously, speaks in a similar vein as Tracy. For him, any statement made by Christian theology in our day, any attempt to find meaning for life after the Shoah, must be considered "blasphemy" if it fails to meet the test of this historical event. All post-Shoah Christian theology must be rooted in historical consciousness and in the realization that salvation can be achieved only in alliance with Jews within history: "But this means that we Christians for our own sakes are from now on assigned to the victims of Auschwitz--assigned, in fact, in an alliance belonging to the heart of saving history, provided the word "history" in this Christian expression is to have a definite meaning and not just serve as a screen for a triumphalist metaphysic of salvation which never learns from catastrophes nor finds in them a cause for conversion...."[40]

Two leading feminist theologians, Elisabeth Schussler-Fiorenza and Rebecca Chopp, have also given special attention to the significance of history for theological reflection after the Shoah. Schussler-Fiorenza insists we cannot speak of the suffering of the victims of the Shoah as a "theological metaphor" for all human suffering. Instead, that suffering "must be named in its political particularity. The ideological heart of Nazi-fascism was racism, its ideological catch-word was 'Untermensch,' the less than human, the sub-human being."[41]

Nazism for Schussler-Fiorenza represented an extreme example of the Western capitalistic form of patriarchy, with origins in Aristotelian philosophy and subsequent mediation through Christian theology. The same ancient philosophical system, imported into Christian theology by Thomas Aquinas and others, that first subjugated women as people with "subhuman" nature combined with religiously-rooted bigotry and a new bio-theology to produce the Nazi cataclysm throughout Europe. Overcoming Biblical and theological anti-Judaism thus becomes the first step in the complicated, rather wrenching process of cleansing Western society of its patriarchal basis.

Rebecca Chopp lays particular stress on the profound connection she perceives between Shoah literature and liberation theology, a relationship she terms unique among Western religious writings. Both in her judgment create new theological space which in turn forces upon Christianity a fundamental reconceptualization of its theology.   Christian theology must grapple not merely with individual suffering, but even more with mass suffering. Liberation theology and <u>Shoah</u> literature equally interrupt and disrupt Christianity and Christian theology with the question and the quest "who is this human subject that suffers history?"[42]

Chopp goes on to add that both liberation theology and <u>Shoah</u> literature force us to understand history not merely in terms of abstract notions of evolution or process but primarily in terms of the suffering realities of that history caused by various forms of human exploitation. The history that now must be the basis of theological reflection is not abstract history, but the history of human victims. And the voices and the memory of the tortured, the forgotten, and the dead must become primary resources for Christian anthropology. And, while Chopp does not explicitly articulate this position, one could surmise that she would identify with the direction taken by Schussler-Fiorenza and Tracy, namely, that Biblical anti-Judaism with its inevitable de-humanization of concrete Jewish persons opened the way for Jewish suffering in the <u>Shoah</u> and for the suffering experiences under imperialist colonialism to which liberation theology has been responding.

The argument being advanced by Tracy, Metz, and Chopp about the significance of human history and ethics in all religious statements after the <u>Shoah</u> was actually surfaced in a preliminary form some years earlier by the Austrian Catholic philosopher Friedrich Heer. He insisted that the church's failure to challenge the Nazis in any effective way is symptomatic of how the church has dealt with other manifestations of evil, in particular war and the possibility of a nuclear holocaust. For him, the main problem springs from the church's withdrawal from history: "The withdrawal of the church from history has created that specifically Christian and ecclesiastical irresponsibility towards the world, the Jew, the other person, even the Christian himself, considered as a human being--which was the ultimate cause of past catastrophes and may be the cause of a final catas-trophe in the future."[43]

As Heer sees it, antisemitism is the product of a longstanding and deepseated cancer within Christianity that began to grow in its classical period. The disregard on the part of Christians for the well-being of the Jewish people throughout history, especially between 1918 and 1945, can only be understood as part of a general disregard for humanity and the world. He attributes this attitude to the dominance in Christian theological thinking of what he calls the "Augustinian principle." This attitude views the world under the aspect of sin and ultimately leads to a sense of fatalism and despair about the world. Heer remains convinced that this fatalistic tendency constitutes every bit as much a danger today as it did in the period of the incubation of Nazism. In fact, he argues that millions of contemporary

Christians share the responsibility for preparing the suicide of the church and of humankind in a new holocaust which may be brought about by nuclear warfare while the churches remain silent bystanders: "There is a straight line from the church's failure to notice Hitler's attempt at a 'Final Solution' of the Jewish problem to her failure to notice today's and tomorrow's endeavors to bring about a 'Final Solution' to the human problem. The murder of millions of Jews during the Hitler era anticipated the murder of millions and perhaps hundreds of millions of human beings who would die if the great war returned--a war that could only end in mass murder and genocide."[44]

The only cure for this centuries-long pattern in Christianity, according to Heer, is to abandon the "Augustinian principle" and replace it with a return to the Hebrew Bible's roots of Christ's own piety and even to older roots-- namely, to the original faith of Israel in which people felt themselves to be both God's creatures and responsible partners in the development of the earth.

There are two reservations I have in connection with this call for the return to history. First of all, it must be sensitive to the profound changes in the nature of the God-humanity relationship introduced by the Shoah. I am not sure that Heer has recognized this. Neither have the liberation theologians on whose writings Rebecca Chopp heavily relies. Secondly, this return to history must be accompanied by new explorations into human consciousness, especially the extent to which consciousness harbors the roots of power and evil. None of the Jewish or Christian thinkers we have examined have adequately probed the link between history and human consciousness. We cannot ignore the Freudian/Jungian revolution in our reflections on the Shoah experience. A sustainable ethic after the Shoah will require a new appreciation of the profound connection between history and human consciousness with respect to both human and divine activity. History after the Shoah, as David Tracy has underscored, will revolve not so much about events as about persons, in particular those who, for whatever reason, society has declared to be "non-persons." And part of the process of probing the linkage between history and human consciousness in this post-Shoah era will involved coming to see how the life process in which we all share is seriously harmed by such declarations against certain groups or individuals.

Another important implication for post-Shoah theological interpretation has been suggested by Darrell Fasching. It is directly tied to Tracy's emphasis on post-Shoah history as the history of non-persons. Fasching insists that Christian faith must now be chutzpah [brazenness--Ed.] faith, to borrow an important term from the Jewish tradition. It must be a faith that, like the covenantal faith of the Hebrew Scriptures, understands the God-humanity relationship as one of mutual trust and challenge. Irving Greenberg has correctly insisted, according to Fasching, that the post-Shoah age allows humans ultimate refuge neither in the sacred or the secular. Rather, continuing in the tradition of chutzpah, both God and humanity need to be questioned. For Fasching, authentic faith after the Shoah can be discovered by one measuring rod along--the deed. True believers are those who decry the creation of "non-persons" and work to make such declarations untenable in society. If this faith model had prevailed in Nazi Germany, Fasching is convinced we would have never witnessed the apostasy of so many Christians and the so-called "German Christian" movement would have gone nowhere.

The primary lesson of the Shoah in the mind of Fasching is the centrality of chutzpah faith for human survival. He is convinced that "the world can no longer afford the luxury of unquestioning faith. Unquestioning faith is pagan faith. Unquestioning faith is a nearly universal characteristic of religion throughout the world. Virtually all forms of religion have asked followers to sacrifice their will and surrender themselves to higher reality. And all faith that asks for a total surrender of will is finally not only pagan but demonic, even if it is faith in Jesus or the God of Jesus. For all such faith is a training ground for fanaticism which blurs the distinction between God and the state and leads to the dehumanization of the chosen victims of the state. The only authentic faith is a questioning faith, a faith prepared to call even God into question. The difference between God and the idol is that idols will brook no dissent. The test of authentic faith is the possibility of dissent against all authority in the name of a human dignity which reflects the image of God."[45]

Fasching's contention deserves serious consideration since it is obvious that many Christians supported the Nazi state out of a sense that faith demanded obedience to civil authority. There are examples, however, of Christians with a rather conservative piety not unlike that criticized by Fasching who risked their lives to the point of death in defiance of Nazi policies. And the liberal Christian record terms of social protest during the Nazi era is not outstanding, to say the least, even though liberals had cast aside many of the elements of traditional Christian piety which Fasching holds to be centrally responsible for generating what he calls mass Christian apostasy during the Shoah period. But, in my judgment, he is on to something quite important in his insistence on the primacy of chutzpah faith after the Shoah even if his claims require some adjustment.

Intimately connected to the above two issues is the question of power. For there are those who regard the rejection of all forms of power by the human community as absolutely critical for the realization of human dignity while other commentators on the Shoah take a directly contrary stand--the judicious use of power is unquestionably necessary for the prevention of any future outbreaks of the massive human annihilation that was the Shoah. Neither the Christians nor the Jews with whom we have interacted in this essay have as yet satisfactorily handled this difficult question. Irving Greenberg has undoubtedly been the most direct in positing the relationship between power and the Shoah, although it has entered Richard Rubenstein's more recent writings as well. For Greenberg it would be immoral to abandon the quest for power. "Power inescapably corrupts," he writes, "but its assumption is inescapable after the Holocaust." The only option in the post-Shoah world that will enable us to avoid the repetitions of the human degradation and evil of the Nazi period is to combine the assumption of power with what Greenberg terms the creation of "better mechanisms of self-criticism, correction and repentance." Only in this way can we utilize power "without being the unwitting slave of bloodshed or an exploitative status quo."[46]

Greenberg is correct in stressing that a willingness to use power is indeed a central demand of the Shoah experience, so long as long-established forms of entrenched power in society with the perduring power to create "non-persons" remain intact. A meaningful religious ethic cannot totally reject the use of power in principle at this moment of history, though it certainly may responsibly determine that certain configurations of power [e.g. nuclear weaponry] are totally immoral even when a threat to continued human survival looms large. In this regard, serious questions need to be raised about the argument put forward by Christian ethicist Stanley Hauerwas that humility must be our primary moral response to the experience of the Shoah. Our vision of the post-Shoah God must be one which excludes any divine underwriting of human pretensions but rather stands "capable of calling us from our false actions of power and control."[47]

Though I would join Hauerwas in underlining humility as a crucial post-Shoah human virtue, I am unwilling to grant it the same pre-eminence. Hauerwas fails to take seriously enough the human co-creational role after the Shoah. This failure could prove decisive in the effort to prevent further designations of groups as non-persons on a mass scale. His emphasis on humility without enhanced responsibility could result in people of faith becoming bystanders rather than central actors in human history.

The more recent attempt to reflect on the meaning of the Shoah-power relationship from a Jewish perspective has come from Marc Ellis in several works.[48] Ellis is openly critical of Greenberg's perspective, though he extends this critique to other major Shoah thinkers including Fackenheim, Wiesel, and Rubenstein: "The dynamic balance between Holocaust and empowerment found in their analyses of the Holocaust is lost when they enter the realities of the post-Holocaust world. Empowerment, almost without restraint, becomes the watchword. Greenberg's analysis of the State of Israel as the answer to the Holocaust, as the sign of deliverance, as the redemption out of nothingness destroys the balance. The Jewish people recently liberated from the hell of Nazi Germany can become, in some minds, reluctant heroic warriors charting the historic course of redemption in a hostile world. Though the forms of oppression vary, the world remains essentially the same--hostile to Jewish interest and survival."[49]

As a Christian ethicist viewing this internal Jewish debate [which admittedly has implications far beyond the Jewish community], it appears to me that both make critical points. What Greenberg is ultimately saying, as I see it, is that after the Shoah we cannot rely on divine intervention in human history to protect us, even if we consider ourselves a covenanted people. The Shoah has shattered the foundations of any such divine-human perspective.   And post-Shoah morality must respond to this unparalleled situation. The Jewish community, and by implication all of human-kind, must assume a far greater responsibility for its continued survival.   And this can only be accomplished through the judicious use of power accompanied by the development of self-correcting mechanisms for preventing unwarranted application of this power.   Ellis, on the other hand, is strongly convinced that Jewish survival, human survival, after the Shoah can be ensured only if Jews tie their destiny to other oppressed peoples of the world, not to the current power elite.   And he leaves little doubt that he would include the Palestinians within the ranks of the oppressed.

Greenberg makes another important point in his reflections on power in my judgment, even though he may do it somewhat obliquely. Power assumes such an important ethical role for Greenberg because of his affirmation of the traditional Jewish priority of community survival over individual human rights.   Catholic ethicist David Hollenbach has noted that this remains a distinctive characteristic of both classical Jewish and Islamic ethics.[50] We in the West have been conditioned for the past several centuries to accord the highest place to individual human rights in our vision of public morality. The general Middle Eastern approach, rooted in a strong sense of community identity, makes us terribly uncomfortable.   But somehow we are going to have to incorporate better this classical Jewish/Islamic vision into our overall moral scheme, without totally sacrificing our cherished commitment to individual human rights, if we are to deal fairly with the power question as it pertains to the current situation in the Middle East.

I believe Ellis has put power aside far too easily. On this basic point, my support goes out to Greenberg.   But, while endorsing the basic thrust of Greenberg's ethic of survival, I have serious difficulties with many of the concrete ways he interprets it in his most recent essay on the subject, "The Ethics of Jewish Power."[51]   Though in an earlier publication on the subject he called for the creation of "better mechanisms of self-criticism, correction and repentance" as the only way to employ power "without being the unwitting slave of bloodshed or an exploitative status quo"[52], his application, or more precisely non-application, of this rule to Israeli activities in the West Bank/Gaza since the start of the Intifada is both puzzling and quite disturbing.   At best, one sees an extremely superficial use of this moral principle as Greenberg discusses particular military activities. Little or none of the moral agonizing recognized by Greenberg in the original essay is present in this "uprising-era" piece.   Such an evident lack of sensitivity gives some credence to Ellis' claim that Greenberg in the end transforms the Shoah into a mandate for Jewish survival at any cost.

In addition to the questionable nature of some of Greenberg's specific judgments from a post-Shoah moral perspective, there are three overarching omissions in his approach. The first is his failure to ask whether there might not be significantly more responsible ways of pre-serving public order. Even some Jewish supporters of Israel acknowledge that terrible mistakes were made from the standpoint of peace-keeping operations. New techniques have been developed which the Israeli army chose to ignore. Secondly, and far more importantly, Greenberg fails to realize that preserving public order is not usually best accomplished through the heavy hand of power alone. The words of the leading Catholic thinker Romano Guardini written out of personal experience of the Nazi era need to be weighed seriously by Greenberg: "In the coming epoch, the essential problem will no longer be that of increasing power--though power will continue to increase at an even swifter tempo--but of curbing it. The core of the new epoch's intellectual task will be to integrate power into life in such a way that man can employ power without forfeiting his humanity, or to surrender his humanity to power and perish."[53]

Finally, nowhere in "The Ethics of Power" does Greenberg make an abiding commitment to pursue a peaceful resolution of the current conflict with the Palestinians--an essential ingredient of any current evaluation of Israel's use of power in the necessary maintenance of public order in the West Bank/Gaza. Devoid of such clear commitment, the misapplications of power that have been part of the Israeli-Palestinian relationship since the Intifada assume an even greater moral seriousness.

There are other theological and ethical issues that continue to be part of the overall religious discussion of the Shoah. To bring this essay to a close, I would simply like to mention some of them without elaboration. They include the issue of the role of religion in the public sphere. Reflecting on the Shoah some Christian writers such as Franklin Littell and Clyde Man-schreck have warned that a Nazi-like commitment to "naked state sov-ereignty" can easily take hold in nations where religious influence has been totally excluded from the public culture.[54] Franklin Littell has also been influential in the recently developing effort to establish criteria for an "early warning system" for genocide and holocaust.[55] Lastly, there has been an ongoing discussion, intensified by recent research, into Christian under-standings of the meaning of the church. Did a certain vision of the church as inherently tied to a conservative political order for its own survival make it possible for Christians to come to regard Jews as "unfortunate expendables" [Nora Levin] or "outside the universe of moral obligation" [Helen Fein] when that survival was threatened?[56]

The centrality of the issues discussed above give ample evidence of the Shoah's continuing relevance for theology in our time. The event was the child of many of the forces most influential in the shaping of contemporary Western culture. And these forces are alive in nearly every part of the world, making the Shoah something far more than a Western phenomenon even though that was its actual locale. Any faith perspective that believes it can avoid the issues raised by the Shoah or summarily dispense with them is opening itself up to self-destruction. Both Christians and Jews for their own well-being, for their mutual enrichment, for the safety and sustainability of creation, must continue to wrestle with them even though we many never penetrate the veil of darkness that covers the event.

For Rosemary Radford Reuther, whose own work Faith and Fratricide: The Theological Roots of Anti-Semitism [1974] may be perceived equally as "foundational" as that of Richard Rubenstein's After Auschwitz: Radical Theology and Contemporary Judaism [1966], in delineating the need for the centrality of a reformulated Christology in light of the Shoah, her current re-examination of both Jewish and Christian thinkers reveals a critique not previously encountered among Christians: the use of Shoah theology as a means of Jewish empowerment in American and in Israel, particularly with regard to the Palestinians.   Here, Reuther moves beyond the Shoah in focusing on the Jewish People now as "normal human beings, capable, like any other people, of taking power in a dominating way and using it to make victims of other people." The questions she asks--"Who is going to be the victim of our liberation? Who is to be enslaved by our redemption?"--are, in essence, part of her theology of consistent universalism, not allowing either the particularism of Jewish thinking or the philosemitism of Christian thinking, either fundamentalist or liberal, to erect barriers to a reality leading to disengagement of Jews, Christians, and/or Arabs.[1]

THEOLOGICAL AND ETHICAL REFLECTIONS ON THE SHOAH:

Getting Beyond the Victim-Victimizer Relationship

Rosemary Radford Reuther

I. Introduction: Redemption through Genocide

In the midst of the Second World War, Adolf Hitler, leader of the German people, conducted a systematic campaign to exterminate European Jewry. This genocidal campaign was directed at all Jews, on the basis of what was presumed to be a shared racial nature. It did not matter if the Jew was male or female, infant or elderly, culturally assimilated into German or other European societies or set apart by traditional Jewish dress, speech and way of life, secular or religious. Even if the Jew was a convert to Christianity did not finally matter, although there was some distinctions made on this ground at first. For Hitler and Nazi ideology, a Jew was a Jew. All belonged to one racial nature, which Nazism regarded as inimical to the national 'purity' of the Aryan race.

In Hitler's paranoid worldview these two races, Aryan and Jew, were set apart, not simply as superior and inferior types of human beings, but as ontologically opposite species of good and evil. The Aryan was exalted above the merely human to the heroic; the Jew was sunk below the creaturely to the pestilent and the demonic. To exterminate the Jew was, in Hitler's mad fantasy world, to redeem the Aryan from the dangers of 'contamination' by a disease of mental, moral and physical weakness and to inaugurate the Third Reich, the Germanic millennial age of undiluted virility.

This crusade of redemption through genocide almost succeeded. Six million Jews were annihilated. This meant not only more than one-third of the Jews of the world at that time, but also ninety percent of the rabbis and religious scholars of Eastern and Western European Judaism. The Shoah pulled up an entire culture by the roots. Although individuals may survive from these communities of European Jewry and return to live in small numbers in places like Warsaw or Amsterdam, the cultural communities of Jewry that existed in these cities before the Second World War can never be reconstituted. The Nazi Shoah was more than the killing of a large number of individuals. It was ethnocide, the effort to destroy a people as a cultural entity.

The more traditional Jews of the Eastern shtetls [villages--Ed.] were the least likely to escape. Although remnants of these people with their traditional culture may have been transplanted to America or to Israel, a void has been left in the heart of the human community of peoples that can never be filled. Like the extinction of one of the species of creation, when a national community is exterminated, a distinct and irreplaceable part of reality has been destroyed, never to be restored.

This enormity happened in the 'heartland' of Western Christian Europe: the land of Goethe, Beethoven, and Mozart; of Kant, Hegel and Schelling; of the founders of modern Christian theology, Schleiermacher, Ritschl and Troeltsch. Germany was the center of the Christian Enlightenment, from which flowed the classics of modern European literature and music, philosophy, theology and Biblical studies. It happened with the passive acquiescence or active collaboration of most European Christians and with no decisive protest from church leadership, Catholic or Protestant.

Many individual Christians sought to save their Jewish neighbors at the risk of their own lives, but official church leadership did not mobilize in united protest. Even the Confessing Church in Germany, under the intrepid leadership of theologians like Karl Barth and Dietrich Bonhoeffer, were primarily concerned to protest against a Nazi 'cultural Christianity' and failed to focus on Nazi antisemitism as an issue.[2]

II. From Story to Theology

For both Jews and Christians in the post-War period, the Shoah throws the viability of their religious traditions into question, but in quite different ways. Yet it took more than two decades for theological reflection on the Shoah to begin to be articulated, and for Jews and some Christians to recognize that theological business as usual could not continue after this fissure had opened up in the world.

For almost two decades there was virtual silence from theologians, Jewish or Christian. Perhaps this was because, before there could be Shoah theology, the Shoah had to be articulated as story. Meaningless chaos must be shaped as meaning, even if only as the meaning of meaninglessness, the speaking about the unspeakable. Elie Wiesel's first book, Night, was published in Yiddish in 1956 and became available in French in 1958 and in English in 1960.

The first Jewish religious thinker to name the Shoah as a major crisis for traditional Jewish theology was Richard Rubenstein in the mid-1960's. Rubenstein, a non-establishment Jewish religious scholar, published his foundational book, After Auschwitz: Radical Theology and Contemporary Judaism in 1966. In this volume, Rubenstein questioned the very possibility of faith in God after the Shoah.

Emil Fackenheim, a German Jew transplanted to Canada courtesy of British internment camps for German refugees, had been writing primarily on Hegel and religious philosophy, with no reference to the Shoah. As he himself admits in an article published in May, 1970, in The Christian Century, before 1967, he was "at work on a theology that sought to show that nothing unprecedented could call into question the Jewish faith--that it is essentially immune to all secular events between Sinai and the Messianic days."[3] Fackenheim took up Rubenstein's challenge and began to write about the possibility of religious faith after the Shoah.

Rubenstein, in a reply to this article by Fackenheim, also published in The Christian Century [July 29, 1970], said that Fackenheim was the first Jewish theologian to "agree with me concerning the unique and decisive character of Auschwitz for Jewish religious life." Rubenstein said "at the time I wrote After Auschwitz, one could search through almost everything written by contemporary establishment [Jewish] theologians without finding the slightest hint that they were living in the same century as Auschwitz or the rebirth of Israel."[4] [There is an unconscious irony in the appearance of this exchange in a journal named The Christian Century, for this journal was given this name in 1900, in order to signify the expected triumph of Christianity in the twentieth century.]

By the early 1970's the Shoah had become a key theme of theological reflection for Jewish and Christian theologians. In 1974 a major conference, held at Saint John the Divine Cathedral in New York City, brought together the leading Jewish and Christian thinkers that had made the Shoah a central lens for viewing and revisioning their religious traditions.[5] For Jews, particularly for American Reform Jews, the Shoah would become the new normative theology, central to modern Jewish identity. For Christian theologians a focus on the Shoah was more the specialty of a few thinkers rather than a central paradigm. But it was increasingly incorporated into the thought of major Christian theologians.

This difference is understandable [if not excusable] since the Shoah challenged traditional Jewish and Christian religious self-understandings in quite different ways. For Jews, the Shoah, as an attempted extermination of Jews as a people, the central issue was theodicy. If God is in charge of the world, and is the God who elected Israel as his people, how could such an event take place? Is faith in the God of Jewish self-understanding still possible after Auschwitz? If not, what is the nature of Jewish collective identity?

For Christianity the issue was less the existence or goodness of God than the goodness and redemptive value of Christianity. If Christianity played a major role in fomenting the Shoah, how can Christians continue to affirm the redemptive essence of Christianity? For Christians the issue was the culpability, not only of Christians, but of key Christian doctrines, in this evil. Christology was the central problem for a Christianity after the Shoah. If faith in Jesus as the Christ, the Messiah of Israel, was a major ideological factor in promoting anti-Judaism in Christian cultures and societies, is such a belief still tenable?

III. Jewish Shoah Theology

For Richard Rubenstein, Auschwitz brings to an end the possibility of belief in the God of traditional Judaism. This God was understood as the Lord of History, providentially in charge of historical events and directing them to an ultimately redemptive end. Belief in the God of providential guidance of history demands a theodicy to justify the ways of God to humanity. The question of theodicy is how evil is possible if God is both good and in charge of history. If God allows evil, then God is not wholly good. But if evil happens because God cannot prevent it, then God is not wholly omnipotent.

Classical theodicy tried to solve this conundrum by declaring that there are hidden reasons for God's permission of evil. Out of evil God brings final good, although His full design is hidden from our eyes. The traditional strategy of the Jewish tradition for explaining the evils that befall the Jewish people is to assert that these evils are punishment for sin. God is chastening His people. When they learn from this chastening and repent of their sins, becoming wholly obedient to God's commandments, then redemption and blessings will follow.

A minority tradition supplemented this interpretation by a martyr theology. Through its sufferings the people of Israel is atoning for the sins of its people, perhaps the sins of all people. Exemplary figures, such as prophets and holy teachers, could be seen as playing the paradigmatic role in this work of atonement. Christianity took its interpretation of Jesus's atoning suffering and death from this martyr theology of first century Judaism.[6]

For Rubenstein no such rationalization of evil as a means to future good can justify the enormous unjust suffering of the Shoah or vindicate divine justice and goodness in the light of so many innocent Jewish victims. No possible sins could justify such vast destruction of Jewish people, people selected only because they were Jews, without regard to any actual particularities of either morality or immorality. If God could be imagined as willing the 'final solution' of destruction of the people of Israel, how can such a God be the God of Israel? The Shoah breaks the link between the God of Israel and the people of Israel as God's chosen people.

For Rubenstein a God who could will the destruction of the Jews in punishment for even the greatest sins cannot be claimed as good. If such a God exists, then He is a cosmic sadist. One cannot honor or hope in such a God, but only recoil from Him in horror. According to Rubenstein, God is dead after Auschwitz. Henceforth Jews must cease to look beyond immanent historical events for meaning and justice, in an effort to make sense out of senseless evil. There is no divine plan that will work out for the best in the end. Such faith in God must be renounced, rather than attempting to justify God's justice in the face of the <u>Shoah</u>.

Rubenstein also believed that Jews should abandon the idea of their special election or chosenness. They should cease to see themselves as paradigmatic of humanity in relation to ultimate reality. Such notions of Jewish specialness have created cycles of self-inflation, gentile jealousy-- expressed either as hostility or as over-identification with Jews--and cataclysmic violence against Jews, leading to crises of Jewish self-doubt. Jews made the mistake of allowing gentiles to 'overhear' this concept of Jewish chosenness and thereby to wish to identify with it.

Rubenstein sees Christianity as the major example of this tragedy of a gentile identification with the Jewish concept of divine chosenness. By attempting to claim this idea for themselves, they must deny this status as still intact for Jews. Christian antisemitism is the negative side of a competitive Christian relationship to Jewish self-understanding of divine election.[7] Rubenstein would affirm Jewish particularity, but as one par- ticularity among others. Jews are unique as every people in their own way are unique. Rubenstein, in these remarks, seeks to 'normalize' Jewish identity, as one cultural community among others.

In keeping with his Freudian interpretation of collective psychology, Rubenstein views civilization pessimistically. In a subsequent book, <u>The Cunning of History</u>, he denies the uniqueness of the <u>Shoah</u>. The <u>Shoah</u> should be seen as an extreme expression of a general trend in modern bureaucratic and technological societies and sovereign states.[8] While moder- nity has brought the human capacity to express technological skills to the highest level or prowess, it is at the same time perfecting the tech- niques of mass murder.

The Nazi extermination of the Jews did not happen through outbreaks of irrational passion, but was the bureaucratic realization of an ideological theory. The technological metropolis is moving, more and more, toward this finale as necropolis, the annihilation of the human through objectification. Rubenstein speaks of himself as becoming a political conservative, suggest- ing that it would be better to avoid preserving too many redundant people through liberal humanitarianism that the state will feel the need to annihi- late.[9]

However, underneath Rubenstein's pessimistic account of history and technological civilization there lurks a romantic impulse to break free of historical alienation and return to identification with spontaneous libidinal 'nature.' The Jew of historic rabbinic Judaism, with his belief in a tran- scendent God of commandments, rewards and punishments, is the alienated Jews, a type of the alienated 'man' of civilization. This Jew was in a state of exile or estrangement from his own embodiment, both from his own body and from the natural world around him.

But, lurking underneath this ethical Jew, with his self-estranging system of law and his punishing God, there remains the natural Jew, longing to be integrated into the rhythms of nature, the circling seasons and the life cycle. This natural or 'pagan' Jewishness Rubenstein sees as derivative from the Canaanite background of ancient Hebrew religion. This paganism Judaism repressed but also preserved in its festivals, by imposing a historical meaning upon the earlier festivals of the agricultural year.

It is through this Freudian lens that Rubenstein interprets the anti-nomian elements in Zionism over against rabbinic Judaism. Rubenstein's views of Zionism seemed to have been particularly influenced by a fringe Canaanite Movement in Zionism which saw the return from exile as a reclaiming of the pre-Jewish Canaanite identity.[10] The return to the land expresses a desire to return to spontaneous relation to the body, both one's own body and its sexuality and to the embodiment of the community in its own national land. The Israelis with their agricultural dances are reclaiming the peasant Hebrew underneath the law-bound urban Jew.

Rubenstein, in his book My Brother Paul, also interpreted Christianity, specifically Pauline anti-nomianism, in terms of this desire to escape from civilization and its discontents.[11] Such a return to the body also shifts the understanding of the divine. The Jew returned from self-estrangement rediscovers the real deity of nature which Judaism rejected, not the Lord of history, but the cosmic Matrix, the devouring primal Mother from which all things spring and to which they return at death.

This concept of the divine Matrix as the real deity of nature coincides with Rubenstein's description of himself as a 'Catholic' rather than a 'Protestant' Jew. What binds him to Judaism is not its ethical command-ments, but rather its cultic life, built on the old agricultural festivals. These are the rituals that bind a community together through collective experiences, not in order to solve the human dilemma of good and evil, but rather to comfort one another in shared affliction in the midst of ultimate meaninglessness.[12]

While other Jewish thinkers agreed that the Shoah must be seen as a major challenge to traditional Judaism, Rubenstein's reading of this crisis through a post-Freudian interpretation of rabbinic law as repression in-furiated most Jews. Although Emil Fackenheim agreed with Richard Rubenstein that the Shoah had created a crisis for traditional Jewish theol-ogy, he vehemently disagreed with Rubenstein's Freudian outlook and his demythologizing of Jewish election. For Fackenheim, it is blasphemous to say that the Shoah is one expression among others of "tendencies of Western civilization in the twentieth century."[13]

As Fackenheim developed his own approach to Shoah theology, he would reject all comparisons between the Shoah and other events of modern mass violence, such as the genocide of American Indians, the enslavement of African Blacks, with its results of mass death, the violence of the war in Vietnam or the bombing of Hiroshima and Nagasaki.

For Fackenheim the Shoah was an evil of a different order than any other human evil. It is evil without remainder or purpose, evil for evil's sake. It stands out beyond all other relative evils as unique, as absolute evil. The Shoah also calls Jews back to Jewish uniqueness and particularity, from all desires to be assimilated into generic universals of human progress. Jewish faith must be rebuilt by recommitment to this unique Jewish status of chosenness and its ongoing continuation.

It is by raising Jewish children after the Shoah that Jews reaffirm their faith in the continuing life of the people Israel. By raising Jewish children Jews refuse to give new victories to Hitler.[14]   This is a conscious and collective commitment. It carried over also to the state of Israel. By committing oneself to the defense of the state of Israel one expresses one's determination that the people Israel shall survive as a nation.

Such commitments to Jewish survival, for Fackenheim, have critical theological significance. Through dedication to Jewish survival, the eclipsed face of God can be restored. The relation between God and Israel has been reversed. Where once the existence of God guaranteed the existence of Israel, today the continued existence of the people Israel guarantees the existence of God. For Fackenheim Jewish survival makes no distinctions between religious and secular Jews. Such distinctions were abolished by the fires of Auschwitz. Simply by continuing to affirm themselves as Jews, by raising Jewish children to continue to affirm themselves as Jews, Jews witness against Satan. They overcome the triumph of Satan in Hitler's death camps, and so prove that the bond between God and the Jewish people is stronger than the power of Satan.

Fackenheim does not dispute Rubenstein's assertion that one cannot construct a theodicy of the Shoah itself. The Shoah eclipses the presence of God and cannot be justified by any redeeming purpose. But the presence of God can be restored through the redemptive acts of Jewish familial and national survival. For Fackenheim, the ongoing existence of the State of Israel became the primary means and expression of this redemption of the God of Israel.

In an essay entitled "The Holocaust and the State of Israel: Their Relation," Fackenheim constructs a theological connection between the two which is total and unbreakable. This is not a relationship of moral causality. Fackenheim would not say that the state of Israel happened because of the Shoah, either in the sense that God allowed the state of Israel to come about to redeem the Jewish people from the Shoah, or in the sense that the world community supported the emergence of this state as recompense for the Shoah. Rather the relation between the two realities is established by the continuous and total response of Jews themselves.

By total commitment to the defense and security of the state of Israel, Jews negate the threat to their existence of the Shoah. This relation between the state of Israel and the Shoah must be exclusive, undiluted by any other concerns for general human goods and evils. As he put it "the heart of every authentic response to the Holocaust---religious or secular--is a commitment to the autonomy and security of the state of Israel."[15]

For Fackenheim the founding of the state of Israel is "the beginning of the dawn of our redemption."[16] In traditional rabbinic thought the Jewish people would be restored to their homeland by an act of divine intervention in history, the coming of the Messiah. This coming might be spurred on by religious acts of prayer, repentance, and strict observance of Torah. Fackenheim concurs with modern Jewish thinkers, such as Rabbi Abraham Isaac Kook, who not only emphasize the efficacy of human redemptive acts in bringing about the Messianic times, but abolish distinctions between religious acts and secular acts such as land settlement.[17]

Human effort, in effect, can overcome divine inaction and make the beginning of redemption within history. Fackenheim believes that the heroic acts that have gone into the founding of the state of Israel cannot be explained by human causation within ordinary historical developments. There is a miraculous element to such extraordinary efforts that could reunite a people scattered all over the world, rent apart by centuries of cultural separations, which could revive an ancient language and make it a modern national language and create a powerful state capable of defending itself against overwhelming odds. Such heroic acts are, for Fackenheim, proof that Zionism is a theophany of the Jewish collective will "in touch with the Absolute."[18]

Fackenheim makes a direct symbolic identification between resistance to Hitler, resistance to the Arabs and resistance to Satan. For Fackenheim the Arabs are the current manifestation of Satan that seek, like the Nazis, the extermination of the Jewish people. By fighting the Arab enemies of Israel, one reverses the victories of Satan, of Hitler, of the past. In his essay Fackenheim paints two complementary pictures of the Jew face to face with absolute evil in the form of the Shoah. One is the calm, dignified rabbi who insists on praying the Kaddish [Memorial Prayer--Ed.] for his flock before the Nazis begin to shoot them down in their mass grave. The second picture is that of a Jewish butcher who leapt out of that grave and sunk his teeth into the throat of the Nazi officer, hanging on until the Nazi died. These two redemptive acts complete one another; the one is that of transcendent goodness in the face of absolute evil, the other is that of the absolute will to refuse to let evil have the final victory.[19]

For Fackenheim, the Israelis today represent, in collective form, the will power of the butcher who leapt out of the grave, while the Arabs are the collective manifestation of the Nazi officer into whose throat they sink their teeth. Through this determination to defeat their enemies, Jewish powerlessness is overcome, and Jewish redemption is inaugurated. Even in the midst of the Shoah, the flame of Jewish will to live sprang up, foreshadowing the will made powerful in the state of Israel.

For example, in 1943, Mordecai Anielewicz, a leader of the Warsaw ghetto uprising, perished in the flames, satisfied that Jewish passivity had been breached and Jewish self-defense had begun. That same year a kibbutz in Palestine was named for him. Five years later a small group of members of Kibbutz Yad Mordecai [Yad=hand--Ed.] held off the Egyptian army in a battle critical for the survival of the Jewish state. In this event Fackenheim sees the spirit of the Warsaw uprising resurrected and present in the battle of Israelis against the Arabs that threatened their state.[20]

Other Jewish thinkers, in their response to the Shoah, were not willing to make such a total and exclusive relation between the negation of Auschwitz and the new power of the state of Israel, nor to sever the redemption of the Jews so completely from concern for the redemption of human communities. The writings of Irving Greenberg in the mid-1970's became the leading example of a more balanced approach, freed from the extremes of both Rubenstein and Fackenheim. His talk, "Cloud of Smoke, Pillar of Fire: Judaism, Christianity and Modernity after the Holocaust" was the keynote address of the Saint John the Divine conference in 1974.[21]

In this address Greenberg discussed the challenges to both traditional Jewish theology and traditional Christian theology by the Shoah. Both Judaism and Christianity, he said, were religions of redemption. Both hope that the evils of human history will be finally overcome by divine redemptive action. Both base their hopes that life will win over death, good over evil, on foundational paradigms of redemption in the past that shape subsequent ways of life and self-understanding.

For the Jews, the foundational paradigmatic event is the exodus from slavery in Egypt and the giving of the covenant on Sinai. For Christians it is Easter, the revelation of the resurrection of the Crucified One. In the light of Easter, the crucifixion is remembered, not as meaningless evil, but as an act of divine atonement for human sin. Both religions insulate themselves from further crises of meaning or revelations of God by living between this foundational paradigm and the expected fulfillment of messianic deliverance at the end of history.

The Shoah challenges both of these Jewish and Christian strategies of insulation from history. For Jews the Shoah threatens the basic faith in a God who has entered into a covenant with the Jewish people. There can be no covenant if their is no covenant people. There can be no God of the covenant if that God could will or allow the people of the covenant to be exterminated.

But the Shoah offers an even more devastating challenge to Christianity, for Christians have not been innocent victims, but collaborators with the Shoah. Christianity was the major source of the 'teaching of contempt' for Jews and Judaism that was translated into secular terms by Nazi racial antisemitism. Christianity did not only hope for a future deliverance from evil, but believed that it had already received the down-payment on the messianic advent in Jesus's death and resurrection. But a Christianity which could use its faith in Christ to foment hatred against Jews, leading to pogroms and to Nazi attempted genocide, is a creed whose claims to possess the beginnings of redemption through this same Christ has lost credibility. Belief in Jesus as the Christ has become a font of evil, not the beginning of redemption.

Greenberg also perceives in the Shoah a challenge to modern secular messianism as well, the redemptive claims of the Enlightenment, of scientific rationalism and liberal universalism. These secular gods of modern civilization failed in the death camps. The claims of progress through science and technology were turned into a means for racist de-struction. Science provided the tools for mass murder. Nor did world Jewry rise to the occasion, according to Greenberg. Jews outside of Europe [in America] proved more concerned about their well-being in their own country than with rescuing their threatened sisters and brothers in Europe.[22]

The failure of human projects of redemption, religious and secular, is experienced as an absence of the divine presence in the modern world. We live in the time of the silence of God. For Greenberg this divine absence and silence does not justify a denial of God's existence. Greenberg speaks more in the mystical language of Elie Wiesel, rather than the demythologizing language of Richard Rubenstein. We have entered into a time of profound silence that no longer knows how to speak adequately about God. The test of adequate language about God has become the burning children of the crematoria. Today any statement about God or about religious truth must be tested by the light of the burning children. Any religious statement that cannot be uttered in the presence of these innocent victims cannot be uttered at all.

For Greenberg the Shoah has shattered all certainties about how God is acting in history. Today we can only have 'moment faiths' that spring from the tentative human acts of redemptive concern. New ways of speaking about God must grow experimentally from such concrete human redemptive acts. Greenberg wishes to speak cautiously of what such acts are, not with the tones of absolute commands issued from Sinai characteristic of Fackenheim. Humans have to demonstrate by real actions on behalf of life that faith in human goodness is still possible. Through building up signs of commitment to life, one can also begin to posit that there is a divine life and goodness that is stronger than evil and violence.

In 1974 Greenberg saw commitment to the state of Israel as one such sign that hope is possible. This shows that Jews have arisen from the Shoah to affirm their collective survival. The state of Israel also brings to an end all those efforts to snuff out Jewish collective life that began 1900 years ago with the Roman victory over the Jewish national uprisings and their destruction of Jerusalem. But, unlike Fackenheim, Greenberg wished to balance concerns for the welfare of Jews in Israel with concerns for the welfare of Jews through the world in the diaspora. He also wished to balance particularity and universalism, concern for Jewish welfare with concern for welfare of others.

Jews today, together with people of all human religious and secular cultures, have to seek to overcome the denigrating stereotypes that denied full and equal human dignity to one another. "This," Greenberg says, "is the overriding command and essential criterion of religious existence today," not to create another matrix of inter-group hostility that could lead to another genocide. Only by joining together in the work of rehabilitation of the image of God in the face of other human beings can we also rehabilitate the presence of God in our midst in history.[23]

Not all major Jewish thinkers, however, were willing to concede the claim that the Shoah had created a major crisis in faith in the God of Israel and the continuing claims of that God on Jewish life through the Torah. Orthodox Jewish theologian, Eliezer Berkovits, would say that the main question raised by the Shoah is not "Where was God?" but, rather, "Where was man?" Berkovits, in his 1973 volume Faith After the Holocaust, explained the possibility of radical evil in history by the nature of God's creative act of a reality separate from Godself.[24] In creating the world God makes a voluntary withdrawal of divine omnipotence from the sphere of creation in order to make room for human freedom and choice.

The Shoah is the extreme example of the human misuse of freedom to make evil choices, rather than good choices. But this extreme example of the human capacity to choose evil does not disturb the fundamental framework for the Jewish understanding of God and the path to which God calls us.

Other less traditional Jewish religious thinkers who had come out of the anti-war movement of the 1960's, such as civil rights activist turned religious thinker Arthur Waskow, sought to make connections between the Shoah and the threat of nuclear war. Waskow seeks to restate the moral and mystical connection between Jewish particularity and universal humanity by seeing the Jewish people as a paradigmatic people who have gone ahead of the rest of humanity and tested the threat of annihilation that now looms over all humanity in nuclear war.

Waskow's symbolic linking of the fires of Auschwitz and the fires of the holocaust that threaten us all in nuclear weapons even suggests a martyr role for the Jewish victims of the death camps. God, in some sense, 'planned' the Shoah to avert the ultimate holocaust from humanity as a whole. By entering the incinerator first and demonstrating its effects, the Jewish victims call all people into solidarity to avoid the "fire next time" that will destroy us all.[25] Such mystical connections in Waskow's thoughts are strained. Can such speculations that the Jews are God's chosen avante garde, to avert humanity's threatened destruction, pass Greenberg's test of religious assertions utterable in the presence of burning children?[26]

IV. Christian Shoah Theology

Christian responses to the Shoah have been slower to develop than Jewish ones. As mentioned before, Christian theologians who have made the Shoah a central theme of their thought remain isolated individuals; they have not become a theological movement. It is true that church bodies, both Catholic and Protestant, have felt the need to respond collectively to the Shoah. During the Second Vatican Council, in the first half of the 1960's, there was a major discussion of how the Shoah must impel Catholic Christianity to take a critical look at its heritage of anti-Judaism.

In the document on the relation of the Catholic Church and other religions, the section on relations to the Jewish people specifically repudiated the ancient Christian charge of deicide. The death of Jesus was said to be the particular responsibility of certain Jews and gentiles in the first century. It is also a paradigm for all humanity's apostasy from God. But there can be no inference from the death of Jesus of any special or inheritable guilt of all Jews.[27]

Protestant responses to the Shoah have focused on the question of mission to the Jews. This was central to the statement of the German Evangelical Church issued in 1975.[28] This statement confessed the historical complicity of Christianity with antisemitism. It also made a link between antisemitism and anti-Zionism. Not only must Christians oppose antisemitism in their own nations, but they must also support the independence and security of the state of Israel. Such support for the state of Israel is not simply a recognition of a human need of the Jewish people, like all people, for a secure homeland, but it is an event in the salvation history of the people of God.

Such a statement suggested that the return of Israel to its national homeland was, in some sense, a fulfillment of prophecy and the beginning of redemption. Yet this German Christian statement failed to reject the thesis of the superior salvific status of Christianity. It did not reject mission to the Jews, but remained committed to the idea that full salvation for the Jews awaits their conversion to Christ. Thus, by implication, the return of the Jews to the Holy Land remains linked with a Christian messianic scenario of a final victory of Christ.[29]

A number of Christian denominations have developed statements on Jewish-Christian relations that seek to repudiate antisemitism. They have also developed educations programs and revisions of liturgical and catechetical material to purge their teachings of negativity to Jews and Judaism.[30] Yet, generally speaking, such revisions of Christian thought, to purge it of antisemitism, have not seen the Christian view of God present in Christ as deeply shaken by such revisions.

For those Christian theologians who have taken the Shoah and the critique of Christian anti-Judaism as central themes of their thought, the issue of Christology has been the critical problem. Is it possible to continue to believe that Jesus is the Christ, the fulfillment of the Jewish hopes for the Messiah, and yet purge Christianity of antisemitism?

In the book which I published in 1974, Faith and Fratricide: The Theological Roots of Anti-Semitism, this question of Christology was central.[31] As I put it in that volume, is it possible to affirm that Jesus is the Christ without at the same time teaching a negated and supercessionary relation to Judaism, as an incomplete faith that failed to accept its own 'fulfillment' in Christ? In that book I defined antisemitism as the "left hand" of Christology. The negation of Judaism is the shadow side of the affirmation that Jesus is the Christ. This relation goes back to the earliest roots of Christian faith. The two are interwoven already in the New Testament.[32]

Christian symbolism constructed a series of negations of Jews and Judaism: Judaism as the 'old' covenant, superceded by the church as the new covenant; Judaism as an ethnic particularistic religion, superceded by Christianity as a universal, inclusive religion; Judaism as outward letter, external conformity to law, in contrast to Christianity as spirit, as obedience to God informed by inward spiritual power or 'grace.' In each of these theological dualisms Christian self-affirmation of its superior and higher spiritual status is built on a corresponding negation of Judaism as its incomplete or even antithetical 'other.'

Christian theology was built from its earliest days, as a break-away Jewish sect that became gentile, on a competitive relation to Judaism over who is the true and final chosen people of God. This religious rivalry was translated in the fourth century, when Christianity assumed power as the favored religion of the Christianized Roman empire, into a series of ec-clesiastical and imperial laws that relegated Jews to a permitted but de-spised status in Christian societies. It is this fifteen centuries of theologi-cally-based hostility to Jews, incarnated in political, social and cultural systems in Christian societies, that is the background of modern European antisemitism.

Foundational doctrines of Christian faith, their belief that Jesus is the Messiah of Jewish hope and that the Church is the New Covenant, the New Israel, that supercedes the old Israel, are the ideological matrix out of which European antisemitism emerged. Thus Christian purgation of antisemitism must struggle both against the effects of its teaching in social antisemitism, but also it must grapple with these teachings themselves.

In the concluding chapter of that volume I outlined what I saw where the key shifts in the interpretation of Christian theology, particularly in Chris-tology, necessary to overcome theological anti-Judaism. I suggested that the key to a Christology without antisemitism is a theology of hope that sees Jesus's messianic identity as proleptic and contextually limited, not as absolute, universal, final and fulfilled. Both of these two steps, to be proleptic and to be contextually limited, are necessary to a reinterpretation of Christian hope without its antisemitic shadow side.

By proleptic, I mean that the experience of Jesus as messianic announcer, crucified by his antagonists in his Jewish and Roman imperial contexts, resurrected in hope, anticipated, but does not fulfill, our final deliverance from antagonistic relations. We can affirm the truth of our hope of that prophetic announcer of God's coming redemption. But the fulfillment, the overcoming of violence and injustice, are as much ahead of us today as they were ahead of that popular Jewish teacher two thousand years ago. Chris-tians as much as Jews struggle with an unresolved history, holding on to our past paradigmatic experience as the basis of our hope that evil will not have the last word and God will win in the end.

But it is not enough to simply admit that salvation is incomplete. Chris-tians must also accept the contextually limited relevance of their theological symbols and the historical experience on which they are based. Remember-ing Jesus, his life and death, are the breakthrough experiences that found our particular people, the Christian people. They are the paradigms drawn from our interpreted experience that mediate hope in the midst of adversity to us. But this does not mean that they are the only paradigms that may do this. Other people with other collective memories continue their struggle for redemption on other grounds; among them, the Jews, for whom Jesus's life, death and anticipated coming again did not become the normative paradigm and who continue to found themselves efficaciously on the Exodus and the Torah as their memory and their Way.

This explication of antisemitism as deeply intertwined with Christology was generally welcomed by Jews, for whom this thesis was somewhat obvious. Jews had long experienced Christian violence toward them as rooted in the assertion that they are "Christ-killers." Many Christians who had been involved in Jewish-Christian dialogue were at first antagonized by this thesis, wishing to see antisemitism as more peripheral rather than central to Christian doctrine. However, several other Christian writers have made the revision of Christology, in light of the Shoah, central to their writings.

One example of this rethinking is the writings of husband-and-wife pair, A. Roy and Alice L. Eckardt, in recent books such as Long Night's Journey into Day: Life and Faith After the Holocaust[1982] and Jews and Christians: The Contemporary Meeting [1986].[33] For the Eckardts, a full and adequate Christian response to the Shoah necessitates fundamental revisions in the interpretation of Christian teachings. All notions that Judaism has either an inferior understanding of ethics or an incomplete capacity to redeem vis-a-vis Christianity must be decisively rejected.

The Eckardts believe that Christianity must rethink the basic understanding of Jesus's resurrection and the claim that Jesus is the Messiah of Israel. Jesus cannot be said to have risen from the dead in a physical sense [and there is no other way to interpret this original Christian belief] or to be in an already achieved messianic status because the world is still unredeemed.[34] The Eckardts take seriously the Jewish view that the coming of the Messiah does not refer simply to a changed spiritual relation to God [as Christianity has tended to see this], but to a decisive shift in human relations that begins the conquest of historical evil. Since this obviously has not happened, it is impossible and indeed meaningless to say that the Messiah has already come.

Jewish rejection of Jesus as the Messiah is not unfaithfulness, but faithfulness to the God and to the understanding of the messianic advent of their tradition. Jews have remained faithful both to the one covenant that God made with them and also to a realistic and wholistic understanding of redemption. This understanding of redemption does not split the spiritual from the physical, the personal from the social, as Christianity has generally done.

This unification of the religious and ethical with the social and the political is, for the Eckardts, a central insight that Christianity needs to relearn from its Jewish 'elder brother.' Although they do not say so, one might see in liberation theologies such an effort by Christians to reclaim the social realism of the Hebrew prophetic tradition. The Eckardts, however, see this reunification of the spiritual and the political as a central element of Jewish self-understanding that Christians must accept, if they are to understand the importance of the state of Israel for contemporary Jewish thought, both religious and secular.

The Eckardts do not want to make absolutist claims for a relationship of Jewish peoplehood to a divinely-given land in Palestine. They say, rather, that no people has an absolute claim to anything. All human claims to states or land are partial and relative. They would strongly reject the sort of fundamentalist Christian Zionism that assimilates a Jewish return to the Holy Land into a Christian dispensationalist eschatology, for by saying that such a return is necessary as part of the fulfillment of prophecy and an ultimate conversion of the Jews to Christianity. They characterize such a theology as antisemitic, since the formation of a Jewish state is celebrated only as a stepping stone to Jewish conversion, the annihilation of the unconverted and the triumph of Christ.[35]

While seeking to avoid "territorial fundamentalism," the Eckardts typically characterize any criticism of the policies of the state of Israel, whether from Palestinians or other Arabs, or from Christian peace activists, such as Quakers, as motivated by antisemitism. They see all criticism of Israel as springing from a hostility to Jewish empowerment and self-determination.[36] They say that "the worst fate that can befall any people is to be bereft of political sovereignty."[37] Jews have a right to a state because every people have a right to a nation-state, to national self-determination.

To reject a Jewish state is an expression of an antisemitic ideology that believes that only the Jews, of all the world's peoples, are to be homeless and powerless wanderers and to lack a home [state] of their own. For the Eckardts the Jews do not have a special God-given right to a state different from other people. They have the same right to a state as other people, for a state is the basis for defending one's national existence against one's enemies.

A somewhat different view of the relation of the state of Israel as a solution to antisemitism is taken by Franklin Littell, whose long commitment to struggle against Christian antisemitism is expressed in his book, The Crucifixion of the Jews [1975].[38] Littell's theology springs from the Anabaptist free church tradition of radical rejection of church-state amalgamation.[39] The authentic calling of the Christian church is to remain a counter-culture that must stand in tension with and prophetic critique of all worldly systems of power. The church is a community set apart from the state to witness to an alternative, redemptive lifestyle of God's messianic age. This Kingdom lifestyle is characterized by pacifism, egalitarianism and communal sharing.

Littell uses this Anabaptist critique of Christendom in his battle against Christian antisemitism. He was influenced in this particularly by the

Barthian theological attack on German Christianity as 'cultural Christianity.' For Barth, the essence of the Christian failure to oppose Hitler was its sellout of the Gospel to a pagan nationalism and idolatrous sacral state.[40] Littell sees the Jews of Medieval Europe as better preserving this counter-cultural ethic, as a people set apart, without power in Christian theocratic states.[41]

However, these free church principles come out oddly in Littell's thought when he turns to the necessity for Christians to give absolute support for Israel as a Jewish state. Such a state he sees as an essential component of Jewish identity. Like the Eckardts, Littell sees the nature of the Jewish people as a wholistic social and political community, not just a spiritual peoplehood divorced from political expression. One of the fundamental mistakes of Christianity is this spiritualization of peoplehood. Littell identifies this communal nature of Judaism with the necessity of a state.

Unlike the Eckardts, Littell gives special or unique status to this Jewish right to a Jewish state. The right of the Jews to a state is not simply a particular expression of a universal right of all people to a state. Rather the Jewish people have a unique right to a state on this particular land. God has chosen the Jewish people as a unique community and promised them this particular land. Thus, only for the Jews is there a valid fusion of spiritual and political identity, of peoplehood, land and political sovereignty. The Jews are set apart from all other people as the only people whose ethnic identity has been mandated by God and who have been given a land in which to express their national identity.[42]

Even more than the Eckardts, Littell scores any criticism of Israel, whether from Arabs or from Quakers, as antisemitism. He also identifies any opposition to a Jewish state as a lingering expression of an ideology that decrees powerlessness and misery for Jews as divine punishment and sees Jewish empowerment as a threat to this ideology.[43] Littell also condemns Islam as an extreme example of a false sacral political order that fuses religion, culture and state. He claims that Israel as a Jewish state challenges the idea of an Islamic state.[44] It is hard to know what Littell means at this point, if Israel is itself a divinely-mandated theocratic state. An Islamic and a Jewish Torah-state would seem more to be rivals in the Middle East, with similar ideas of religious law and theocratic politics.

One of the most systematic efforts to rethink Christian theological claims in the light of a sorry history of Christian antisemitism has come from Episcopal theologian Paul van Buren. Van Buren is developing a four-part magnum opus, A Theology of the Jewish-Christian Reality, three volumes of which have appeared: Discerning the Way [1980]; A Christian Theology of the People Israel [1983], and Christ in Context [1988].[45]

Van Buren's theology is deeply shaped by Protestant Neo-orthodoxy. Neo-orthodoxy rejected the liberal universalism of nineteenth century Enlightenment theologians, like Schleiermacher. The doctrine of original sin was taken with radical seriousness. All human beings are fallen and have lost any natural connection with God. This view of the human condition leads to a positivist Christological monism. Only through Christ is their authentic revelation of God and redeeming relation to God. Such a view left no room for a positive evaluation of non-Christian religions. Judaism, at best, could only have a preparatory role in the economy of salvation. But, without faith in Christ, the Jews remain in darkness.[46]

Van Buren has transferred this monistic idea of historical revelation to God's covenant with the people Israel. God [the only God that Jews and Christians know] has made Himself known in only one way, as the God who chose the people Israel as His people.[47] The covenant of God with Israel at Sinai is God's foundational and normative work at the center of creation and the redemption of creation. All other work of God in history [it is not apparent in van Buren that God is at work in nature at all] flows exclusively from this one elect center.

Van Buren uses the metaphor of light and darkness for the relation of this one revelatory center, the covenant of God with Israel, to the gentile world. He draws his use of this metaphor, not only from Christian theology, but also from Jewish messianic Kabbalism.[48] The covenant of God with Israel is both the one place where the true God is revealed and also the center from which creation is being healed from its brokenness. The Gentile, lacking any natural relation to God, is by nature sunk in darkness, both spiritually and morally. Gentiles exhibit the godless nature of humanity as idolatrous and morally perverse. The Gentile, then, is the 'natural' human or 'pagan.'[49]

God, however, is not only the God of Israel, but the creator and redeemer of all nations. God has chosen to reach out to the gentiles through His covenant with Israel. Israel is called to be God's unique people, walking in the Way of Life which God has given them in the Torah. But Israel is also called to be the light to the nations, to communicate its revelation of God and the healing of the nations to the gentiles. This extension of the covenant of God with Israel to the nations is specifically the role of the Christian Church.

Christianity, or the Christian Church, is not a 'new covenant' of God with a new people, which supercedes the covenant of God with Israel. That covenant is eternal and unchangeable. Rather, the Christian church is an extension of the one covenant of God with Israel to the gentiles. The dispensation of salvation to the gentiles is, in a sense, a new work of God in history, but in a strictly auxiliary and dependent relation to the sole covenant of God with Israel.[50]

Van Buren completely rejects the title of Christ for Jesus. Jesus was not the Messiah of Israel.[51] The appropriation of this title for Jesus is an error that manifests how deeply Christianity misinterpreted its own mandate. Jesus is central for Christianity, but not as Messiah of Israel, or as the basis of a new covenant superceding that of Israel. Jesus is the paradigmatic expression of the extension of the covenant of God with Israel to the gentiles. Jesus is where Israel is summed up in one person and given to the gentiles. The gentiles plug into the covenant of God with Israel through their relation to Jesus as Israel-for-us. Jesus is central to the salvation of Christians [gentiles connected to God's covenant], but Jesus is unnecessary for the salvation of Jews, who are the primary possessors of this covenant.[52]

By seeing itself as a 'new covenant,' superceding the covenant of God with Israel, Christianity fell into error, cut itself off from its Jewish roots and therefore lost the source of the authentic interpretation of its mission. This error was compounded by an antisemitic teaching of contempt for Jews and Judaism. Christianity responded with hostility when Jews refused to accept this false concept of Jesus as the Messiah and the Church as the New Israel, superceding the Jewish people. Christians called on the Jews to abandon faithfulness to the Torah in favor of a new way of salvation through Christ alone.

Such a gospel of Christ could only be rejected by the Jews with a resounding 'No!' This rejection of the Christian gospel is not unfaithfulness, but rather the expression of the faithfulness of the Jewish people to its God. Christians must come to recognize Jewish rejection of this type of Christian gospel as a witness to truth, recalling the Christian church to its true identity and mission.[53]

The culmination of Christian self-deception, expressed in hostility to Jews, was the Shoah, the effort to destroy the Jewish people entirely, so that all memory of their negation of a secularized Christian triumphalism could be erased. Van Buren parallels the crucifixion of Christ and the Shoah, Golgotha and Auschwitz. Both represent the power of Satan, or the evil impulse that resists God's love. But they are also the places where God Himself entered into history and was present in the suffering of the faithful man of Israel, Jesus, and in the suffering of the people of Israel.[54]

The state of Israel is a resurrection sign, the sign that God's faithfulness to life against death perseveres. By aligning itself in solidarity with the Jewish remembrance of the six million, but also in support for the state of Israel, the Church participates in this saving hope on the other side of the horror of human resistance to God.

> In so far as the Church seeks to enter into the Jewish memory of the six million, in so far as the Church shares with Jews the determination that there shall never be another Holocaust, in so far as the Church holds most dear the Jewish State as one precious affirmation of Jewish life after so many deaths, it plays a minor part in the affirming of those dead that their death is not the ultimate fact for them, that God's cause for his people continues.[55]

Once the Christian church has returned to its true, auxiliary relationship to the covenant with Israel, then Israel will be able to recognize and claim the Christian Church as its own vehicle for its mission to the gentiles. Heretofore, it has not been able to do this because of Christian hostility and misinterpretation of its relationship to the people Israel. The Christian church and its teachers must humble themselves and become disciples of the Jewish tradition in order to regain their true place in God's economy of salvation.

The central expression of Jewish faithfulness to their covenant with God is faithful obedience of the commandments of the Torah. The core of the Christian false gospel was the effort to invalidate the Torah as mere legalism with salvific efficacy. Van Buren believes that Christians do not need to observe the Torah because Jesus is their Torah. But the Torah remains central to the ongoing response of Israel to its covenantal relation to God. Jewish apostasy is non-observance of Torah.[56]

God's covenant with Israel includes the promised land. The land has been given by God to Israel in perpetuity, whether or not they are actually present in it. No other people, whether they have dwelt there for centuries or millennia, have any true right to this land. Jewish presence in the land normatively takes the form of a Jewish state. Such a Jewish state cannot be like other states. It is called to a higher destiny, not only to be an exemplar of all other nations, but also the place where creation itself is being healed. The Jewish state is the beginning of the redemption of creation, the overcoming of fallen creation's resistance to God manifest in Golgotha and Auschwitz.

The Jewish state must realize its redemptive nature by becoming a Torah state. This is why Israel cannot be governed by a secular constitution. It is called to take on the full yoke of the Torah as its law in order to fulfill its redemptive task, both for itself and for the healing of creation.[57] By implication, this also means encouraging the state of Israel to become fully a theocratic state, where the commandments of Torah are enforced as state law. The fact that most Israelis are secular and vehemently antipathetic to further extensions of the power of the rabbinate over their lives apparently does not concern van Buren.

The true Jew is the Torah-observant Jew. The non-observant Jew is not only apostate from God's command's, but threatens the redemption of creation that flows from Torah observance. Thus it is for the sake, not only of Jews, but of all creation to encourage Jews to become Torah-observant. Van Buren's ideas of becoming Torah-observant center on things like food and sabbath laws. There is no acknowledgement at all that there is any injustice involved in the relation of the state of Israel to the Palestinians, whom van Buren calls "the strangers in the land," and that doing justice to the Palestinians might be a part of becoming faithful to the Torah.[58]

The role of the Christian church is to extend the revelation of God in the covenant with Israel, and the healing work of God in and through Israel, to the nations. Christianity does this by preaching the Gospel, rightly understood, to the nations. This is the 'good news' that, in Jesus, God has extended the covenant with Israel to them. Christianity should also render service to the people Israel, both in atonement for its past sins of antisemitism and also as an expression of its authentic subsidiary relation to Israel. It should do this by becoming an extension of the Anti-Defamation League, combatting antisemitism among gentiles.

Christians should also raise money for the defense of the state of Israel and defend Israel against all anti-Zionist criticism. All suggestions that the state of Israel is less than just in its relation to the Palestinians, or in its relations to third world nations, are simply lies, according to van Buren.[59] Christians should learn the truth [presumably from the government of Israel] and take it upon themselves to combat such calumny.

Christian Shoah theologians as a whole are concerned to combat Christian antisemitism, to define and remove the roots of this antisemitism in Christian theology. However, Rosemary Radford Reuther and Paul van Buren represent opposite strategies for defining and uprooting the theological source of Christian antisemitism. Van Buren wishes to do this by monocentric particularism. The one true God of creation and redemption is available through only one people in whom He is revealed, and in one land through which His redemptive intent is manifest. Redemption of the nations and the rest of the world is an extension of this one covenant, in a strictly subsidiary relation to it.

Rosemary Radford Reuther, by contrast, would solve the dilemma of Christian competitive negation of Judaism, and other religions, by moving to a consistent universalism which would allow every human culture, and its quest for truth and justice, to have its own validity. God as the center of creation and redemption is not manifest through only one center, through one people and one land, but as the center for all peoples and all lands, defined in distinct and different ways. Christianity is just as relative and particularistic as Judaism; it is not the universal truth over against ethnocentric particularism.

The relation between the universal and the particular cannot be found by universalizing one particular people and their culture, either as a Judaism extended to all the world through the Christian Church, as van Buren would have it, or by a universalizing of Christianity in a supercessionary relation to Judaism. Each human cultural community has its own particularity and limits. It must enter into dialogue with other cultural communities, both as peers and as 'others,' whose various world visions are not reducible to one language. One universal culture or religion is neither possible nor necessary.

Yet, in order to live in peace and justice on one planet, the different human cultures and religions need to find concrete ways of affirming their mutual respect for one another. There also must be some working concensus on what justice and human rights mean as the basis of an international rule of law by which all people must be judged in their treatment of others, both within and between their national communities.[60]

V. Post-Shoah Theology: Jewish and Christian

Although Shoah theology began to be articulated less than twenty-five years ago, by the end of the 1980's it was heading into an impasse. Its credibility as a fruitful avenue of theological and ethical thought is in jeopardy. This, in my opinion, is because it has become too uncritically a tool of Jewish empowerment, in America, but especially on behalf of the state of Israel, discarding any moral critique of the possible misuse of such power.

Christian Shoah theologians particularly have tended to compensate for antisemitism by a hyperbolic philosemitism that is unwilling to allow that Jews in power can be like anyone else in power; namely, abusers of power. Such compensatory philosemitism betrays an unwillingness on both sides, Jewish and Christian, to accept that Jews are normal human beings, capable, like any other people, of taking power in a dominating way and using it to make victims of other people.

The imagery of former powerlessness and victimization is constantly rehearsed to claim that such use of power is necessary for 'survival' and that, without more weapons and more land, 'another Holocaust' is around the corner. Anyone who suggests that the time has come to concede human rights and some areas of national self-determination to the Palestinians who remain in the present occupied territories are accused of desiring this future Shoah and being opposed to the rights of Jews to defend themselves from annihilation.

With the fourth largest army in the world, including nuclear armaments, and after months of concentrated military, economic and cultural assault on an unarmed Palestinian people, this rhetoric of survival has lost its credibility. It is time to say Yesh G'vul, 'there is a limit,' in the slogan of the Israeli army reservists who refuse to serve in the occupied territories. Jews have had a tragic history of powerlessness and victimization, but this history does not justify the victimization of another people, the Palestinians, a people who have had little to do with that past history of Jewish oppression, but who have become the main victims of Jewish power in Israel.

In mid-June, 1989, Lieutenant-General Dan Shomron, Chief of Staff of the Israeli Defense Forces, warned rightist politicians that the Palestinian uprising could not be resolved militarily, "short of mass deportation, or starvation and genocide."[61] Shomron himself did not suggest that such military measures should cease in favor of political negotiations, but went on to recommend harsher measures against uprising leaders, such as doubling the length of administrative detention and expulsion without trial. That a term like "genocide" could be used as one of the 'options,' in what is increasingly being termed in Israel "the final solution to the Palestinian question," is an indication of how far Jewish power in Israel has moved into the shadow of its worst antithesis.

A younger Jewish theologian who has sought to find a way forward from this impasse of a Shoah theology is Marc Ellis. In his book, Toward a Jewish Theology of Liberation, Ellis seeks to rescue Shoah theology from its misuse as a tool of abusive power, particularly in relation to the Palestinian people.[62] Ellis affirms the original insights of Jewish and Christian Shoah theology. In theologians like Irving Greenberg the deep probing of the questions of divine power and presence in history led to tentative ways of affirming life and hope through a concern for all threatened life.

But, increasingly in the 1980's, Greenberg's own thought became focused on the justification of Jewish empowerment as an end in itself, impervious to the possibility of serious ethical failing.[63] Ellis affirms Jewish empowerment as good and necessary to rescue Jews from abject vulnerability. But he asks the Jewish community to take ethical responsibility for the use and abuse of this power, to stop using the rhetoric of past powerlessness to cover up present power and to refuse to face the possibility that they, too, like any other people, can become abusers of power.

Ellis sees a parallelism between a Christian abuse of its theological and political empowerment by victimizing the Jews, and the current Israeli victimization of Palestinians. A similar parallelism was suggested by Yeheskel Landau, Israeli founder of Religious Zionists for Peace, Oz V'shalom. In his reply to my paper at a conference at Bethel College, Newton, Kansas [April 10, 1989], Landau compared my earlier book, Faith and Fratricide, and my recent book The Wrath of Jonah, by saying, "Rose-

mary is very consistent. In her previous book she showed how antisemitism is the left-hand of Christology. In her new book she has show
how anti-Palestinianism is the left-hand of Zionism."

Ellis believes that, just as Christians after Auschwitz could find no
authentic basis to reclaim the moral content of their tradition, and to go
forward, except through solidarity with the Jewish people, so Jews, both in
Israel and in the Diaspora cannot reclaim the moral basis of their tradition
today for the future except by reaching out in solidarity with the human and
national rights of he Palestinian people. Ellis quotes the Catholic theologian
Johannes Baptist Metz's statement:

> We Christians can never go back behind Auschwitz. To go
> beyond Auschwitz, if we see clearly, is impossible for us by
> ourselves. It is possible only together with the victims of Ausch-
> witz.[64]

Ellis paraphrases this statement for Jews today:

> We Jews can never go back behind empowerment. To go
> beyond empowerment, if we see clearly, is impossible for us by
> ourselves. It is possible only with the victims of empowerment.[65]

Ellis calls for a new framework for Jewish theology capable of a
positive future. Shoah theology, emerging from reflection on the death
camps, represents the Jewish people only as they were then, helpless and
suffering. But it does not and cannot speak to the people the Jews have
become--powerful and often oppressive.

Shoah theology, Ellis says, spoke radically about the question of God in
the midst of a threatened annihilation and argued rightly for Jewish empowerment. But it lacks the framework to face the costs of that empowerment. It has not ethical guidelines for a Jewish state with nuclear weapons,
supplying military arms to authoritarian states, such as Guatemala, unjustly
expropriating the land and houses of Palestinian peasants and torturing
resisters to the occupation.[66]

The new framework for theology that Ellis delineates is a theology of
solidarity with the Palestinian people. This is not simply a generic call for
solidarity with all victims. Rather it demands that people in power take
responsibility for the particular victims of their particular power. Jews are
not simply to flee back again into general humanitarianism which pays no
attention to who they are in particular. Rather, by taking responsibility for
who they are as a particular people at this time in history, they also have to
take responsibility for that people who their power has victimized most
specifically, namely, the Palestinian people.[67]

For Ellis, this theology of solidarity means a de-absolutization of the state of Israel. This does not mean a disregard or abandonment of the state of Israel by diaspora Jews. Rather, there must be a more mature relationship to it. As Jews in the Diaspora need to de-absolutize the power of gentiles to make room for their own equal rights as citizens, so in Israel they need to de-absolutize the redemptive claims of the Jewish state in order to make room for Palestinian civil rights within Israel and Palestinian national rights along side Israel.[68]

As Ellis was defining what he saw as a post-Shoah theology of solidarity with the Palestinians, a parallel theology was being developed by Palestinian Christian theologian, Naim Ateek. In his 1989 book Justice and Only Justice: A Palestinian Theology of Liberation, Ateek showed how militant Zionist use of the Bible as the basis for expropriating land where Palestinians once lived has thrown the validity of the Bible, particularly the Hebrew Scriptures, and its God, into question for Palestinian Christians. Palestinians experience themselves as the victims at the expense of the other. Each have to concede space to live to the other and to be able to forgive each other's past misdeeds. Each have to learn to enter into the perspective of the other. Israelis claim they need security, and Palestinians say they seek justice, but neither security nor justice is possible for one without the other. Israelis need to acknowledge that security for them is possible only through justice to the Palestinians. Palestinians need to realize that justice will be possible for them only through acknowledging Israeli fears of insecurity, even if these fears appear irrational to a disarmed, landless and stateless people, suffering under Israeli military might.

A post-Shoah theology, in effect, must critically examine the shadow side of all monistic theologies of liberation and redemption. We must ask "Who is going to be the victim of our liberation? Who is to be enslaved by our redemption?" A theology of solidarity beyond the victim-victimizer relation must seek a path of hope freed from this shadow side. Whenever the Messiah of one people triumphs only by cursing another people; whenever our promised land is claimed by expropriating the land of an earlier people, whether ancient Canaanites, modern Palestinians, Indians in America, or Blacks in South Africa, not only is redemption incomplete, but the seeds have been planted for new evils, new holocausts.

Christians and Jews, Israelis and Palestinians, must recognize that power constructed as domination over others always creates violence, injustice and hatred. Christians have been amply guilty of this in the past, both toward Jews, toward other peoples whom they have conquered and colonized and toward each other. The very possibility of power, much less oppressive power, is new to Jews. It is difficult for them, perhaps, to change rhetorical gears and to deal with the fact that they, too, cannot only gain power but use it unjustly.

Marc Ellis has suggested the moral health of the Jewish community demands this shift to a new self-understanding that accepts responsibility for the costs of power. Dialogue and solidarity between Christians and Jews today cannot be based solely on the innocent victim-guilty victimizer relation of the remembered pogroms and death camps. It must be a mutually self-critical collaboration of peoples, both of whom know that they are capable of abuse of power. Each are seeking to regain their prophetic voice toward injustice, both in their own societies and in relation to each other.

This, I think, also means that Jews and Christians must overcome their antagonism to Arabs and to Muslim people. They must extend their dialogue to the Muslim world and the Arab people as well, without in any way being blind to the parallel tendencies to violence and competitive domination in that culture as well.

In all such relations we must seek a conversion that shifts from an ethic of competitive power, in which the victory of one is possible only through the defeat and humiliation of the other. We must seek a theology and ethic of co-humanity that fosters a quest for mutual justice between neighbors who must learn to live together in one land and on one earth. This quest must curb the tendencies of all three monotheistic faiths to foster triumphalistic self-affirmation through hatred and negation of the others. It must call forth and develop the best of all three religious traditions, Judaism, Christianity, and Islam, of compassion, forgiveness and mutual regard for the neighbor as oneself.

For John Roth, the construction of a proper methodology with which to approach the Shoah is predicated upon four interwoven acts: asking the right questions, listening for the right words of God, understanding those words, and doing that which is required to mend the world. For him [and for others], it is the works of Elie Wiesel which have yielded those all-important insights of understanding and doing which frame the above-mentioned responsibilities, insights such as the importance of questions over answers, particularly the question of "why;" the inter-relationship of language to life; the "sins" of passivity, indifference, neutrality, and inactivity; the importance of protest against evil and injustice; and the demand for an accounting even from God because one is involved in the human community. As with a number of other contributors, Roth cannot divorce theology from ethics, either before, during or after the Shoah.

ASKING AND LISTENING, UNDERSTANDING AND DOING:

Some Conditions for Responding to the Shoah Religiously

John K. Roth

I. Introduction

"I pray to the God within me that He will give me the strength to ask Him the right questions."--Moshe, in Elie Wiesel's Night

Born in Turin, Italy, a Jew named Primo Levi took his degree in chemistry from the university there in 1941. He was arrested two years later for resisting fascism. Deported from Italy to Auschwitz, Levi was sent to Monowitz, one of the main camp's many forced labor satellites. Liberated in late January, 1945, he eventually found his way back to Italy, resumed his career as a chemist, and also became an acclaimed author who wrote about the Shoah with an honesty that few others have matched.

Only once did I meet Primo Levi and hear him speak. He gave the featured address at the annual Shoah commemoration in my hometown, Claremont, California. On that occasion, as on so many others, he showed himself to be life-affirming. And yet, on that night, as on so many others, darkness shadowed Levi's words as he reflected on memory. In what was apparently a suicide attempt, a fall down a stairwell in April, 1987, cost him his life.

Primo Levi's best-known book about the Shoah is Survival in Auschwitz. It is a classic memoir about his year there, which Levi called "a journey towards nothingness."[1] Although Levi's writings speak about many things, rarely do they say much directly about God. Survival in Auschwitz, however, contains a striking exception to that rule. It came to mind almost immediately when, as a philosopher and a Christian, I began to craft this essay about asking and listening, understanding and doing, which are crucial conditions for responding religiously to the Shoah, the Nazi attempt to annihilate Jewish life root and branch, and to destroy millions of others whom the Nazis took to be lebensunwertes Leben ["life unworthy of life"].

As Levi describes it, the scene that came to my mind took place on a Sunday afternoon in October, 1944. All the prisoners in Levi's part of the camp were ordered to their crowded quarters. As in all the huts--Levi's was number forty-eight out of sixty--everyone received a "card with his number, name, profession, age and nationality" and obeyed the order to "undress completely, except for shoes."[2] Levi and his comrades then waited for the "selection." It would sentence some to the gas chambers. Others would be reprieved to work a while longer.

Levi's account goes on to describe how the SS "inspectors" eventually reached hut forty-eight to process his group. The procedure was as random and capricious as it was quick and simple. One by one, each prisoner ran a few steps and then surrendered his identity card to an SS man who, in turn, passed the card to a man on his right or left. "This," writes Levi, "is the life or death of each of us. In three or four minutes a hut of two hundred men is 'done,' as is the whole camp of twelve thousand men in the course of the afternoon."[3] Not quite "done," however, because in the part of the camp where Levi worked, it usually took two or three days before those "select-ed" actually went to the gas.

Meanwhile, the prisoners could figure out whose card went left, whose went right, and what the difference meant. Thus, Levi continues by noting what he observed that evening, after the meager portion of soup had been served and devoured, and how he felt about what he saw and heard:

> Silence slowly prevailed and then, from my bunk on the top row, I see and hear old Kuhn praying aloud, with his beret on his head, swaying backwards and forwards violently. Kuhn is thank-ing God because he had not been chosen.
> Kuhn is out of his senses. Does he not see Beppo the Greek in the bunk next to him, Beppo who is twenty years old and is going to the chamber the day after tomorrow and knows it and lies there looking fixedly at the light without saying anything and without even thinking any more? Can Kuhn fail to realize that next time it will be his turn? Does Kuhn not understand that what has happened today is an abomination, which no propitiatory prayer, no pardon, no expiation by the guilty, which nothing at all in the power of man can ever clean again?
> If I were God, I would spit at Kuhn's prayer.[4]

II. Asking

Another Shoah survivor, Elie Wiesel, writes in ways akin to, but also quite different from, Primo Levi's. For example, at the beginning of his classic memoir, Night, which details Wiesel's experiences as a manchild in Auschwitz at fifteen, he introduces one of his teachers. His name was Moshe, and the year was 1941. Although the Shoah was under way, it had not yet touched Wiesel's hometown of Sighet in what was then Hungary. One day the twelve-year-old Wiesel asked his teacher, "And why to you pray,

Moshe?" His teacher replied, "I pray to the God within me that He will give me the strength to ask Him the right questions."[5]

Together, Elie Wiesel and Primo Levi might make one consider that "the right questions" include asking God: "Did You spit at Auschwitz?" "In particular, did You spit at a prayer of thanks offered by one who 'has not been chosen'?" To those questions others might be added: If God did spit at Auschwitz, if God did spit at a prayer of thanks offered by one "who has not been chosen," did God do more than that? And if, in either case, God failed to spit, did God do anything else instead?

Care should be taken before one even considers responding to such potent questions, for they may be beyond answering, even by God. Elie Wiesel suggests as much in one of his gem-like dialogues. Following another "selection," Wiesel invites meditation on some last words between a mother and her daughter:

> Where are we going? Tell me. Do you know?
> I don't know, my little girl.
>
> I am afraid. Is it wrong, tell me, is it wrong to be afraid?
> I don't know; I don't think so.
>
> In all my life I have never been so afraid.
> Never.
>
> But I would like to know where we are going. Say, do you
> know? Where are we going?
> To the end of the world, little girl. We are going to the end
> of the world.
>
> Is that far?
> No, not really.
>
> You see, I am really tired. Is it wrong, tell me, is it wrong
> to be so tired?
> Everybody is tired, my little girl.
>
> Even God?
> I don't know. You will ask Him yourself.[6]

The Jewish theologian, Irving Greenberg, applies--perhaps even to God--a telling principle when one considers "answers" to "the right questions" raised by the Shoah: "No statement," he contends, "no statement, theological or otherwise, should be made that would not be credible in the presence of....burning children."[7] That criterion--could any other be more demanding?--makes every statement problematic. In the Presbyterian church where

I worship, for example, it is customary for the reader of Scripture to begin with an admonition to "listen, listen closely for the Word of God." What do we Christians hear, what should we hear, if we "listen, listen closely for the Word of God" after the Shoah?

A sound response to that question deserves deep and thoughtful consideration. But surely, at the very least, it directs us Christians toward repentant responsibility that changes and corrects anti-Jewish elements in the Christian tradition that helped to create what Primo Levi rightly called "an abomination." Heeding such a call--Christian Scripture would say it entails being "doers of the Word, not hearers only" [James 1:22]--will not by any means set everything right, but it is an imperative shirked at everyone's peril, including God's.

The latter point deserves emphasis because of a principle stressed by Emil Fackenheim, another leading Jewish thinker. Adolf Hitler, argues Fackenheim, should have no "posthumous victories."[8] Fackenheim makes that point in relation to Jewish faithfulness after the Shoah. Fully comprehended, it becomes an imperative for Christians, too. For Fackenheim shows that social reality decisively includes Christianity, even, indeed perhaps especially, after Auschwitz. As a Jew, he is convinced that the world's mending requires not only Christianity's elimination but its reconstruction. That reconstruction depends on asking the right questions and on listening for the right responses. It also depends on understanding that becomes doing what is right.[9]

As a Christian, one reason I go to church is that I hear things there that I do not hear elsewhere. A case in point involves a poem included in a recent sermon by my Pastor, John Najarian. The poem's author was Rainer Maria Rilke. He did not live to witness the Shoah's consuming fire, but, in 1899, this German-speaking writer penned a verse worth hearing after Auschwitz. Listening to it with post-Shoah ears, the poem's premonitions anticipate some Jewish and Christian voices among the defenseless who perished under the Nazis. Rilke may speak, too, for those Jews and Christians living after Auschwitz who try to be faithful to Emil Fackenheim's principle that Hitler shall have no posthumous victories.

> What will you do, God, when I die?
> When I, your pitcher, broken, lie?
> When I, your drink, go stale or dry?
> I am your garb, the trade you ply,
> you lose your meaning, losing me.
>
> Homeless without me, you will be
> robbed of your welcome, warm and sweet.

I am your sandals: your tired feet
will wander bare for want of me.

Your mighty cloak will fall away.
Your glance that on my cheek was laid
and pillowed warm, will seek, dismayed,
the comfort that I offered once--
to lie, as sunset colors fade
in the cold lap of alien stones.

What will you do, God? I am afraid.[10]

Responding to the Shoah religiously is an awesome task. Properly, it can cause one to be afraid. "I would like to know where we are going," Elie Wiesel writes for his little sister, who, in all of her life, has never been so afraid and never shall be again. Her "we" may include God as well as humankind. But if Christians and Jews can muster the right determination, the answer may not be "To the end of the world, little girl. We are going to the end of the world." Instead, the response might be, "We are going to mend the world." That, I believe, is the direction that should map the asking and listening, the understanding and doing, that are basic conditions for responding to the Shoah religiously. To consider in more detail how that mapping might work, Christians especially can profit by listening to Jewish voices. Elie Wiesel's is an example.

III. Listening

Elie Wiesel insists that the essence of being Jewish is "never to give up--never to yield to despair."[11] Keeping that imperative is anything but easy, as Twilight shows. Its story does so by exploring "the domain of madness," which is never far from the center of Wiesel's consciousness, and by illuminating, in particular, Maimonides' conviction--its serves as the novel's epigraph--that "the world couldn't exist without madmen."[12]

Arguably the most complex of Wiesel's novels, Twilight defies simple summary. One of its dominant themes, however, emerges when Raphael Lipkin's telephone rings at midnight. This survivor of the Shoah, now a university scholar, hears an anonymous voice denouncing Pedro: "Professor, let me tell you about your friend Pedro. He is totally amoral. A sadist. He made me suffer. And not just me, there were many others."[13] Pedro is Raphael's friend indeed. More than once he has saved Raphael from the despair that repeatedly threatens to engulf him.

They first met in September 1945. Raphael had returned to Rovidok, the Eastern European town that had once been his home. There, on Sabbath afternoons well before Pedro had entered Raphael's life, he initially encountered madness. Raphael would go to the town's asylum to visit an old man who had become his friend. Although Raphael did not understand all the old man had to say, his friend's impassioned vision never left him. Some time later, an encounter with madness of another kind--it, too, never left him--invaded Raphael's Rovidok. Germans occupied that place in September 1939. Raphael was among those who had to watch them hang an old Jew--it seems the victim was Raphael's friend from the asylum--for resisting the occupation.

This death was but the first of many losses Raphael witnessed in Rovidok and elsewhere. All too soon nothing remained for him there. That town could never be his home again. So Raphael left with Pedro, who worked for a clandestine Jewish organization that helped survivors. Pedro's help was more than physical. Akin to Raphael's old friend from the asylum, he taught the young Lipkin: "It may not be in man's power to erase society's evil, but he must become its conscience; it may not be in his power to create the glories of the night, but he must wait for them and describe their beauty."[14]

Much later, the midnight calls keep coming. What's more, the caller seems to know too much. Eventually suggesting where the "truth" about Pedro can be found, the calls lure Raphael to upstate New York. There a Dr. Benedictus--only gradually does Raphael sense that, in spite of his name and calling, this "healer" may be the malevolent caller--administers the Mountain Clinic. It "caters to patients, men and women--mostly men-- whose schizophrenia is linked in some mysterious way, to Ancient History, to Biblical times."[15]

Raphael seeks the truth about Pedro as he encounters persons who think they are Biblical characters such as Adam, Cain, the Messiah, and even God. Their madness, which is rooted in an inability to come to terms with humanity or God after Auschwitz, is compounded for Raphael by the attempt that is underway to discredit Pedro. Thus, Raphael edges toward the abyss that awaits him: "What am I to do?" Raphael asks a Pedro who is both there and not there. "To whom shall I turn for a little light, a little warmth? Madness is lying in wait for me and I am alone."[16]

The madness that lies in wait for Raphael would destroy him, and, if he were truly left alone, Raphael might succumb to it. Perhaps that is what the telephone voice intended by calling Pedro into question and Raphael toward despair. Recognition of that possibility, recollection that "Pedro taught me to love mankind and celebrate its humanity despite its flaws," renewed realization that Pedro's "enemy is my enemy"--such forces rally Raphael's resistance.[17]

By reaffirming a summons to save, Raphael's battle against madness that destroys does not ensure a tranquil equilibrium. A different kind of madness, the moral madness without which the world could not exist, is the prospect instead. "The caller tried to drive you out of my life," Raphael tells the absent Pedro. "He failed. Does that mean I've won? Hardly. I cry into the night and the night does not answer. Never mind, I will shout and shout until I go deaf, until I go mad."[18]

Twilight is not the first time a man named Pedro has appeared in Elie Wiesel's novels and provided saving inspiration. Differing from his name-sake in Twilight because he is not Jewish, another Pedro is a decisive presence in The Town Beyond the Wall. This novel, the one most closely linked to Twilight, begins fittingly with an epigraph from Dostoevsky: "I have a plan--to go mad."[19] It also starts at twilight and under circumstances that can drive one to madness that destroys.

Once Michael's home, Szerenszevaros ["the city of luck"] is now in the vise of Communist victors over Nazi tyrants. Secretly returning to see whether anyone can be found, Michael stands before his former home. Ages ago, a face watched silently there while Jews were sent away. The face, seeking a hatred from Michael to match its own hidden guilt, informs the police. Michael finds himself imprisoned in walls within his past, tortured to tell a story that cannot be told: there is no political plot to reveal; his captors would never accept the simple truth of his desire to see his homeland once more; his fried, Pedro, who returned with him, must be protected.

Michael holds out. He resists an escape into one kind of madness by opening himself to another. His cellmate, Eliezer, dwells in catatonic silence. But Michael hears and heeds the advice that he knows his fried Pedro would give him: "That's exactly what I want you to do: re-create the universe. Restore that boy's sanity. Cure him. He'll save you."[20]

What of such a plan? Twilight, as well as The Town Beyond the Wall and some thirty more of Wiesel's books, follows Night. All of Night's sequels, in one way or another, explore ways in which the world might be mended. Nonetheless, we know that in the order of things dawn, day, and especially twilight leave night close by. Yet even if, as Wiesel contends, "everything to do with Auschwitz must, in the end, lead into darkness," questions remain concerning what that darkness might be and whether the leading into darkness is indeed the end.[21] For if The Town Beyond the Wall concludes with Michael's coming "to the end of his strength," it also ends with "the night....receding, as on a mountain before dawn."[22] Similarly, as Twilight moves toward night, "from far away, a star appears. Uncommonly bright...."[23]

Twilight and The Town Beyond the Wall are both about friendship, another theme that is never far from the center of Wiesel's vision. Both Michael and Raphael have friends named Pedro. In each case, Pedro serves as a special kind of teacher. These relationships transcend the physical limits of space and time. Even when absent from The Town Beyond the Wall or from Twilight, the two Pedros are very much present for their friends. Michael and Raphael take courage from the challenging encouragement that each one's Pedro provides.

Michael and Raphael have learned from the men named Pedro. What they have discerned resonates with lessons I am trying to learn as a Christian and a philosopher who seeks to ask the right questions and to listen so that understanding follows and becomes doing what is right. Considering further, then, the authorship of Elie Wiesel as it moves from Night to Twilight, with journeys to The Town Beyond the Wall and meetings with Pedro among the multitude of encounters in between, here are ten of his major insights--two sets of five that focus first on understanding and then on doing. Simple and yet complex, complex and yet simple, each point is central, I believe, to Wiesel's way of thinking and living. None of the insights is an abstract principle; all are forged in fire that threatens to consume. For those reasons these themes from Wiesel have integrity, credibility, and durability that make them worthy guidelines for all seasons.

IV. Understanding

Elie Wiesel seeks understanding--but not too much. While wanting people to study the Shoah, he alerts them to the dangers of thinking that they do nor can or even should know everything about it. While wanting people to meet as brothers and sisters, he cautions that such meetings will be less than honest if differences are glossed over, minimized, or forgiven. While wanting humankind and God to confront each other, he contends that easy acceptance is at once too much and too little to accept. Wiesel's understanding is never facile, obvious or automatic. Nevertheless, its rhythm can be learned. Five of his movements follow.

1.   "The Holocaust demands interrogation and calls everything into question. Traditional ideas and acquired values, philosophical systems and social theories--all must be revised in the shadow of Birkenau."[24] The first lesson Wiesel teaches is that the Shoah is an unrivaled measure because nothing exceeds its power to evoke the question "Why?" That authority puts everything else to the test.

Whatever the traditional ideas and acquired values that have existed, whatever the philosophical systems and social theories that human minds have produced, they were either inadequate to prevent Auschwitz, or, worse, they helped pave the way to that place. The Shoah insists, therefore, that how we think and act needs revision in the face of those fact, unless one wishes to continue the same blindness that eventuated in the darkness of Night. The heeded revisions, of course, do not guarantee a better outcome.

And yet failure to use the <u>Shoah</u> to call each other, and especially ourselves, into question diminishes chances to mend the world.

2. "The questions remain questions."[25] As the first lesson, Elie Wiesel does not place his greatest confidence in answers. Answers--especially when they take the form of philosophical systems and religious dogmas-- make him suspicious. No matter how hard people try to resolve the most important issues, questions remain and rightly so. To encounter the <u>Shoah</u>, to reckon with its disturbing "Whys?"--without which humanity itself is called into question--that is enough to make Wiesel's case.

Typically, however, the human propensity is to quest for certainty. Wiesel's urging is to resist that temptation, especially when it aims to settle things that ought to remain unsettled and unsettling. For if answers aim to settle things, their ironic, even tragic, outcome is often that they produce disagreement, difference, division, and death. Hence, Wiesel wants questions to be forever fundamental.

People are less likely to savage and annihilate each other when their minds are not made up but opened up through questioning. The <u>Shoah</u> shows as much: Hitler and his Nazi followers "knew" they were "right." Their "knowing" made them killers. Questioning might have redeemed them as well as their victims.

Wiesel's point is not that responses to questions are simply wrong. They have their place; they can be essential, too. Nonetheless, questions deserve lasting priority because they invite continuing inquiry, further dialogue, shared wonder, and openness. Resisting "final solutions," these ingredients- -especially when they drive home the insight that the best questions are never put to rest but keep us human by luring us on--can create friendships in ways that answers never can.

3. "And yet--and yet. This is the key expression in my work."[26] Elie Wiesel's writings, emerging from intensity that is both the burden and the responsibility of <u>Shoah</u> survivors, aim to put people off guard. Always suspicious of answers but never failing for questions, he lays out problems not for their own sake but to inquire, "What is the next step?" Reaching an apparent conclusion, he moves on. Such forms of thought reject easy paths in favor of hard ones.

Wiesel's "and yet--and yet" affirms that it is more important to seek than to find, more important to question than to answer, more important to travel than to arrive. The point is that it can be dangerous to believe what you want to believe, deceptive to find things too clear, just as it is also dishonest not to strive to bring them into focus. His caution is that it is insensitive to overlook that there is always more to experience that our theories admit, even though we can never begin to seek comprehension without reasoning and argument. And so Elie Wiesel tells his stories, and even their endings resist leaving his readers with a fixed conclusion. He wants them instead to feel his "and yet--and yet," which provides a hope that people may keep moving to choose life and not to end it.

4. "There is a link between language and life."[27] The Shoah was physically brutal. That brutality's origins were partly in "paper violence," which is to say that they depended on words. Laws, decrees, orders, memoranda, even schedules for trains and specifications for gas vans and crematoria-- all of these underwrite Wiesel's insistence that care must be taken with words, for words can kill.

Wiesel uses words differently. He speaks and writes to recreate. His words, including the silences they contain, bring forgotten places and unremembered victims back to life just as they jar the living from complacency. Doing these things, he understands, requires turning language against itself. During the Nazi era, language hid too much: Euphemisms masked reality to lull. Rhetoric projected illusions to captivate. Propaganda used lies to control. All of those efforts were hideously successful. In our own day, as Wiesel points out, we bid farewell by saying, "Relax." "Have fun." "Take it easy." Seemingly innocuous, such language is certainly a far cry from words possessed by genocidal intent. And yet innocuous words may not be as innocent as they seem. They are likely to distract and detract from needs that deserve concern and care.

Language and life are linked in more ways than words can say. After-Auschwitz-priorities nonetheless enjoin that words have to decode words, speech must say what speech hides, writings must be unwritten, and set right what has been written. None of this can be done perfectly once and for all. The task is ongoing, but only as it is going on will lives be linked so that "and yet--and yet" expresses hope more than despair.

5. "Rationalism is a failure and betrayal."[28] Although Elie Wiesel is hardly an enemy of reason and rationality, he does stand in a tradition that takes reason to have no function more important than assessing its own limitations. And yet Wiesel's critique of reason is grounded somewhat different from that of philosophers such as David Hume or Immanuel Kant. Theirs' depended on theory. Wiesel's rests on history and on the Shoah in particular.

The Shoah happened because human minds became convinced that they could figure everything out. Those minds "understood" that one religion had superseded another. They "comprehended" that one race was superior to every other. They "realized" who deserved to live and who deserved to die. One can argue, of course, that such views perverted rationality and mocked morality. They did. And yet to say that much is to say too little, for one must ask about the sources of such perversity. When that asking occurs, part of its trail leads to reason's tendency to presume that indeed it can, at least in principle, figure everything out.

With greater authority than any theory can muster, Auschwitz shows where such rationalism can lead. Wiesel's antidote is not irrationalism; his rejection of destructive madness testifies to that. What he seeks instead is the understanding that lives in friendship--understanding that includes tentativeness, fallibility, comprehension that looks for error and revises judgment when error is found, realization that knowing is not a matter of fixed conviction but of continuing dialogue.

V. Doing

Elie Wiesel's lessons about understanding urge one not to draw hasty or final conclusions. Rather his emphasis is on exploration and inquiry. It might be objected that such an outlook tends to encourage indecision and even indifference. To the contrary, however, one of Wiesel's most significant contributions runs in just the opposite direction. His perspective on understanding and on morality is of one piece. Thus, dialogue leads not to indecision but to an informed decisiveness. Tentativeness becomes protest when unjustified conviction asserts itself. Openness results not in indifference but in the loyalty of which friendship is made and on which it depends. Wiesel's doing is demanding, but it, too, has a rhythm that can be learned. Here are five of its movements:

1. "Passivity and indifference and neutrality always favor the killer, not the victim."[29] Elie Wiesel will never fully understand the world's killers. To do so would be to legitimate them by showing that they were part of a perfectly rational scheme. Though for very different reasons, he will not fully understand their victims, either; their silent screams call into question every account of their dying that presents itself as a "final solution." But Elie Wiesel insists that understanding should be no less elusive where indifference--including its accomplices, passivity and neutrality--prevails. Too often indifference exists among those who could make a difference, for it can characterize those who stand between killers and victims but aid the former against the latter by doing too little, too late.

Where acting is concerned, nothing arouses Wiesel more than activating the inactive. This goal is illustrated in his play, Zalman, or the Madness of God. Inside the Soviet Union, an old rabbi, his assistant Zalman, a doctor, a daughter, a grandson, and a son-in-law, the chairman of a synagogue, and the rest of a fearful congregation--along with the troupe of observers--actors--are confronted by choices imposed upon them by an oppressive government intent on forcing them into silent submission. Traveling visitors from the West--some Jewish, some not--wish to witness Russian Jews at prayer.

Concerned about appearance, government officials decide to permit the visit, but warnings are issued to the local Jews. There must be no disturbances, no protests, nothing to suggest discontent. Almost everyone is willing to go along. The old rabbi, however, provoked by Zalman or the madness of God, chooses differently. He breaks the silence and testifies to the suffering of his people.

It is a dramatic scene, but nothing changes much--at least on the surface--except that futility gains some ground. The government investigates; the Jews' anxiety increases for a time. No plot is discovered, and fear subsides to a more normal level. The doctor dares to seek out the visiting actors to drive home the protest made by the rabbi. Unfortunately, they have already gone their way silently. Although the possibility remains that the rabbi can have a significant relationship with his grandson, his family may be more lost to him than ever, and there is no assurance that the madness of his moving protest has not pushed him into a permanent disorientation that will be useless, Zalman begins to doubt that his provocation was worth the pain and disintegration and emptiness it has caused. Madness compounds itself.

Such is the strand of hopelessness that runs through this drama. Yet threads of hope are intertwined with that strand. Slim though they may be, those threads direct one to the power of a challenge that resists indifference, passivity, and neutrality by saying: The rabbi must not be left alone; his sacrifice must not be in vain. Indifference makes such threads delicate and fragile. Passivity and neutrality show them to be more easily ignored or forgotten than carried forward into action. And yet the possibility they contain provides the premise on which Wiesel's unwritten third act awaits is post-<u>Shoah</u> direction.

2. "<u>It is given to man to transform divine injustice into human justice and compassion.</u>"[30] Abraham, Isaac, and Jacob--along with Adam and Eve, Cain and Abel, Joseph, Moses, and Job--this time they are not patients in <u>Twilight's</u> Mountain Clinic but Biblical "messengers of God." Seeds of error, deception, and guilt were born with Adam. Bias, favoritism, hurt feelings, vengeance, and murder form the tale of Cain and Abel. Promises, tests, obedience, trust, survival, hope--these did not add up to a world of rationality and justice for Abraham and Isaac, but they exist.

Jacob fought to secure a blessing, and the world has shaken to the core trying to understand its nature and what it might portend. Wily Joseph escaped the jealousy of his brothers, worked his way to the top, handled Potiphar's wife beautifully, made himself a Just Man. His success was too much; unfairly, his people paid the price. Leadership and the law--these things associate with Moses, but even this man--closest of all to God and his people--glimpsed the future from so far away that he had to wonder. As for

Job, maybe life had been unfairly good to him and so his testing was to be commensurate.

Like Wiesel himself, these Biblical messengers understood that human thought and action have enacted and exacerbated too many of the threatening portents that accompany the freedom to choose that makes existence human. They also wrestled with the fact that human existence neither accounts for nor completely sustains itself. Their dearly-earned reckoning with that reality led them to a profound restiveness. It revealed, in turn, the awesome injunction that God intends for humankind to have hard, even impossible, moral work until and through death.

One may not see life the way those Biblical messengers saw it. Whatever one's choices in that regard, it is nevertheless as hard as it is inhuman to deny that injustice too often reigns divine and that moral work is given to us indeed. Elie Wiesel presumes neither to identify that work in detail for everyone nor to insist, in particular, where or how one should do it. Those are the right questions, though, and he wants one to explore them. That exploration, he urges, is not likely to be done better than through the Shoah lenses. Enhancing vision sensitively, they can help to focus every evil that should be transformed by human justice and compassion.

3. "If I still shout today, if I still scream, it is to prevent man from ultimately changing me."[31] While "and yet--and yet" may be the key expression in Wiesel's writings, a close contender could be phrased "because of-- in spite of." Here, too, the rhythm insists that, no matter where one dwells, there is and must be more to say and do. On this occasion, though, the context is more specific, for the place where "because of--in spite of" becomes crucial is the place where despair most threatens to win. So because of the odds in favor of despair and against hope, in spite of them, the insistence and need to rebel in favor of life are all the greater. And not to be moved by them is to hasten the end.

How this understanding's logic works in tandem with doing can be illuminated further by noting Wiesel's observation that many of those freed from the Nazi camps believed that the world must not have known about them. Disabused of that naivete, some still clung to the idea that if they told what had happened, the effect would be sobering and transforming. That hope, too, proved illusory, for the story has been told, responsibility has been assessed, and, if anything, the Shoah is more widely a part of human memory than ever. The labor, however, has not been sufficient to check the violence, suffering, and indifference that waste life away. Instead, the threats of population riddance and nuclear destruction persist. Not even antisemtism has been eclipsed.

At times, Wiesel hints that humanity's eventual destruction is to be the price--as yet unpaid--for Auschwitz. That counsel of doom will not be his last word, however, as is evidenced by The Testament. This novel traces the odyssey of Paltiel Kossover, a character who represents hundreds of Jewish intellectuals condemned to death by Joseph Stalin in 1952. The Shoah does not stand center stage in The Testament, but, as is usual in Wiesel's writings, casts its shadow before and after all the action. This book, moreover, contains Wiesel's most fundamental answer to the question he must face repeatedly, a question that elicits a response incorporating the rhythm of "because of--in spite of:" Have things gone so far that memory and protest rooted in the Shoah are futile?

Arrested and questioned, Paltiel, whose name means "God is my refuge," expects to disappear without a trace. He is encouraged by his KGB inter-rogator to write an autobiography in which, the official hopes, the prisoner will confess more than he does by direct questioning. Kossover can sustain his life by writing about it, but he has no reason to think his testament will ever reach anyone he loves. Even less can he assume that his telling the tale of his own experiences will in any way influence history. Still, he tries his best, and what his best amounts to involves an ancient story--often repeated by Wiesel--that serves as The Testament's prologue.

It speaks of a Just Man who came to Sodom to save that ill-fated Biblical place from sin and destruction. Observing the Just Man's care, a child approached him compassionately:

> "Poor stranger, you shout, you scream, don't you see that it is hopeless?

> "Yes, I see."

> "Then why do you go on?"

> "I'll tell you why. In the beginning, I thought I could change man. Today, I know I cannot. If I still shout today, if I still scream, it is to prevent man from ultimately changing me."

Kossover does not escape the Soviet prison, but his testament finds a way out. It reaches and touches the poet's son. Stranger things have happened in our day, and thus Wiesel insists, again by way of analogy, that the enormous loss of the Shoah is not all that remains. A future still awaits our deter-mination, especially if the rhythm "because of--in spite of" is heard, understood, and enacted.

4. "As a Jew, I abide by my tradition. And my tradition allows, and indeed, commands, man to take the Almighty to task for what is being done to His people, to His children--and all men are His children--provided the

questioner does so on behalf of His children, not against them, from within the community, from within the human condition, and not as an outsider."[32] Some of Elie Wiesel's most forceful writing involves tales of the Hasidim. Many features impress him as he traces this Jewish movement from its flowering in eighteenth-century Europe to its presence in the death camps and to its surprising influence in a world that came close to destroying Hasidic ways completely. One of the rhythms of understanding and doing stressed by Wiesel derives, at least in part, from an Hasidic awareness of the relationships between "being for" and "being against."

As Wiesel portrays its Eastern European development, Hasidism combines a genuine awe of God with direct and emotional reactions toward God. It found God eluding understanding, but also as One to whom people could speak. The Hasidim argued with God, protested against God, feared, trusted, and loved God. All of this was done personally and passionately, without compromising God's majesty and beyond fear of contradiction. Levi Yitzhak of Berditchev, for example, understood his role as that of attorney-for-the-defense, reproaching God for harsh treatment of Jews. Joining him was Rebbe [Rabbi--Ed.] Israel, Maggid [Story-teller--Ed.] of Kozhenitz, the author of one of Wiesel's favorite Hasidic prayers: "Master of the Universe, know that the children of Israel are suffering too much; they deserve redemption, they need it. But if, for reasons unknown to me, You are not willing, not yet, then redeem all the other nations, but do it soon!"[33]

Nahman of Bratzlav holds another special place in Wiesel's heart. Laughter is Nahman's gift: "Laughter that springs from lucid and desperate awareness, a mirthless laughter, laughter of protest against the absurdities of existence, a laughter of revolt against a universe where man, whatever he may do, is condemned in advance. A laughter of compassion for man who cannot escape the ambiguity of his condition and of his faith."[34] And one more example, Menahem-Mendl of Kotzk, embodied a spirit whose intense despair yielded a righteous anger and revolt so strong that it was said, "a God whose intentions he would understand could not suit him."[35] This rebel embraced life's contradictions both to destroy and to sustain them. Short of death, he found life without release from suffering. At the same time, he affirmed humanity as precious by living defiantly to the end. Wiesel implies, too, that Mendl hoped for something beyond death. His final words, Wiesel suggests, were: "At least I shall see Him face to face." Wiesel adds, "We don't know--nor will we ever know--whether these words expressed an ancient fear or a renewed defiance."[36]

Love, mercy, challenge, irony, laughter, anger, rebelliousness--Hasidim's spirit and Elie Wiesel's have them all but with a difference than transforms. Anything can be said and done, indeed everything must be said and done, that is for children, women, and men. Wiesel understands this to mean that a stance against God is sometimes enjoined. But he hastens to add that such a stance needs to be from within a perspective that also affirms

God. Otherwise we run the risk of being against humankind in other ways all over again. Those ways include succumbing to dehumanizing temptations which conclude that only human might makes right, that there is human history as we know it and nothing more, that, as far as the Shoah's victims are concerned, Hitler was victorious.

For....against: the rhythm involves taking stands. Spiritually, this means to be against God when being for God would put one against humankind. Spiritually this also means to be for God when being against God would be against humankind by siding with forces that tend, however inadvertently, to legitimize too much the wasting of human life. Wiesel and his Hasidim are fiercely humanistic. Their humanism, however, remains tied to God. The lesson here is that, without enlivening and testing those ties, and, in particular, their ways of being for and against humankind, a critical resource for saving life and mending the world will be lost.

5. "By allowing me to enter his life, he gave meaning to mine."[37] Another of Elie Wiesel's novels, The Oath, tells of a community that disappeared except for one surviving witness. It is a tale about that person's battle with a vow of silence. Azriel is his name, and Kolvillag, his home in Eastern Europe, was destroyed in a twentieth-century pogrom prompted by the disappearance of a Christian boy. Ancient animosity renewed prejudice. Prejudice produced rumor; rumor inflamed hate. Accused of a ritual murder, Azriel and his fellow Jews were soon under threat.

Not unlike Twilight's old madman from Rovidok, a strange, mystical member of the community--Moshe, whose character and voice are felt, one way or another, in so many of Wiesel's writings--surrenders himself as the guilty party though no crime has been committed. However, he does not thereby satisfy the authorities and "Christians" of the town. Madness intensifies. The Jews begin to see that history will repeat, and they prepare for the worst. Some arm for violence; most gather strength quietly to wait and endure.

Permitted to speak to the Jews assembled in their ancient synagogue, Moshe envisions Kolvillag's destruction. He knows the record of Jewish endurance, its long testimony against violence, but this seems to have done little to restrain men and women and even God from further vengeance. So Moshe persuades his people to try something different: "By ceasing to refer to the events of the present, we would forestall ordeals in the future."[38] The Jews of Kolvillag become Jews of silence by taking his oath: "Those among us who will survive this present ordeal shall never reveal either in writing or by the word what we shall see, hear and endure before and during our torment!"[39]

Next comes bloodshed. Jewish spirits strain upward in smoke and fire. Only the young Azriel survives. He bears the chronicles of Kolvillag--one created with his eyes, the other in a book entrusted to him for safekeeping by his father, the community's historian. Azriel bears the oath of Kolvillag as well. Torn between speech and silence, he remains true to his promise.

Many years later, Azriel meets a young man who is about to kill himself in a desperate attempt to give his life significance by refusing to live it. Azriel decides to intervene, to find a way to make the waste of suicide impossible for his new friend. The way Azriel chooses entails breaking the oath. He shares the story of Kolvillag in the hope that it will instill rebellion against despair, concern in the place of lethargy and indifference, life to counter death.

The oath of silence was intended to forestall ordeals in the future. Such forestalling, Wiesel testifies, must give silence its due; it must also break silence in favor of speech and action that recognizes the fatal interdependence of all human actions. "By allowing me to enter his life, he gave meaning to mine." Azriel's young friend echoes the lesson that Elie Wiesel has shared so generously with those who listen closely for what he has to say. Rightly understood, that listening--and the asking it provokes--becomes a mandate for doing unto others what Azriel did for the boy he saved.

A Postscript

"And why do you pray, Moshe?" Responding to the Shoah religiously entails listening, understanding, and then acting in ways inspired by Moshe's reply to Elie Wiesel's asking: "I pray to the God within me that He will give me the strength to ask Him the right questions." In that spirit let these words from a sixteenth-century English hymn provide an ending that is just the beginning:

> God be in my head,
> And in my understanding;
> God be in mine eyes,
> And in my looking.
> God be in my mouth,
> And in my speaking;
> God be in my heart,
> And in my thinking.
> God be at mine end,
> And at my departing.
>
> Amen.

NOTES

INTRODUCTION

WHY THIS BOOK?

Steven L. Jacobs

1. For a thorough analysis and discussion of the importance of "Shoah versus Holocaust" terminology, see Zev Garber and Bruce Zuckerman, "Why do They Call the Holocaust 'The Holocaust:' An Inquiry into the Psychology of Labels," in Modern Judaism, Volume 9, Number 2, May, 1989, pages 197-211.

2. Alan Rosenberg and Gerald E. Myers [Editors]. Echoes from the Holocaust: Philosophical Reflections on a Dark Time. Philadelphia, Temple University Press, 1988.

3. Samuel Pisar. Of Blood and Hope. Boston, Little, Brown and Company, 1979.

4. The current debate among German historians [e.g. Ernest Nolte, etc.] about the role of Nazism and the Shoah in the overall drama of German and Western world history, as well as the reunification of Germany in 1990, have raised unease among Jews and others the world over. To be sure, right-wing militant fascism has existed in both parts of Germany since the end of the Second World War, counterbalanced, only in part, by proper recognition of primary German responsibility for the murderous deaths of Jews, Gypsies, homosexuals, and others. To date, however, neither the historical debate nor the implications of German reunification have triggered theological reflections by either Jews or Germans. In time, these topics, too, may serve as sources of serious religious debate among religious thinkers in both communities.

REVISIONISM AND THEOLOGY

Two Sides of the Same Coin

Harry James Cargas

1. On Cargas himself and his attempts to foster Jewish-Christian dialogue, see my "Harry James Cargas: Appreciation and Response," in Journal of Reform Judaism, Spring, 1985, pages 33-43. On the subject of ritual murder, see R. Po-Hsia, The Myth of Ritual Murder: Jews and Magic in Reformation Germany. New Haven, Yale University Press, 1988.

2. Arthur R. Butz. The Hoax of the Twentieth Century. Torrance, Institute for Historical Review, 1976.

3. Edward R. Flannery. The Anguish of the Jews: Twenty-Three Centuries of Anti-Semitism. New York, The Macmillan Company, 1965.

4. Rosemary Radford Reuther. Faith and Fratricide: The Theological Roots of Anti-Semitism. New York, The Seabury Press, 1974.

5. Count Arthur de Gobineau. The Inequality of the Races. Los Angeles, The Noontide Press, 1966. Translated by Adrian Collins, M.A.

6. John F. Morley. Vatican Diplomacy and the Jews During the Holocaust, 1939-1943. New York, Ktav Publishing House, 1980.

EVIL AND EXISTENCE

Karl Barth, Paul Tillich and Reinhold Niebuhr
Revisited in Light of the Shoah

Alan Davies

1. Arthur A. Cohen. The Tremendum: A Theological Interpretation of the Holocaust. New York, Crossroad, 1988.

2. For example, in his December 13, 1949, radio address on antisemitism, later translated and published as "The Jewish Problem and the Christian Answer," in Against the Stream: Shorter Post-War Writings, 1946-52. London, SCM Press, 1954, pages 195-201. Barth describes the contemporary Jewish situation following [page 196] as "the greatest catastrophe in their history."

3. Cited in Eberhard Busch, Karl Barth: His Life from Letters and Autobiographical Texts. Philadelphia, Fortress Press, 1975, page 290. Translated by John Bowden.

4. Karl Barth. Community, State and Church: Three Essays. New York, Anchor Books, 1960, page 143.

5. Otto Weber. Karl Barth's Church Dogmatics: An Introductory Report. Philadelphia, Westminster Press, 1953, page 187. Translated by Arthur C. Cochrane.

6. Immanual Kant. Religion Within the Limits of Reason Alone [1974] Book I.

7. Karl Barth, "The Doctrine of Creation," Church Dogmatics. Edinburgh, T. & T. Clark, 1961, Volume III, Part 3, pages 295 ff. Translated by G. W. Bromiley and R. J. Ehrlich.

8. Ibid., page 349.

9. Ibid., page 353.

10. Ibid., page 523.

11. See John Hick. Evil and the God of Love. New York, Harper and Row, 1966, pages 141-150.

12. Karl Barth, "The Christian Community in the Midst of Political Change," Against the Stream, page 115.

13. Church Dogmatics, Volume III, Part 3, page 343.

14. Ibid., page 347.

15. Emil L. Fackenheim. Encounters Between Judaism and Modern Philosophy: A Preface to Future Jewish Thought. New York, Basic Books, 1973, page 223.

16. Ernst Zundel, a neo-Nazi propagandist of major proportions, is the author of various tracts, including Did Six Million Really Die? and [under a pseudonym] The Hitler We Loved and Why. He has been tried and convicted twice in Canada for publishing and circulating information that he knew was false and inimical to the public interest [under Section 177 of the Criminal Code of Canada]. For further details of his career, see my article, "A Tale of Two Trials: Antisemitism in Canada 1985," in Holocaust and Genocide Studies, Volume 4, Number 1, 1989, pages 77-88. Arthur Butz, a professor of electrical engineering at Northwestern University, Evanston, Illinois, is the author of the new antisemitic classic The Hoax of the Twentieth Century, a work that belongs on the same shelf as Edouard Drumont, La France Juive., etc.

17. For a critique of Barth's theological anti-Judaism, see my book, Anti-Semitism and the Christian Mind: The Crisis of Conscience After Auschwitz. New York, Herder and Herder, 1969, pages 113-126.

18. Church Dogmatics, Volume III, Part 3, page 363.

19. Ibid., page 364.

20. Ibid.

21. Ibid., page 367.

22. Karl Barth. The German Church Conflict. London, Lutterworth Press, 1965, page 30. Translated by P. T. A. Parker. Hirsch is cited in Gunda Schneider-Flume. Die politische Theologie Emanuel Hirsch, 1918-1933. Bern, Herbert Lang, 1971, page 160.

23. Cf. Heinz Zahrnt. The Question of God: Protestant Theology in the Twentieth Century. New York, Harcourt, Brace and World, 1966, pages 112-122. Translated by R. A. Wilson.

24. Cf. Wilhelm and Marion Pauck. Paul Tillich: His Life and Thought. New York, Harper and Row, 1976, Volume I, page 108.

25. Paul Tillich, "The Demonic," in The Interpretation of History. New York, Charles Scribner's Sons, 1936, page 78.

26. Ibid., pages 79-80.

27. Ibid., page 81.

28. Ibid.

29. Ibid., page 80.

30. Ibid., page 120. See, also, Ronald H. Stone. Paul Tillich's Radical Social Thought. Atlanta, John Knox Press, 1980, pages 58-61.

31. Ibid., pages 120-121.

32. Cf. James Luther Adams. Paul Tillich's Philosophy of Culture, Science, and Religion. New York, Harper and Row, 1965, page 32, footnote 26.

33. Tillich, The Interpretation of History, page 94.

34. Ibid., page 95.

35. Paul Tillich. The Courage to Be. New Haven, Yale University Press, 1952, pages 57-63.

36. Paucks, Op. cit., page 127.

37. Paul Tillich. The Socialist Decision. New York, Harper and Row, 1977, Chapter 2. Translated by Franklin Sherman.

38. Ibid., page 30.

39. Ibid., page 22.

40. Paucks, Op. cit., page 127.

41. Tillich, Op. cit., pages 160-161. See the careful discussion of Tillich on this subject in A. James Reimar. The Emanuel Hirsch and Paul Tillich Debate: A Study in the Political Ramifications of Theology. Lewiston-/Queenston, The Edwin Mellen Press, 1989, pages 223 ff.

42. Cited in D. Mackenzie Brown. Ultimate Concerns: Tillich in Dialogue. New York, Harper and Row, 1965, page 59.

43. See Hannah Arendt. Eichmann in Jerusalem: A Report on the Banality of Evil. New York, Viking Press, 1963, pages 135-136.

44. Brown, Loc. cit.

45. Ibid., page 180.

46. See Paul Tillich, "The Jewish Question: Christian and German Problem," in Jewish Social Studies, Volume XXXIII, Number 4, 1971, pages 253-271.

47. Jacob Bohme [1575-1624]; Friedrich Schelling [1775-1854]. Tillich, it should be noted, wrote a dissertation on Schelling, now available in English: Mysticism and Guilt-consciousness in Schelling's Philosophical Development. Lewisburg, Bucknell University Press, 1974. Translated by Victor Nuovo.

48. Zahrnt, Op. cit., page 336.

49. For a good account of this issue, see Michael R. Marrus. The Holocaust in History. Toronto, Lester and Orpen Dennys, 1987, pages 40 ff.

50. Reinhold Niebuhr. The Nature and Destiny of Man: A Christian Interpretation. New York, Charles Scribner's Sons, 1941, Volume I, page 254, footnote 4.

51. See, for example, his polemic against the use of Kantian, Hegelian and Whiteheadian analogies in modern Protestant theology in his post-World War II book, The Self and the Dramas of History. New York, Charles Scribner's Sons, 1955, pages 96-97.

52. Ibid., page 181.

53. Ibid., page 182.

54. Ibid., page 184.

55. Ibid., page 180.

56. Ibid., page 120, footnote 12.

57. Ibid., page 263.

58. Ibid.

59. "In modern international life Great Britain with its too strong sense of security....and Germany with its maniacal will-to-power, are perfect symbols of the different forms which pride takes among the established and the advancing social forces. The inner stability and eternal security of Great Britain has been of such long duration that she may be said to have committed the sin of Babylonia and declared, 'I shall be no widow and I shall never know sorrow.' Germany on the other hand suffered from an accentuated form of inferiority long before her defeat in the World War. Her boundless contemporary self-assertion which literally transgresses all bounds previously known in religion, culture and law is a very accentuated form of the power impulse which betrays a marked inner insecurity."

60. Ibid., page 219.

61. Cf. Richard Wightman Fox. Reinhold Niebuhr: A Biography. New York, Pantheon Books, 1985, page 191.

62. Reinhold Niebuhr. Man's Nature and His Communities: Essays on the Dynamics and Enigmas of Man's Personal and Social Existence. New York, Charles Scribner's Sons, 1965, page 19.

63. Reinhold Niebuhr, "Jews After the War," reprinted in Love and Justice: Selections from the shorter writings of Reinhold Niebuhr. Philadelphia, Westminster Press, 1957, page 133. Edited by Dr. B. Robertson.

64. Reinhold Niebuhr. The Children of Light and the Children of Darkness: A Vindication of Democracy and a Critique of its Traditional Defense. New York, Charles Scribner's Sons, 1944, page 142.

65. Ibid., page 143.

66. Niebuhr, "Jews After the War," page 135.

67. Reinhold Niebuhr. Faith and History: A Comparison of Christian and Modern Views of History. New York, Charles Scribner's Sons, 1949, page 132.

68. See, for example, his comments in his essay, "The Relations of Christians and Jews in Western Civilization," in Pious and Secular America. New York, Charles Scribner's Sons, 1958, pages 109-111.

69. Niebuhr, Man's Nature and His Communities, pages 23-24.

70. Ibid.; Niebuhr was actually quoting from the London Times Literary Supplement.

71. Will Herberg. Judaism and Modern Man: An Interpretation of Jewish Religion. New York, Meridian Books, 1959, page 77.

72. Niebuhr, Faith and History, page 162.

73. Kurt Gerstein, officer in the SS, attempted to inform the free world of the Nazi atrocities, with, unfortunately, little success.

SUFFERING, THEOLOGY AND THE SHOAH

Alice Lyons Eckardt

1. The use of the term "extermination" is extremely problematic since we normally restrict its use to animal or insect vermin. But that is exactly how the Nazis were using the German equivalent term, categorizing Jews as vermin, non-human, or more precisely anti-human, which had to be exterminated for the good of the "real" human race. By using the term do we fall into the Nazi way of thinking just slightly? Or may we reinforce an unconscious attitude in this direction in others? Yet if we use a more innocent term such as "killing," we obscure the radical nature of the Nazis "Final Solution." Even "annihilate," which is an accurate term as far as totality is concerned, removes the odiousness of the prey that is associated with the word exterminate.

2. This particular incident took place [probably not by accident but by Nazi design] on Rosh Ha-Shanah [Jewish New Year--Ed.] when the story of the Akedah [Binding of Isaac] is read in the synagogue services. [Cf. later discussion of the Akedah]. For a full account, see H. Zimmels, The Echo of

the Holocaust in Rabbinic Literature, New York, Ktav Publishing House, 1972, pages 112-113; and Irving Rosenbaum, Holocaust and Halakhah, New York, Ktav Publishing House, 1976, pages 3-5.

3. Hannah Arendt, "Radical Evil: Total Domination," in Roger W. Smith [Editor], Guilt: Man and Society, New York, Doubleday and Company, 1971, page 227. Arendt insists that "there are no parallels to life in the concentration camps. Its horror can never be fully embraced by the imagination for the very reason that it stands outside of life and death."

4. Many survivors have sought to express this incomprehensibility. Andre Stein's essay, "A Chronicle: The Necessity and Impossibility of 'Making Sense' at and of Auschwitz," is a masterful attempt to probe the world of the extermination camps as the victims experienced it and tried to take it in. They had to recognize that there was no continuity between Auschwitz or Sobibor and any previous existence, even that of the Nazi ghettos. Their previous life came to seem more like hallucinations or fantasies than remembrances of real places and people. [See Jewish Social Studies, Volume XLV, Numbers 3-4, 1983, pages 323-336.] Elie Wiesel describes his discovery that the SS could always devise a more naked and refined cruelty than that which the prisoners had already experienced and which they had assumed was the ultimate in suffering. [See One Generation After, New York, Random House, 1970, pages 46-47.] Wiesel has frequently spoken and written about the total "otherness" of the world of the camps, which he calls the "Kingdom of Night." Can scholars and philosophers encompass this Kingdom in their schemas? "Auschwitz, by definition, is beyond their vocabulary." [See Legends of Our Time, New York, Avon Books, 1968, page 19.] Emil Fackenheim comments, "We cannot comprehend [the Holocaust} but only comprehend its incomprehensibility." [See To Mend the World, New York, Schocken Books, 1982, page 238.]

5. Thomas Idinopulos, "Art and the Inhuman: A Reflection on the Holocaust," in The Christian Century, Volume XCI, Number 35, October 16, 1974, page 955.

6. The Nazi camp system was extremely complex, encompassing concentration, labor, exchange, transit, and extermination camps, as well as a few that combined the functions of labor and death camps [Auschwitz and Maidanek in particular]. But the concentration camp system had gradations with Category III being the most brutal and lethal. [Mauthausen is the prime example of such a camp. For Jews and "protective custody" prisoners-- whose return was "not desired"--Mauthausen was a virtual death sentence.] Furthermore, the camps underwent frequent transformations from one type to another and experienced different conditions that radically altered the possibilities of survival. Labor camps were often as deadly as the worst of the concentration camps.

7. Reinhold Niebuhr was a firm advocate of the second of these.

8. Haas proposes that any formal system that enables people to make evaluations of what is right and wrong is an ethic, regardless of its content. "Moral" indicates the values "we think an ethic ought to incorporate or develop....," but that content is shaped by language and culture and can be remolded. [See "The Morality of Auschwitz: Moral Language and the Nazi Ethic," in Holocaust and Genocide Studies, Volume 3, Number 4, 1988, pages 383-384; Morality After Auschwitz, Philadelphia, Fortress Press, 1988, pages 2-3 and passim.]

9. Jacob Katz. Exclusiveness and Tolerance. New York, Behrman House, 1983, pages 86-87.

10. Elie Wiesel. Somewhere a Master, New York, Summit Books, 1982, page 42. Lurianic Kabbalah differed from Spanish Kabbalah in that it put much more emphasis on human initiative and responsibility.

11. See Paul's Epistle to the Romans 5:3-5.

12. See J. Christopher Baker. Suffering and Hope. Philadelphia, Fortress Press, 1988, pages 47-48.

13. Cited in W. H. C. Frend. Martyrdom and Persecution in the Early Church. Oxford, Basic Blackwell, 1965, page 196.

14. Points 11-13 are to be found in Irenaeus, Schleiermacher, and liberal Protestantism. In the Irenaean-Schleiermachian-liberal Protestant theological tradition the justification of God's goodness and omnipotence along with the existence of evil and the inflicting and experiencing of suffering depend on humanity's "capacity not to sin and God's capacity to bring about good out of all evil--perhaps even to permit or ordain evil so that good may be experienced, by contrast, in human life....[Hence], evil is not 'damnable....but a calling forth of God's compassion on account of [humanity's] weakness and vulnerability'....all evil remains mysteriously under the subjection of God's providential creativity and foreknowledge, and is functionally vital to humanity's moral growth." [See Carter Heyward. The Redemption of God. Washington, D.C., University Press of America, 1982, pages 112-116. Underlining added.]

15. Heyward, Op. cit., page 125.

16. Heyward, Ibid., pages 107-108.

17. See Face to Face, Volume XIV, Spring, 1989, for a number of very helpful articles on Christian and Jewish views of redemption and salvation, which are relevant to our present topic.

18. Traditionally, they are always identified as "Just Men." I have not seen any Jewish feminist develop the theme as related to "Just Women." The number is not always given as thirty-six; the numbers thirty, forty-five, and 330 have been mentioned by various rabbis. Kabbalah gave widest acceptance to the number thirty-six.

19. In fact, the Akedah became the foundation for the wide-ranging attack on the remnants of idolatry in Biblical Israel.

20. The Akedah received much attention in the crisis the Jewish people faced following the first war against Rome [after 70 C.E.]. For more on this, see Robert Hayward, "The Present State of Research into the Targumic Account of the Sacrifice of Isaac," in Journal of Jewish Studies, Oxford, Volume XXXII, Number 2, 1981.

21. God's directive threatened to abrogate the promise God had made to Abraham regarding his future progeny, and undercut the commandment not to kill that was subsequently issued at Mount Sinai.

22. These stories are the only accounts that have survived from the many that had been recorded by Jason of Cyrene about those heroes of faith. See II Maccabees 6:18-31 and 7:1-41 in The Apocrypha, and Shalom Speigel, The Last Trial [New York, Behrman House, 1979, pages 13-14].

23. A poetic version of their martyrdom was made part of the synagogue liturgy for Yom Kippur [Day of Atonement--Ed.] and the Tisha B'Av [Ninth of Av, Day of Mourning--Ed.].

24. Cited in Spiegel, Op. cit., page 15, from Yalkut [Midrashic anthology--Ed.], Deuteronomy 26, #938; also cited by Alexander Feinsilver from Babylonian Talmud Gittin 57b, The Talmud for Today [New York, St. Martin's Press, 1980], pages 179-180.

25. Nathan Hanover, The Abyss of Despair [Yeuven Metzulah], New Brunswick and London, Transaction Books, 1983, pages 52, 55, and 64. Translated by Abraham J. Mesch. One rabbi forbade Jewish fighters to attack the Polish nobles of Tulczyn, who had betrayed the community to the Cossacks because such an attack would result in Catholic kings in other nations taking vengeance on Jews in their domain.

Hanover reported that rabbis of the threatened communities exhorted Jews to take all appropriate measures to prevent catastrophe: to escape or bribe their enemies if possible, to remain constant to Judaism despite their fear, to "indulge in sincere repentance so that the evil decree would not come to pass," but to be prepared for martyrdom if necessary.

26. Abraham Ibn Ezra's twelfth century commentary on Genesis 22:19 calls attention to the fact that Abraham "acted 'contrary to Scripture,' 'for he slaughtered and abandoned' Isaac on the altar." See Spiegel, Op. cit., page 47.

27. Spiegel, Ibid., pages 46, 49, 35, 38, 43-44, and 57; underlining added. In some accounts God was said to have used "the dew of resurrection" to revive Isaac after he had been killed. This also provided assurance that the Holy One will revive the dead in the future because of the merit of Isaac [pages 47, 130, 48, and 111]. Spiegel's full length study should be seen in its entirety; there is no way to do justice to its extensive scholarship in a summary fashion.

28. Spiegel, Ibid., pages 22, 24, 26-27, and 47. The poem is translated and published on pages 141-151.

29. As with most Christian themes, there were Jewish antecedents for this idea as well, apart from the Isaac story. In the Graeco-Roman period a number of Jewish writings and sects came to emphasize the value of the martyr's blood to expiate sin and "to guarantee that God would avenge the death of His servant....This was a strong tradition, and it was to influence the Christian theology of righteous suffering...." See Frend, Op. cit., page 57.

30. Frend, Ibid., page 81. Cf. Isaiah 53: he was "despised and rejected by men" yet "he has borne our griefs and carried our sorrows; ....he was wounded for our transgressions....was bruised for our iniquities; upon him was the chastisement that made us whole, and with his stripes we are healed....he bore the sin of many, and made intercession for the transgressors."

31. The Interpreters' Bible, 5:631.

32. In Alexandria during the fourth-fifth centuries Bishop Cyril wrote that "Christ willingly submitted to suffering and through suffering was led to triumph....The cross itself is a glorious moment." See Robert Wilken, Judaism and the Early Christian Mind. New Haven, Yale University Press, 1971, page 199.

33. Frend, Op. cit., pages 81 and 197, citing II Clement.

34. Cited in Alice L. Eckardt, "The Reformation and the Jews," in Shofar, Volume 7, Number 4, Summer, 1989, page 39.

35. W. H. C. Frend sums up the whole theology of martyrdom in this early period of the church:

> They were seeking by their death to attain to the closest possible imitation of Christ's Passion and death....Christ himself suffered in the martyr. The martyr was a "true disciple of Christ"....one who "followed the Lamb wheresoever he goes," namely to death....Death was the beginning of true discipleship [and its crown] was the climax of the Christian's earthly life, a reward which all should "earnestly desire," but it was a reward to be accepted "in meekness," not grasped at, and by implication, not provoked...." [pages 197-199].

Nevertheless, there were some "who deliberately courted death." As Ignatius of Antioch travelled to Rome as a prisoner to be executed, he wrote to the churches of Asia Minor in "a state of exaltation bordering on mania." Not only would death make him a true disciple of Christ, and bind him to his Master, but it would serve as expiatory suffering to help overthrow Satan in the Last Times [pages 197-199].

36. Frend, Ibid., pages 14-15 and 19-20. Othmar Perler's comments on the influence of IV Maccabees are cited: from the third century on, "in both East and West the Maccabees were regarded....as the prototypes of martyrdom and a source of inspiration to confessors....Christians....regarded themselves as the Maccabees' descendants" [page 20]. The Shepherd of Hermas was regarded as scripture by the church at Lyon, and he made the Jewish martyrdom tradition his ideal, even without including the imitation of Christ's passion [pages 196-197].

The Christian tradition that the saints of the early church, most of whom were martyrs for the faith, are able to intercede with God for the faithful or repentant believer and even that their relics have power to heal and perform other miracles is at least indirectly related to the heritage of Jewish martyrdom.

37. Epistle to Barnabas; Irenaeus; Tertullian, Augustine; see Spiegel, Op. cit., pages 84-85 and 38. There are other parallels as well: the role of Satan, and the theme of resurrection of the dead [pages 103-108 and 109-113].

38. Spiegel, Ibid., pages 114, 115, and 116. An additional difference is that the church held Jesus' sacrifice to be made on behalf of individuals; the synagogue held Isaac's "sacrifice" [or merit] to be on behalf of the entire people Israel.

39. See Heyward, Op. cit., pages 122-123 and 121-122.

40. Compare views in Acts of the Apostles and Pauline letters that not only express expectation of persecution but also acceptance with rejoicing: e.g., the disciples rejoice that they have been found worthy to suffer for the name

[Acts 5:41]; Paul believed that suffering and death were the basis of his right to be called an apostle [II Corinthians 4:11; 6:9; and 11:23]; Paul preached that only through afflictions did one attain the kingdom of God [Acts 14:22; I Thessalonians 3:4].

41. Almost every one of the apostolic Fathers has something to say regarding the suffering of Jews as deserved. Origen [185-254] claimed "that Jews suffer here and will hereafter 'on account of their unbelief and other insults which they heaped upon Jesus'." Hippolytus [170-236] concludes that "the trail of Jewish crimes leading to deicide is 'the cause of their present condition involved in these myriad troubles'." [See Clark Williamson, Has God Rejected His People?, Nashville, Abingdon Press, 1982, pages 98 and 104.] John Chrysostum [c. 344-407] vehemently asserted that for the "odious assassination of Christ" there is "no expiation possible....no pardon;" the loss of temple and nation, and the dispersion of the people was God's work. [See Edward Flannery, The Anguish of the Jews, New York/Mahwah, Paulist Press, 1985, page 51.] Cyril, Bishop of Alexandria [385-412] saw the Jewish exile, destruction of Temple, Jerusalem, and the land as punishment for disobedience to God, specifically their failure to "understand the shadow of the Old Testament" [See Wilken, Op. cit., pages 86-87].

In the East, Jacob of Sarug [ca. 449-521] argued that the Cross was the turning point in Jewish history; while previously they had been most favored of peoples, afterwards they became the most rejected. Jerusalem's fall was a result of their rejecting the Son and willingly continuing to do so. [See Homily V; translation from the Syriac by Alison Salveson.]

42. Jacob Katz, Exclusiveness and Tolerance, Chapter VII.

43. Cited in Encounter Today, Paris, Volume VII, Number 2, 1972, page 84. The date and occasion of this quotation [along with its sources] are, unfortunately, not given.

44. Gershon Greenberg, "Orthodox Theological Responses to Kristallnacht," paper presented to the Eighteenth Annual Scholars Conference on the Church Struggle and the Holocaust, Washington, DC, March, 1988.

45. A Jew of Poland recalled all too vividly how, as a youngster, he pleaded with his father to take the whole family to Palestine. The father, not knowing what he should do, asked his rabbi. The rabbi advised him to wait--wait until the Messiah would lead them all to Eretz Yisrael [Land of Israel--Ed.]. All but the boy perished while waiting. [Personal conversation, 1979].

46. Gershon Greenberg, Op cit. Wasserman followed his teacher Chofetz Chaim in maintaining that settlement of the Land by apostates was a destruction [a churban] of Eretz Yisrael. He held these views until his death.

47. Cited by Pesach Schindler, "Faith During Auschwitz and the Paradox of Tikkun [Mending--Ed.] in Hasidic Documents," in Conservative Judaism, Volume XXXI, Number 4, Summer, 1977, pages 31 and 32. A sixteen year old Dutch Jew, living in Brussels with papers identifying him as a Gentile, came to very similar conclusions, although with much more anguish and uncertainty as he did so. Although he did not see the agony of those years as the end of the Jewish exile, he nevertheless did anticipate that the return to Zion would be "the raising of a banner for the future...." [See Moshe Flinker, Young Moshe's Diary, Jerusalem, Yad Vashem, 1976, pages 56, 108, and 112].

48. Ignaz Maybaum, The Face of God After Auschwitz [Amsterdam, Polak and Van Gennep, 1965], pages 61-67 passim; and Dow Marmur, "Holocaust as Progress: Reflections on the Thought of Ignaz Maybaum," Remembering the Future, I [Oxford, Pergamon Press, 1989], page 956.

49. Reeve Robert Brenner, The Faith and Doubt of Holocaust Survivors [New York, The Free Press/London, Collier Macmillan, 1980], pages 226, 206-207, and 229. Compare also the letter a survivor wrote to the Jewish Chronicle of London to denounce the "thoughtless dayanim [judges--Ed.] and rabbanim [rabbis--Ed.] who claim that the Holocaust was retribution for the sins of the Jewish people" [24 November 1989].

50. Friedlander, "The Misuses of the Holocaust" in European Judaism, Volume 17, Number 1, Summer, 1983, page 61; and "Destiny and Fate," in Arthur A. Cohen and Paul Mendes-Flohr [Editors], Contemporary Jewish Religious Thought [New York, The Free Press/London, Collier Macmillan, 1988], pages 139-140.

Nevertheless, death-camp survivor Eugene Heimler is willing to affirm that "Jewish destiny lies in the [recurring] testing. Because after the testing comes the Covenant...." The six million "paid the ultimate sacrifice in order to awaken the world's conscience and thus enable the impossible, the un-paralleled to happen in history: a scattered people returning from all over the globe and out of the dust and destruction recreating their country." [See Heimler, "Messages: Extracts from a new book," in European Judaism, Volume 17, Number 1, Summer, 1983, page 12.

51. Richard L. Rubenstein and John K. Roth. Approaches to Auschwitz. Atlanta, John Knox Press, 1987, pages 280.

52. Andre Neher. The Exile of the Word. Philadelphia, Jewish Publication Society of America, 1981, pages 132 and 135.

53. Brenner, Op. cit., page 207.

54. Neher, Op. cit., pages 191 and 196. According to the Talmudic tradition, Nahor's son Uz was Job. [Genesis 22:20]

55. Neher, Ibid., pages 132, 178, 179, and 178.

56. Martin Buber was led to ask: "Can one still speak to God after Oswiecim and Auschwitz? Can one still, as an individual and as a people, enter at all into a dialogue relationship with Him?....Dare we recommend to the survivors....'Call to Him, for He is kind, for His mercy endureth forever'?" [Cited by Harold M. Schulweis, in Abraham Ezra Millgram [Editor], Great Jewish Ideas, New York, B'nai B'rith, 1964, page 212.]

57. Emil Fackenheim, The Human Condition After Auschwitz [The B. Rudolph Lectures in Judaic Studies, Syracuse University, 1971], page 10; and "Commanded to Hope," in Michael A. Ryan [Editor], The Contemporary Explosion in Theology [Metuchen, Scarecrow Press, 1975], page 59, underlining added. See also Fackenheim, "From Bergen-Belsen to Jerusalem" [Jerusalem, Institute of Contemporary Jewry and World Jewish Congress, 1975], page 14.

58. Pesach Schindler, consultation, Jerusalem, June 18, 1976. Irving Greenberg stresses the voluntary nature of the covenant in the age after Auschwitz. Though Jews now know the possible lethal consequences of being identified with the covenant people, they have chosen voluntarily to resume the covenant relationship because of their love affair with God and the covenant. [See The Voluntary Covenant, New York, National Jewish Resource Center, 1982]. But see also Greenberg, "The Ethics of Jewish Power," Perspectives [New York, NJRC, January, 1984].

59. See Alice L. Eckardt, "Power and Powerlessness: The Jewish Experience," in Israel Charny [Editor], Toward the Understanding and Prevention of Genocide [Boulder/London, Westview Press, 1984], pages 190-191.

60. Tucker further argues that "all redemptions are destined to be partial redemptions, challenging us to further work as 'God's partners in creation'." [See Gordon Tucker, "Contemporary Jewish Thought on the Messianic Idea," in Face to Face, Volume XIV, Spring, 1989, pates 28-29 and 30. John Macquarrie points out that "when the end is removed to the distant future....it shares in the negativity of the 'not yet' and it becomes neutralized and ineffective." [See "Eschatology and Time," in Frederick Herzog [Editor], The Future of Hope, page 115 and cited by Baker, Op. cit., page 89.]

61. Elie Wiesel, Messengers of God: Biblical Portraits and Legends. New York, Random House, 1976.

62. See Note 2. Albert Friedlander asks, "Can we understand this [father]? Should we understand....?" [See "Stations Along the Way: Christian and

Jewish Post Holocaust Theology," in Common Ground, London, #2, 1978, page 13.]

63. Wiesel, Messengers of God, pages 233-234; Neher, The Exile of the Word, pages 219-220.

64. Wiesel reminds us of a Jewish legend in which God points out that the difference between a group of pure and a group of impure people is that the pure ones had protested. God says that the others should have protested: "against Me, against Man, against everything wrong. Because protest in itself contains a spark of truth, a spark of holiness, a spark of God." [See Jewish Legends: Teachers Study Guide, New York, Archdiocese of New York and Anti-Defamation League of B'nai B'rith, n.d., page 8.]

65. Irving Abrahamson [Editor], Against Silence: The Voice and Vision of Elie Wiesel [New York, Holocaust Library, 1985], Volume III, pages 310, 93, and 267. Wiesel wrote elsewhere, "....there comes a time when only those who do not believe in God will not cry out to him in wrath and anguish. ["Why I Write," New York Times Book Review, April 14, 1985, page 14.]

66. Neher comments that Wiesel's work has wrought a "Copernican revolution in the realm of the Bible." [See The Exile of the Word, page 215.]

67. Interview with Harold Flender, March/April, 1970, reprinted in Against Silence, Volume III, pages 198 and 199.

68. See, for example, how Jurgen Moltmann uses Wiesel's account of the young boy hanging on the gallows as "a shattering expression of theologia crucis" [See The Crucified God, New York, Harper and Row, 1974, pages 273-274]. For an extensive survey and critique of Moltmann's theology, and of the continuation of pre-Shoah Christian theology, see Alice L. Eckardt and A. Roy Eckardt, Long Night's Journey into Day: A Revised Retrospective on the Holocaust. Detroit, Wayne State University Press and Oxford, Pergamon Press, 1988. Also, see Charlotte Klein [Editor], Judaism in Christian Theology. Philadelphia, Fortress Press, 1978.

69. Johannes Baptist Metz. The Emergent Church. New York, Crossroad, 1981, page 19; and "Facing the Jews: Christian Theology After Auschwitz," in Elisabeth Schussler-Fiorenza and David Tracy [Editors], The Holocaust as Interruption [Edinburgh, T. & T. Clark, 1984], pages 27 and 28; underlining added.

70. Robert McAfee Brown, "The Holocaust: The Crisis of Indifference," in Conservative Judaism, Volume XXXI, Numbers 1-2, Fall-Winter, 1976-1977, page 18.

71. Eugene Fisher bravely suggests that, since "Jesus' death is a divine gift bringing all humanity closer to God's love, [and since the] sense of hope amidst despair is true because of the death of [that] one Jew long ago, Christians will inevitably ask themselves, might it not be also true, and much more so, of the deaths of six million Jewish women, men and children....?" [See "Mysterium Tremendum: Catholic Grapplings with the Holocaust and its Theological Implications," in SIDIC, Volume XXII, Numbers 1 & 2, 1989, page 13.]

I find two difficulties here: [1] Traditionally, Jesus' death atones for human sin because he is the Messiah/Christos: he does not become Messiah because he is crucified.   Thus to try to read any atoning or redemptive function into the death of the six million requires making them a predetermined messianic people, for only then could their deaths have salvational power. But is that what the church really believes about the Jewish people? Is that what even those Jews who are willing to talk about "chosenness" mean by that term? [2] What about all the Jews who are ready to tell God to find another people for that role if it involves Shoah-like suffering? Would Christians be reimposing a special status on Jews who no longer desire this? Gordon Tucker warns that "when you honor a person or a nation with supernatural status, the fate of their natural form, their bodies, their history on earth, becomes less and less objects of concern" [See Tucker, Op. cit., page 28.]

72. John Paul II in "John Paul II: On the Holocaust," [Washington, DC, National Conference of Catholic Bishops, 1988], page 8; and cited by Sergio Minerbi, "The Kidnapping of the Holocaust" in the Jerusalem Post, 25 August 1989, page 6.

73. John Cardinal O'Connor, "Yad Vashem Revisited," in Face to Face, Volume XIV, Spring, 1988, pages 47-48; underlining added. O'Connor writes that he was influenced by Richard Cardinal Cushing with regard to the "potential of suffering." O'Connor lists two other ways by which suffering can be a power for good apart from "supernaturalizing" it: Jews can inspire others through their endurance of their suffering [in and since the Shoah] with patience, resignation, hope, faith, and love; and can humanize suffering and turn it into dialogue rather than a sword. [The second of these he attributes to having learned from Elie Wiesel.]

Professor Ulrich Simon of King's College, London, argues in a very similar way to O'Connor: While the "martyrs" of the Nazi era have "paid a debt," taking our place, "their heroism could not satisfy the tragic desolation of our existence" without their being "offered by the eternal high priest to the Father." "If the death of Christ is the universal sacrifice for sin which 'takes away' the sin, then expiation and reconciliation have an objective and infinite value." [See Atonement, Cambridge, James Clark and Company, 1987, page 96.]

74. If we conclude it ought not, then we are free to question whether our assumptions regarding an ethic of suffering really represents external morality/divine reality.

75. True, the idea of sacrificial suffering can lead individuals to endanger themselves and even give up their lives on behalf of someone else. This kind of voluntary sacrificial action merits the highest respect and praise. But no such action should be commanded or demanded or involuntarily imposed. It then ceases to be genuinely sacrificial.

76. Lawrence Langer, "Beyond Theodicy: Jewish Victims and the Holocaust," in Religious Education, Volume 84, Number 1, Winter, 1989, pages 50-51 and 52.

77. Terrence Des Pres. The Survivor. New York/Oxford, Oxford University Press, 1976, page 100.

78. Cf. Eliezer Berkovits, Faith After the Holocaust. New York, Ktav Publishing House, 1973, Chapters IV and V.

79. I did not list the Palestinian Arabs here out of lack of sympathy for their situation, but because I think their situation is far more complex and even more ambiguous than most of the other disinherited.

80. Consider: Any theodicy that makes blacks "God's contemporary suffering servant has to be rejected." "....any theodicy that breeds quietism thereby sustains oppression." "....[A] morally viable and defensible theodicy [must] become the foundation of a moral commitment to human liberation from the plague of unjust suffering. This is the only road along which the divine righteousness can be saved, sustained, and honored."
[See William Jones, Is God a White Racist?, Garden City, Doubleday/
Anchor, 1973, as cited and paraphrased by A. Roy Eckardt, Black-Woman-Jew: Three Wars for Human Liberation, Bloomington, Indiana University Press, 1989, pages 23 and 24.]

In this volume, Eckardt provides extensive coverage of these liberation movements' views. For other consideration of this discussion, see Alice L. Eckardt and A. Roy Eckardt, Long Night's Journey into Day, Revised Edition, 1988, pages 116 and passim.

81. Des Pres, Op. cit., page 6.

82. Hans Jonas, "The Concept of God After Auschwitz," in Albert Friedlander [Editor], Out of the Whirlwind: A Reader of the Holocaust. New York, Schocken Books, 1976, pages 470-476 passim.

Jonas's view offer quite a contrast to Cardinal O'Connor's conviction. Which is closer to the truth? We do not know. All we can do is to consider what the ethical, behavior, and other consequences of either persuasion will be--on the large scale, that is.

83. J. Christaan Baker, Suffering and Hope, page 16; and Langer, Op. cit., pages 53, 54, and 52.

MYSTERIUM TREMENDUM:

Catholic Grapplings with the Shoah and Its Theological Implications

Eugene J. Fisher

1. Portions of this work were previously published in the journals: SIDIC, Volume 2, Number 1, 1989, pages 10-15 and Ecumenical Trends, Volume 17, Number 2, 1988, pages 24-27.

2. Helga Croner and Leon Klenicki [Editors], Issues in the Jewish-Christian Dialogue [New York, Paulist Stimulus Books], page 135; David Tracy, "Religious Values After the Holocaust: A Catholic View," in Abraham Peck [Editor], Jews and Christians After the Holocaust [Philadelphia, Fortress Press, 1982], page 87; Arthur Cohen, The Tremendum: A Theological Interpretation of the Holocaust [New York, Crossroad, 1981].

3. For surveys from a Catholic point of view of this literature, now quite extensive, see John T. Pawlikowski, O.S.M., What Are They Saying About Christian-Jewish Relations [New York, Paulist Press, 1980]; Michael McGarry, C.S.P., Christology After Auschwitz [New York, Paulist Press, 1977]; and Eugene Fisher, "Ani Ma'amin: Theological Responses to the Holocaust," in Interface, National Conference of Catholic Bishops, December, 1980, pages 1-8.

4. Commission of the Holy See for Religious Relations with the Jewish People, "Guidelines for the Implementation of the Concilar Declaration Nostra Aetate, Number 4," Rome, December 1, 1974.

5. Cf. Pinhas E. Lapide, "The Sermon on the Mount: A Jewish Reading," in Christianity and Crisis, May 24, 1982, pages 139-142.

6. Even the details of Jesus' Sermon to "turn the other cheek" [Matthew 5:39] draws on the Hebrew Scriptures: "It is good for a person to bear the yoke....let him give his cheek to the smiter and be filled with insults. For the Lord will not cast off forever, but....have compassion according to the

abundance of steadfast love" [Lamentations 3:27-31]. The context of this saying in the Babylonian exile makes it all the more strong.

7. It needs to be recalled, of course, that Lieutenant Waldheim's commanding officer was executed after the Second World War for the massive atrocities his unit committed against Jews and Yugoslav partisans.

8. John Paul II, "To the Jewish community of Australia," Sydney, November 26, 1986. Reprinted in Eugene Fisher and Leon Klenicki [Editors], Pope John Paul II on Jews and Judaism [Washington, DC, United States Catholic Conference Publication Numbers 151-2], page 96.

9. See, for example, the results of my 1976 analysis of Catholic teaching materials regarding Jews and Judaism, summarized in Faith Without Prejudice: Rebuilding Christian Attitudes [New York, Paulist Press, 1977], page 9.

10. H. Vorgrimler [Editor], Commentary on the Documents of Vatican II, Volume II [New York and London, 1967], pages 76 and 77.

11. March 6, 1982.

12. Elie Wiesel, Ani Ma'amin: A Song Lost and Found Again. New York, Random House, 1973.

13. Emil Fackenheim, God's Presence in History [New York, Harper and Row, 1970], page 87.

14. Bishop James Malone, "The State of Christian-Jewish Relations," in Origins, December 6, 1984.

15. For example, See Fackenheim, Op. cit., page 96. Fackenheim's notion of the Shoah as a revelatory moment has been sharply criticized by some Jewish thinkers. Michael Wyschogrod, for example, maintains: "There is no salvation to be extracted from the Holocaust....If there is hope after the Holocaust, it is because to those who believe....the divine promise sweeps away the crematoria and silences the voice of Auschwitz." [See, "Faith and the Holocaust," in Judaism, Volume 20, Summer, 1971, page 294.] Jacob Neusner declares flatly: "Jews find in the Holocaust no new definition of Jewish identity because we need none. Nothing has changed. The tradition endures." [See, "The Implications of the Holocaust," in The Journal of Religion, Volume 53, Number 3, July, 1973, page 308.]

16. Irving Greenberg, "Cloud of Smoke, Pillar of Fire: Judaism, Christianity, and Modernity After the Holocaust," in Eva Fleischner [Editor], Auschwitz: Beginning of a New Era? [New York, Ktav Publishing House, 1973], pages 43, 48, and 49.

17. Press communique on the meeting with Jewish leaders, Rome, September 1, 1987, page 3.

18. Pope John Paul II, Address to Jewish Leaders, Miami, FL, September 11, 1987.

19. One will note, in the above, that I did not deal with the theology of the emergence of a Jewish State in the Holy Land as a "fulfillment" of Biblical prophecies, but, rather, as a "sign of the times," a statement of the Jewish people's faith in God which should evoke in Christians a similar spiritual affirmation of hope out of despair of our age. While I acknowledge that there are those in both the Christian and Jewish communities who would see in the modern state of Israel such a fulfillment, my own approach to Israel as historical event ["sign of the times"] does not require that view. Neither does such a fundamentalist approach to the Biblical text appeal to Catholic Biblical scholarship.

20. Daniel Polish, "A Painful Legacy," in Ecumenical Trends, Volume 16, Number 9, October, 1987, pages 153-155.

21. Bishops' Conference for Ecumenical and Interreligious Relations, National Conference of Catholic Bishops, April 24, 1987.

22. Ibid.

23. Interview with Stanislau Musial, S.J., in 30 Days, July-August, 1989, page 9.

24. Ibid.

25. Michael McGarry, C.S.P., conveniently summarizes the historical, theological, ethical and definitional "Relevance of the Shoah" in Ecumenism, Number 94, June, 1989, pages 20-23.

26. See my "The Evolution of a Tradition: From **Nostre Aetate** to the **Notes**," in Fifteen Years of Catholic-Jewish Dialogue 1970-1985 [Rome, Libreria Editrice Lateraneuse, 1988], pages 239-254.

27. Pontifical Commission for Religious Relations with the Jews, "Guidelines and Suggestions for Implementing **Nostre Aetate**, Number 4," December 1, 1974, contained in Ibid., pages 293-298.

28. Ibid., page 294.

29. Text and commentary in Ibid., pages 306-318.

30. For collections of the papal texts, with commentary, see Eugene Fisher, John Paul II and the Holocaust [Washington, DC, United States Catholic Conference Publications, 1988], and Eugene Fisher and Leon Klenicki [Editors], John Paul II on Jews and Judaism, 1979-1987 [Washington, DC, United State Catholic Conference Publications, 1987].

31. Ibid., page 10.

32. Ibid.

33. Copies are available from the United States Catholic Conference Office of Publishing and Promotion Services, Washington, DC, Publication Number 211-X.

34. God's Mercy Endures Forever [Washington, DC, United States Catholic Conference Publishing and Promotion Services, 1989, Publication Number 247--0], page 1.

35. Ibid.

IN THE PRESENCE OF BURNING CHILDREN:

The Reformation of Christianity After the Shoah

Douglas K. Huneke

1. Adolf Hitler. Mein Kampf [Boston, Houghton, Mifflin Company, 1971. Translated by Ralph Mannheim.], page 640.

2. Paul Althaus, from a lecture presented at the University of Leipzig, May 28, 1937. Quoted in Robert P. Ericksen, Theologians Under Hitler [New Haven, Yale University Press, 1985], page 103.

3. Quoted in Ericksen, Ibid., page 87.

4. Raul Hilberg, The Destruction of the European Jews [New York, New Viewpoints, 1973], page 188.

5. Elie Wiesel, Night [New York, Hill and Wang, 1972], pages 41 and 43.

6. Irving Greenberg, "Cloud of Smoke, Pillar of Fire: Judaism, Christianity, and Modernity After the Holocaust," in Eva Fleischner [Editor], Auschwitz: Beginning of a New Era? Reflections on the Holocaust [New York, Ktav Publishing House, 1977], page 23.

7. Jules Isaac, Jesus and Israel [New York, Holt, Rinehart and Winston, 1971. Edited by Claire Huchet-Bishop and translated by Sally Gran.], pages 401-404.

8. Cited as an "Appendix and Practical Conclusion," in Ibid., pages 404-405.

9. Paul van Buren, "The Status and Prospects for Theology," an address to the Theology Section of the American Academy of Religion, Chicago, November 1, 1975.

10. Regrettably, the first Seelisberg Point actually speaks of "the Old and New Testaments," thereby fueling the triumphalist misconception that the new supplants the old; that the new is superior to and the completion of the old. Only in recent years have there been challenges and some changes to the artificially imposed and archaic use of "Old" and "New" to distinguish the Hebrew and Christian Scriptures.

11. Richard L. Rubenstein and John K. Roth, Approaches to Auschwitz: The Holocaust and Its Legacy [Atlanta, John Knox Press, 1987], page 205.

12. Wiesel, Op. cit., pages 71-72.

13. Elie Wiesel, The Oath [New York, Random House, 1973], page 138.

14. Helmut Gollwitzer [Editor], Dying We Live: The Final Messages and Records of the Resistance [New York, Pantheon Books, 1956], page xiv.

15. Perry London conducted pioneering research on Nazi era rescuers. I have expanded his first two findings on adventurousness and moral parental role models. His findings are contained in "The Rescuers: Motivational Hypotheses About Christians Who Rescued Jews From the Nazis," in J. Macaulay and L. Berkowitz [Editors], Altruism and Helping Behavior [New York, Doubleday and Company, 1975].

16. Henri J. M. Nouwen, Reaching Out: Three Movements of the Spiritual Life [New York, Doubleday and Company, 1975], pages 46-47.

17. Jules Isaac, Op. cit., page 402.

18. Hitler, Op. cit., page 307.

19. Ibid., page 402.

20. Ellis Rivkin, What Crucified Jesus? [Nashville, Abingdon Press, 1984], page 124.

21. Ibid.

22. Stanley Milgram, Obedience to Authority: An Experimental View [New York, Harper Colophon, 1969], page 6.

23. Ibid., page 8.

24. Dietrich Bonhoeffer, The Cost of Discipleship [New York, Macmillan Publishing Company, 1974], page 45.

25. Ibid., page 47.

26. Helmut Thielicke, "Why the Holocaust," in Christianity Today, 27 January 1978, page 521.

27. Ibid.

28. Wendell Berry, Sabbaths [San Francisco, North Point Press, 1987], page 83.

HOW THE SHOAH AFFECTS CHRISTIAN BELIEF

Thomas A. Idinopulos

1. The view of Henry Wieman, cited in Bernard M. Loomer, "Christian Faith and Process Philosophy," in The Journal of Religion, Volume XXIX, Number 3, July, 1949.

2. Jacques Maritain, A Christian Looks at the Jewish Question [New York, 1939], page 87.

3. Jacques Maritain, "The Mystery of Israel," reprinted in Joseph Evans and Leo Ward [Editors], The Social and Political Philosophy of Jacques Maritain [New York, 1965], pages 194-212.

4. Jacques Maritain, Blessed Are the Persecuted," reprinted in The Range of Reason [New York, 1952], pages 219-226.

5. Thomas Lask, The New York Times, December 15, 1970.

6. David Magarshak, Dostoevsky [New York, 1962], page 32.

7. Cited in Lawrence Langer, The Holocaust and the Literary Imagination [New Haven, Yale University Press, 1975], page 1.

8. George Steiner, Language and Silence [New York, 1966], page 123.

9. Cited in Langer, Op. cit., page 74.

A CONTEMPORARY RELIGIOUS RESPONSE TO THE SHOAH

The Crisis of Prayer

Michael McGarry

1. On the subject of God's silence, see, also, Andre Neher, The Exile of the Word: From the Silence of the Bible to the Silence of Auschwitz. Philadelphia, The Jewish Publication Society of America, 1981. Translated by David Maisel.

2. Pope John Paul II, "To the Jewish Community of Australia," November 26, 1986. Reprinted in Eugene Fisher and Leon Klenicki [Editors], Pope John Paul II on Jews and Judaism [Washington, DC, United States Catholic Conference, 1987], page 96. Shoah is the Vatican's and others' preferred term for the "Holocaust" and so it will be used throughout this essay. Literally, shoah is Hebrew for "catastrophe" or "disaster." "Holocaust" bears connotations of a holy offering made to God....the exact opposite of that to which it refers. On this point, see Zev Garber and Bruce Zuckerman, "Why Do We Call the Holocaust 'the Holocaust'? An Inquiry into the Psychology of Labels," in Proceedings, Remembering for the Future: The Impact of the Holocaust on the Contemporary World [Oxford, Pergamon Press, 1988], Volume II, pages 1879-1892. [Hereafter, referred to as RF.]

3. See Arthur A. Cohen, The Tremendum: A Theological Interpretation of the Holocaust. New York, Crossroad, 1981.

4. See the excellent treatment and summary in Richard L. Rubenstein and John K. Roth, Approaches to Auschwitz: The Holocaust and Its Legacy [Atlanta, John Knox Press, 1987], pages 199-338; John T. Pawlikowski, "Christian Ethics and the Holocaust: A Dialogue with Post-Auschwitz Judaism," in Theological Studies, Volume 49, 1988, pages 649-669; Abraham J. Peck [Editor], Jews and Christians After the Holocaust [Philadelphia, Fortress Press, 1982]; James E. Moore, "A Spectrum of Views: Traditional Responses to the Holocaust," in Journal of Ecumenical Studies, Volume 26, 1988,m pages 212-224 [Hereafter, referred to as JES.]; Alan L. Berger, "Holocaust and History: A Theological Reflection," in JES, Volume 25, 1988, pages 194-211.

5. See Phillip Lopate, "Resistance to the Holocaust," in Tikkun, Volume 4, May/June 1989, pages 55-64, and the responses in the same issue. See S. T. Meravi, "Remembrance of Things Past," in The Jerusalem Post International Edition, June 2, 1989, page 13, for the incipient discussion on the multi-

plication, taste, and meaning of Shoah Memorials. This discussion is only beginning.

6. See Rose Thering, O.P., Ph.D., Jews, Judaism, and Catholic Education [South Orange, NJ. Seton Hall University Press, 1986], page 71. See also Eugene Fisher, Seminary Education and Christian-Jewish Relations: A Curriculum and Resource Handbook [Washington, DC, National Catholic Education Association, 1983].

7. See Michael McGarry, "Problems American Catholics Have in Dealing with the Holocaust," in RF, Volume I, pages 417-428.

8. See Robert N. Bellah and others, Habits of the Heart: Individualism and Commitment in American Life [Berkeley, University of California Press, 1985].

9. "Notes on the Correct Way to Present the Jews and Judaism in Preaching and Catechesis in the Roman Catholic Church," Paragraph #25, in Helga Croner [Editor], More Stepping Stones to Jewish-Christian Relations: An Unabridged Collection of Christian Documents 1975-1983 [New York, Paulist Press, 1985], page 231.

10. "A Catholic document on the Shoah and anti-Semitism will be forthcoming, resulting from....serious [joint Catholic-Jewish] studies." Pope John Paul II, "The Miami Address to Jewish Leaders," Origins, Volume 17, September 24, 1987, page 243.

11. Emil L. Fackenheim, To Mend the World: Foundations of Future Jewish Thought [New York, Schocken Books, 1982], page 256.

12. By "prayer," I mean here the believer's personal and communal communication to God of praise, gratitude, contrition for sins, and petition. These four attitudes form the outline of most traditional Christian understandings of prayer.

13. See Michael McGarry, "The Relevance of the Shoah for Christians Today, " in Ecumenism, Volume 94, June, 1989, pages 20-22.

14. Rubenstein and Roth, Op. cit., page 285.

15. Fackenheim, Op. cit., pages 218-219.

16. Ibid., page 254.

17. Ibid., pages 289-291.

18. See David Wyman, The Abandonment of the Jews: America and the Holocaust 1941-1945 [New York, Pantheon Books, 1984]; Robert W. Ross, So It Was True: The American Protestant Press and the Nazi Persecution of the Jews [Minneapolis, University of Minnesota Press, 1980]; Deborah Lipstadt, "Finessing the Truth: The Press and the Holocaust," in Dimensions Volume 4, 1989, pages 3 and 10-15.

19. See Frederick C. Holmgren, "The God of History: Biblical Realism and the Lectionary," in RF, Volume I, pages 799-811.

20. For a survey of some traditional Jewish interpretations of the Shoah as somehow God's punishment "upon the Jewish people on account of its lack of faith and its laxity in the observance of God's commandments," see the fine survey by Norman Solomon, "Does the Shoah Require a Radically New Jewish Theology?" in RF, Volume 1, pages 1053-1068, especially pages 1058-1061. For an analysis of Christian applications of the "punishment theory," see Richard V. Pierard, "Varieties of Antisemitic Response to the Holocaust Within American Conservative Protestantism," in RF, Volume I, pages 447-460.

21. See Irving Greenberg's still watershed article, "Cloud of Smoke, Pillar of Fire: Judaism, Christianity and Modernity After the Holocaust," in Eva Fleischner [Editor], Auschwitz: Beginnings of a New Era: Reflections on the Holocaust [New York, Ktav Publishing House, 1977], pages 7-56.

22. Rosemary Radford Reuther, Faith and Fratricide: The Theological Roots of Anti-Semitism [New York, Seabury Press, 1974], page 230.

23. For a Catholic-Jewish discussion on the uniqueness of Jesus intimacy with the Father, his "Abba experience," see Father John T. Pawlikowski, O.S.M., and Rabbi Eugene B. Borowitz, 1987 Lecture Series: Proceedings of the Center for Jewish-Christian Learning [Saint Paul, MN, College of Saint Thomas, 1987].

24. Luke 22:39-44.

25. See Samuel Terrien, The Elusive Presence: Toward a New Biblical Theology [New York, Harper and Row, 1978], pages 361-372.

26. Paul M. van Buren, A Theology of the Jewish-Christian Reality, Part I: Discerning the Way [San Francisco, Harper and Row, 1980], page 116.

27. Etty Hillesum, An Interrupted Life: The Diaries of Etty Hillesum, 1941-1943 [New York, Pantheon Books, 1983. Translated by Arno Pomerans.], pages 127 and 146-147.

28. See Ellis Rivkin. What Crucified Jesus? The Political Execution of a Charismatic. Nashville, Abingdon Press, 1984.

29. Rubenstein and Roth, Op. cit., pages 290-338.

30. Elie Wiesel, Night [New York, Hill and Wang, 1960; Bantam Books, 1982. Translated by Stella Rodway], pages 61-62.

31. Jurgen Moltmann, The Crucified God: The Cross of Christ as the Foundation and Criticism of Christian Theology [New York, Harper and Row, 1974], page 275.

32. The theme of God's suffering is found throughout the theological literature on the Shoah. See, for example, Marcus Braybrooke, "The Suffering of God: New Perspectives in the Christian Understanding of God since the Holocaust," in RF, Volume I, pages 702-708; Robert S. Frey, "The Holocaust and the Suffering of God," in RF, Volume I, pages 613-621; Dorothee Solle, "God's Pain and Our Pain: How Theology has to Change after Auschwitz," in RF, Supplementary Volume, pages 448-464. See also Moltmann, Op. cit.; David Tracy, "Religious Values After the Holocaust: A Catholic View," in Peck, Op. cit., pages 87-107.

33. John Shea, Stories of God: An Unauthorized Biography [Chicago, Thomas Moore Press, 1979], pages 89-116, especially page 102.

34. Supplementing John Shea's helpful categories is the suggestion of the creative retrieval of the hutzpah k'lapei Shamaya [the tradition of arguing with God]. On this, see Belden Lane, "Hutzpa K'lapei Shamaya: A Christian Response to the Jewish Tradition of Arguing with God," in RF, Supplementary Volume, pages 233-247. Of course, this theme grounds many of Elie Wiesel's writings; see, for example, his The Trial of God [New York, Random House, 1978. Translated by Marion Wiesel.]

35. Elie Wiesel, A Jew Today [New York, Random House, 1978. Translated by Marion Wiesel.], pages 144-145. Quoted in Rubenstein and Roth, Op. cit., page 287.

36. Jacques Ellul. Prayer and Modern Man. New York, Seabury Press, 1970.

37. Ibid., page 99.

38. Ibid., page 102.

39. Quoted in Fackenheim, Op. cit., page 289-290.

40. van Buren, Op. cit., page 118.

41. This draws on what Fackenheim has identified as the "commanding voice of Auschwitz," the "614th commandment," that the Jews survive as Jews. See his The Jewish Return into History [New York, Schocken Books, 1979], Chapter 2.

42. Good Friday Liturgy, Intercessions.

THE SHOAH: CONTINUING THEOLOGICAL CHALLENGE FOR

CHRISTIANITY

John T. Pawlikowski

1. Uriel Tal, Christians and Jews in Germany: Religion , Politics and Ideology in the Second Reich, 1870-1914 [Ithaca, Cornell University Press, 1975], page 305.

2. Alexandre Donat, The Holocaust Kingdom [New York, Holt, Rinehart and Winston, 1965], pages 230-231.

3. Cf. John T. Pawlikowski, The Challenge of the Holocaust for Christian Theology [New York, Anti-Defamation League, 1982]; "Christian Perspectives and Moral Implications," in Henry Friedlander and Sybil Milton [Editors], The Holocaust: Ideology, Bureaucracy, and Genocide [Millwood, Kraus International Publications, 1980], pages 295-308; "The Holocaust: Its Implications for the Church and Society Problematic," in Richard W. Rosseau, S.J. [Editor], Christianity and Judaism: The Deepening Dialogue [Scranton, Ridge Row Press, 1983], pages 95-106; "The Holocaust: Its Implications for Public Morality," in Franklin H. Littell, Irene G. Shur, and Claude Foster, Jr. [Editors], The Holocaust: In Answer.... [West Chester, Sylvan Publishers, 1988], pages 287-297; and "Implications of the Holocaust for the Christian Churches," in Alex Grobman and Daniel Landers [Editors], Genocide: Critical Issues of the Holocaust [Chappaqua, NY, Rossel Books, 1983], pages 410-418.

4. Emil Fackenheim, The Jewish Return into History [New York, Schocken Books, 1978], page 246.

5. On non-Jewish victims, cf. Bohdan Wytwycky, The Other Holocaust: Many Circles of Hell [Washington, DC, The Novak Report, 1980]; Frank Rector, The Nazi Extermination of Homosexuals [New York, Stein and Day, 1981]; Richard S. Lukas, Forgotten Holocaust: The Poles Under German Occupation, 1939-1944 [Lexington, University Press of Kentucky, 1986]; Gabrielle Tyrnauer, "The Gypsy Awakening," in Reform Judaism, Volume 14, Number 3, Spring, 1986, pages 6-8; Richard Plant, The Pink Triangle:

The Nazi War Against Homosexuals [New York, Henry Holt, 1986]; Ian Hancock, The Pariah Syndrome [Ann Arbor, Karoma Publishers, 1987].

6. Uriel Tal, "Forms of Pseudo-Religion in the German Kulturbereich Prior to the Holocaust," in Immanuel, Volume 3, Winter, 1973-1974, page 69.

7. Uriel Tal, Christians and Jews in Germany, pages 302-303.

8. Michael Ryan, "Hitler's Challenge to the Churches: A Theological-Political Analysis of Mein Kampf," in Franklin H. Littell and Hubert G. Locke [Editors], The German Church Struggle and the Holocaust [Detroit, Wayne State University Press, 1974], pages 160-161.

9. David Tracy, "Religious Values After the Holocaust: A Catholic View," in Abraham J. Peck [Editor], Jews and Christians After the Holocaust [Philadelphia, Fortress Press, 1982], page 101.

10. David Hartman. A Living Covenant: The Innovative Spirit in Traditional Judaism. New York, The Free Press, 1985.

11. David Hartman, "New Jewish Religious Voices II: Auschwitz or Sinai?" in The Ecumenist, Volume 21, Number 1, November/December, 1982, page 8.

12. Richard L. Rubenstein, After Auschwitz: Radical Theology and Contemporary Judaism [Indianapolis, Bobbs-Merrill, 1966]; also, cf., "Some Perspectives on Religious Faith After Auschwitz, " in Littell and Locke, Op. cit., pages 256-268.

13. Richard L. Rubenstein and John K. Roth, Approaches to Auschwitz: The Holocaust and Its Legacy [Atlanta, John Knox Press, 1987], pages 311-312.

14. Steven Katz, Post-Holocaust Dialogues: Critical Studies in Modern Jewish Thought [New York, New York University Press, 1983], page 176.

15. Emil Fackenheim. The Jewish Return into History. New York, Schocken Books, 1978.

16. Arthur Cohen. The Tremendum: A Theological Interpretation of the Holocaust. New York, Crossroad, 1981.

17. Ibid., page 97.

18. Irving Greenberg, "The Voluntary Covenant," in Perspectives #3 [New York, National Jewish Resource Center, 1982], page 14.

19. Ibid., page 15.

20. Ibid.

21. Ibid., page 16.

22. Ibid., pages 17-18.

23. D. H. Lawrence, Selected Poems [London, Penguin Books, 1967], page 144.

24. Robert McAfee Brown, "The Holocaust as a Problem in Moral Choice," in Harry James Cargas [Editor], When God and Man Failed: Non-Jewish Views of the Holocaust [New York, Macmillan Publishing Company, 1981], page 94.

25. Elie Wiesel, Messengers of God [New York, Random House, 1976], page 235.

26. Robert Heilbroner. An Inquiry into the Human Prospect. New York, W. W. Norton and Company, 1980

27. John T. Pawlikowski. Christ in Light of the Christian-Jewish Dialogue. New York/Ramsey, Paulist Press, 1982.

28. John T. Pawlikowski. Jesus and the Theology of Israel. Wilmington, Michael Glazier, 1989.

29. Johannes Baptist Metz, "Facing the Jews: Christian Theology After Auschwitz," in Elisabeth Schussler-Fiorenza and David Tracy [Editors], The Holocaust as Interruption [Edinburgh, T. & T. Clark, 1984], pages 43-52.

30. Paul van Buren. A Theology of the Jewish-Christian Reality: Part 3: Christ in Context. San Francisco, Harper and Row, 1988.

31. Richard L. Rubenstein and John K. Roth, Op. cit., page 297.

32. Franklin Sherman, "Speaking of God After Auschwitz," in Worldview, Volume 17, Number 9, September, 1974, page 29. Also cf. Sherman's essay on the same theme is Paul D. Opsahl and Marc H. Tanenbaum [Editors], Speaking of God Today [Philadelphia, Fortress Press, 1974].

33. Marcel Dubois, "Christian Reflections on the Holocaust," in SIDIC, Volume 7, Number 2, 1974, page 15.

34. Ibid.

35. Douglas Hall, "Rethinking Christ," in Alan T. Davies [Editor], Antisemitism and the Foundations of Christianity [New York, Paulist Press, 1979], page 183.

36. Jurgen Moltmann, "The Crucified God," in Theology Today, Volume 31, Number 1, April, 1974, page 9.

37. A. Roy Eckardt, "Christians and Jews: Along a Theological Frontier," in Encounter, Volume 40, Number 2, Spring, 1979, page 102.

38. Stanley Hauerwas, "Jews and Christians Among the Nations," in Cross Currents, Volume 31, Spring, 1981, page 34.

39. David Tracy, "The Interpretation of Theological Texts," unpublished lecture, Indiana University, 1984, pages 16-17.

40. Johnnes Baptist Metz, The Emergent Church [New York, Crossroad, 1981], pages 19-20.

41. Elisabeth Schussler-Fiorenza and David Tracy, "The Holocaust as Interruption and the Christian Return to History," in Schussler-Fiorenza and Tracy, Op. cit., page 86.

42. Rebecca Chopp, "The Interruption of the Forgotten," in Schussler-Fiorenza and Tracy, Op. cit., page 20.

43. Fredrich Heer, God's First Love [New York, Weybright and Talley, 1970], page 406.

44. Fredrich Heer, "The Catholic Church and the Jews Today," in Midstream, Volume 17, Number 5, May, 1971, page 29.

45. Darrell J. Fasching, "Faith and Ethics After the Holocaust: What Christians Can Learn From Jews," in Remembering the Future: Jews and Christians During and After the Holocaust: Theme I, Papers Presented at an International Scholars' Conference, Oxford, England, 10-13 July 1988 [Oxford, Pergamon Press, 1988], page 606.

46. Irving Greenberg, "The Third Great Cycle in Jewish History," in Perspectives, September, 1981, pages 24-25.

47. Stanley Hauerwas, Op. cit., page 34.

48. Marc H. Ellis, Toward a Jewish Theology of Liberation [Maryknoll, Orbis Books, 1987]; "From Holocaust to Solidarity: Perspectives on a Jewish Theology of Liberation," in Christian-Jewish Relations, Volume 21, Number 1, Spring, 1988, pages 31-36.

49. Marc H. Ellis, Toward a Jewish Theology of Liberation, page 37.

50. David Hollenbach, Justice, Peace & Human Rights: American Catholic Social Ethics in a Pluralistic Context [New York, Crossroad, 1988], page 115.

51. Irving Greenberg and David Elcott, "The Ethics of Jewish Power: Two Views," in Perspectives. New York, The National Jewish Center for Learning and Leadership, April, 1988.

52. Irving Greenberg, "The Third Great Cycle," pages 24-25.

53. Romano Guardini, Power and Responsibility [Chicago, Henry Regnery, 1961], page xiii.

54. Cf. Franklin H. Littell, "Foundations and Traditions of Religious Liberty," in Journal of Ecumenical Studies, Volume 14, Number 4, Fall, 1977, page 10; Clyde L. Manschreck, "Church-State Relations: A Question of Sovereignty," in Clyde L. Manschreck and Barbara Brown [Editors], The American Religious Experiment: Piety and Practicality [Chicago, Exploration Press, 1976], page 121.

55. Franklin H. Littell, "Early Warning," in Remembering the Future: Theme II, pages 2125-2133.

56. Cf., John T. Pawlikowski, "The Vatican and the Holocaust: Unresolved Issues," Paper presented at Baruch College, The City University of New York, March, 1989; Helen Fein, Accounting for Genocide: National Responses and Jewish Victimization [Chicago, University of Chicago Press, 1984], page 33; Nora Levin, The Holocaust [New York, Schocken Books, 1973], page 693; and Otto Kulka and Paul Mendes-Flohr [Editors], Judaism and Christianity Under the Impact of National Socialism [Jerusalem, The Historical Society of Israel and the Zalman Shazar Center for Jewish History, 1987.]

THEOLOGICAL AND ETHICAL REFLECTIONS ON THE SHOAH:

Getting Beyond the Victim-Victimizer Relationship

Rosemary Radford Reuther

1. See, also, a critique of her position by David Biale in his review of The Wrath of Jonah by Rosemary Radford Reuther and Herman J. Reuther [New York, Harper and Row, 1989] in Tikkun, Volume 4, Number 3, pages 99-102, under the title, "The Philo-Semitic Face of Christian Anti-Semitism."

2. Arthur C. Cochrane, The Church's Confession Under Hitler [Philadephia, Westminster Press, 1962], pages 206-208.

3. Emil L. Fackenheim, "The People of Israel Lives," in The Christian Century, May 6, 1970, page 563.

4. Reader's Response: Richard L. Rubenstein, The Christian Century, July 29, 1970, pages 919-921.

5. The Jewish speakers at this conference were Irving Greenberg, Alfred Kazin, Yosef Yerushalmi, Emil Fackenheim, Seymour Siegel, Shlomo Avineri, Paul Jacobs, Milton Himmelfarb, Arthur Waskow, Edith Wyschogrod, Lionel Rubinoff, Paul Ritterband, Charles Silberman, and Elie Wiesel. The Christians were Alan T. Davies, Rosemary Radford Reuther, Walter Burghardt, Gregory Baum, Johannes Hoekendijk, Aarne Siirala, John T. Pawlikowski, Claire Huchet-Bishop, Thomas Hopko, Eva Fleischner, Michael Ryan, and Charles Long. Gabriel Habib of the Middle East Council of Churches sent a statement. The talks are printed in Eva Fleischner [Editor], Auschwitz: Beginning of a New Era? Reflections on the Holocaust [New York, Ktav Publishing House, 1977].

6. For the idea of a suffering prophet or teacher in First Century Judaism, see H. A. Fischel, "Martyr and Prophet," in Jewish Quarterly Review, Volume 37, 1946/47, pages 265 ff. and 363 ff.

7. Richard L. Rubenstein, After Auschwitz: Radical Theology and Contemporary Judaism [Indianapolis, Bobbs-Merrill, 1966], pages 9-11, 56-58, 85, and passim.

8. Richard L. Rubenstein, The Cunning of History: Mass Death and the American Future [New York, Harper and Row, 1975], page 21.

9. Ibid., pages 95-97.

10. Rubenstein, After Auschwitz, pages 131-142 and 154. On the Canaanite Movement in the Jewish Yishuv [Settlement--Ed.] in the early 1940's, see Akiva Orr, The UnJewish State: The Politics of Jewish Identity in Israel [London, Ithaca Press, 1983], page 95.

11. Richard L. Rubenstein. My Brother Paul. New York, Harper and Row, 1972.

12. Rubenstein, After Auschwitz., pages 196 and 22.

13. Note 2, above.

14. In Rubenstein's reply to Fackenheim [Note 3, above], he points out, somewhat nastily, that raising Jewish children is indeed an ethical decision for Fackenheim since his wife is a Christian, and so, according to Jewish law, his children are not Jews and must be converted to Judaism in order to become Jews.

15. Emil L. Fackenheim, "The Holocaust and the State of Israel: Their Relation," in Fleischner, Op. cit., pages 205-214.

16. The phrase is found in a prayer for the state of Israel by Israeli Chief Rabbi, quoted by Fackenheim, Ibid., page 205.

17. See Abraham Isaac Kook, "The Land of Israel," in Arthur Hertzberg [Editor], The Zionist Idea: A Historical Analysis and Reader [New York, Meridian, 1960], page 190.

18. Fackenheim, Op. cit., page 208.

19. Ibid., pages 212-214.

20. Ibid., page 214.

21. Fleischner, Op. cit., pages 7-55.

22. For the relation of American Jewish organizations to the rescue of European Jewry during World War II, see the study by Shoah survivor Leon Wells, Who Speaks for the Vanquished? American Judaism and the Holocaust [New York, Peter Lang, 1987].

23. Irving Greenberg, "Cloud of Smoke, Pillar of Fire: Judaism, Christianity and Modernity After the Holocaust," in Fleischner, Op. cit., page 44.

24. Eliezer Berkovits. Faith After the Auschwitz. New York, Ktav Publishing House, 1973.

25. Arthur Waskow, "Between the Fires," in Tikkun, Volume 2, Number 1, pages 84-86.

26. See my reply to Waskow's article in Tikkun, Volume 2, Number 5, pages 5-6.

27. "Declaration on the Relationship of the Church to Non-Christian Religions," in Walter Abbott [Editor], Documents of Vatican II [New York, America Press, 1966], pages 663-666.

28. "Rat der Evangelischen Kirche in Deutschland," in Christen und Juden: Eine Studie des Rates der Evangelischen Kirche in Deutschland [Gutersloh, Gutersloher Verlagshaus Gerd Mohn, 1975].

29. For the history and ideology of Christian Zionism, see Regina Sharif, Non-Jewish Zionism: Its Roots in Western History [London, Zed Press, 1983]; and Rosemary Radford Reuther and Herman J. Reuther, The Wrath of Jonah: The Crisis of Religious Nationalism in the Israeli-Palestinian Debate [San Francisco, Harper and Row, 1989], pages 74-91.

30. For Christian documents on Jewish-Christian relations published between 1963 and 1976, Helga Croner [Editor], Stepping Stones to Further Jewish-Christian Relations: An Unabridged Collection of Christian Documents [London, Stimulus Books, 1977].

31. New York, Seabury Press, 1974.

32. Ibid., pages 64-66.

33. Long Night's Journey into Day [Detroit, Wayne State University Press, 1982]; and Jews and Christians: The Contemporary Meeting [Bloomington, Indiana University Press, 1986].

34. Long Night's Journey into Day, pages 125-133.

35. Jews and Christians, pages 79-81.

36. Ibid., page 78.

37. Long Night's Journey into Day, page 134.

38. Franklin H. Littell. The Crucifixion of the Jews. New York, Harper and Row, 1975.

39. Franklin H. Littell. The Anabaptist Concept of the Church. Hartford, American Society of Church History, 1952.

40. Franklin H. Littell. The German Phoenix. New York, Doubleday and Company, 1960.

41. Littell, The Crucifixion of the Jews, page 68.

42. Ibid., pages 95-96.

43. Ibid., page 88.

44. Ibid., pages 83-84.

45. All three volumes published by Harper and Row.

46. See Karl Barth, Christ and Adam: Man and Humanity in Romans 5 [New York, Macmillan Publishing Company, 1956].

47. van Buren, Christian Theology of the People Israel, pages 70-76 and 116-128.

48. See Reuther and Reuther, The Wrath of Jonah, pages 43-47.

49. van Buren, Op. cit., page 350.

50. Ibid., pages 268-294.

51. Ibid., pages 33-37.

52. Ibid., pages 161-162 and 195-197.

53. Ibid., pages 272-274.

54. van Buren, Christ in Context, pages 176-183.

55. Ibid., page 179.

56. van Buren, Christian Theology of the People Israel, pages 316-319.

57. Ibid., 127-128 and 312-313.

58. Ibid., pages 338-341.

59. Ibid., page 337.

60. One example of such an effort to provide international standards of human rights is the Universal Declaration of Human Rights, adopted by the United Nations General Assembly, December 10, 1948. Two additional covenants, one dealing with economic, social and cultural rights and the second with civil and political rights were adopted December 16, 1966. Ratified by 46 and 44 nations respectively, the covenants went into force in 1976. See The International Bill of Human Rights, Introduction by Peter Mayer [Glen Ellen, Entwhistle Books, 1981].

61. An example of such a construction of criticism of Israel is the review of the book by Reuther and Reuther, The Wrath of Jonah, by David Biale, in Tikkun, Volume 4, Number 3, 1989, pages 99-192.

62. A report on Shomran's statement appeared in the Los Angeles Times, June 18, 1989, page 1.

63. Maryknoll, Orbis Press, 1987; New Edition with Postscript on the Palestinian Uprising and the Future of the Jewish People, 1989.

64. Irving Greenberg, "On the Third Era of Jewish History: Power and Politics," in Perspectives [New York, National Jewish Resource Center, 1980], and "The Third Great Cycle of Jewish History," in Perspectives [New York, National Jewish Resource Center, 1981]. Ellis' critique of Greenberg's more recent views are in his book, Toward a Jewish Theology of Liberation, pages 26-36.

65. Johannes Baptist Metz, The Emergent Church: The Future of Christianity in a Post-bourgeois World [New York, Crossroads, 1981], page 19; quoted in Ellis, Ibid., pages 24 and 123-124.

66. Ibid., page 124.

67. Ibid., pages 132-136.

68. Maryknoll, Orbis Press, 1989.

ASKING AND LISTENING, UNDERSTANDING AND DOING:

Some Conditions for Responding to the Shoah Religiously

John K. Roth

1. Primo Levi, Survival in Auschwitz: The Nazi Assault on Humanity [New York, Collier Books, 1976. Translated by Stuart Woolf], page 13.

2. Ibid., page 116.

3. Ibid., pages 116-117.

4. Ibid., page 117.

5. Elie Wiesel, Night [New York, Bantam Books, 1986. Translated by Stella Rodway], page 3.

6. Elie Wiesel, A Jew Today [New York, Random House, 1978. Translated by Marion Wiesel.], pages 144-145.

7. Irving Greenberg, "Cloud of Smoke, Pillar of Fire: Judaism, Christianity, and Modernity After the Holocaust," in Eva Fleischner [Editor],

Auschwitz: Beginning of a New Era? Reflections on the Holocaust [New York, Ktav Publishing Company, 1977], page 23. This important essay is reprinted in John K. Roth and Michael Berenbaum [Editors], Holocaust: Religious and Philosophical Implications [New York, Paragon Publishers, 1989].

8. See, for example, Emil L. Fackenheim, God's Presence in History: Jewish Affirmations and Philosophical Reflections [New York, Harper and Row, 1972], pages 67-98.

9. See Emil L. Fackenheim, To Mend the World: Foundations of Future Jewish Thought [New York, Schocken Books, 1982], pages 278-294.

10. Rainer Maria Rilke, Poems from the Book of Hours [New York, New Directions, 1975. Translated by Babette Deutsch.], page 31.

11. Wiesel, A Jew Today, page 164.

12. Elie Wiesel, Twilight [New York, Summit Books, 1988. Translated by Marion Wiesel.], pages 202 and 209.

13. Ibid., page 179.

14. Ibid., page 118.

15. Ibid., page 37.

16. Ibid., page 11.

17. Ibid., page 201.

18. Ibid., page 202.

19. See Elie Wiesel, The Town Beyond the Wall [New York, Avon Books, 1970. Translated by Stephen Becker.], page 3.

20. Ibid., page 182.

21. See Elie Wiesel's review of Auschwitz by Bernd Naumann. The review first appeared in Hadassah Magazine, January, 1967, and is reprinted in Irving Abrahamson [Editor], Against Silence: The Voice and Vision of Elie Wiesel [New York, Holocaust Library, 1985. Three Volumes.], Volume II, page 293.

22. Wiesel, The Town Beyond the Wall, page 189.

23. Wiesel, Twilight page 217.

24. Elie Wiesel, "Forward," in Harry James Cargas, A Christian Response to the Holocaust [Denver, Stonehenge Books, 1981], page iii.

25. Elie Wiesel, "Telling the Tale," in Abrahamson, Op. cit., Volume I, page 234. This text is from an address to the Forty-Ninth General Assembly of the Union of American Hebrew Congregations, November, 1967.

26. Elie Wiesel, "Exile and the Human Condition," Ibid., Volume I, page 183. This text is from a lecture to the International Young Presidents Organization, Madrid, Spain, April, 1980.

27. Ibid., page 182.

28. Elie Wiesel, "The Use of Words and the Weight of Silence," in Abrahamson, Ibid., Volume II, page 79. This text is from an interview conducted by Lily Edelman which appeared in the National Jewish Monthly, November, 1973.

29. Elie Wiesel, "Freedom of Conscience: A Jewish Commentary," in Ibid., Volume I, page 210. This text is from an address at the Bicentennial Conference on Religious Liberty, Philadelphia, 27 April 1976.

30. Elie Wiesel, Messengers of God: Biblical Portraits and Legends [New York, Random House, 1976. Translated by Marion Wiesel.], page 235.

31. Elie Wiesel, One Generation After [New York, Avon Books, 1972. Translated by Lily Edelman.], page 95. See also Elie Wiesel, The Testament [New York, Summit Books, 1981. Translated by Marion Wiesel.], page 9.

32. Elie Wiesel, "The Trial of Man," in Abrahamson, Op. cit., Volume I, page 176. This text is from a lecture at Loyola University, Chicago, which Wiesel delivered on 12 April 1980.

33. Elie Wiesel, Souls on Fire: Portraits and Legends of Hasidic Masters [New York, Random House, 1972. Translated by Marion Wiesel.], page 133.

34. Ibid., page 198.

35. Ibid., page 245.

36. Ibid., page 254.

37. Elie Wiesel, The Oath [New York, Random House, 1973. Translated by Marion Wiesel.], page 16.

38. Ibid., page 239.

39. Ibid., page 241.

GLOSSARY

Aggadah: [Hebrew] Post-Biblical Jewish literature which includes stories, chronicles, sayings, moral instructions, admonitions and chastisements, as well as consolations.

Akedah: [Hebrew] Reference to the Binding of Isaac as depicted in Bereshit [Genesis], Chapter 22. Oft-times mistakenly referred to in Christian literature as the "Sacrifice" of Isaac, precursor to the death of Jesus.

Aliyah: [Hebrew] Immigration to Israel. Literally a "going up" to the Land of Israel. [Its opposite if **yeridah**, literally a "going down" from the Land of Israel.]

Anamnesis: [Greek] Literally "remembering." Its Hebrew equivalent is **zikkaron**. For Eugene Fisher, Volume II, both Judaism and Christianity are religions of remembering.

Ani Ma'amin: [Hebrew] Literally "I believe...." The opening words to Maimonides' [1135-1204] "Thirteen Articles of Faith," traditional included in the Jewish siddur, prayer book.

Antinomianism: An early Christian interpretation which held that salvation is directly contingent upon faith only rather than obedience to any moral law.

Antisemitism: Hated of the Jewish People and the Jewish Religious Faith, Heritage, and Tradition. Throughout history, the forms antisemitism has taken have included expulsion, ghettoization, forced religious conversion, denial of civil rights, and extermination/annihilation. [Preferred spelling here is without the hyphen; to use it is to imply its opposite: That there is such a thing as "S/semitism," which is non-existent.]

Apocalypse: The idea of the revelation of the End of Days as well as the Day[s] of Judgment. Important to all three monotheistic religious traditions, Judaism, Christianity, and Islam.

Apostasy: The abandonment of the beliefs of one's faith community.

Aryan: The term wrongly employed by the Nazis to designate any "pure-blooded" Caucasian, male or female, possessing no Jewish ancestors, primarily, but, also, one possessing neither Polish or Slavic "blood."

Ashkenazim: German Jews and their descendants. Though the term can be found in the Scriptures [Genesis 10:3; Jeremiah 51:27], it has been used since the ninth century in the above way.

Atheism: The philosophical position that either there is no God or that the proofs which have thus far been presented to prove the existence of God are themselves faulty.

Auschwitz: [German; Polish: Oswiecim; Yiddish: Ushpitzin]. Town thirty miles west of Cracow, Poland. Premier Nazi concentration camp which saw the extermination of between four and five million prisoners, more than one and one-half million of them Jews. It has, also, become the symbolic reference to the entire concentration/extermination camp system of the Nazis.

Bat Kol: [Hebrew] Literally, "daughter of a voice." The term is found in rabbinic literature, especially the Talmud to denote the Divine Voice, available to be heard by anyone.

Bayt Ha-Knesset: [Hebrew] One of the primary functions/roles of the synagogue--to be a "House of Assembly and Gathering."

Bayt Ha-Midrash: [Hebrew] One of the primary functions/roles of the synagogue--to be a "House of Study and Learning."

Bayt Ha-Tefillah: [Hebrew] One of the primary functions/roles of the synagogue--to be a "House of Prayer and Worship."

Bayt Ha-Mikdash: [Hebrew] Literally, "House of the Holy." Reference to the ancient Temple in Jerusalem. Destroyed once by the Babylonians in 586 B.C.E., and, again, by the Romans in 70 C.E.

Beviat Ha-Mashiach: [Hebrew] Literally, the "coming of the Messiah." This term is taken from Maimonides "Thirteen Articles of Faith," and is the general referent to that future moment when, according to Jewish Religious Tradition, he will make his appearance known to the House of Israel. [See above, **Ani Ma'amin.**]

Bureaucracy: According to Webster's New World Diction of the American Language, College Edition, [c] 1959, "the administration of government through departments and subdivisions managed by sets of officials following an inflexible routine....the concentration of authority in administrative bureaus." Particularly relevant in understanding the Nazi administration of the Shoah.

Christology: Christianity's unique faith-claim of the distinctiveness of Jesus as the Christ according to the New Testament texts, and, thus, the very heart and essence of the Christian religious tradition.

Churban: [Hebrew] Literally, "destruction." One of the possibly appropriate words used to describe the wanton murder and callous slaughter of the Jews by the Nazis and their minions during the years 1939-1945.

Chutzpah: [Hebrew] Literally, "brazenness" or "audacity." Sometimes regarded as a uniquely Jewish trait, though in point of fact, not specifically applicable to only one group or individual.

Conservative Judaism: Also known as "Positive-Historical Judaism," this Jewish Religious Movement represents the so-called "middle of the road" approach to religious questions and practices.

Covenant Theology: That theological understanding, originally, of the unique relationship between God and the Children of Israel/Jewish People, first entered into at Mount Sinai, whereby the Jews agreed to observe God's laws as set forth in the Torah in return for Divine protection and favor. Today, there are those theologians who speak of the Jewish Covenant at Sinai and the Christian Covenant through Jesus at Golgotha.

Creed: An authoritative statement of religious belief describing the essence of the group's and/or individual's faith.

Das Nichtige: [German] Literally, "The Nothingness;" a theological reference by Swiss thinker Karl Barth, with far broader religious and philosophical implications. [See the essay by Alan Davies in Volume II.]

Deicide: Literally, "God killer." The ages-old charge against the Jewish People, over which so much innocent blood has been shed, that the Jewish People and its leaders were primarily responsible for the death of Jesus at the hands of the Romans who were only their willing tools. Its roots lie in the New Testament accounts of the events themselves and the invidious statement, "His blood be upon us and upon our children." Despite serious scholarship to the contrary, and the contemporary Roman Catholic position that the death of the Christ was attributable to no one group alone, either historically or since, this charge continues to rear its ugly head even in our own day.

Diaspora: One of the terms, without value-judgment, used to describe the world-wide Jewish communities living outside the Land of Israel.

Die Endlosung: [German] Literally, the "Final Solution," that is, the Nazis' "Final Solution to the Jewish Problem"--extermination or annihilation of approximately six million Jewish men, women, and children, with a world plan to obliterate the Jewish People from the face of the earth.

Displacement Theology: The idea, still prevalent in some Christian denominations, that, with the appearance of Jesus as the Christ, and the rise of Christianity, both Judaism and the Jewish People have been "displaced" from their position as God's favored elect.

Dogma: The authoritative affirmation of the beliefs and principles of one's faith community.

Einsatzgruppe [pl. en]: [German] The "Mobile Killing Units" of the SS under the direct authority of Heinrich Himmler, Chief of the SS, responsible for the murder of those Jews found in areas conquered by the Wehrmacht. Oft-times, the Jews themselves were forced to dig their own graves, strip themselves naked, lie down in the trenches and pits and wait to be machine-gunned to death. No regard whatsoever was shown for men, women, children, the aged or the very young.

Einsatzkommando: [German] One of the SS men who considered it their "honorable duty" to put an end to the Jews by such "special operations" as described above.

El Mistater: [Hebrew] Literally, the "Hidden Face of God." Following the idea of German-Jewish philosopher Martin Buber [1878-1965] concerning the "eclipse of God" during the Shoah, for one awful moment in history, God "chose" to "turn His face away" from humankind with the Shoah as result. This concept, interestingly enough, is also found in Jewish rabbinic literature during earlier historical epochs.

En Sof: [Hebrew] Literally, "infinity" or "nothingness." In Jewish mystical literature and tradition, it is the "expanse of God" or "holy nothingness" beyond humanity's full ability to comprehend and understand--the "realm of God."

Eretz Yisrael: [Hebrew] Literally, the "Land of Israel" as distinct from the state and/or government and/or people of Israel. Sacred to all three religious traditions, Judaism, Christianity, and Islam.

Ethics: The system or code by which the morality of a nation-state or any group is put into practice.

Ethnocide: The effort to destroy a people as a cultural entity. [See the essay by Rosemary Radford Reuther in Volume II.]

Evil: That which causes harm to an individual or group usually innocent. In religious circles, the most difficult questions revolve around the role/-place/function of evil in a God-controlled world.

Existentialism: That philosophical understanding usually associated with such thinkers as Jean-Paul Sartre and Albert Camus that our world is one of random accident and chance, that whatever happens happens, and we make our way in the world as best we can. Though some have attempted to develop a "religious existentialism," incorporating both the concept of randomness with an interactive God, others feel they are both mutually-exclusive and mutually incompatible.

Fascism: A political system, usually run by a dictator, supported by one party which brooks no dissent, and characterized by intense nationalistic fervor and oppression of both dissidents and minorities.

Galut: [Hebrew] Literally, "exile." That Jewish understanding usually associated with both religious and secular Zionism which regards those Jews who <u>choose</u> to live outside the Land of Israel as living in exile."

Gemilut Hasadim: [Hebrew] Literally, "deeds of loving-kindness." One of the goals of the Jewish Religious Tradition is to heighten human consciousness to better look for ways to perform such deeds.

Genocide: Term coined by the late Raphael Lemkin [1901-1959] Polish-American jurist and "father" of the United Nations Treaty on Genocide to describe the conscious attempt to destroy a people's identity culturally, spiritually, and physically.

Geulah: [Hebrew] Literally, "redemption." That moment in the Jewish journey when universal peace will be achieved and the Jews will have returned to their homeland to dwell in harmony with their neighbors.

Ghetto: Originally from the Italian word 'giotto', that restricted area of settlement, usually in the worst section of the city. Jews were forced into such environments starting in Italy in the Middle Ages, though the term has expanded to include other groups as well.

Gog & Magog: According to the New Testament Book of Revelations [20:8], those nations, under the leadership of Satan, who will contend against God in the coming cataclysm.

Grace: The fullest expression of Divine love and blessing for all of humanity, largely unmerited, and not always understandable by human beings.

Halakhah: [Hebrew] Literally, "The Way." The system of Jewish Law as culled by the Rabbis from the Torah itself and elaborated upon in the Talmud and subsequent and additional Jewish resource literatures. For the Orthodox Jew, Jewish Law governs all facets and aspects of daily and religious living, coming as it does directly from God and interpreted authoritatively by rabbinic spokesmen. Conservative Judaism likewise affirms its sanctity, but attempts to give it a more human cast through its Law and Standards Committee of the Rabbinical Assembly. Reform Judaism has long rejected its sovereignty, acknowledging, instead, that "the past shall exercise a vote, not a veto."

Hallel Psalms: Specifically, Psalms 113-118. Recited in the Jewish worship services for Passover, Shavuot, Sukkot, and Hanukkah.

Heilsgeschichte: [German] According to both Jewish and Christian religious traditions, the working out of human history understood as moving towards an ultimate salvation/redemption.

Hesed: [Hebrew] Literally, "lovingkindness." [See **Gemilut Hasadim.**]

Heshbon Ha-Nefesh: [Hebrew] Literally, "the accounting of the soul." When one's life's journey is at its end, according to Jewish religious tradition, one's good and bad deeds are judged by God and the scale tips one way or the other in terms of admittance into the afterlife.

Hester Panim: [Hebrew] Literally, "[God's] Hidden Face." [See **El Mistater.**]

Higher Criticism: The so-called "scientific study of the Bible," using the best insights of the various academic disciplines. Growing originally out of 19th Century German Protestant scholarship, it was understood by Jews as "higher antisemitism" and an attack on their own religious legitimacy. Roman Catholics, too, saw it in a similar light.

Historikerstreit: [German] Literally, the "historians' fight." The movement, among a small circle of contemporary German historians [e.g. Ernest Nolte and Michael Sturmer, among others], to view the Shoah in a far broader context and thus diminish both its uniqueness and minimize an overall sense of German guilt.

Holocaust: Up until recently, the universally-acknowledged English word used to describe the wanton murder of nearly six million Jews by the Nazis and their collaborators. Said to have first been used by the noted writer and Nobel Prize winner Elie Wiesel. Its origin is an Anglicization of the Greek translation of the Hebrew word 'olah, the totally-consumable offering by fire to God as depicted in the Torah. In recent years, the term itself has become increasingly problematic for obvious reasons.   Current thinking is to use the Hebrew term **Shoah** instead.

Hubris: [Greek] Literally, "pride." The excessive, ego-inflating pride that enables one both to perceive himself/herself and to act as if he/she were as God. Understood to be sinful in all three Western religious traditions.

Ideology: Strongly held beliefs, opinions, ideas, values, etc. whether of an individual, group, nation-state, or religious community.

Immanent: The religious belief that the God who is addressed in prayer is close at hand and responsive to human concerns.

Incarnation: The religious belief, primarily of Christianity, following the New Testament, that out of God's love for humanity, He sent His divine son, Jesus, to earth giving him both human form and human nature.

Intifada: [Arabic] Literally, "uprising." The militant response of Palestinians living in the West Bank of Israel to Israeli military and political rule. Begun in December, 1987, it has witnessed the deaths of hundreds of innocent men, women, and children, both Palestinian and Israeli. Perceived by some as a national liberation movement and by others as a terrorist campaign, it continues to be one of the major stalemates to a lasting peace in the Middle East.

Judenrein: [German] Literally, "Jew-free." The ultimate objective of Hitler's extermination policies towards Jews was to free the world of all physical, cultural, and religious evidence of the presence of the Jewish People and Faith.

K'lal Yisrael: [Hebrew] Literally, "all Israel." That term used to designate the world-wide Jewish People in its collective presentation.

Kabbalah: [Hebrew] Literally, "received tradition." The mystical tradition and literature of religious Judaism, arising, perhaps, as early as the 1st Century of the Common Era, and continually influencing all streams of religious expression.

Kabbalat Shabbat: [Hebrew] Literally, "reception of the Sabbath." The onset of the Sabbath according to Jewish religious tradition occurs on Friday Evening at sundown with appropriate blessings, customs, and festive meal.

Kaddish: [Hebrew] Literally, "holy prayer." Aramaicized prayer usually understood to be the "Mourner's Prayer" recited by survivors after the funeral of a loved one either during the Worship Service or at home.

Kadoshim: [Hebrew] Literally, "holy ones," plural form. Reference to the near six million Jews murdered and slaughtered by the Nazis and their cohorts. The use of this religiously-relevant term raises anew the theological problems with which these two volumes are ultimately concerned.

Kibbutz: [Hebrew] Literally, "collective, gathering." The collective farming settlement begun in Palestine in the 1920's prior to the re-creation of the State of Israel in 1948.

Kiddush Ha-Shem: [Hebrew] Literally, "sanctification of the [Divine] Name." The term applied to those Jews who died a martyr's death. Understood now as applicable to all who died as a result of the Shoah.

Kiddush Ha-Hayyim: [Hebrew] Literally, "sanctification of life." The very opposite of the above **Kiddush Ha-Shem.** Understood in the contemporary Jewish world both as an historic Jewish value and a post-Shoah Jewish imperative.

Kristallnacht: [German] Literally, "Night of the Broken Glass/-Crystal." On November 9-10, 1938, the Nazis attacked Jewish businesses [844], homes [171], and synagogues [267] as well as the Jews themselves [72 killed or severely injured] while the state police did nothing to intervene and the government closed its eyes. This "pogrom" was presumably a spontaneous response to the assassination of the Third Secretary of the German Embassy in Paris, Ernst Vom Rath, by a Polish Jew Hershel Grynszpan. A fine of $1,000,000,000 RM [Reich Marks] was imposed upon the Jews of Germany to pay for the damages and clean up operations.

Lebensraum: [German] Literally, "living room." The German understanding, actually given voice prior to World War I, and furthered by Adolf Hitler, that the German people had a/the "natural right" to claim/reclaim those territories both needed for expansion as well as those areas where the majority of the population was German-speaking and, thus, Aryans.

Lebensunwerte Leben: [German] Literally, "life unworthy of life." That German/Nazi understanding that there existed those sub-populations-- the aged, infirm, feeble-minded, handicapped, as well as Jews, Gypsies, homosexuals, and others--who usefulness to the State [economically, politically, militarily, etc.] was nil and thus could be destroyed.

Lecha Dode: [Hebrew] Literally, "Come, my beloved." Title of a popular hymn sung in the synagogue on Friday Evening welcoming the Sabbath.

Limpieza de Sangre: [Spanish] Literally, "purity of blood." A concept which arose in the 15th Century in both Spain and Portugal that only those who were "pure Christians" could perform even the most humble of societal tasks, but especially the more important ones. Its relevance to Nazi ideology is obvious.

Lubavitch Hasidim: Hasidic sect who trace their origins to the town of Lubavitch in Russia. Also known as **Habad Hasidim**, their understanding of traditional Orthodox Judaism is a merging of the intellectual of normative Judaism with the emotional ecstasy of Hasidic Judaism.

Lurianic Kabbalah: An interpretation of the Jewish mystical tradition based on the writings and teachings of Isaac ben Solomon Luria [1534-1572], also known as "Ha-Ari," the sacred lion. His interpretations of the mystical were infused with a hungering for the advent of the Messiah.

Marranos: [Spanish] Literally, "pigs." Term used to designate those new converts to Christianity who were formerly Jews during the Middle Ages. From the Christian perspective, they were not to be trusted as true and sincere converts. From the Jewish perspective, they were equally understood to be "secret Jews" who converted for their physical survival as well as their children, but secretly practiced the rituals of Judaism.

Masada: The summer palace of King Herod in the Judean desert which saw the ultimate suicide of 960 Zealot defenders, men, women, and children. against the Romans at the end of a protracted four-year struggle [66-70].

Medinat Yisrael: [Hebrew] Literally, the "State of Israel." The official term for the contemporary nation-state founded in 1948. Distinguished from **Eretz Yisrael**, the Land of Israel. [See above.]

Megillah: [Hebrew] Literally, "scroll." Generally, any scroll of ancient Jewish text. **Ha-Megillah** or **Megillat Esther** is that associated with the festival of **Purim** and tells the story of the Book of Esther found in the Torah.

Messianism: That religious strain in both Judaism and Christianity which gives voice to the community's yearning for the appearance of the Messiah in Judaism or the return of the Messiah in Christianity. Jewish and Christian thinking on this subject, however, are substantively different.

Metaphysics: A branch of the discipline of philosophy concerned with both first causes and ultimate reality.

Midrash: [Hebrew] Literally, "that which is drawn out." Jewish interpretive literature of a non-legal nature. Commentary on the Torah as well as additional sermonic and story literature "filling in the gaps," so to speak, in the literary record. Some of it is quite fanciful--allowing the Rabbis, the creators of the literature, to give free rein to their imaginations. Others of it are quite insightful morally, ethically, spiritually, psychologically, as well as intellectually.

Mikveh: [Hebrew] [Pl.: **Mikvaot**] Jewish ritual baths used for a variety of religious occasions [e.g. after menstruation, prior to a wedding, conversion, etc.] Early **mikvaot** have been found at **Masada**.

Minhag: [Hebrew] [Pl. **Minhagim**] Jewish religious customs of a given Jewish community at a given historical moment. It is said in Jewish religious life that "the **minhag** of one generation becomes the law of the next."

Mitzvah: [Hebrew] [Pl. **Mitzvot**] Literally, "commanded act" by God to the Jewish People. According to the Rabbis, there are 613 **mitzvot** found through the Torah of both a moral-ethical and ritual-ceremonial nature, of equal sanctity. The **mitzvot** of the Torah given by God ultimately become in the eyes of the Rabbis the legal system--**Halakhah**--of the Jewish Religious Tradition. The word has also taken on a popular form in describing any "good deed."

Monism: The philosophical-theological idea or concept that there exists only one ultimate thing--in religious thought, obviously God.

Morality: Actions which are in accord with the principles of right conduct of a given group, community, religion, or nation-state

Moshav: [Hebrew] Literally, a "settlement." Existing in Israel and distinct from the **kibbutz**, the members of the agricultural **moshav** own their own homes but pool their resources for the purchase of needed farming items and the sale of whatever they produce.

Mussellmann [er] [German] Literally, "muscleman/men." German Nazi term of irony to describe the zombie-like slaves in the concentration and extermination camps, more often than not prior to their murder.

Mysterium Tremendum: [Latin] Literally, "tremendous mystery." Term made "popular" by the late Arthur Cohen [and others] to, somehow, label the Shoah and extend its implications into both the philosophical and theological realms. [A parallel term also used is **caesura**, indicating a break in the natural order and rhythm of things.]

Mystery: That thing, event, idea, etc., for which past and present explanations are not satisfactory. In theological terms, a **mystery** may very well be beyond human comprehension.

Mysticism: That branch of religious expression which sees it as possible to commune with and experience God without recourse to the intellectual and verbal.

Mythology: The collected "stories" of a given religious tradition and/or community often shrouded in the past and expressed in "larger than life" personages.

National Socialism: The "politically correct" term to describe the political philosophy of the Nazis.

Nationalism: Intense patriotic devotion to one's nation-state and its ideals, beliefs, and practices perceived as beyond reproach.

Nazi: Contraction of the German **Nationalsozialistiche Deutsche Arbeiterpartei** [National Socialist German Workers Party]; also abbreviated as **NSDAP**. Founded in 1919 and ultimately given free rein under the organizing genius of Adolf Hitler later to become **Fuhrer** of Germany. It was formally abolished and declared outlawed by the Nuremberg Trials in 1945.

Neturei Karta: [Aramaic] Literally, "guardians of the city." Orthodox Jews already in Jerusalem in Palestine prior to the founding of the State of Israel in 1948. They are intensely opposed to the political rebirth of Israel believing its contravenes the work of the coming Messiah to bring it about.

Nihilism: In philosophical and theological thought, the belief that there is no objective basis for either knowledge or truth. In politics, the belief that all currently-existing political institutions must be destroyed to make way for new ones.

Nostre Aetate: [Latin] Literally, "In Our Time." The 1965 Vatican Declaration on the Roman Catholic Church and the Jewish People which has led to a strengthening and furthering of the inter-religious dialogue between these two faith communities.

Oleh: [Hebrew] [Pl. **Olim**] Literally, "one who ascends." The term used to describe someone who makes **aliyah**, immigration, to Israel and becomes a citizen of that country.

Ontology: The philosophical and metaphysical concern with the nature of being and reality.

Original Sin: The theological concept, found in both Judaism and Christianity, that, as a result of the sin of Adam and Eve in the Garden of Eden, subsequent humanity is born with a "taint" and must work diligently to return to a state of **grace** in God's favor.

Orthodox Judaism: The most traditional and fundamentalist expression of religious Judaism. Orthodox Jews believe the Torah is literally the Word of God and only those who are its authentic and authoritative spokesmen, the Rabbis, can interpret those words for succeeding generations. Orthodox Jews equally claim their religious practices are the only authentic Jewish ritual and ceremonial practices.

Paganism: Religious expression, polytheistic in origin, nature-god oriented, predating Judaism, and today describing a philosophy which is neither Jewish, Christian or Muslim.

Passion of Christ: The suffering of Jesus on the Christ prior to his death. Said to be freely chosen and substitutionary for all humanity.

Pentateuch: [Greek] Literally, "Five Books." Reference to the First Five Books of the Torah: **Bereshit** [Genesis], **Shemot** [Exodus], **Vayikra** [Leviticus], **Bamidbar** [Numbers], and **Devarim** [Deuteronomy].

Pharisees: Anglicization of the Hebrew **Perushim**, "separatists." Religious and political party of the Second Temple Period whose interpretations of the Jewish religious tradition emphasized a "liberal" approach and emphasis on teaching, prayer, ethical behavior, and legal norms. The forerunners of the Rabbis.

Philosophy: The intellectual and academic discipline concerned with such "ultimate questions" as good and evil, knowledge, aesthetics, etc.

Pintele Yid: [Yiddish] Literally, "point Jew." A term of compliment for the Jew who attempts to scrupulously observe all the myriad practices of the Jewish religious tradition.

Pirke Avot: [Hebrew] Literally, "Sayings of the Fathers." Ethical tractate of moral maxims of the Rabbis from the 3rd Century B.C.E. [Before the Common Era] to the 3rd Century C.E. included in the **Talmud** and studied by Jewish religious families on Sabbath afternoons.

Pogrom: [Russian] Literally, "destruction." Historically, in Russia, used to describe an attack, organized, abetted, and oft-times inspired by the authorities which pitted the serfs against the small Jewish enclaves in their midst. More often than not, the Jews witnessed the wanton slaughter and deaths of their own without any retribution whatsoever.

Predicate Theology: A rethinking and re-focusing of theological questions from the author or subject of an act to the act or object itself. For example, the question is not whether God is good, but what is the nature of goodness. [See, for example, Harold Schulweis, Evil and the Morality of

God, Cincinnati, Hebrew Union College Press, 1984, as well as the essay by Peter J. Haas in Volume I.]

Race: An anthropological term used to categorize the different biological divisions of humankind, based on specific characteristics, for example, skin pigmentation. Adapted by the Nazis to the plane of history.

Racism: Discrimination--and worse--against a given biological sub-population based on the above specific characteristics.

Reconstructionist Judaism: The newest Jewish religious movement based upon the philosophy of Rabbi Mordecai Kaplan's [1881-1984] major work Judaism as A Civilization, which called for a "reconstruction" of American Jewish life in all areas, with religious Judaism serving as the hub of a wheel which spokes radiated to all facets and aspects of Jewish living. Kaplan was a professor at the [Conservative] Jewish Theological Seminary of America and was influenced by the writings of American pragmatic philosopher John Dewey [1859-1952].

Reform Judaism: Perhaps the most "liberal" wing of the Jewish religious tradition. Having its start in Sessen, Germany, in 1810 as a movement for liturgical change, it has flowered in the United States and today numbers almost two million adherents. It is also the most welcoming of non-Jews and has pioneered in the area of interfaith dialogue.

Refusenik: [Russian/English] Literally, "one who has been refused." Term used to described those Jews who were **refused** permission to emigrate to either Israel or the United States by the previous Soviet Union.

Resurrection: The belief, central to Christianity, thought originally brought to it from the **Pharisees**, that Jesus was **resurrected** three days after his death on the cross.

Revelation: The belief of Judaism, Christianity, and Islam that, out of God's love for humanity, he chooses to **reveal** himself to us: Though Moses, Sinai, and the prophets for Jews, through Jesus for Christians, and through Mahomet for Muslims. The Hebrew Scriptures, Christian Bible, and Qur'an are the setting down of those revealing moments.

Revisionism: The pseudo-scholarly, antisemitic attempt to "prove" that the Shoah never took place as it has been reported, that it is a "fiction" of the Zionist Jews, who continue to manipulate others, non-Jews, as well as the historical record to win support and allegiance for the beleaguered State of Israel.

Ritual Murder: Already at play in the Middle Ages, the utterly false notion that Jews periodically kidnap and murder Christian children to drain their blood for the making of the **matzot** [unleavened cakes] need for Passover. This libel has been a mainstay of the antisemites up to and including our own day.

SA: [German] **Stormabteilung** or "Storm Troopers." The original Nazi "goon squads," which later become eclipsed into the **Gestapo** [Geheime **Statspolizei**] or "Secret State Police." The **Gestapo** were the original persecutors of Jews and played a central role in their annihilation and extermination during the Shoah.

Sadducees: The conservative, priestly party of the Second Temple/Roman Period who wished to support and maintain that status quo of Judaism as a cultic religious community. Opposed to the **Pharisees**.

Salvation: The religious belief that the ultimate goal of faith is to be redeemed from death and/or everlasting hell and attain freedom, **grace**, and eternal afterlife in God's presence.

Sanhedrin: Hebrew word derived from Greek origin which identifies the Supreme Court of ancient Israel during the Roman period. Composed of 71 Rabbis, it has headed by a Presiding Judge and rendered both civil and religious decisions and solutions to complexities of the developing Jewish legal tradition. No longer extent in Jewish life after the 4th Century C.E.

Satan: The ultimate personification of evil in Christian religious tradition. Said to have originally been an angel in the heavenly court who found disfavor in God's eyes.

Scylla & Charybdis: Taken from Greek mythology and understood to have been two sea monsters who lured sailors and ships to their death and destruction. The idiom "between **Scylla & Charybdis**" is equivalent to "between a rock and a hard place" [i.e. between two difficult choices, both of which have both positive and negative consequences].

Second Generation: The term now used to describe the children of Shoah survivors, children of severely-diminished families who are now adults themselves. Many of them continue to struggle with the Shoah, some psychologically, others religiously.

Sefirot: [Hebrew] Literally, "numbers." An essential term in Jewish Kabbalistic and mystical literature to denote the various emanations from God which ultimately become his attributes.

Sephardim: [Hebrew] Literally, "Spaniards." Since the onset of the Middle Ages, the term used by Jews to designate those Jews who trace their ancestry to Spain, Morocco, Italy, Egypt, Palestine, and Syria, as well as the Balkans, Greece, and Turkey.

Shearith Yisrael: [Hebrew] Literally, the "Saving Remnant of Israel." That community of Jews who survives the tragic destruction of large numbers of its own people, and because of its commitments, religious and other, rebuilds itself. After the Shoah, all contemporary Jewish communities throughout the world are "saving remnants."

Shechinah: [Hebrew] Literally, the "Presence." Term used to denote the "Indwelling Presence of God." That is, God's immanence, nearness, to humanity; approachable and reachable.

Shema Yisrael: [Hebrew] Literally, "Hear, Israel!" Taken from **Devarim** [Deuteronomy} 6:4, "Hear, Israel! Adonai is our God, Adonai alone," this sentence has become the Affirmation of God's Unity and is included in all Jewish worship services. It is as close as the Jewish religious tradition comes to a creedal formulation.

Shevirat Ha-Kelim: [Hebrew] Literally, the "breaking of the vessels." Term taken from Jewish Kabbalistic mystical literature to describe the human condition in its estrangement from God. These vessels which held the divine sparks or emanations have been shattered because of human error and can only be put back together through human commitment to God.

Shoah: [Hebrew] Literally, "Destruction, Devastation." The Hebrew, Biblical term now preferred more and more to describe the wanton murder and callous slaughter of almost six million Jewish men, women, and children during the years 1939 and 1945 by the Nazis and their assistants. A singularly unique event in the history of the Jewish People as well as all humankind.

Shofar: [Hebrew] Literally, "ram's horn." Reminder of the **Bereshit** [Genesis] story whereby Abraham sacrificed a ram rather than his son Isaac. Used in ancient Israel as both a military instrument and a call to gather the community. Associated today with the High Holy Days of **Rosh Ha-Shanah** [New Year] and **Yom Kippur** [Day of Atonement].

Shtetl: [Yiddish] Literally, "small town." Term used to denote the village where Jewish lived in Eastern Europe, primarily Russia and Poland.

Shulchan Aruch: [Hebrew] Literally, "Set/Prepared Table." The abstracted and organized Code of Jewish Laws taken from the **Talmud** and elsewhere, originally prepared and added to by Joseph Caro [1488-1575]. Together with the commentary of Moses Isserles [1525-1572], it has become authoritative in Orthodox Jewish religious life.

Shutafut: [Hebrew] Literally, "partnership." The classical rabbinic idea in Jewish religious life that God and humanity are co-partners in the very process of creation. God needs us every bit as much as we need God to bring about a world of which he would be proud.

Sitz im Leben: [German] Literally, "seat in life." Term used to denote one's "situation in life," that is, description of reality as it is, not as we would like it to be.

Social Darwinism: Philosophy popular in the 1920's in both America and Europe where Charles Darwin's twin emphasis on survival of the fittest and evolution of the species were adapted onto the plane of history. The Nazis perverted even this questionable understanding and saw all of history as a battleground between the Aryan, of whom they were its finest representatives, and the Jews, the most evil and lowest ordered among the species.

Socialism: Political philosophy whereby ownership, production, and distribution of goods are held by the collective rather than the individual.

Sonderkommando: [German] Literally, "special commando." Those Jews assigned the grisly task of removing the bodies from the various gas chambers and taking them either to the crematoria or for burial. Their own life expectancy was less than three months, after which they themselves were murdered to prevent witnesses.

SS: [German] Contraction of **Schutzstaffeln,** "Protection Squad." Originally organized as a body guard unit for the **Fuhrer,** it became one of the primary instruments under Heinrich Himmler's direction of the implementation of the Shoah.

Surplus Population: Term used in the writings of Helen Fein, Richard Rubenstein, and others to designate those groups "falling outside the universe of moral obligation," and, thus, liable for Shoah in the case of the Jews and genocide in the case of others.

Synoptic Gospels: Reference to the first three Gospel accounts of Jesus life and death--Matthew, Mark, and Luke--governed primarily by a similar point of view.

Talmud: [Hebrew] Literally, "Teaching." The encyclopedic collection of rabbinic literature following several centuries after the close of the **Mishnah** [the first compilation of Jewish laws completed around 200 C.E.] covering all aspects of Jewish life, based on both discussions in the various rabbinic academies as well as rendered legal decisions. There are both a Babylonian and Palestinian versions, the former ultimately becoming more authoritative in subsequent Jewish religious life.

Talmud Torah: [Hebrew] Literally, "study of the Torah." Term used to designate both the intensive Jewish religious study, especially the **Talmud**

itself, as well as a unique educational system of schools set up for such a purpose.

Teaching of Contempt: Term first suggested by the late French Jewish historian Jules Isaac [1877-1963] to describe the anti-Jewish and antisemitic teachings of Christianity over the course of the centuries. Isaac believed, and rightly so, that such "teaching of contempt" was an indirect contributor to the Shoah which he himself experienced firsthand. His monumental work Jesus et Israel and Genese de l'antisemitisme were said to have influenced directly Pope John XXIII and led directly to the Vatican Declaration **Nostre Aetate.**

Teleology: The philosophical study of the final cause of things and events.

Teshuvah: [Hebrew] Literally, "return." The religious belief of Judaism that the sincere penitent who recognizes the error of his/her ways and **returns** to the path of Jewish life will be accepted by God with open heart and open arms. One finds such an expression in the classic statement, "The gates of repentance are always open."

Theodicy: The religious and philosophical position which attempts to reconcile the goodness of God with the existence of evil in the world.

Theology: The study of the nature of God, God's relationship with the world, and matters pertaining to both.

Theophany: A religious event characterized by the appearance of God to humanity. Jews speak of the **theophany** at Sinai, not necessarily indicating the physical appearance of God.

Tifutzah: [Hebrew] Literally, "dispersion." Parallel term for the **Diaspora** of Jews living throughout the world outside the Land of Israel. Term itself is value-neutral.

Tikkun Olam B'Malchut Shaddai: [Hebrew] Literally, "repairing the world beneath the sovereignty of God." The ethical ideal of Jewish life which impels social action and demands that Jews involve themselves in improving society wherever they find themselves.

Torah She B'al Peh: [Hebrew] Literally, "Torah which is upon the mouth." The Oral Tradition of Rabbinic interpretation later set down in such primary texts as the **Mishnah** and **Talmud.** The so-called "Oral Tradition" continues to be authoritative today for Orthodox Jews, less so for Conservative, Reform, and Reconstructionist Jews.

Torah She B'michtav: [Hebrew] Literally, "Torah which is written down." The written text of the Hebrew Scriptures which begins with **Bereshit** and ends with **Divre Hayamim Bet** [II Chronicles].

Tosafot: [Hebrew] Literally, "addenda." The additional rabbinic commentaries on the **Talmud** compiled by the French Rabbis from the 12th to the 14th Centuries.

Totalitarianism: The political philosophy which has as its goal the complete domination of all aspects of the life of its citizens, usually under the leadership of a dictator, benevolent or otherwise.

Transcendence: The religious belief that God is above and beyond the realm of human approachability.

Tzaddik: [Hebrew] [Pl. **Tzaddikim**] Literally, "righteous or holy man." According to Jewish literary and mystical tradition, in each and every generation, the world is sustained by "thirty-six righteous men" [Hebrew: **Lamed-Vav Tzaddikim**] who, by virtue of their goodness and holiness, bring joy to God. They are, however, unknown to themselves as well as to the rest of humankind.

Unique: Singularly distinct. The issue with regard to the Shoah is whether or not this historical event is **unique** in both Jewish and world history, calling forth new and different responses, or "simply" another in a long list of antisemitic and genocidal world events not mandating significantly different responses.

Untermensch: [German] Literally, "underman." Term of opprobrium used to designate Jews, Poles, Gypsies, Slavs, and others, as "sub-human"- -to be disposed of by the Nazis at will and to be enslaved as necessity dictated.

Volk: [German] Literally, "people." The almost mystical reverence shown by the Nazis for the "purely German person and people," the **Aryan**. The German term **blut und boden** ["blood and soil"] equally stresses this idea and its impact upon a generation of Germans willing to do Hitler's bidding.

Weltanschauung: [German] Literally, "worldview." A perspective on the human condition from one's own individual or collective viewpoint, taking into consideration political, economic, religious, and other factors.

Xenophobia: The psychological fear of the different. Said to be at the root of antisemitism in particular and all prejudice in general. Part of the psychological make-up of most human beings, though its conscious manifestation and translation into acts of hatred is a learned response.

Yad Vashem: [Hebrew] Literally, "a hand and a name." Refer-ence taken from the Biblical book of **Yishayahu** [Isaiah], **Yad Vashem** is the Israeli Shoah Memorial Authority created in 1953 to memorialize this tragedy of the Jewish People as well as to do significant archival gathering and research into these events.

Yahadut: [Hebrew] Literally, "Judaism." The Hebrew term for the religious expression of those committed to the belief in the One God of Israel.

Yeshiva: [Hebrew] [Pl. **Yeshivot**] A traditional Jewish parochial school whose primary curriculum consists of the study of the **Talmud** together with other rabbinic literatures.

Yiddish: A cognate, folk language of Hebrew, consisting of linguistic elements of Hebrew, French, Italian, German, and Slavic. Spoken primari-ly by those Jews coming from Eastern Europe [Poland and Russia] and their descendants. A significant literature also arose using **Yiddish** beginning in the late 18th and early 19th Centuries.

Yishuv: [Hebrew] Literally, "settlement." Term used to designate the Jewish community of Palestine prior to 1948 and Israel subsequent to it.

Yordeh: [Hebrew] [Pl. **Yordim**] Literally, "one who goes down, emigre." Term used to indicate that citizen of Israel who leaves Israel, settles somewhere else, and may or may not become a citizen of her/his adopted country.

Zikkaron: [Hebrew] Literally, "remembering." Its Greek equivalent is **anamnesis.** For Eugene Fisher, Volume II, both Judaism and Christianity are religions of remembering.

Zykon B: [German] The trade name of the actual crystalline gas pellets used in the gas chambers in the concentration and extermination camps. Upon contact with the air, **Zykon B**, a pesticide, becomes gaseous suffocating those in its immediate confined space. Death was said to take place within fifteen to forty-five minutes depending upon the size of the gas chamber.

* * * * *

THE BOOKS OF THE TORAH

The Five Books of Moses

Bereshit   Genesis

Shemot	Exodus
Vayikra	Leviticus
Bamidbar	Deuteronomy

Nevi'im: The Prophets

Yehoshua	Joshua
Shofetim	Judges
Shmuel Alef	I Samuel
Shmuel Bet	II Samuel
Melachim Alef	I Kings
Melachim Bet	II Kings
Yishayahu	Isaiah
Yirmiyahu	Jeremiah
Yehezkel	Ezekiel

"The Twelve"

Hoshai'ah	Hosea
Yoel	Joel
Amos	Amos
Ovadiah	Obadiah
Yonah	Jonah
Micha	Micah
Nachum	Nahum
Havakkuk	Habakkuk
Tzfaniah	Zephaniah
Haggai	Haggai
Zechariah	Zechariah
Malachi	Malachi

Ketuvim: The Writings

Tehillim	Psalms
Mishlei	Proverbs
Iyov	Job
Shir Ha-Shirim	Song of Songs/Canticles
Rut	Ruth
Aicha	Lamentations
Kohelet	Ecclesiastes
Esther	Esther
Daniel	Daniel
Ezra	Ezra
Nehemiah	Nehemiah
Divrei Ha-Yamim Alef	I Chronicles
Divrei Ha-Yamim Bet	II Chronicles

* * * * *

THE JEWISH HOLIDAYS

Biblical - Major

Shabbat	Sabbath
Pesach	Passover
Sefirat Ha-Omer	Counting of the Omer
Shavuot	Weeks
Rosh Ha-Shanah	New Year
Yom Kippur	Day of Atonement
Sukkot	Booths
Shemini Atzeret	8th Day of Solemn Assembly
Rosh Hodesh	New Moon

Biblical-Minor

Hanukkah	Festival of Dedication
Purim	Festival of Esther/Lots

Rabbinic

Lag B'Omer	33rd Day of the Omer
Tisha B'Av	9th Day of Av/Collective Day of Mourning
Simchat Torah	Celebration of the Torah
Tu B'Shevat	15th Day of Shevat/Jewish
Arbor Day	

Contemporary

Yom Ha-Shoah	Shoah Remembrance Day
Yom Ha-Atzmaut	Israeli Independence Day

* * * * *

THE MONTHS OF THE JEWISH CALENDAR

Tishri	September-October
Heshvan	October-November
Kislev	November-December
Tevet	December-January
Shevat	January-February
Adar [& Adar Bet/II]	February-March
Nisan	March-April
Iyar	April-May

Sivan	May–June
Tammuz	June–July
Av	July–August
Elul	August–September

BIBLIOGRAPHY

Abrahamson, Irving [Editor]. Against Silence: The Voice and Vision of Elie Wiesel. New York: Holocaust Library, 1985.

Ateek, Naim. Justice and Only Justice: A Palestinian Theology of Liberation. Maryknoll: Orbis Press, 1989.

Barth, Karl. The German Church Conflict. London: Lutterworth Press, 1965.

Barth, Karl. Church Dogmatics. Ediburgh: T. & T. Clark, 1961.

Bekker, J. Christaan. Suffering and Hope. Philadelphia: Fortress Press, 1987.

Bonhoeffer, Dietrich. The Cost of Discipleship. New York: Macmillan Publishing Company, 1974.

Brenner, Reeve Robert. The Faith and Doubt of Holocaust Survivors. New York: The Free Press, 1980.

Charny, Israel [Editor]. Toward the Understanding and Prevention of Genocide. Boulder: Westview Press, 1984.

Cochrane, Arthur C. The Church's Confession Under Hitler. Philadelphia: Westminster press, 1962.

Davies, Alan T. [Editor]. Antisemitism and the Foundations of Christianity. New York: Paulist Press, 1979.

Des Pres, Terrence. The Survivor. New York: Oxford University Press, 1976.

Donat, Alexandre. The Holocaust Kingdom. New York: Holt, Rinehart and Winston, 1965.

Eckardt, Alice L. and A. Roy. Jews and Christians: The Contemporary Meeting. Bloomington: Indiana University Press, 1986.

Eckardt, Alice L. and A. Roy. Long Night's Journey into Day: A Revised Retrospective on the Holocaust. Detroit: Wayne State University Press, 1988.

Ellis, Marc. Toward a Jewish Theology of Liberation. New York: Orbis Books, 1987.

Ellul, Jacques. Prayer and Modern Man. New York: Seabury Press, 1970.

Ericksen, Robert P. Theologians Under Hitler. New Haven: Yale University Press, 1985.

Fackenheim, Emil L. The Human Condition After Auschwitz. Syracuse: Syracuse University Press, 1971.

Fein, Helen. Accounting for Genocide: National Responses and Jewish Victimization. Chicago: University of Chicago Press, 1984.

Fisher, Eugene. Faith Without Prejudice: Rebuilding Christian Attitudes. New York: Paulist Press, 1977.

Flinker, Moshe. Young Moshe's Diary. Jerusalem: Yad Vashem, 1976.

Friedlander, Albert [Editor]. Out of the Whirlwind. New York: Schocken Books, 1976.

Friedlander, Henry and Sybil Milton [Editors]. The Holocaust: Ideology, Bureaucracy, and Genocide. Millwood: Kraus International Publications, 1980.

Gollwitzer, Helmut [Editor]. Dying We Live: The Final Messages of the Resistance. New York: Pantheon Books, 1956.

Grobman, Alex and Daniel Landes [Editors]. Genocide: Critical Issues of the Holocaust. Chappaqua: Rossel Books, 1983.

Guardini, Romano. Power and Responsibility. Chicago: Henry Regnery, 1961.

Haas, Peter. Morality After Auschwitz. Philadelphia: Fortress Press, 1988.

Hancock, Ian. The Pariah Syndrome. Ann Arbor: Karoma Publishers, 1987.

Hartman, David. A Living Covenant: The Innovative Spirit in Traditional Judaism. New York: The Free Press, 1985.

Heer, Friedrich. God's First Love. New York: Weybright and Talley, 1970.

Herberg, Will. Judaism and Modern Man: An Interpretation of the Jewish Religion. New York: Meridian Books, 1959.

Heyward, Carter. The Redemption of God. Washington, DC: University Press of America, 1982.

Hick, John. Evil and the God of Love. New York: Harper and Row, 1966.

Hillesum, Etty. An Interrupted Life: The Diaries of Etty Hillesum 1941-1943. New York: Pantheon Books, 1983.

Isaac, Jules. Jesus and Israel. New York: Holt, Rinehart and Winston, 1971.

Katz, Steven. Post-Holocaust Dialogues: Critical Studies in Modern Jewish Thought. New York: New York University Press, 1983.

Katz, Jacob. Exclusiveness and Tolerance. New York: Behrman House, 1983.

Klein, Charlotte. Anti-Judaism in Christian Theology. Philadelphia: Fortress Press, 1978.

Langer, Lawrence. The Holocaust and the Literary Imagination. New Haven: Yale University Press, 1975.

Levi, Primo. Survival in Auschwitz: The Nazi Assault on Humanity. New York: Collier Books, 1976.

Levin, Nora. The Holocaust. New York: Schocken Books, 1973.

Littell, Franklin H., Irene G. Shur, and Claude Foster, Jr. [Editors]. The Holocaust: In Answer.... West Chester: Sylvan Publishers, 1988.

Littell, Franklin H. and Hubert G. Locke [Editors]. The German Church Struggle and the Holocaust. Detroit: Wayne State University Press, 1974.

Lukas, Richard S. Forgotten Holocaust: The Poles Under German Occupation, 1939-1944. Lexington: University Press of Kentucky, 1986.

Macaulay, J. and L. Berkowitz. Altruism and Helping Behavior. New York: Doubleday and Company, 1975.

Maybaum, Ignaz. The Face of God After Auschwitz. Amsterdam: Polak & Van Gennep Ltd, 1965.

Milgram, Stanley. Obedience to Authority: An Experimental View. New York: Harper and Row, 1969.

Morley, John F. Vatican Diplomany and the Jews During the Holocaust, 1939-1943. New York: Ktav Publishing House, 1980.

Neher, Andre. The Exile of the Word. Philadelphia: The Jewish Publication Society of America, 1981.

Niebuhr, Reinhold. The Nature and Destiny of Man: A Christian Interpretation. New York: Charles Scribner's Sons, 1941.

Pauck, Wilhelm and Marion. Paul Tillich: His Life and Thought. New York: Harper and Row, 1976.

Pawlikowski, John T. Jesus and the Theology of Israel. Wilmington: Michael Glazier, 1989.

Plant, Richard. The Pink Triangle: The Nazi War Against Homosexuals. New York: Henry Holt, 1986.

Rector, Frank. The Nazi Extermination of Homosexuals. New York: Stein and Day, 1981.

Remembering the Future: The Impact of the Holocaust on the Contemporary . Oxford: Pergamon Press, 1988.

Reuther, Rosemary Radford and Herman J. The Wrath of Jonah: The Crisis of Religious Nationalism in the Israeli-Palestinian Conflict. San Francisco: Harper and Row, 1989.

Rivkin, Ellis. What Crucified Jesus? Nashville: Abingdon Press, 1984.

Rosenbaum, Irving J. Holocaust and Halakhah. New York: Ktav Publishing House, 1976.

Ross, Robert W. So It Was True: The American Protestant Press and the Nazi Persecution of the Jews. Minneapolis: University of Minnesota Press, 1980.

Roth, John K. and Michael Berenbaum [Editors]. The Holocaust: Religious and Philosophical Implications. New York: Paragon House Publishers, 1989.

Rubenstein, Richard L. and John K. Roth. Approaches to Auschwitz: The Legacy of the Holocaust. Atlanta: John Knox Press, 1987.

Rubenstein, Richard L. My Brother Paul. New York: Harper and Row, 1972.

Schussler-Fiorenza, Elisabeth and David Tracy [Editors]. The Holocaust as Interruption. Edinburgh: T. & T. Clark, 1984.

Spiegel, Shalom. The Last Trial. Philadelphia: The Jewish Publication Society of America, 1967.

Tal, Uriel. Christians and Jews in Germany: Religion, Politics and Ideology in the Second Reich, 1970-1914. Ithaca: Cornell University Press, 1975.

Tillich, Paul. The Socialist Decision. New York: Harper and Row, 1977.

Tillich, Paul. The Interpretation of History. New York: Charles Scribner's Sons, 1936.

van Buren, Paul. A Christian Theology of the People Israel. New York: Harper and Row, 1983.

van Buren, Paul. Discerning the Way. New York: Harper and Row, 1980.

van Buren, Paul. Christ in Context. New York: Harper and Row, 1988.

Wells, Leon. Who Speaks for the Vanquished? American Judaism and the Holocaust. New York: Peter Lang Press, 1987.

Wiesel, Elie. The Town Beyond the Wall. New York: Avon Books, 1970.

Wiesel, Elie. Twilight. New York: Summit Books, 1988.

Wiesel, Elie. The Oath. New York: Random House, 1973.

Wiesel, Elie. One Generation After. New York: Avon Books, 1972.

Wiesel, Elie. The Testament. New York: Summit Books, 1981.

Wiesel, Elie. Night. New York: Bantam Books, 1960.

Wiesel, Elie. Somewhere a Master. New York: Summit Books, 1982.

Wiesel, Elie. Souls on Fire. New York: Vintage Books, 1973.

Wiesel, Elie. A Jew Today. New York: Random House, 1978.

Wiesel, Elie. One Generation After. New York: Random House, 1970.

Wiesel, Elie. Messengers of God: BIblical Portraits and Legends. New York: Random House, 1976.

Wiesel, Elie. The Trial of God. New York: Random House, 1978.

Wiesel, Elie. The Gates of the Forest. New York: Avon Books, 1966.

Wiesel, Elie. Legends of Our Time. New York: Avon Books, 1968.

Wiesel, Eli. Ani Ma'amin: A Song Lost and Found Again. New York: Random House, 1973.

Wyman, David. The Abandonment of the Jews: America and the Holocaust 1941-1945. New York: Pantheon Books, 1984.

Wytwycky, Bohdan. The Other Holocaust: Many Circles of Hell. Washington, DC: The Novak Report, 1980.

Zahrnt, Heinz. The Question of God: Protestant Theology in the Twentieth Century. New York: Harcourt, Brace and World, 1966.

Zimmells, H. The Echo of the Nazi Holocaust in Rabbinic Literature. New York: Ktav Publishing House, 1977.

SOME QUESTIONS FOR POSSIBLE FURTHER REFLECTION AND FUTURE DISCUSSION

1. Having read all of the essays in this volume, what appear to be the primary concerns/dominant issues of these writers?

2. Why do you think no women are publicly advocating the historical revisionist/improvisationist position?

3. Is the question of **evil** the fundamental religious question when confronting the Shoah?

4. After consulting a biography of Karl Barth, what possible reasons can you suggest as to why he fails to mention the Shoah in his writings?

5. Are Tillich's "daemonic versus satanic," Barth's "das Nichtige" and Niebuhr's emphasis on "original sin" both possible and plausible--if incomplete--religio-theological explanations of the Shoah?

6. Can Pope John Paul II's use of the term "saving warning" to describe the Jewish experience during and after the Shoah serve as a bridge of reconciliation between these two faith-communities?

7. Can the use of the term "gift" both to describe Jesus' voluntary suffering on the cross and the experience of the Jewish People during and after the Shoah serve as that bridge of reconciliation?

8. Will the beatification of Edith Stein, murdered and martyred during the Shoah, further dialogue between Jews and Roman Catholics?

9. Why do you think it is the suffering of mothers and children during the Shoah which evoke our deepest emotions and horror?

10. What steps would you suggest for Christianity to overcome its tragic legacy of antisemitism?

11. How do you respond to Idinopulos's conviction that Jesus' death did not defeat sin but led to its further increase?

12. Who "owns" the Shoah? The survivors? Their children? The educators?

13. Which view of God holds the most promise for our post-Shoah world: A "commanding" God? A "compelling" God? An "agonizing" God? A God "to whom we are drawn?"

14. Can a "theology of divine vulnerability and suffering" serve as a dialogue model for Jews and Christians after the Shoah? What about "chutz-pah faith?"

15. What role does power--political, religious, and other--now need to play in the construction of any post-Shoah theology?

16. Reuther's critique of Jewish Shoah theology as an uncritical means of American and Israeli Jewish empowerment, paralleling Ellis in Volume I, is a particularly serious one. How do you respond to it?

ABOUT THE CONTRIBUTORS

HARRY JAMES CARGAS: Harry James Cargas, Professor of Literature and Language and of Religion at Webster University, Saint Louis, is the author of twenty-four books, including five on the Shoah. Among these are Harry James Cargas in Conversation with Elie Wiesel, A Christian Response to the Holocaust, and Reflections of a Post-Auschwitz Christian. He serves on numerous boards, including the Catholic Institute for Holocaust Studies, the Anne Frank Institute, the Simon Wiesenthal Center, and is the only Catholic ever appointed to the International Advisory Committee at Yad Vashem in Jerusalem. He also serves on the Executive Council, International Philosophers for the Prevention of Nuclear Omnicide, on the Advisory Board of the Institute for Ultimate Reality and Meaning, and is the Executive Secretary of Canine Assistance for the Disabled.

ALAN DAVIES: Alan Davies is a member of the Department of Religious Studies, Victoria College, University of Toronto. He is the author of Anti-Semitism and the Christian Mind [1969]; Infected Christianity: A Study of Modern Racism [1988]; and the Editor of Antisemitism and Foundations of Christianity [1979]. Currently, he is editing a volume on antisemitism in Canada.

ALICE L. ECKARDT: Alice Lyons Eckardt was Maxwell Fellow in Holocaust Studies at the Oxford Centre for Postgraduate Hebrew Studies, 1989-1990, and is Professor Emerita of Religious Studies, Lehigh University, Bethlehem, PA. Her books include Long Night's Journey into Day: A Revised Retrospective on the Holocaust [1988, with A. Roy Eckardt] and Jerusalem: City of the Ages [1987]. She served on the Executive Committee of the international conference "Remembering the Future" held at Oxford and London in July, 1988, on the Editorial Advisory Board of the three volumes of papers from that conference published by Pergamon Press, 1989. She is a member and past Chairperson of the Christian Study Group on Judaism and the Jewish People, the Executive Editorial Review Board of Holocaust and Genocide Studies, the Editorial Board of the Holocaust Library, the Board of Directors of the Anne Frank Institute of Philadelphia, PA, and the National Advisory Board of the Foundation to Sustain Righteous Gentiles.

EUGENE J. FISHER: Dr. Eugene J. Fisher is the Executive Secretary for Catholic-Jewish Relations of the National Conference of Catholic Bishops [NCCB] and Consultor to the Vatican Commission for Religious Relations with the Jews, the only American on the Commission. He received his Ph.D. from New York University in Hebrew Culture and Education, where his dissertation was entitled, "The Treatment of Jews and Judaism in Current Roman Catholic Teaching." He is the author or editor of several books, including Faith Without Prejudice: Rebuilding Christian Attitudes Toward Judaism [1977]; The Formation of Social Policy in the Catholic and Jewish Traditions and Liturgical Foundations of Social Policy in the Catholic and Jewish Traditions [1980 and 1983; co-edited with Rabbi Daniel Polish]; Homework for Christians Preparing for Christian-Jewish Dialogue [1982]; and Seminary Education and Catholic-Jewish Relations [1983]. His memberships include the Catholic Biblical Association, the National Association of Professors of Hebrew, the Society of Biblical Literature, and the National Conference of Christians and Jews.

DOUGLAS K. HUNEKE: Douglas K. Huneke is the Pastor of Westminster Presbyterian Church, Tiburon, CA. He served for eight years as the Presbyterian University Pastor at the University of Oregon, Eugene, OR. For five years he was a member of the Honors College faculty at that university. In 1976-1977, he was granted a sabbatical leave to study and write on the implications of the Shoah and the on the life and writings of Elie Wiesel. He spent a major portion of his leave at the former extermination camps in Poland and East Germany, and studied at the Shoah memorial and research center, Yad Vashem, in Jerusalem. He is a Visiting Lecturer at San Francisco Theological Seminary. In 1980, he was awarded a Faculty Research Grant by the Oregon Committee for the Humanities [NEH] to research the moral and spiritual development of Christians who rescued Jews and other endangered persons during the Nazi era. In 1981, he was awarded an additional grant from the Memorial Foundation for Jewish Culture to continue gathering the accounts of rescue. He is the author of The Moses of Rovno, the biography of the German, Nazi-era rescuer Herman Graebe [New York, Dodd Mead, 1986].

THOMAS A. IDINOPULOS: Thomas J. Idinopulos [Ph.D. University of Chicago] is Professor of Religious Studies at Miami University, Oxford, OH, writing and teaching on the politics and religion of Jewish, Christian, and Muslim communities of the Middle East. He also serves as Consulting Editor to the Middle East Review, and is the author of The Erosion of Faith: An Inquiry into the Origins of the Contemporary Crisis in Religious Thought [1971]; and Co-Editor of Mysticism, Nihilism, Feminism: New Critical Essays in the Theology of Simone Weil [1984]. In 1986, he received the Associated Church Press Excellence Award for his writing in the Christian Century, and, in 1988, in recognition of his work in Israel, was nominated as a Fellow to the Patriarchal Institute for Patristic Studies, Vlatadon Monastery, Thessaloniki, Greece.

MICHAEL MCGARRY: Reverend Michael McGarry, C.S.P., Rector of the Paulist Fathers's seminary in Washington, DC, writes frequently on Jewish-Christian relations, theology after the Shoah, and the meaning of the Shoah for Christians today. He is the author of Christology After Auschwitz. Father McGarry serves on the Advisory Committee to the Secretariat for Catholic-Jewish Relations of the National Conference of Catholic Bishops, and is host of the nationally syndicated program, "Religious Book World."

JOHN T. PAWLIKOWSKI: John T. Pawlikowski, O.S.M., a Servite priest, is Professor of Social Ethics at the Catholic Theological Union in Chicago, a constituent of the cluster of theological schools at the University of Chicago. He was appointed a member of the United States Holocaust Memorial Council by President Carter in 1980, a position he still holds. He has authored numerous books and articles on Christian-Jewish relations, the Shoah, and social ethics, including The Challenge of the Holocaust for Christian Theology [1982] and Jesus and the Theology of Israel [1989]. In 1986 he received the "Righteous Among the Nations Award" from the Holocaust Museum in Detroit. He has also been active in the Polish-Jewish dialogue as well as the new Christian-Jewish-Muslim trialogue.

ROSEMARY RADFORD REUTHER: Rosemary Radford Reuther is a Christian liberation theologian teaching at Garrett-Evangelical Theological Seminary and Northwestern University. She holds a B.A. in Religion and Philosophy from Scripps College and an M.A. and Ph.D. from Claremont Graduate School in Claremont, CA, in Classics and Early Christianity. She is the author or editor of twenty-one books and numerous articles on religion and social justice, among them Faith and Fratricide: The Theological Roots of Anti-Semitism [1974] and The Wrath of Jonah: The Crisis of Religious Nationalism in the Israeli-Palestinian Conflict [1989, together with Herman J. Reuther].

JOHN K. ROTH: John K. Roth is the Pitzer Professor of Philosophy at Claremont McKenna College, where he has taught since 1966. His seventeen books include A Consuming Fire: Encounter with Elie Wiesel and the Holocaust; Approaches to Auschwitz: The Holocaust and Its Legacy [with Richard L. Rubenstein]; and, most recently, Holocaust: Religious and Philosophical Implications [with Michael Berenbaum]. In 1988, he was named Professor of the Year in the United States by the Council for the Advancement and Support of Education [CASE] and the Carnegie Foundation for the Advancement of Teaching.

ABOUT THE EDITOR

STEVEN L. JACOBS: Steven L. Jacobs serves as the Rabbi of Temple B'nai Sholom, Huntsville, Alabama, and teaches Jewish Studies at Oakwood College, Huntsville, and Mississippi State University, Starkville.   He received his B.A. [With Distinction] from the Pennsylvania State University, and his B.H.L., M.A.H.L., D.H.L. and rabbinic ordination from the Hebrew Union College-Jewish Institute of Religion, Cincinnati, Ohio. In addition to serving congregations in Steubenville, Ohio, Niagara Falls, New York, Birmingham and Mobile, Alabama, and Dallas, Texas, he has taught at Spring Hill College, Mobile, University of Alabama, Tuscaloosa, Uni-versity of Alabama at Birmingham, Birmingham-Southern College, and Samford University, Birmingham.   Author of more than fifty scholarly articles and reviews dealing primarily with the Shoah, his books include Shirot Bialik: A New and Annotated Translation of Chaim Nachman Bialik's Epic Poems [Columbus, Alpha Publishing Company, 1987] and Raphael Lemkin's Thoughts on Nazi Genocide: Not Guilty? [Lewiston, The Edwin Mellen Press, 1992]. He serves on the Alabama State Holocaust Advisory Council and as an Educational Consultant to the Center on the Holocaust, Genocide, and Human Right, Philadelphia.   He is also the Editor of the papers of the late Raphael Lemkin, Father of the United Nations Treaty on Genocide.